C0-BJU-654

# Grounding Religion

Now in its third edition, *Grounding Religion* explores relationships between the environment and religious beliefs and practices. Established scholars introduce students to the ways religion shapes and is shaped by human-earth relations, surveying a series of key issues and questions, with particular attention to issues of environmental degradation, social justice, ritual practices, and religious worldviews.

Case studies, discussion questions, and further readings enrich students' experience. This third edition features updated content, including revisions of every chapter and new material on religion and the environmental humanities, sexuality and queer studies, class, ability, privilege and power, environmental justice, extinction, biodiversity, and politics.

An excellent text for undergraduate and graduate students alike, it offers an expansive overview of the academic field of religion and ecology as it has emerged in the past fifty years and continues to develop today.

**Whitney A. Bauman** is Professor of Religious Studies at Florida International University (FIU) in Miami, Florida, USA.

**Richard Bohannon** is Associate Professor of Individualized and Interdisciplinary Studies at Metropolitan State University in Saint Paul, Minnesota, USA.

**Kevin J. O'Brien** is Professor of Religion at Pacific Lutheran University in Tacoma, Washington, USA.

# Grounding Religion

## A Field Guide to the Study of Religion and Ecology

Third Edition

**Edited by Whitney A. Bauman, Richard Bohannon and Kevin J. O'Brien**

LONDON AND NEW YORK

Designed cover image: Getty Images—SAKDAWUT14

Third edition published 2024
by Routledge
4 Park Square, Milton Park, Abingdon, Oxon, OX14 4RN

and by Routledge
605 Third Avenue, New York, NY 10158

*Routledge is an imprint of the Taylor & Francis Group, an informa business*



First edition published by Routledge 2011

Second edition published by Routledge 2017

*British Library Cataloguing-in-Publication Data*
A catalogue record for this book is available from the British Library

*Library of Congress Cataloging-in-Publication Data*
Names: Bauman, Whitney, editor. | Bohannon, Richard (Richard R.), editor. | O'Brien, Kevin J. (Kevin James), 1977– editor.
Title: Grounding religion : a field guide to the study of religion and ecology / edited by Whitney A. Bauman, Richard Bohannon, and Kevin J. O'Brien.
Description: Third edition. | Abingdon, Oxon ; New York, NY : Routledge, [2024] | Includes bibliographical references and index.
Identifiers: LCCN 2023014818 | ISBN 9781032194967 (hbk) | ISBN 9781032194950 (pbk) | ISBN 9781003259466 (ebk)
Subjects: LCSH: Human ecology—Religious aspects.
Classification: LCC GF80 .G76 2024 | DDC 201/.77—dc23/eng/20230811
LC record available at https://lccn.loc.gov/2023014818

ISBN: 978-1-032-19496-7 (hbk)
ISBN: 978-1-032-19495-0 (pbk)
ISBN: 978-1-003-25946-6 (ebk)

DOI: 10.4324/9781003259466

Typeset in Times New Roman
by Apex CoVantage, LLC

# Contents

# Figures

# Contributors

**Whitney A. Bauman** (he/him) is Professor of Religious Studies at Florida International University (FIU) in Miami, FL. He is also co-founder and co-director of Counterpoint: Navigating Knowledge, a nonprofit based in Berlin. He is the recipient of a Fulbright Fellowship and a Humboldt Fellowship, and in 2022, he won an award from FIU for Excellence in Research and Creative Activities. His publications include *Religion and Ecology: Developing a Planetary Ethic* (Columbia University Press 2014). His next monograph is titled *A Critical Planetary Romanticism: Literary and Scientific Origins of New Materialism* (Columbia University Press, forthcoming 2023).

**Richard Bohannon** (he/him) is Associate Professor of Individualized and Interdisciplinary Studies at Metropolitan State University in Saint Paul, MN. He is the editor of *Religions and Environments: A Reader in Religion, Nature and Ecology* (Bloomsbury Academic 2014) and the author of *Public Religion and the Urban Environment: Constructing a River Town* (Bloomsbury Academic 2012).

**Brian G. Campbell** is Executive Director of the Iowa Environmental Council, a statewide coalition focused on climate change, environmental justice, clean water, and clean energy. Prior to this role, he earned a PhD in American religious cultures and spent over a decade working in higher education as a sustainability director and a professor. Brian grew up in the American South. His most recent research project was co-producing the podcast *Mid-Americana: Stories from a Changing Midwest*, highlighting the diverse people and places in the region he now calls home.

**Miguel A. De La Torre** is Professor of Social Ethics and Latine Studies at the Iliff School of Theology in Denver. A Fulbright scholar, he has taught in Indonesia, Mexico, South Africa, and Germany and lectured in Costa Rica, Cuba, Palestine, Thailand, and Taiwan. He served as the 2012 president of the Society of Christian Ethics and is the recipient of the 2020 AAR Excellence in Teaching Award and the 2021 Martin E. Marty Public Understanding of Religion Award. He has published forty-one books and over a hundred articles, including many for popular media. Recently, he wrote the screenplay to a documentary on immigration, which has screened in over eighteen film festivals winning over seven awards.

**Laura M. Hartman** is Associate Professor of Environmental Studies at Roanoke College in Salem, VA. She teaches classes about environmental justice, climate justice, gender studies, animal ethics, and related topics. Her research interests include transportation justice, church parking lots, consumption, and climate engineering. She is the author of *The Christian Consumer: Living Faithfully in a Fragile World* (2011) and editor of *That All May Flourish: Comparative Religious Environmental Ethics* (2018).

**Nicole Hoskins** (she/her) is Assistant Professor of Religion and Black Studies at the University of Scranton. Her research is focused on black women's resistive practices to environmental racism. She is working on a book project titled *Blackness Weathered: Decolonial Ethics for the Earth.*

**Laurel Kearns** (she/her) is Professor of Ecology, Society, and Religion at Drew Theological School and University in Madison, NJ. Her research is focused on religious involvement in ecological issues and movements, with a particular interest in environmental justice, climate change, and food. In addition to co-editing and contributing to *EcoSpirit: Religions and Philosophies for the Earth* (2007) and the Religion and Nature section of *Bloomsbury's Religion in North America* online compendium, she has written many chapters and articles. She is a co-founder of the Green Seminary Initiative and serves on the board of the Parliament of World Religions. Her decades-long involvement in religious environmentalism has roots in the island where she was born and raised, Sanibel, Florida, which, like most islands, is significantly impacted by climate change.

**Sarah Withrow King** (she/her) has spent twenty years in advocacy, working to raise awareness of injustice and to reduce suffering (ask her about the time she rescued chickens in Austria). She is the co-founder of CreatureKind, a non-profit that helps Christians recognize faith-based reasons for caring about the well-being of fellow animal creatures used for food and to take practical action in response. The author of *Animals Are Not Ours* (Cascade) and *Vegangelical* (Zondervan), Sarah holds an MTS with a concentration in Christian faith and public policy from Palmer Theological Seminary. She is fueled by CrossFit, the *New York Times* crossword, and really ridiculous action movies. Sarah lives with her family and a pack of rescued companion animals in the Willamette Valley, on the traditional lands of the Chelamela and Kalapuya tribes.

**Dana Lloyd** (she/her) is Assistant Professor of Global Interdisciplinary Studies at Villanova University, where she is also affiliated with the Center for Peace and Justice Education. Her research is at the intersection of religious studies, legal studies, Indigenous studies, and environmental humanities. She is the author of the forthcoming book *Land is Kin: Sovereignty, Religious Freedom, and Indigenous Sacred Sites* (University Press of Kansas, 2023).

**Catherine L. Newell** (she/her) is Associate Professor of Religious Studies at the University of Miami. Her research focuses on how scientific paradigms frequently owe their genesis to a religious idea or spiritual belief. Her first book,

*Destined for the Stars: Faith, the Future, and the Final Frontier* (University of Pittsburgh 2019), finds the roots of the US space program in religious ideas about manifest destiny. Her second book, *Food Faiths: Diet, Religion, and the Science of Spiritual Eating* (Lexington, forthcoming), examines how individuals in contemporary society use scientific concepts about food and diet as the basis for a spiritual practice.

**Amanda M. Nichols** (she/her) is Postdoctoral Research Fellow in the Environmental Studies Program at University of California, Santa Barbara. Nichols earned her PhD in religion and nature in 2021 from the University of Florida. Her research, which falls broadly at the intersections of environmental history and religious and gender studies, illuminates the contributions of women to environment-related or environment-focused social movements, especially around nuclear technologies. In addition to her research, Dr. Nichols serves as the managing editor of *Journal for the Study of Religion, Nature and Culture*; the treasurer for the International Society for the Study of Religion, Nature, and Culture; an editor for *Journal of Posthumanism*; a board member of the Feminist Theory and Religious Reflection Unit at the American Academy of Religion; and a production editor for Equinox Publishing.

**Maria Nita** (she/her) is Lecturer in Religious Studies at the Open University. Her anthropological and historical research is concerned with the intersection between climate activism and contemporary culture, with a focus on spirituality, green Christian practices, public rituals, and ecological art and performance more broadly. She is the author of *Praying and Campaigning with Environmental Christians* (2016) and the editor of *Festival Cultures: Mapping New Fields in the Arts and Social Sciences* with Jeremy H. Kidwell (2022).

**Kevin J. O'Brien** (he/him) is Professor of Religion at Pacific Lutheran University in Tacoma, Washington. His teaching and research focus on the intersections of ethics, climate, environment, religion, and social justice. His publications include *An Introduction to Christian Environmentalism* with Kathryn Blanchard (2014), *The Violence of Climate Change* (2017), and *Environmental Ethics and Uncertainty* with Whitney A. Bauman (2020).

**Lisa D. Powell** (she/her) is Professor of Theology and Director of Women and Gender Studies at St. Ambrose University in Davenport, IA, where she specializes in theologies of liberation. She is the author of *The Disabled God Revisited: Trinity, Christology, and Liberation* (T&T Clark, 2023) and *Inconclusive Theologies: Sor Juana Inés de la Cruz, Kierkegaard, and Religious Discourse* (Mercer University Press, 2014). She is a contributing author to a number of edited volumes, including *Karl Barth and Liberation Theology* (T&T Clark, 2023) and *The Routledge Companion to Christian Ethics* (Routledge, 2022), and she has published articles in a variety of journals, including *The Journal of Feminist Studies in Religion, The Journal of the Society of Christian Ethics*, and *Theology Today*.

**Kate Rigby** is Alexander von Humboldt Professor of Environmental Humanities at the University of Cologne, where she leads a research hub for Multidisciplinary Environmental Studies in the Humanities. Her research lies at the intersection of environmental literary and religious studies, and her books include *Dancing with Disaster: Histories, Narratives, and Ethics for Perilous Times* (2015), *Reclaiming Romanticism: Towards an Ecopoetics of Decolonization* (2020), and *Meditations on Creation in an Era of Extinction* (2023). She was the founding president of the Association for the Study of Literature, Environment, and Culture (Australia–New Zealand) and the founding coordinator of the Australia-Pacific Forum on Religion and Ecology.

**Terra Schwerin Rowe** (she/her) is Associate Professor in the Department of Philosophy and Religion at the University of North Texas. Her first book, *Toward a Better Worldliness: Economy, Ecology and the Protestant Tradition* (Fortress 2017), focuses on the challenge of climate change for Christian traditions. Her current research narrows in on energy and extraction—and Christianity and petroleum in particular. Her book *Of Modern Extraction: Experiments in Critical Petro-theology* (Bloomsbury, 2023) charts new methodologies at the intersection of energy humanities and the study of religion. She is currently co-chair of the Energy, Extraction, and Religion seminar at the AAR and a member of the Petrocultutres Research Group.

**Stefan Skrimshire** (he/him) is Associate Professor of Theology and Religious Studies at the University of Leeds. His work bridges Christian political theology and continental philosophy and is in broad dialogue with the environmental humanities. He is the author of *Politics of Fear, Practices of Hope* (Continuum, 2008), the editor of *Future Ethics: Climate Change and Apocalyptic Imagination* (Continuum 2010), *Extinction and Religion* (with Jeremy Kidwell, Indiana University Press, forthcoming), and of numerous articles and chapters relating to theological and philosophical dimensions of the climate and ecological emergency.

**Sarah McFarland Taylor** is the award-winning author of *Green Sisters: A Spiritual Ecology* (Harvard University Press) and *Ecopiety: Green Media and the Dilemma of Environmental Virtue* (NYU Press). She is Associate Professor of Religious Studies, American Studies, and Environmental Policy and Culture at Northwestern University, and she specializes in the study of media, religion, environment, and public moral engagement. The director of the Calling Off the Apocalypse Project (CAP), based at Northwestern University, Taylor works with students, academic professionals in both STEM and the humanities, and entertainment industry mediamakers to teach and promote effective climate communication that engages both climate deniers and climate fatalists in productive ways.

**Emma Tomalin** is Professor of Religion and Public Life at the University of Leeds. A sociologist whose work is focused on religion, public life, global development, and gender, she has conducted research in South and Southeast Asia,

East Africa, and the United Kingdom. Among other books, she is the author of *Bio-divinity and Biodiversity* (2009) and *Working in Gender and Development* (2011) and the editor of *The Routledge Handbook of Religions and Global Development* (2015).

**Carol Wayne White** (she/her) is Professor of Philosophy of Religion at Bucknell University and the author of *Poststructuralism, Feminism, and Religion: Triangulating Positions* (2002), *The Legacy of Anne Conway (1631–70): Reverberations from a Mystical Naturalism* (2009), and *Black Lives and Sacred Humanity: Toward an African American Religious Naturalism* (2016), which won a Choice Award for Outstanding Academic Titles. She has received awards and fellowships from Oxford University, the John Templeton Foundation, and the NEH. Her current research explores the tenets and insights of religious naturalism expressed in contemporary American nature poets and writers in formulating a decolonizing model of eco-poetics.

# Preface to the Third Edition

When we submitted the manuscript for the second edition of this textbook in 2015, the editors did not know who would win the 2016 election in the United States or whether the United Kingdom would leave the European Union. We did not know what a coronavirus was. We did not know anything about the Dakota Access Pipeline or the Standing Rock reservation. We had never heard of #MeToo and were not paying much attention to the Black Lives Matter movement. We were paying even less attention to tensions between Ukraine and Russia.

So, a lot has happened in seven years.

We hope that this new edition will help readers understand how all of the events just mentioned, and so much else going on in the world, are connected to the study of religion and ecology.

This edition has ten entirely new chapters. One introduces environmental humanities, which has become an increasingly important part of the study of religion and ecology. The other nine are on intersections and issues we find increasingly important in the field: indigeneity, poverty, disability, privilege, vegetarianism, energy, extinction, biodiversity, and politics. Four others—on gender, animals, justice, and hope—have been rewritten by new authors. The remaining five—on religion, ecology, sexuality, climate change, and place—have been revised by their original authors.

We also expanded the methodologies in the book, including activist arguments alongside and in conjunction with scholarship. These chapters draw on a more diverse set of sources as the field of religion and ecology works to be more anticolonial and antiracist.

What remains unchanged from previous editions is the conviction that the 21st century calls everyone who can to think critically about religion, ecological systems, and the interconnections between them. In turbulent times, with an unpredictable future ahead of us all, we remain confident that such thinking matters.

# Acknowledgments

This book is largely about observing and analyzing connections. As editors, our most cherished connections are to the people who make our research, our writing, and our teaching possible. In this third edition, we have depended upon all the people who made the previous two editions possible and begun to learn from new colleagues, friends, and interlocutors.

*Grounding Religion* would be impossible without the hundreds of scholars of religious studies, ethics, theology, philosophy, history, sociology, and anthropology who have developed the case that religions matter in and to the rest of the natural world. Thanks to these scholars, recent decades have seen an expanding array of resources on the intersection between religious and environmental issues that sheds light on both the traditionally understood "religions" and on other practices and belief systems that are less frequently recognized as religious. As the bibliographies throughout this book demonstrate, we attempt to build on and appreciate that work. We particularly thank those who created and continue to sustain the Religion and Ecology Group at the American Academy of Religion; the International Society for the Study of Religion, Nature, and Culture; and the Forum on Religion and Ecology.

We would also like to thank the American Academy of Religion, which provided a Collaborative Research Grant for a 2009 colloquium, of which the first edition of this book was a surprising and welcome product. Those who contributed papers and conversation then remain cherished colleagues: Evan Berry, Brian G. Campbell, Forrest Clingerman, Eleanor Finnegan, Sarah Fredericks, Laura M. Hartman, Greg Hitzhusen, Willis Jenkins, Luke Johnston, Elizabeth McAnally, Sam Mickey, Tovis Paige, Sam Snyder, Gavin van Horn, Joseph Witt, Devi Dillard-Wright, and Greg Zuschlag.

Many other mentors and friends have also been essential to our growing understanding of religion and ecology, including Dave Aftandilian, Trevor Bechtel, Kate Blanchard, Christopher Carter, Elonda Clay, Marion Grau, John Grim, Melanie Harris, Noreen Hertzfeld, Catherine Keller, Lois Lorentzen, Jim Maritiam, Bobbi Patterson, Larry Rasmussen, Sarah Robinson, Rosemary Radford Ruether, Whitney Sanford, Lisa Sideris, Bron Taylor, Mary Evelyn Tucker, and Joe Witt.

We are especially grateful to the authors in this edition, who represent a wealth of intelligence, research, and positive change. Those who had worked with us on previous editions—Brian G. Campbell, Laura M. Hartman, Laurel Kearns, and Carol Wayne White—were willing to update, rethink, and restructure their contributions based on changes in the field and the world. Those who are new to this edition—Miguel A. De La Torre, Nicole Hoskins, Sarah Withrow King, Dana Lloyd, Catherine L. Newell, Maria Nita, Amanda M. Nichols, Lisa D. Powell, Kate Rigby, Terra Schwerin Rowe, Stefan Skrimshire, Sarah McFarland Taylor, and Emma Tomalin—offered crucial new insights and perspectives. We thank all of them for their diligent work and for putting up with our many, many emails.

Finally, thanks to our editorial contacts at Routledge: Jasti Bahvya, Iman Hakimi, Ceri McLardy, and Rebecca Shillabeer. Their help throughout the process and commitment to the project has been essential.

# Introduction

*Whitney A. Bauman, Richard Bohannon, and Kevin J. O'Brien*

This book is about critically studying the intersection between religion and ecology while recognizing the complexity and importance of each concept.

Religion matters. The majority of the world's people still identify as belonging to or shaped by a religious belief system; questions about the public role of religious morality in politics and society remain hugely controversial; and threats of terrorism, xenophobic nationalisms, and violent extremism motivated by religious belief have become a background part of contemporary life.

And religion is complicated. Every religious and spiritual tradition contains multitudes. People who share religious identities express their commitments in different ways, and even those who do not identify as religious are influenced by the practices, teachings, and structures of religious traditions.

The non-human, natural world in all its diversity, which we will refer to as ecology, also matters. Humans emerged from and depend utterly upon on earth's ecological systems; even our technologies and cultures are themselves products of the natural world. In the 21st century, we are also increasingly aware that the ecological systems upon which we depend are threatened by the institutions and people of the industrialized world. The air, soil, water, and climate of earth have been changed and are, in many ways, less hospitable to human life than they were before.

And ecology, too, is complicated. The word itself can refer to a branch of biology, an activist movement, a generalized complex system, or the local or global non-human world. Even if we could find agreement on what "nature" or "ecology" is, different cultures have vastly different ideas about how it should be treated and understood and how we should assess the impact of industrialized humans upon it.

Religion and ecology are important, and they are complicated. They become even more important and more complicated when we study the ways they matter to one another, the ways the religious world influences and is influenced by ecological systems. The chapters that follow are meant to inspire questions about this intersection, to help you think critically about the role of each in shaping the other and everything else. The chapters investigate places where religion and ecology meet, introduce ongoing debates within the academic field of religion and ecology, and raise some of the important questions yet to be answered.

DOI: 10.4324/9781003259466-1

## Connecting Religion and Ecology in a Context of Environmental Degradation

Two assumptions are shared throughout the book: (1) there is an important connection between religion and ecology, and (2) this connection is particularly important today because of climate change, species extinction, and environmental injustices.

### *The Intersection of Religion and Ecology*

There is a widespread, and false, assumption that people who are devoutly religious do not care about the environment. Religious people are understood to focus their attention exclusively on a narrow set of cultural rules, on a heaven beyond this reality, and/or on nirvanistic salvation from natural cycles of renewal. At its extreme, this understanding leads some to believe that people of faith are all antagonistic to ecological science and the natural environment. More moderately, many assume that religion is a distinct sphere that should not and does not interact with science and public policy. From this view, religion should have nothing to do with studies of the natural world or claims to environmental responsibility.

This imagined divide between religion and science can be traced to the history of the two terms, which came to their present meanings during the growth of European colonization. The idea of religion (as we will discuss in Chapter 1) was developed as European colonizers came into contact with other cultures. They labeled some aspects of those cultures "religious" in an effort to categorize and control other peoples. At the same time, European scientists began to develop a methodology that distinguished their work from both the "superstition" of other cultures and the "faith" of Western spiritual traditions. This created a divide between the domains of religion and science. In the 18th and 19th centuries, modern Western university disciplines were developed to reify this division, separating natural sciences from social and humanistic studies. The former included all physical and biological subjects, studying nature and bodies. The latter included the humanities and religious studies and focused on art, culture, language, and the human spirit.

But this strict division between religion and the natural world is untenable. It ignores the complexity of religious and cultural traditions, all of which are connected to and influenced by the natural world. It ignores the fact that all of culture and spirituality takes place in the context of bodies and that scientists can only understand nature through human contexts.

When one looks closely at any religious tradition, one always finds considerations of and connections to the natural world. The Buddha's enlightenment took place outdoors, under a bodhi tree. The Muslim Qur'an and the Hebrew Bible both repeatedly stress that communities are shaped by land. The most sacred site on earth for many Hindus is the Ganges River. The parables of Jesus in Christian scriptures frequently draw on images from the natural world, prominently featuring mustard seeds, trees, seas, and wildlife. Most indigenous traditions include trickster figures that move between plant, human, animal, and ancestral worlds. These are just a small sample of the many ways in which recognized, mainstream religions have long been concerned with and related to ecological systems.

Other connections between religion and the natural world extend beyond traditional categories. Many people inside and outside of traditional religious structures experience a profound sense of holy or numinous realities in the natural world. Gardeners, kayakers, anglers, trail runners, and surfers frequently describe their activities and passions in spiritual terms. The outdoors and the wilderness feel sacred to many people, whether they explain this as a connection to a transcendent divine creative force or the immanent reality of ecological interdependence. Many people also feel stirring wonder at the realities of cosmology: our 4.5-billion-year-old Earth is a tiny speck in the vast 13.7-billion-year-old universe, and every person and creature that has ever existed is made from the dust of stars. While some might describe such experiences as spiritual rather than religious, we are not terribly interested in that distinction. Instead, we focus on the inevitable connection between the spiritual/religious realm of human cultures and the non-human world.

*Grounding Religion*, therefore, assumes that religion and ecology are interrelated, and so the scholarly study of religion must include attention to the ways religious and spiritual traditions relate to environmental issues and priorities. Religions do not simply appear and exist on their own, *sui generis*. They emerge and evolve in conversation with other social and natural forces. Religions, in turn, shape how human beings choose to think about, relate to, and treat the natural world. Religions matter and materialize in the natural world through collective human actions. So human cultures matter greatly to how the very concept of "nature" gets constructed, and the natural world itself matters in how the concept of "religion" is constructed.

### *The Contemporary Importance of Religion and Ecology*

Understanding the intersection of religion and ecology is particularly important in today's context of environmental degradation and its multiple, overlapping crises and injustices.

The climate is rapidly changing, following patterns that have been predicted by scientific models for decades but are nevertheless shocking political and cultural systems and endangering lives. The burning of fossil fuels, which has been a defining characteristic of industrialization, emits billions of tons of greenhouse gases like carbon dioxide and methane each year. These gases trap heat, impacting the wildly complex system of the planet's climate and therefore influencing every ecosystem and every creature on earth. The heat in the atmosphere affects the temperature in the oceans, which affects the currents, which affect the breeding of fish, which affects the health of bears, which affects the health of forests, and so on. These gases also persist in the atmosphere, and so the climate will continue changing more severely and unpredictably in the future.

Another, related example of environmental degradation is the destruction of biodiversity and species extinction. The development and extraction of resources from land decimates ecosystems and habitats, leading to a rate of species loss that is estimated as much as a thousand times faster than it would be without human activity. Life on earth is currently suffering through its sixth mass extinction event;

the fifth was sixty-five million years ago and eradicated the dinosaurs. Biodiversity is threatened in rainforests as trees are burned, in prairies as invasive species are introduced, in rivers as dams are built, and in crop fields as one species is grown and all others treated as weeds to be killed.

Although the impacts of climate change and biodiversity loss are planet-wide, they are not equally distributed. In human communities, the poor and marginalized are most likely to suffer from extreme weather events and to be dependent upon specific species as key food sources and cultural touchstones. This is a particular injustice because the poor and marginalized tend to have contributed the least to the problem. Those without significant political and economic power have put very few greenhouse gases into the atmosphere and yet are most likely to be driven from their homes by the floods and droughts of climate change. Indeed, the number of climate migrants and climate refugees is increasing every year. Those in non-industrialized cultures tend to have generations-long, sustainable relationships with their local ecosystems, and yet outsiders' actions destroy the forests and waters and the animals with which their cultures developed.

Other environmental problems are also inequitably distributed. Neighborhoods, reservations, and habitats where poor and marginalized communities live are more likely than others to have polluted air, water, and land. The people most directly impacted by waste dumped in rivers and oceans are those who drink unfiltered water and eat local fish. Urban populations suffer increased rates of asthma and other respiratory illnesses as they breathe more automotive and industrial exhaust. Countries in the majority/two-thirds/less-developed world are increasingly treated as a dumping ground for the waste and wasteful industries of the wealthy. In summary, poor, indigenous, black, and brown people are more likely to feel the effects of environmental crises than are wealthy, white people.

Environmental degradation exacerbates and exposes the injustices of political and economic structures both globally and locally. While environmental degradation is sometimes discussed as a problem caused by "humanity," this conceals the deep inequity between who has caused and who is suffering these problems. Treating the human race as a single environmental agent conceals the histories of colonialism, genocide, slavery, and economic inequities.

This book assumes not only that environmental degradation and injustices are a real and complicated set of problems, but also that these problems form a vital context for discussing religion. If religion and spirituality are going to be relevant to life today, they need to respond to the realities of climate change, extinction, pollution, and inequality. If faith traditions and spiritual practices are to fulfill their role as moral guides, they need to reflect on the ethical implications of these trends and inspire people to more just and sustainable lives.

## The Academic Field of Religion and Ecology

These two assumptions—that religious traditions are related to the natural world and that this relationship is particularly important given contemporary environmental degradation—are not unique to this book but rather emerge from the academic field of religion and ecology.

This field has roots in centuries of scholarship but began to take explicit shape in the 1960s. Since then, scholars have explored the implications of religious ideas for responding to environmental degradation; proposed new applications of long-standing spiritual traditions to environmental questions; and developed new moral and religious models for relationships between human communities, other animals, and the rest of the natural environment. Religion and ecology as a field is deeply interdisciplinary, incorporating the work of philosophers, ethicists, theologians, sociologists, historians, and many others. In addition, the field frequently draws upon the natural sciences, incorporating the findings of biologists, physicists, cosmologists, geneticists, and ethologists about the interconnectedness of reality, the origins of human cultural systems, and the character of the world to which religion responds and relates. Religion and ecology is also characterized by moral commitments to environmental sustainability and human justice. So the field challenges simplistic divides between humanities and sciences, between humanity and the natural world, between environment and justice, and between thought and action.

Because it has developed among so many conversations, even naming this academic field is difficult. The editors of this book have chosen "religion and ecology," but colleagues we respect refer to it as "religion and nature." They assert—with many good reasons—that "nature" is a broader category than "ecology," allowing for more two-way reflection (from sciences/nature to religion and from religion to nature). They also argue that "religion and ecology" has focused too exclusively on a static list of world religions. "Religion and nature" signals, for some, a more inclusive perspective that also attends to less-recognized religious movements, such as neopaganism or spiritual environmentalism and minority viewpoints within all traditions. Others focus on even broader categories, such as "environmental humanities," within which "religion and ecology" and "religion and nature" both fit.

This book uses "religion and ecology" for two reasons. First, this name has the longest history and institutional structure: the group that studies these issues within the American Academy of Religion, the premier organization for scholars of religion in North America, calls itself Religion and Ecology, with the support of the influential Forum on Religion and Ecology at Yale University. The second reason is more philosophical: while we appreciate the breadth of the term "nature," we value the specificity of "ecology" even more. Ecology calls particular attention to systems of interconnection, to the energy and material exchange between organisms, and to the relationships between the living and nonliving.

The debate over what to call the field is just one way that religion and ecology continues to evolve. As scholars understand more about the natural world, study the history and range of religious ideas and practices, and expand our views of what counts as "religion" and "ecology," academic studies change. Even more importantly, the field responds to a changing world; environmental degradation is an ongoing process, and so scholarly understanding of it continues to develop. There is no static "environment" or "ecology" or "nature." There is also no static "religion." Spiritual beliefs and practices are part of ever-changing human cultures, and all religions reflect internal debates and adaptations to new experiences. So the study of religion and ecology is about the intersection of two ever-changing concepts, ensuring that there is always more to learn. This book is in its third edition for that reason, and we suspect that by the time you read these words, we will be thinking about ideas or trends that have changed since we finished writing. Nevertheless, we predict that the big questions of how to think about religion, nature, and justice will remain relevant.

## The Integrative Methodology of Religion and Ecology

As diverse as it is and as much as it changes, scholarship in religion and ecology is broadly characterized by its focus on intersections and integration, bringing disparate perspectives together and insisting that scholars combine multiple ideas and perspectives rather than having to choose between them. This is demonstrated in the previous section by the synthesis between ideas about nature and culture, the sciences and the humanities, and justice and environmentalism.

Another integration can be seen in the way the field treats religion itself. Some scholars of religion insist on a choice between "worldviews"—the attitudes and views of religious leaders, sacred texts, and traditions—on the one hand, and "lived religions"—the practices and actions of religious people in their day-to-day lives—on the other. There are ancient roots for such a choice in debates between Platonic ideals and Aristotelian natural philosophy, and more recent precedent in the tension between Hegelian idealism and Marxist materialism. But religion and ecology refuses the choice; it is committed to understanding both theory and practice, both ideas and actions, and both worldviews and lived religion as complementary and mutually informative.

One cannot study religion without paying attention to worldviews. Religious people have spent thousands of years consciously and subconsciously developing stories and explanations of how and why things came to be along with controversial belief systems about the future of humanity in relation to the world around us and the gods and/or God structuring it. These cosmologies and teachings shape the thoughts, emotions, ideals, and values of millions of peoples. Worldviews also have vital environmental implications: how we understand the relationship between human beings and the rest of the world will shape our decisions about how to treat other beings and one another. For example, it matters a great deal whether people believe that the human species is a product of an evolutionary process just like every other species or a unique and distinct creation with a special role to play in an ordered chain of being.

However, the lived experience of religious people cannot always be explained by their broad worldviews. The religion of a devout Buddhist in contemporary China cannot be reduced to the Four Noble Truths and the teachings of the Buddha; rather, every life needs to be studied and appreciated on its own terms, in its own context. The attitudes of Evangelical Christians toward environmental issues should not be derived solely by reading the Bible and their pastors' sermons; it is also important to talk to the people in the pews and pay attention to their behavior. The Indonesian Muslim who also adheres to Javanese cosmology and medicine cannot be reduced to a single framework of belief. So a study of the environmental impacts of religious belief cannot focus only on broad generalizations about beliefs; it is important to also learn from specific practices and behaviors, from what people do.

To study only worldviews would allow religious leaders and powerful spokespeople to exclusively define religions, ignoring people's diverse perspectives and practices. At the same time, to study only lived religion would make it impossible to connect people within and across faiths. Observations of lived religions need the connections made possible by worldviews, while worldviews need the details and differences provided by a lived religions approach. So the methodology of religion and ecology synthesizes the two, building connections between thought and action, between ideas and practices.

Another synthesis in religion and ecology comes in the assumption that activists need scholars and scholars need activists. This may surprise some people, particularly those who distinguish the scholarly world of academics from the "real" world of practical concerns outside it. It is true that, just as there is a reason to distinguish worldviews and lived religion, there are differences between scholarship and practical action. The academic world is designed to develop intellectual skills, to provide space and time for students and scholars to nurture habits of critical thinking and analysis. Activists, by contrast, seek to make concrete change, working on a clear and often urgent timescale that encourages them to accept basic goals and ideas as given.

However, this distinction should not and cannot be absolute. The academic world is not just abstract; it is also a key place for generating behavior-changing ideas. At its best, a university is a community that asks you to question every assumption and provides the tools of analysis needed for creative solutions to ecological and social problems. Furthermore, the academic world itself is a space of lived experiences: students and their teachers develop habits of action and habitats for thinking. These can be instruments for social and environmental change in positive or negative directions, both on- and off-campus. In other words, academics is part of the real world, and so it makes a practical difference. That difference can be positive if academics train and inspire others to think critically about the world they have come to know and to make constructive changes to it.

Similar to critical theories that deal with race, gender, sex, sexuality, and class, scholars in the field of religion and ecology explicitly seek to make the world better. This field exists not just to develop theories and ideas but also to help people imaginatively consider how religion and/or the study of religion might build a better future for our species and our planet. This book is no exception; we invite you to study religious worldviews and environmental practices because we hope it will help you to make the world better.

Within *Grounding Religion*, you will find different approaches to balancing activism and scholarship. Some of the chapters are focused on scholarship, primarily posing questions and exposing complexities, with activist goals more subtly in the background. Others are very explicitly making arguments about specific changes that should be made in cultural systems and, potentially, in your life. But even the most activist chapters are influenced by deep thinking, just as the most scholarly chapters hope to make positive change. To study religion and ecology is to repeatedly practice striking a balance by identifying connections, reflecting critically, and contemplating what needs to change.

## Format of the Book

The first section, on religion and ecology, features introductory overviews of these central terms and an exploration of how they fit into the broader academic structure of environmental humanities. The second section, "Intersectional Locations," examines the concepts of indigeneity, gender, sexuality, poverty, race, disability, and privilege as they interact with both religion and ecology. The third section then examines eight focal issues that help to complicate, enrich, and explore the academic field of religion and ecology: climate change, animals, vegetarianism, energy, justice, extinction, diversity, politics, and place. The book then concludes with a reflection on the interplay between despair and hope. As you read through these chapters, you will notice many different styles and approaches. This is by design, and we hope it will leave you with a window into the diversity of scholarship in our field.

However, we also hope you will notice the commonalities across the chapters. All explore the intersections between religion and ecology broadly understood. All emphasize how important these intersections are in the context of contemporary environmental degradation. All synthesize attention to environmental health and human justice, working toward an antiracist and anticolonial approach to religion and ecology. All attend to both broad worldviews and lived religious experiences. And all bring rigorous scholarship into dialogue with activist awareness. In summary, all are part of the diverse and exciting field of religion and ecology.

This book is a "field guide" because it is designed to help you find your way around the study of religion and ecology. We hope that *Grounding Religion* will help you to see more and think more deeply about what you encounter in the world and to wrestle with the complexity and importance of religion and ecology.

No field guide can possibly include everything, and so we make no claim to have covered every relevant issue, idea, or term. Instead, the editors and authors aim to offer an introduction and a pedagogical tool. We expect those who read this book to continue applying what you learn here to other issues, intersections, and concepts. Above all, we hope that readers will continue the questioning and thinking essential for an academic study of religion and ecology.

# Part I

# Concepts

# 1 Religion

## What Is It, Who Gets to Decide, and Why Does It Matter?

*Whitney A. Bauman, Richard Bohannon, and Kevin J. O'Brien*

### Introduction

Max Weber, an early and influential sociologist, started his major treatise on the "Sociology of Religion" (1978 [orig. pub. 1922]) by noting that the term "religion" cannot be defined at the beginning of a study but only after one's research is complete. He then proceeded to write over five books on the subject but never achieved enough clarity or completion to reach a definition.

"Religion," it turns out, is a tricky word.

This chapter does not attempt to do what Weber neglected and will not offer a single, authoritative definition. Instead, we will explore a range of ways in which this tricky word is used by a range of people. This allows something more important than the clarity of a definition: critical analysis of the many ways people think about religion and the interests and dynamics that inform them when they do so. By reviewing seven different—and in some cases competing—perspectives, we will begin to introduce the diversity of ways that religion is practiced, studied, and criticized.

Whatever else it is, religion encompasses not only big traditions like Christianity and Hinduism and Buddhism but also newer phenomena like Scientology and neopaganism. In addition to those institutional and traditional structures, religion also includes daily practices and ideas that range from saying prayers, going to temples, talking to invisible spiritual beings, hugging trees, pouring out libations for deceased elders, and holding one's breath while driving past a graveyard. When we talk about religion, we are talking about all of this and far more.

This chapter assumes that such complexity is worth engaging, that whatever religion is, it matters. Religion shapes human life and therefore the world. It shapes global politics, it informs many individuals' lives and livelihoods, and it influences politics, culture, art, and language. It also shapes the environment. Basic ideas about how people relate to one another and the non-human world—which come from religion for many people—have impacted technology, colonization, and consumption. As human beings have become more and more populous on the planet, our religions are, more and more, shaping the air, water, and land of the earth.

DOI: 10.4324/9781003259466-3

**Religion Is a Unified and Unifying System**

We will start with a definition from the French sociologist Emile Durkheim (1858–1917). His perspective has been highly influential ever since he published it:

> A religion is a unified system of beliefs and practices relative to sacred things, that is to say, things set apart and forbidden—beliefs and practices which unite into one single community all those who adhere to them.
>
> (1995 [1912]: 46)

This definition emphasizes two aspects of religion: (1) it separates some aspects of life from others, marking the "sacred" off from the rest of "profane" reality, which (2) serves the social function of uniting a community. Consider the ways many Jewish people treat Saturday as a holy day, a day to worship and not to work. In Durkheim's definition, this is quintessentially religious: it separates one day out from the rest of the week as particularly sacred and uses that day to build community as Jews gather in temples and synagogues and spend time with their families. The community is united by a common understanding of the Sabbath, a day that is "set apart."

One important aspect of Durkheim's definition is that he is not particularly interested in whether any religion is "true" in a metaphysical sense. Instead, he emphasizes that religion is a social phenomenon, a creation of human beings and an institution that structures human life. As a founding figure in the field of sociology, Durkheim is primarily interested in the function of religion within social structures. In other words, rather than asking a question about the reality of religion per se (what philosophers might call a metaphysical or an ontological question), he takes religion as a social fact (something people believe in and live by).

So a student of religion learning from Durkheim would not try to identify what is "really" sacred. Instead, the task is to observe different ideas of the sacred in different traditions. For example, many Muslims and Christians consider their foundational texts—the Qur'an and the Bible—to be uniquely sacred. Hindus and Buddhists tend to have a wider range of texts but agree on the sacredness of particular times—Diwali and Vesak, for example. Many Indigenous traditions focus on the sacredness of particular places and ecosystems rather than texts or seasons. Durkheim's perspective helps us to see that, amid all this diversity, each tradition is distinguishing the sacred from the profane and thereby creating and solidifying communities.

## BOX 1A

Think of a community of which you are a part, whether it is explicitly religious or not, and consider what is "sacred" to that community. Are there objects or times or places or texts that are treated as special? Do those sacred things serve to unify the community?

Durkheim based his theory on a study of Aboriginal peoples from Australia, whom he believed practiced the most "ancient" religion in existence. He assumed that the oldest religions would reveal the roots from which all others had developed. As we will see in the next section, these assumptions are problematic. Nevertheless, his argument that religion serves a basic function in every culture has been very influential. Such thinking helped to inform the idea that there is a list of "world religions," an idea that has shaped the way most people in the Western world learn and think about religion for the last century. Traditional lists of the major religions tend to include Baha'i, Buddhism, Christianity, Confucianism, Daoism, Hinduism, Indigenous traditions, Islam, Jainism, Judaism, and Sikhism.

Within each of these religious traditions is a vast array of diversity, with widely divergent levels of commitment, approaches to practice, and relationships to the rest of the world. Islam is practiced very differently in Indonesia than it is in Saudi Arabia; traditions indigenous to South America are very different from those indigenous to New Zealand; a liberal Christian church in suburban Texas may feel no doctrinal or political connection to a conservative church Christian next door. From a Durkheimian perspective, though, every religion has a common function. Indeed, the fact that people in one religious context feel so different from others suggests that each religion is doing its job by creating unique and coherent communities.

This understanding has informed important projects linking religious communities to environmental projects. One example is the Forum on Religion and Ecology, an organization currently based at Yale University. In the 1990s, the Forum ran a series of ten conferences, each focused on a major world religion's intersection with environmental issues. Buddhists and Hindus studied the ways that the idea of karma can apply in ecological contexts; Muslims discussed examples of environmental stewardship in the life of the Prophet Muhammad; Christians and Jews identified scriptures that emphasize care for the land. The basic idea was Durkheimian: identify what is most sacred to a particular community and use it to bring them together around an environmental cause. We see these themes in the Forum's mission statement:

> The religions of the world transmit ecological and justice perspectives in their scriptures, rituals, and contemplative practices as well as in their moral and ethical commitments. We seek to identify those perspectives in the service of finding comprehensive and collaborative solutions to our global environmental crises.
>
> (The Forum on Religion and Ecology 2022)

### Religion Is a Western Construct

Critics of Durkheim argue that he made grand assumptions about religions beyond his own expertise and experience. His study of Australian religion was based on the ethnography of another European scholar rather than his own primary research or the perspectives of the Aboriginal peoples themselves. The peoples he wrote about would not have used terms directly comparable to "sacred" and "profane" and likely would not have thought of "religion" as a distinct part of their culture. So, critics suggest, Durkheim did not capture any universal truths about religion; he instead projected his own culture and ideas onto others.

Such analysis, which assumes that defining religion is itself an act of cultural creation and an exertion of power, informs the second approach we will study. Tomoko Masuzawa, a historian at the University of Michigan, makes no sweeping claims about religion and argues that there are deep problems with any list of "world religions." She writes,

> These so-called great religions of the world—though what makes them "great" remains unclear—are often arranged by means of one or the other of various systems of classification. . . . What these systems do, regardless of the variation, is to distinguish the West from the rest, even though the distinction is usually effected in more complicated ways than the still frequently used, easy language of "East and West" suggests.
>
> (2005: 2)

Unlike Durkheim, who sought to understand the broad phenomenon of religion as a universal characteristic of human societies, Masuzawa stresses that the very idea of religion is a cultural product. It has, she notes, been particularly used by people of European descent to assert power over others. In particular, lists of "world religions" tend to emphasize the difference between Eastern and Western traditions and suggests that Western ideas and communities are more progressive and more essential to humanity's future. As a classification system created over time by European men, world religions and the notion of "religion" as it is most commonly used tend to serve the interests of European, Christian cultures.

Masuzawa's broadest point is that all classifications systems are social constructions. Classifications that distinguish "religion" as a part of human cultures and list the most prominent "religions" in the world are made up by people and tend to serve the interests of the people who made them up. So any definition of religion or argument about what "counts" as religion involves power struggles.

**BOX 1B**

Can you think of other systems of classification that are taken for granted but might also be influenced by colonial categories? Do you see colonial influences in the ways educational systems are classified? Racial groups? Languages? What else?

Masuzawa demonstrates that much of the early modern study of religion was based on a hierarchy of religions that began with those seen as the most "primitive" and ended with those seen to be most "advanced" and "civilized." Most often, the pinnacle of this hierarchy was Christianity. This thinking informed Emile

Durkheim, who was himself Jewish but nevertheless developed a theory of religion that reflects the Catholic Church of his home country, France. It also informed his assumption that Aboriginal religion would be more "basic" and therefore easier to understand than European religions. He assumed his culture was the most developed and complicated, and this prevented him from recognizing the fullness and richness of others.

Furthermore, a colonial approach to religion fails to take account of how much any given tradition is made up of multiple others. Christianity cannot be examined outside of its relationship to Judaism, Islam, and the religions of the ancient Near East, not to mention the Indigenous religions it came into contact with through colonization. Similarly, Buddhism, Jainism, and Hinduism cannot be examined without understanding the ways they cross-pollinate across history. Drawing on the careful historical perspective Masuzawa demonstrates, we need to understand religion as an idea and every religious tradition as a construct that is always being contested and negotiated.

This does not mean we give up on trying to understand religion; Masuzawa is herself a scholar of religion. But she does offer reasons to attend to the power dynamics inherent in any such study. For example, traditions like Japanese Shinto and South Asian Hinduism are referred to as "religions" because of a Western classification system that has been globalized by economic and cultural colonization. Shinto and Hinduism might helpfully be understood as religions, but we cannot assume that they will fulfill all the expectations Westerners bring to that term. Many Hindus do not even think of themselves as "Hindu" (itself a Western term) but primarily affiliate with their geographic region of origin and its ritual traditions. Many practitioners of Shinto are also active Buddhists and would not understand these two "religions" as demanding an either-or choice.

The postcolonial perspective that Masuzawa provides also helps us to see how "religion" distorts most Indigenous peoples' experience of daily life. For many Indigenous peoples, there is no strict separation between culture, daily life, politics, and something like religion. Furthermore, unlike in monotheistic traditions, which tend to emphasize the distinction between the sacred and this world, most Indigenous traditions are animistic, understanding the entire natural world, including humans, as participating in a single sacred reality. The sacred is found in the intertwining of all things, the combination of the many agential, valuable creatures who come together in life. Western concepts of "religion" do not do a good job accounting for the integration of spirituality with landscapes and non-human animals.

Masuzawa's perspective suggests the need for caution at the intersection of religion and ecology. If the former idea has been shaped by colonialism and Western power, then it is worth treading lightly with any claims about what "world religions" or "religious people" should do about environmental degradation. It is also worth analyzing what cultural ideas and power are in the background when we talk about the environment and ecology, which we will discuss more in Chapter 3. From Masuzawa's perspective, all ideas are constructed in a cultural context and bear the imprint of the assumptions and interests of the people who created them. This is a crucial reminder as we continue to explore a range of ideas about religion.

**Religion Is About Ultimate Concern**

As social scientists, Tomoko Masuzawa and Emile Durkheim both understand religion as a phenomenon to be observed and characterized analytically, with methodologies and tools that can be externally verified. Others approach religion more experientially, defining the term based on their own spiritual lives and assuming that external forces beyond humanity shape our belief systems and practices.

One such perspective comes from the German American theologian Paul Tillich (1886–1965). Tillich wanted to understand religion in global and universal terms, not confined to any one tradition. He offered this brief but influential definition: "Religion is the state of being grasped by an ultimate concern" (1988 [1958]: 42). Here religion is understood primarily in terms of that to which people devote themselves. Religion is about one's "ultimate concern," whatever one is willing to give one's life for, the most important thing in reality, that against which all else is measured.

Influenced by his own Lutheran Christian tradition, Tillich believed in God and in the Christian story of God's revelation and incarnation in Jesus Christ. However, in an attempt to reach beyond the specifics of his own faith, he characterized God as "the Ultimate," a less culturally distinct term in which he hoped more people could recognize their highest truth. Tillich assumed that all people, not just Christians, are shaped by some ultimate concern.

For Tillich, all people are "grasped by" the same Ultimate: Muslims, Christians, Jews, and Hindus might name God differently, but they are all talking about the same reality. His approach also suggests that while many Buddhists and Confucians, atheists, and others do not believe in or align themselves to a singular god, they could still live in service to some capital-T "Truth," such as compassion, justice, or community.

Tillich wanted his definition to inspire personal reflection; he wanted his readers to ask what was acting as the "ultimate concern" in their lives. What is at the center of who you are? What do you treat as the primary source of truth and goodness and clarity? When do you allow—and when do you resist—being "grasped" by that ultimate concern? When do you, instead, occupy yourself with something less than ultimate, something that is less than your highest ideal? In the terms of Christian theology, Tillich is asking people to recognize when they fall into idolatry, giving allegiance to things that are less than God, less than Ultimate.

**BOX 1C**

Do you feel comfortable with the questions just asked in relationship to your own, "ultimate concern"? Are they questions you have ready answers for? Would you feel comfortable talking about those questions with your family, friends, or neighbors? Why or why not?

In his 2015 letter on climate change, *Laudato Si'*, Pope Francis uses a similar understanding of religion to make an environmental argument. He writes,

> A spirituality which forgets God as all-powerful and Creator is not acceptable. That is how we end up worshiping earthly powers, or ourselves usurping the place of God, even to the point of claiming an unlimited right to trample his creation.
>
> (Francis 2015: ¶75)

Note the way this quote links idolatry to environmental degradation. People "trample creation" because they have begun to spend their time on things that are less than God. In the terms of Tillich's definition, the pope explains environmental degradation by the fact that people are making something less than the Ultimate their central concern. The universalism of Tillich's approach is also reflected in Pope Francis' letter. He seeks to appeal to more than just Catholics or Christians, instead addressing himself to "every person living on this planet" and calling for a response to climate injustice from people of all faiths (Francis 2015: ¶3).

Another environmental application of Tillich's definition sees the environmental cause itself as an ultimate concern. People who do not believe in an "Ultimate God" could still embrace the idea that the earth's integrity should be an ultimate concern around which people should unite. António Guterres, the secretary general of the United Nations, said in 2020 that "making peace with nature is the defining task of the 21st century. It must be the top, top priority for everyone, everywhere" (2020). While this is not an explicitly religious claim, Tillich's definition makes it possible to understand it in religious terms. Guterres is calling for an ultimate focus on environmental justice and implicitly criticizing anyone who would attend instead to less important matters. According to Tillich, this is a religious argument.

The power of Tillich's definition is that it creates universal common ground: if there is an Ultimate with which everyone can have a direct relationship, then all human beings have something fundamental in common. If one believes, as both Tillich and Pope Francis do, that there is a divine source of Truth that grasps everyone everywhere, then it is possible to call for a global movement to solve big problems like the destruction of biodiversity and the unjust distribution of toxic waste. Asking people to evaluate their ultimate concerns and to serve something truly Ultimate is, in this approach, a key path to environmental change.

## Religion Is Not a Helpful Category for All Cultures

One limitation of Tillich's definition is that in seeking a universal and encompassing understanding of religion, he largely ignores the many differences between religious traditions and the wildly diverse cultures and contexts in which they are expressed. He assumes that everyone has an "ultimate concern" that can and should animate their lives, but he does not pay much attention to the particularities that come from specific identities and add richness, character, and specificity to each person's experience.

A different perspective comes from the author and consultant Mary Lou Fox, an Ojibwe teacher and language activist who is the founding director of the Ojibwe

Cultural Foundation in Ontario, Canada. When asked about her understanding of religion, Fox says that the term does not translate into her culture:

> If you ask me to differentiate between religion and religion of Indian people, we really don't have a religion per se, but really it's a way of life and we call it *anishinaabe bimadiziwin*. It's just the way you live and it's something that's really twenty-four hours a day. It's your thinking and it's not like just on Sunday that you go to church or that you pray at a certain time. But really they say that every act should be an act of thanksgiving and praise.
>
> (Quoted in Smith 1995: 25)

One could perhaps fit this approach into Tillich's definition. In that reading, Fox treats the way of life of the Ojibwe people, *Anishinaabe bimadiziwin*, as ultimate, and so she is concerned with praising and thanking the world around her at all times. However, that understanding ignores the way she frames her own beliefs and practices.

Fox explicitly says, "We don't have a religion." Instead, she focuses on the way of life of her people. In contrast to Tillich's view, Fox makes no appeal to an ultimate or universal concern. In contrast to Durkheim, she resists any separation of the sacred from the rest of life. So, she suggests, religion is not a helpful concept for her culture.

As explained by Theresa Smith, in whose book Fox is quoted, the Anishinaabeg culture in the region known today as the Great Lakes is best understood as a "lifeway," a holistic system that does not distinguish between the spheres of life like family, work, and religion (1995). Ojibwe lifeways are characterized by relationships to people, to land, to animals, and to *manitouk*, which are other-than-human Thunderers in the sky and Mishebeshu in the water. The relationships between these different beings lead to fascinating stories from which all people can learn, but they are uniquely resonant to Ojibwe people when communicated in the Ojibwe language.

Mary Lou Fox resists the category of religion because she is not focused on finding common ground between peoples across cultures. Rather, she focuses on the particularity of her own community, defining their lifeway and the ways it shapes their experiences and behavior.

This impulse to focus on the particular rather than the universal, the local rather than the global, has a clear analogue in environmentalism. A movement called bioregionalism argues that the biggest problems of the 21st century came from the globalization of industrial cultures, related to attempts by European and European-descended people to understand, encompass, and control the planet as a whole. Bioregionalists argue that the same universal and global thinking cannot solve the problems it has created, and so they call for people to learn to inhabit the specific ecosystems in which they live, frequently seeking to learn from Indigenous communities about how to do so.

For example, the Standing Rock Reservation became a focal point for environmental organizing in 2016 when the Lakota and Dakota people who live there declared that their land and water were threatened by the proposed construction of the Dakota Access Pipeline. Tribal members gathered on the shores of the Mississippi for "ceremony, prayer, and water protection," which the media labeled a protest (Whyte 2017: 158). Thousands of people from all over the world camped alongside the water protectors in support, the world paid attention, and the pipeline was delayed. This was not an intervention in the global problem of climate change but rather a very specific effort to protect a place and the lifeways of the people native to it (Estes 2017). Such local efforts are, for many bioregionalists and many Indigenous people, the only path forward to resist the colonial exploitation of globalization.

Mary Lou Fox offers a reminder that the category of "religion" does not work for all people and cultures and that there is much to learn from and much to respect in Indigenous communities who think of themselves, the non-human world, and the sacred in other terms.

**Religion Is a Response to Pain**

Not all universal definitions of religion come from Europeans. Another prominent definition is written by the Japanese Zen Buddhist monk D. T. Suzuki (1870–1966): "Religion is the inmost voice of the human heart that under the yoke of a seemingly finite existence groans and travails in pain" (1963: 24).

Like Tillich, Suzuki bases his understanding of religion in a universal human experience. But instead of transcendence and connection beyond the self, Suzuki focuses on the internal experience of suffering. While Tillich suggested that the universal human experience is the quest for meaning and purpose, Suzuki suggests that the most fundamental human need is to relieve suffering.

One can see the influence of Suzuki's Buddhist background here. The first noble truth of the Buddha's teachings is *dukkha*, the reality of suffering. In other words, Buddhism teaches that the first step along the path to enlightenment is accepting that everyone who lives experiences disappointment and pain. It makes sense, then, that Suzuki would understand religion as a response to the troubling reality that all things "groan and travail." In Buddhism, the truth of *dukkha* leads to an explanation and a set of practices: most Buddhists understand suffering to be caused by attached desire, and they perform practices like prayer and meditation in hopes of reducing attachments.

What all religious beliefs and practices have in common, Suzuki suggests, is that they help people to deal with the inevitability of suffering. For example, many Jews and Muslims emphasize the importance of law and tradition as a way to bring order to the otherwise chaotic world and its troubles. Baha'i scriptures teach that suffering is a test from God through which the faithful can grow. Scientology suggests that the right information provided by the church can free its followers from the thoughts and emotions that hurt them.

Suzuki treats religion as something internal; it is an emotional, affective phenomenon created by "the human heart." Religion helps people to process their own suffering and, hopefully, to be more empathetic and responsive to the suffering of others. Religion is not accountable to some distant "Ultimate" and does not have to create cohesion across an entire society. Instead, it is about the alleviation of pain. The fundamental religious question from this perspective is this: why are beings suffering and what can we do to reduce that suffering?

The environmental implications of this perspective are demonstrated by the Buddhist scholar and activist Joanna Macy, who has been prominent in the environmental movement since the 1980s. Macy has spent her career helping to develop perspectives, rituals, and stories that help activists remain grounded and committed in the face of the enormous environmental and social challenges they face. She suggests that the sheer scope of these problems can be overwhelming. The destruction of ecosystems, the inequality of social systems, and the uncertainty of the future are scary and painful; many people are tempted to turn away, to ignore the problem and seek comfort in material possessions or distractions. A popular response to the pain of the earth and its creatures is denial. However, Macy argues that denial never works, that it never actually helps anyone to truly deal with suffering.

Instead, she argues, Buddhism teaches that the proper response to suffering and pain is to be fully present to it. In environmental terms, this means facing the travails of the planet with eyes wide open. "Grief can ambush us at any time, and our power doesn't have anything to do with being immune to that. It derives rather from our capacity to suffer with—the literal meaning of compassion." Honestly facing the pain of climate change, species extinction, and injustice will allow environmentalists to "discover who you really are, to let all the falseness that we imprison ourselves in be stripped away" (Macy 2000: 255).

The power of this approach to environmental issues is that it focuses on the suffering of real creatures. Mass extinction and climate change can feel like abstractions, too big to fully understand or even think about. If the purpose of environmentalism is not to "solve" big problems but to do what one can about the specific suffering of beings, the issues become less overwhelming. Perhaps the religious approach to extinction is not to try to save every species everywhere, but to save one habitat and prevent the creatures in it from suffering needlessly. Perhaps the best way to get people to care about climate change is not to show graphs of global temperatures but to talk about the pain of a particular group of refugees driven from their home by a flood.

For Macy and Suzuki, suffering is a fundamental reality of existence, and the role of religion is to help people deal constructively with it. This view, focused on the ways religion responds to an immanent experience, insists that all people are religious in some way because all people find a way to deal—healthily or otherwise—with suffering. Whatever we do when faced with the suffering of other people and creatures is our religion.

## Religion Is the Sigh of the Oppressed

While Suzuki's definition suggests that every human being and every human culture is in some way religious, others suggest that religion is something that people can—and perhaps should—opt out of. Perhaps the most famous such definition comes from the 19th-century German philosophers Karl Marx and Friedrich Engels, who had expansive theories about history, politics, and economics. This included an understanding of religion, which they define this way:

> Religion is the sigh of the oppressed creature, the heart of a heartless world, just as it is the spirit of a spiritless situation. It is the opium of the people. The abolition of religion as the illusory happiness of the people is required for their real happiness.
>
> (1964 [1844]: 42)

Like Durkheim, Marx and Engels understood religion as a social system that functions for a purpose. But unlike him, they believed that this purpose was not constructive and was not essential. Like Suzuki, they thought of religion as a way of making difficult experiences more tolerable. But unlike him, they believed that this was a problem. While making suffering more tolerable may be useful and necessary at times, they believed that it ultimately keeps people from making important changes in their societies. Religion may soothe and comfort the poor masses, they argued, but in doing so, it legitimates the economic imbalances that keep them poor. It creates illusions that distract people from how painful their reality has become.

As materialists, Marx and Engels insisted that all belief systems and social structures, including religions, develop out of the actual conditions in which people live. What people believe and do is a product of how they work, where they live, and how their basic needs are provided for. Religion is a product of oppressive systems, serving as an opiate, medicinal pain relief. It brings short-term comfort but also slows people down and inhibits their initiative. Religion makes it less likely that people will revolt and so supports the status quo.

While the previous quote refers to the "abolition" of religion, Marx and Engels believed that this would occur gradually and inevitably as the need for illusions and opiates lessened. They even opposed some of their radical peers who argued that religion should be illegal in a socialist society. Instead, they believed that the priority should be creating new and less oppressive social conditions. When that is done, religion will no longer be necessary; when people are no longer oppressed, they will not require "the sigh of the oppressed creature." The prediction of a secular, communist future has not occurred on the time scale Marx and Engels seemed to expect, but their critique of religion nevertheless remains vitally important.

**BOX 1D**

In what communities or media have you heard arguments against religion, arguments that religious belief is dangerous or backwards? Who tends to make such arguments, and why? What do you think can be learned from them?

Though Marx and Engels were not particularly optimistic about what religious people could do for liberation, many theologians and religious studies scholars draw from their work. Perhaps the most famous example are Latin American liberation theologians, who apply Marxist categories to relate the suffering of the poor and marginalized in their home countries to the suffering of Jesus. Gustavo Guitierrez (1988), for instance, argues for the "preferential option for the poor" within Christian theology. He argues that if Jesus were alive today, he would be with the poor, the starving, criminals, and outcasts. All religious thinking, then, should start from the perspective of the "least of these." Theologian Leonardo Boff extends this "option for the poor" to other animals and the rest of the natural world. He argues that in a world of environmental degradation, Jesus would stand with all the poor of the earth, not just the human ones (1995).

Other environmental thinkers follow the example of Marx and Engels to present religion as dangerous because it can lull people into a false sense of security. While very few environmentalists advocate for the "abolition" of religion, many argue that promises of otherworldly salvation distract people from the problems of this world. For example, many climate activists note that religious people are prominent among those who argue against the scientific evidence for climate change.

One such critical voice is the scholar Bron Taylor, who is concerned that the most mainstream and powerful religions in the world are "ancient dreams . . . for which there is no evidence and many reasons to doubt" (Taylor 2010: 221). Noting that the world's dominant religions were formed long before contemporary scientific understandings of the world and long before human beings were a dominant force in global systems, he suggests that they are largely incompatible with nature as most people now understand it and that they distract people from the important crises now facing human societies. Taylor focuses more positively on new religious movements which he groups under the heading "Dark Green Religion." These are beliefs and practices based on a commitment to the earth itself as sacred. Taylor understands nascent neopagan and activist spiritualities as moving toward a new religion that is "firmly grounded in an evolutionary-ecological worldview . . . in what we can confidently say is the real world" (Taylor 2010: 221).

While his thinking is not explicitly Marxist and he is more convinced that religion can be constructive, Taylor's approach to religion bears some resemblance to the previous definition. Like Marx and Engels, he worries that religion can be illusory and so distract people from reality; like them, he worries that religion can prevent social change. This critical perspective is an important part of any consideration of religion and ecology.

## Conclusion: Religion Matters

It might be tempting to argue that if the thinkers cited here can have such divergent perspectives on religion, the term has become meaningless. Perhaps religion can just be defined any way one wants?

The authors of this chapter see it differently. We learn from the thinkers cited here that it is possible to communicate about what religion is, what it does, and what it might be. Of course, there are multiple perspectives on these issues because the world is wildly diverse and people have vastly different experiences. But the questions matter a great deal. The task of studying religion is to engage these questions while learning from others, to be open to new possible answers from all directions.

Definitions of religion matter because they work as filters through which we see things. If you believe that all religions are about an "ultimate concern"—as did Tillich—or that they demarcate "the sacred"—as did Durkheim—then you will start asking religious people what they consider "sacred" or most worthy of concern. You will likely assume that whatever they discuss with you is central to their religious experience. If you attend more to the power dynamics inherent in discussions of religion—as Masuzawa and Marx did—then you will focus your attention on the historical conditions that frame any given conversation. If you assume that religion is a response to suffering—as do both Marx and Suzuki, in different ways—then you will pay particular attention to how each spiritual system addresses, mitigates, or disguises the key sources of suffering in human life. If you focus on the lifeway of your own community—as Fox did—then you will be cautious about assuming that you have any expertise in the belief systems and practices of others. Different definitions highlight different aspects of religion.

Another question posed by these definitions concerns what counts as a religion. If we assume with Durkheim that religion is a unifying social force centered around demarcating the sacred from the profane, then we will start looking for organized groups of people who clearly distinguish one category of things as special and holy and separate from the rest of the world. When seeking religious responses to environmental degradation, we will likely look to organized structures like the Roman Catholic Church, the Religious Society of Friends, the Rabbinical Assembly, or the World Union for Progressive Judaism. These are important groups, and it is valuable to research how each of these institutions has developed a response to environmental degradation in light of what their leaders consider most sacred.

However, not all religious activities are reflected in such organizational structures. Masuzawa would likely point out that looking for institutional structures biases one in favor of Western institutions that thrive in currently existing political structures and so excludes many non-Western and non-industrialized cultures. Mary Lou Fox reminds us that it is possible to forego such broad perspectives and instead attend to the particular lifeways of a place-based community. To engage the spirituality of a particular Indigenous community or a Christian house church leads to different understandings of religious environmentalism than a broad institutional analysis.

Tillich and Suzuki's more inclusive definitions of religion offer a helpful corrective, freeing us to see religion in *any* attempt to make meaning or respond to suffering. It is easy to see how many communities, whether or not they are formally organized, could be recognized as "religious" from these perspectives. This makes the field of religion and ecology much broader. Indeed, these definitions can be used to characterize the environmental movement itself as religious. When they respond to the suffering of polar bears and polluted neighborhoods, appeal to the integrity and beauty of Mother Earth, or declare an ecosystem sacred, environmentalists can be understood to be acting religiously.

**BOX 1E**

Do you think it makes sense to call environmentalism and/or the climate justice movement religious? What difference might it make to the goals and cause of activists if they understood their work this way?

Finally, Marx and Engels' perspective can inform skepticism about whether religious groups will respond constructively to environmental crises. According to their definition, religion is fundamentally opposed to any real social change, and so people concerned with environmental degradation should seek to understand and study religion as a product of the problem rather than part of the solution.

There is no one way to think about religion, no single definition or perspective or even rejection of the term that makes sense from all sides. This means that anyone studying the intersection of religion and the environment needs to take complexity seriously, to keep multiple possibilities and perspectives in mind.

But this complexity brings us back to our starting point: religion (or something like it) is important. However it is understood and framed, the religious world is a major force in shaping how human beings interact with the world, and it is continually being reshaped by changing social and ecological contexts. Amid all the disagreements, this idea unites all the perspectives discussed here, it unites scholars of religion and ecology, and it unites the contributors to this book. Whatever definition we use, religion matters.

## References

Boff, L. (1995) *Ecology and Liberation: A New Paradigm*, trans. J. Cumming. Maryknoll, NY: Orbis Books.

Durkheim, E. (1995) *The Elementary Forms of Religious Life*, trans. K. E. Fields. New York: Free Press.

Estes, N. (2017) "Fighting for Our Lives: #NoDAPL in Historical Context," *Wicazo SA Review*, pp. 115–22.

Francis (2015) *Laudato Si': On Care for Our Common Home*. Vatican City: Vatican Press.

The Forum on Religion and Ecology. (2022) "Mission and Vision," https://fore.yale.edu/ (accessed November 17, 2022).

Guterres, A. (2020) "The State of the Planet," Speech at Columbia University, New York, December 2.

Gutierrez, G. (1988) *A Theology of Liberation: History, Politics, and Salvation*, trans. and ed. S. C. Inda and J. Eagleson. Maryknoll, NY: Orbis Books.

Macy, J. (2000) "Encouraging Words for Activists," in S. Kaza and K. Kraft (eds) *Dharma Rain: Sources of Buddhist Environmentalism*. Boston: Shambhala, 252–6.

Marx, K., and Engels, F. (1964) *On Religion*, ed. R. Niebuhr. New York: Schocken.

Masuzawa, T. (2005) *The Invention of World Religions: Or, How European Universalism was Preserved in the Language of Pluralism*. Chicago: University of Chicago Press.

Smith, T. S. (1995) *The Island of Anishnaabeg*. Moscow: University of Idaho Press.

Suzuki, D. T. (1963) *Outlines of Mahayana Buddhism*. New York: Schocken.

Taylor, B. (2010) *Dark Green Religion: Nature Spirituality and the Planetary Future*. Berkeley, CA: University of California Press.
Tillich, P. (1988) *The Spiritual Situation in Our Technical Society*, ed. J. M. Thomas. Macon, GA: Mercer University Press.
Weber, M. (1978) "The Sociology of Religion," in G. Roth and C. Wittich (eds) *Economy and Society*. Berkeley, CA: University of California Press.
Whyte, K. P. (2017) "The Dakota Access Pipeline, Environmental Injustice, and U.S. Colonialism," *Red Ink* 19(1): 154–69.

## Further Reading

Baugh, A. (2017) *God and the Green Divide: Religious Environmentalism in Black and White*. Oakland: University of California Press.
Berry, E. (2015) *Devoted to Nature: The Religious Roots of American Environmentalism*. Oakland: University of California Press.
Berry, T. (2009) *The Sacred Universe: Earth, Spirituality, and Religion in the Twenty-First Century*. New York: Columbia University Press.
Boff, L. (1995) *Ecology and Liberation: A New Paradigm*, trans. J. Cumming. Maryknoll, NY: Orbis.
Gottlieb, R. S. (2006) *A Greener Faith: Religious Environmentalism and Our Planet's Future*. New York: Oxford University Press.
Gould, R. K. (2005) *At Home in Nature: Modern Homesteading and Spiritual Practice in America*. Berkeley, CA: University of California Press.
Smith, J. Z. (2004) *Relating Religion: Essays in the Study of Religion*. Chicago: University of Chicago Press.

# 2 Grounding Religion in the Environmental Humanities

*Kate Rigby and Laurel Kearns*

In October 2014, a little-known invasion took place in Australia.

On the 17th of that month, spring in the Southern Hemisphere, a group of thirty Pacific Islanders in traditional garb paddled a flotilla of kayaks and canoes into Newcastle harbor. Although their beautiful hand-carved watercraft were dwarfed by the massive freighters that usually fill Australia's largest coal port each day, the kayaks prevented ten ships from departing. With the motto, "Not Drowning, Fighting," these Pacific Climate Warriors had come to protest the climate-wrecking coal industry that was already beginning to wreak havoc in their island nations.

This protest action, supported by hundreds of local Australian climate activists, was followed by a series of presentations in the major cities of Perth, Brisbane, Sydney, Canberra, and Melbourne, as well as further demonstrations at large financial institutions heavily invested in Australia's lucrative multinational coal mining and export industries. During a Pacific Warrior event in Melbourne, the packed audience was palpably startled when one of the most engaging and energetic protesters, Mikaele Maiava from Tokelau, informed us that where he came from, they were all "hard-core Christians" who took the Bible seriously.

Maiava went on to offer a reading of the biblical flood narrative, in which God promises Noah and his descendants never again to cause waters to flood the world. To Maiava, this meant that current sea level rises must be caused by *humans*—some humans, that is, with others bearing the brunt—and that it is therefore up to us, all of us, whether as protesters or perpetrators or both, to rectify this calamitous and unjust situation. At this, the audience appeared to relax somewhat. But it seemed that Maiava's profession of Christian faith was less well-taken than the traditional dance with which he began or than his description of the ancient ritual of burying the umbilical cords of newborns under a tree on the shore of their natal island. For this audience at least, it appeared that while indigenous spiritualities were expected, affiliation with an institutionalized religion, perhaps particularly Christianity, was questionable.

This incident is telling on a number of counts. To begin with, it points to the important role that religion might play in some sites and forms of environmental activism. Indeed, the Newcastle port protest was itself given a biblical resonance by being likened to the battle of "David versus Goliath," and it earned the Pacific

DOI: 10.4324/9781003259466-4

Climate Warriors, who organized the protests, the 2020 Pax Christi International Peace Award.[1]

More generally, this story highlights the relevance of religious studies to research in the environmental humanities, a field that is expressly concerned with "fundamental questions of meaning, value, responsibility and purpose in a time of rapid, and escalating, change" (Rose et al. 2012: 1). For most of human history, and still today for some 84% of the world's population, these questions have been framed in part through religious worldviews, narratives, and practices. At the same time, the wave of tension that rippled around the room when Maiava proclaimed that his fellow Pacific Climate Warriors were all "hard-core Christians" is also symptomatic of the neglect of, or even hostility toward, religion in much of the environmental movement and in much environmental humanities research, conducted as it has been overwhelmingly by white middle-class scholars in secular institutions of the Global North. In addition, the divide between "religion," viewed as problematic, and indigenous traditions or earth-based spiritualities, celebrated and welcomed, can also be traced in this literature.[2]

This chapter will offer an introduction to the environmental humanities as a multi-, inter-, and transdisciplinary research field and then explore how the study of religion and ecology might contribute to its further development, and vice versa, especially with reference to the cultivation of forms of more-than-human flourishing and the pursuit of eco-justice. We conclude with a specific example from our own work that demonstrates how the reimagining of Christian texts and traditions in the face of escalating socio-ecological damage is both inspiring and being inspired by faith-based environmental activism.

## Locating the Environmental Humanities

The environmental humanities bring the study of meaning, cultures, values, and ethics to bear on questions of human relationships to non-human systems, beings, and one another. This includes environmental philosophy, aesthetics, and ethics (also sometimes referred to as eco-philosophy or, in the deep ecological tradition, ecosophy); religion and ecology; environmental history; environmental literary and cultural studies (also referred to as ecocriticism); ecolinguistics; environmental anthropology/sociology; and environmental (or more-than-human) geography. Toward the end of the millennium, these green strands began to be woven together to create new interdisciplinary formations, often also including conversations and collaborations with the natural sciences, in what is now widely seen as the beginnings of the environmental humanities as a distinct research field transgressing established disciplinary boundaries.

As Emmett and Nye observe in their "critical introduction" to the environmental humanities, "because of its wide range," this emerging field "is difficult to pin down, and it has different profiles depending on the scholarly strengths at the institutions where it has emerged" (2017: 6). A brief account of three such institutions is illustrative.

From 1991 to 1995, the Massachusetts Institute of Technology (MIT) hosted the MacArthur Workshop on Humanistic Studies of the Environment. This workshop had a foundation in science and technology studies and located "ecological problems in the behaviour of human institutions, beliefs and practices" (Emmett and Nye 2017: 3). The focus here was how humanistic perspectives could supplement and respond to the findings of scientists who were studying environmental issues.

A different kind of working group convened at the Centre for Resource and Environmental Studies at the Australian National University in 1999. The emphasis here was on crossing and transcending disciplinary boundaries, "cross-cutting the divides that impede our understanding and action" (Rose and Robin 2004). This meant moving across not only the boundaries dividing the arts, humanities, and social sciences from the natural sciences but also those that separate privileged Western knowledge systems from other ways of knowing, including nonmodern and indigenous ontologies, epistemologies, and ethics.[3] Conjoining research expertise in environmental ethics, ecopolitical theory, and ecocritical literary and cultural studies, as well as environmental history and anthropology, the Australian environmental humanities developed a pronounced decolonial perspective, which can also be traced in the premier journal in the field, *Environmental Humanities*, co-founded by Deborah Bird Rose and her Australian co-editors in 2012.

A third example is the Environmental Humanities Initiative at Arizona State University (ASU), which traces its origins to 2006. Unlike the previous two, this initiative included scholars of religion from its foundations, explicitly including "religion and ecology; religion and conflict; spirituality and ecology" among its research areas.[4] Since 2013, ASU has hosted the North American Humanities for the Environment (HfE) Observatory, one of several created around the world "to identify, explore, and demonstrate the contributions that humanistic and artistic disciplines can make to understanding and engaging with global environmental challenges."[5]

**BOX 2A**

The three institutions just discussed offer different balances between natural science, social science, humanities, and indigenous forms of knowledge to understand environmental issues. What ways of knowing do you think are most important in studying the environment? Why?

While these institutions show a development of environmental humanities over time, what remains consistent is a commitment to a rich and complex understanding of human beings as part of studying the environment. In the scientific journal *Nature Climate Change*, a group of scholars emphasized the importance of this project. They offer a succinct definition of the field of environmental humanities, which addresses

> fundamental questions of value, responsibility, rights, entitlements, needs, duty, faith, care, government, cruelty, charity and justice in a world marked by (1) significant differences in people's customs and aspirations,

> (2) manifest inequalities in people's living conditions and material prospects, and (3) complex material and moral interdependencies among people and non-humans stretched across space and unfolding through time. Addressing these questions involves reasoned argument predicated on sometimes starkly opposed principles, as long-standing debates over the moral significance of animals graphically demonstrate. The environmental humanities illuminate peoples' complex and divergent understandings of life—human and non-human—on Earth. They also pay close attention to human faculties beyond cognition and reason, dealing with such things as love, trust, fear, care, commitment, devotion and loyalty.
>
> (Castree et al. 2014: 765)

This elaboration of the environmental humanities demonstrates the breadth of the field. It also demonstrates that practitioners increasingly understand religion and the study of religion as an essential part of understanding human dimensions of environmental problems. It opens with a list of values, including "faith," that many people across the world derive from religious worldviews and ethics.

The importance of religion was also recognized in a 1991 letter signed by thirty-four well-known international scientists, such as Carl Sagan, E. O. Wilson, and Stephen Jay Gould and several Nobel Laureates. The "Open Letter to the Religious Community" stated that "(p)roblems of such magnitude and solutions demanding so broad a perspective must be recognized from the outset as having a religious as well as a scientific dimension" and that "(e)fforts to safeguard and cherish the environment need to be infused with a vision of the sacred" (Sagan et al. 1990).

## Mind the Gap!

In summary, religion is an important part of environmental action, environmental studies, and environmental humanities because it is an important part of how human beings make sense of the world and are motivated to change it. But unfortunately, there is currently a gap between mainstream environmental humanities and the study of religion and ecology.

In a 2007 article, Joern Fischer and co-authors noted a gap—which has only grown wider since—between "our current trajectory and meaningful sustainability targets" (Fischer et al. 2007: 621). They note that accelerating biodiversity loss, climate change, and toxic pollution are all signs that "[h]uman action in the world emerges from a complex dialectic among the living world itself, the social contexts of human life and action, and the conceptualizations through which human life is made meaningful." For this reason, they argue, "enhanced collaboration among natural and social scientists and scholars of human contexts, symbols and meanings would signal the beginning of a new paradigm for addressing the sustainability gap" (623). We agree with this argument and want to extend it by also attending to the gap between the environmental humanities and the study of religion and ecology.

Book-length introductions to the environmental humanities began to appear in 2015, and of the major introductory anthologies published over the next three years, only one includes a chapter dedicated to religion and ecology (Rigby 2016). Emmett's and Nye's landmark "critical introduction" to the field (2017) includes some mentions of religion but does not discuss the study of religion as a research area. Only recently has consideration of religion begun to feature more centrally in the environmental humanities, notably in Hubbell's and Ryan's textbook *Introduction*, which features the excellent chapter "Ecological religious studies: faith in nature" (2021: 129–46). Recognition nonetheless remains patchy. Cohen's and Foote's *Cambridge Companion to Environmental Humanities* (2021), for example, lacks a section on religion, while Matthias Schmidt's and Hubert Zapf's German-language anthology, *Environmental Humanities*, references religion only in association with classical antiquity (2021).

**BOX 2B**

Where in your life do you encounter discussions of religious practices, traditions, and beliefs? Are there parts of your life where people do not talk about religion or take it seriously? Why do you think that is?

Similarly, looking from the other side of the divide, it is only recently that scholars in religion and ecology have begun to explicitly engage with the environmental humanities as a new interdisciplinary formation (e.g., Yü and Maaker 2021).[6] In our view, this dialogue is long overdue and has much to offer. For the vast majority of the world's population for the vast majority of human history, culture, understandings of work, and relationships with other creatures and to the rest of the world have been significantly shaped by religious texts, tenets, traditions, and practices. The neglect of religion represents a major blind spot in the environmental humanities. Part of the reason is that this field has been developed preponderantly in the Global North, where educated people can too often dismiss religion as narrow, private, and even backward rather than a vital part of contemporary cultures and their origins. By the same token, studies of religion and ecology stand to be enriched by the new concepts and methodologies that have emerged within the inter- and transdisciplinary experimentation of the environmental humanities, such as the field of multispecies studies, as discussed in a following section.

### Resituating Religion in the Environmental Humanities

Studies of religion and ecology have long been a site for multidisciplinary exchange, connecting historical, hermeneutical, theological, comparative, anthropological and sociological approaches to religion and spirituality in the horizon of ongoing environmental damage and injustice. In a series of field-defining conferences on the "Religions of the World and Ecology," hosted by the Harvard Divinity School between 1996 and 1998, scholars of religions from different disciplines were also brought into conversation with religious leaders and environmental scientists, as well as artists and writers.[7] These conferences led to the foundation of the Forum on Religion and Ecology (FORE), led by Mary Evelyn Tucker and John Grim, now located at Yale. Affiliated organizations have developed around the world, such as the European Forum for the Study of Religion and Environment and the Australia-Pacific Forum on Religion and Ecology. Meanwhile, in 2006, the International Society for the Study of Religion, Nature, and Culture (ISSRNC) was created with an explicit commitment to fostering interdisciplinary and international exchange and an orientation to the diversity of spiritual experience and expression beyond the bounds of organized religion.[8]

The potential contribution of religion and ecology to the interdisciplinary weave of the environmental humanities was also evident in one of the earliest and most influential publications in the field, Lynn White Jr.'s slim article, "The Historical Roots of our Ecologic Crisis," published in *Science* in 1967. Here, White argues that "[w]hat people do about their ecology depends on what they think about themselves in relation to things around them. Human ecology is deeply conditioned by beliefs about our nature and destiny—that is, by religion" (1205).

**BOX 2C**

Lynn White's famous article argues, "Since the roots of our [environmental] trouble are so largely religious, the remedy must also be essential religious, whether we call it that or not" (1207). What parts of that claim seem true, and what seem questionable? How might one go about testing his assumptions and his argument?

Despite the fact that White ends his article with an acknowledgment that Christianity has better and more earth-affirming traditions that could be tapped, his nuanced critique was widely mistaken as a blanket condemnation of Christianity. This contributed, in part, to the widespread suspicion of Christianity and other monotheistic faiths among many environmentalists. That suspicion was evident among the audience at the Pacific Climate Warriors event in Melbourne mentioned at the beginning of this chapter.

What is less frequently remarked is how White's method of analysis and argumentation "effectively lays out the entire project of the environmental humanities as an inter- or trans-disciplinary undertaking" (Rigby 2016: 276).[9] A pioneering scholar in the cultural history of science and technology, White also drew heavily on the sociology of Max Weber (Riley 2014) and on religious studies. He prefigures research in environmental history that recognizes that human cultures are shaped by the places where they develop: specifically, he argues that the thick, sticky, clayey soils of Northern Europe encouraged people to develop new technologies that reshaped Northwestern European farmers' relations with one another, their domesticated animals, and the land. White, therefore, uses science, history, sociology, and religion to explain the change in medieval European minds giving rise to the modern Western idea that "Man and nature are two things, and man is master" (White 1967: 1205), which he believed led to environmental crisis.

White's method also incorporates an ecocritical dimension in his attention to textual reinterpretations, as well as raising eco-philosophical questions about the underlying assumptions informing the Western alliance of science and technology. In particular, his identification of the dualistic and "anthropocentric" (1205) dimension of the mentality that came to predominate in modern Western society prefigures the "deep ecological" critique initiated by Arne Naess (1973) and Routley and Routley (1979). At the same time, White pre-empts more recent critiques of environmentalists who romanticize "wilderness," which, in his view, "advocates deep-freezing an ecology, whether San Gimignano or the High Sierra, as it was before the first Kleenex was dropped" (White 1967: 1204). This celebration of "untouched wilderness" is a distinctly modern Western phenomenon, which contributed to the settler-colonial exclusion of First Peoples from their ancestral lands and a failure to recognize their role in shaping and sustaining their environs (Guha 1989; Langton 1996; Gilio-Whitaker 2019).

White's call for the recovery of an animistic sensibility also prefigures the efflorescence of animist studies within the field of religion and ecology (e.g., Harvey 2006), while his advocacy of St. Francis, who "tried to substitute the idea of the equality of all creatures, including man, for the idea of man's limitless rule of creation" as the "patron saint of ecologists" (White 1967: 1206), resonates with subsequent articulations of a bio-inclusive or trans-species principle of eco-justice within both religious studies and faith-based environmental activism.

In short, Lynn White's foundational essay demonstrates both the importance of religion in explaining environmental degradation and the importance of thinking that crosses disciplinary boundaries to incorporate the richness and complexity of human experience.

## Eco-justice and the Promise of Multispecies Religious Studies

Perhaps the most fruitful and important site of cross-fertilization between religious studies and ecology and environmental humanities comes in considerations of justice, in which religious ideas frequently appear.

Presbyterian minister William Gibson founded the Eco-Justice Project in 1974 out of the Center for Religion, Ethics, and Social Policy at Cornell University (Kearns 2013). As Gibson explained in the Center's journal, *The Egg*, eco-justice advocates are inspired by the Hebrew prophetic tradition, believing that the "God of justice, engaged in deliverance from bondage and oppression, is also the God of creation, who cares for all creatures and engages in the work of protecting and restoring the earth as well as the poor" (quoted in Gibson 2004: 28). Within Judaism, the concept of Tikkun Olam, the repair of the world, has been extended to include concepts of eco-justice (Troster 2004). More recently, the papal encyclical *Laudato Si'* explores the concept of "integral ecology" envisioning both humans and all of creation thriving (Francis 2015).

According to faith-based eco-justice advocates, human beings are called to actively participate in this work through their personal relations with more-than-human others and through collective endeavors to counter systemic forms of domination. Further biblical support for this position was found in the core Christian ethos of neighbor-love, based on the Parable of the Good Samaritan (Luke 10:25–37), which they understand as extending not only to human beings but also to more-than-human others: "the near one and the far one; the one removed from me by distances in time and space, in convictions and loyalties [. . . the neighbor is] man and is angel and is animal and inorganic being, all that participates in being" (H. Richard Niebuhr, quoted in Rasmussen 2013: 221).

The related term "environmental justice" came to prominence in the 1982 United Church of Christ–led campaign protesting the proposed dumping of toxic chemicals in Warren County, North Carolina, but its perspectives on the connection between race, class, and environmental toxics can already be seen in the Memphis Sanitation Workers strike of the civil rights movement (Glave 2010). The 1987 publication of "Toxic Wastes and Race" brought heightened attention to the disproportionate placement of hazardous and toxic waste sites in and consequent impact on communities of color and lower economic status across the United States.[10] This helped to inspire the 1991 First National People of Color Environmental Leadership Summit, which was sponsored by the United Church of Christ's Commission on Racial Justice and produced a historic set of Principles of Environmental Justice. The first principle highlights the significance of religious/spiritual/indigenous worldviews: "Environmental Justice affirms the sacredness of Mother Earth, ecological unity and the interdependence of all species, and the right to be free from ecological destruction." (For more on the environmental justice movement and its contemporary expressions, see Chapter 15 of this book.)

Interestingly, while the Christian concept of eco-justice was bio-inclusive, seeking justice for all of life, secularized discussions and organizing around environmental justice have frequently been focused more exclusively on justice for human beings. Much of the early literature on environmental justice omitted mention of faith-based groups, of which there were many. This follows the pattern of the Environmental Humanities analyzed earlier: religion is mainly left out or only mentioned in a general acknowledgment of the role of social, cultural, and religious/spiritual values. One finds far more mentions of indigenous cultures, values, and worldviews; many environmental activists and scholars tend to equate religion with traditions presumed to be hostile to valuing the sacred interconnectedness of humans and nature. This leaves little motivation to address the efforts of faith-based groups and perspectives, at least those based in monotheism, despite the fact that practitioners in these communities have long extended concern over the impact of environmental degradation to more-than-human others.

The devastating impacts of anthropogenic climate disruption, toxic pollution, and ecological unravelling on both vulnerable human communities and an array of other life-forms, along with the emergence and spread of new zoonotic diseases, such as COVID-19, suggests that it is no longer prudent to consider the pursuit of social justice apart from the ethical dimension of human relations with other beings. In the era sometimes referred to as the Anthropocene,[11] at a time when human activities are profoundly reshaping earth's future, a bio-inclusive eco-justice perspective that takes religion seriously offers a distinct advantage over more narrowly human-centered formulations of environmental justice.

Such a bio-inclusive orientation resonates with an exciting trend in the environmental humanities known as multispecies studies. Proceeding from the understanding that all living beings "emerge from and live their lives within multispecies communities," multispecies studies push "humanistic" scholars to think beyond our own species. It brings together diverse bodies of knowledge from across the arts, literature, philosophy, sciences, and beyond the academy, in order to examine what it means to "live with others in entangled worlds of contingency and uncertainty" and to explore, "how can we do the work of inhabiting and co-constituting worlds well?" (van Dooren et al. 2016: 1).

While much research in multispecies studies is informed by indigenous philosophies, the potential role of religion in enhancing multispecies coexistence remains largely unexplored. Although some religious texts and traditions are undoubtedly highly anthropocentric, there is considerable scope for diverse faith-based groups to contribute to shaping visions and practices of multispecies community, such as Muslim interpretations of the Qur'anic verse 6.38: "There is no animal on land, nor a bird flying with its wings, but are communities like you." By the same token, while scholars of religion and ecology have done important work on human-animal relations (e.g., Waldau and Patton 2006), few have as yet located their work within a multispecies framework, which concerns human entanglements, both moral and material, with a greater diversity of non-human others (including inorganic ones, such as rivers, rocks, or tornados) in specific places over time.

There is much to be learned from the multispecies approach for the study of religion and ecology and much to be learned from religious people and communities who are already working at this intersection. For example, the multi-faith nonprofit Faith in Place does environmental and community advocacy in Chicago. One initiative involves native species restoration work on the city's South Side, which contains many toxic/hazardous waste sites. At first, the work of planting native plant species and removing invasives appealed primarily to white, often more suburban participants and failed to attract significant participation from local communities and congregations of color. Faith in Place staff member Veronica Kyle recognized the need to expand the imagination of what community meant and connected the project to the migration stories of the elders in these communities. She helped to create story circles that related the migration of families to the area to the migrations of birds and butterflies, species that particularly benefit from the habitat restoration project. In her organizing, she asked communities about what they wanted from their neighborhoods and what it felt like to be welcomed, and many mentioned access to familiar foods. These story circles helped to contextualize the work of welcoming and supporting birds and butterflies by planting their favorite foods and increased local participation in the project of co-creating a multispecies community (Kyle and Kearns 2018).

**BOX 2D**

Do you know of initiatives in your community, or elsewhere, that try to get people involved in environmental action with a multispecies orientation? How do they appeal to particular cultures, traditions, values, or ideas within specific communities? How could they?

Studying and advocating for the environment requires humanistic inquiry because human beings are a part of the natural environment and changing human imaginaries and practices requires careful study of our cultures, expressions, ideas, and ethics. Religion is an essential part of our socio-cultural world, as religious traditions inform many people's deepest values and have significantly shaped the cultures in which we all live. As ecological crises continue to deepen, and climate change impacts come hard and fast, the environmental humanities will be enriched by attention to how religious texts, traditions, tenets, and practicing communities afford ways of working though experiences of trauma and grief, as well as frameworks for solidarity, resilience, and transformation.

## Notes

1 On the role of faith in the activism of the Pacific Climate Warriors, see Ledderucci 2021. For the comparison to David and Goliath, see https://world.350.org/pacificwarriors/2014/10/20/coal-ships-stopped-the-warriors-have-risen/.

2 A great deal of sociological scholarship explores the "spiritual but not religious" category, reflective of a broader distancing from organized religions. Additionally, within both religious studies and sociology/anthropology, there is great debate over the usefulness of the colonial concept of "religion" and definitions of religion. Something similar can be said about the term spirituality, which covers a large range of activity. See Taylor 2009 for a more in-depth exploration.

3 Whereas "transdisciplinary" is sometimes used to refer to research that crosses disciplinary boundaries within the academy, here it refers to research that is co-created with knowledge-holders from beyond the academy.

4 "About the Environmental Humanities," ASU Global Institute of Sustainability and Innovation, https://sustainability-innovation.asu.edu/environmental-humanities/about/ (accessed July 19, 2022).

5 "North American Observatory: Building Resilience in the Anthropocene," https://sustainability-innovation.asu.edu/research/project/humanities-for-the-environment-north-american-observatory-building-resilience-in-the-anthropocene/ (accessed July 14, 2022).

6 *The Routledge Handbook on Religion and Ecology* (Jenkins et al. 2017) has a section on environmental humanities, but each chapter deals only with a single discipline (history, literature, philosophy, and art) rather than with EH as a new inter- and transdisciplinary field.

7 Religions of the World and Ecology Conference Series, Harvard 1996–1998, Yale Forum on Religion and Ecology, https://fore.yale.edu/Event-Listings/Religions-World-and-Ecology-Conference-Series/Religions-World-and-Ecology-Archive (accessed July 20, 2022).

8 See, e.g., *Dark Green Religion*, published by ISSNRC's founding president, Bron Taylor, in 2009. See also the ISSNRC's website www.issrnc.org/ (accessed July 29, 2022)

9 On White as a forerunner of environmental humanities, see also (Bergmann, Rigby and Scott 2023, 5–6)".

10 "A Movement is Born: Environmental Justice and the UCC," United Church of Christ, www.ucc.org/what-we-do/justice-local-church-ministries/justice/faithful-action-ministries/environmental-justice/a_movement_is_born_environmental_justice_and_the_ucc/ (accessed 7/19/22). The pattern of disproportionate environmental burdens placed on communities of color continues: A 2017 study, "Fumes Across the Fence-Line," by the Clean Air Task Force, documents that "African Americans are exposed to 38 percent more polluted air than White Americans, and they are 75 percent more likely to live in communities that border a plant or factory." www.washingtonpost.com/climate-environment/interactive/2021/environmental-justice-race/ (accessed July 19, 2022).

11 First proposed by ecologist P. J. Crutzen and atmospheric chemist E. F. Stoermer (2000), this term has been hotly debated in the environmental humanities, on the grounds that it veils significant differences among humans in terms of both responsibility and vulnerability. See, e.g., Horn and Bergthaller (2020).

## References


Bergmann, S., Rigby, K., and Scott P. M. (2023) "Introduction," in S. Bergmann, K. Rigby and P. M. Scott (eds), *Religion, Materialism and Ecology* (London: Routledge), 1-12. London: Routledge.

Castree, N. et al. (2014) "Changing the Intellectual Climate," *Nature Climate Change* 4: 763–8.

Cohen, J., and Foote, S. (eds) (2021) *The Cambridge Companion to Environmental Humanities* (Cambridge Companions to Literature). Cambridge: Cambridge University Press.

Crutzen, P. J., and Stoermer, E. F. (2000) "The 'Anthropocene'," *Global Change Newsletter* 41: 17–18.

Emmett, R. S., and Nye, D. E. (2017) *The Environmental Humanities: A Critical Introduction.* Cambridge, MA: MIT Press.

First National People of Color Environmental Leadership Summit. (1991) "Principles of Environmental Justice," www.ejnet.org/ej/principles.html (accessed June 8, 2022).

Fischer, J. et al. (2007) "Mind the Sustainability Gap," *TRENDS in Ecology and Evolution* 22(12): 621–4.

Francis, P. (2015) *Laudato Si': Encyclical letter of the Holy Father Francis.* Vatican City: Vatican Press.

Gibson, W. (ed) (2004) *Eco-Justice: The Unfinished Journey.* New York: State University of New York Press.

Gilio-Whitaker, D. (2019) *As Long as Grass Grows: The Indigenous Fight for Environmental Justice, from Colonization to Standing Rock.* Boston: Beacon Press.

Glave, D. (2010) *Rooted in the Earth: Reclaiming the African Environmental Heritage.* Chicago: Chicago Review Press.

Guha, R. (1989) "Radical American Environmentalism and Wilderness Preservation: A Third World Critique," *Environmental Ethics* 11(1): 71–83.

Harvey, G. (2006) *Animism: Respecting the Living World.* New York: Columbia University Press.

Horn, E., and Bergthaller, H. (2020) *The Anthropocene: Key Issues for the Humanities.* London: Routledge.

Hubbell, J. A., and Ryan, J. C. (2021) *Introduction to the Environmental Humanities.* 1st ed. London: Routledge.

Jenkins, W., Tucker, M. E., and Grim, J. (eds) (2017) *The Routledge Handbook of Religion and Ecology.* Abingdon: Routledge.

Kearns, L. (2013) "Religion and Environmental Justice," in R. Bohannon (ed), *Religions and Environments: A Reader in Religion, Nature and Ecology*. New York: Bloomsbury, 297–312.

Kyle, V., and Kearns, L. (2018) "The Bitter and the Sweet of Nature: Weaving a Tapestry of Migration Stories," in M. Krasny (ed) *Grassroots to Global: Broader Impacts of Civic Ecology*. Ithaca, NY: Cornell University Press, 41–64.

Langton, M. (1996) "What Do We Mean by Wilderness? Wilderness and Terra Nullius in Australian Art," *Sydney Papers* 8: 11–31.

Ledderucci, C. (2021) "Pacific Climate Warriors and Local Narratives on Climate Change: An Analysis of a Faith-Informed Indigenous Rhetoric," in J. M. Luetz and P. D. Nunn (eds) *Beyond Belief*. Cham: Springer, 289–311.

Naess, A. (1973) "The Shallow and the Deep, Long-Range Ecology Movement," *Inquiry* 16: 95–100.

Rasmussen, L. (2013) *Earth-Honoring Faith: Religious Ethics in a New Key*. Oxford: Oxford University Press.

Rigby, K. (2016) "Religion and Ecology: Towards a Communion of Creatures," in S. Oppermann and S. Iovino (eds) *Environmental Humanities: Voices from the Anthropocene*. London: Rowman & Littlefield Publishers, 273–94.

Riley, M. T. (2014) "A Spiritual Democracy of All God's Creatures: Ecotheology and the Animals of Lynn White Jr," in Stephen D. Moore (ed) *Divinanimality: Animal Theory, Creaturely Theology*. New York: Fordham University Press, 261–80.

Rose, D., and Robin, L. (2004) "The Ecological Humanities in Action: An Introduction," *Eco-Humanities Corner, Australian Humanities Review* 31–2.

Rose, D., van Dooren, T., Chrulew, M., Cooke, S., Kearnes, M., and O'Gorman, E. (2012), "Thinking Through the Environment, Unsettling the Humanities," *Environmental Humanities* 1(1): 1–5.

Routley, R., and Routley, V. (1979) "Against the Inevitability of Human Chauvinism," in K. E. Goodpaster and K. M. Sayre (eds) *Ethics and the Problems of the 21st Century*. South Bend, IN: Notre Dame University Press, 36–59.

Sagan, C. et al. (1990) "An Open Letter to the Religious Community," http://earthrenewal.org/open_letter_to_the_religious_.htm (accessed July 19, 2022).

Schmidt, M., and Zapf, H. (eds) (2021) *Environmental Humanities. Beiträge zur geistes- und sozialwissenschaftlichen Umweltforschung*. Internationale Schriften des Jakob-Fugger-Zentrums. 1st ed. Göttingen: V&R Unipress.

Taylor, B. (2009) *Dark Green Religion: Nature Spirituality and Planetary Future*. Berkeley: University of California Press.

Troster, L. (2004) "Repairing the Order of Creation: A Jewish Perspective on Environmental Ethics," *Environmental Practice* 6(1): 2–6.

United Church of Christ Commission for Racial Justice. (1987) "Toxic Wastes and Race in the United States: A National Report on the Racial and Socio-Economic Characteristics of Communities with Hazardous Waste Sites," www.ucc.org/wp-content/uploads/2020/12/ToxicWastesRace.pdf (accessed July 23, 2022).

van Dooren, T., Kirksey, E., and Münster, U. (2016) "Multispecies Studies: Cultivating Arts of Attentiveness," *Environmental Humanities* 8(1): 1–23.

Waldau, P., and Patton, K. (2006) *A Communion of Subjects: Animals in Religion, Science and Ethics*. New York: Columbia University Press.

White, L. Jr. (1967) "The Historical Roots of Our Ecologic Crisis," *Science* 155(3767): 1203–7.

Yü, D. S., and de Maaker, E. (2021) *Environmental Humanities in the New Himalayas: Symbiotic Indigeneity, Commoning, Sustainability*. London: Routledge.

## Further Reading


Adamson, J., and Davis, M. (eds) (2016) *Humanities for the Environment: Integrating Knowledge, Forging New Constellations of Practice*. 1st ed. London: Routledge.

Barnhill, D. G., and Gottlieb, R. S. (2001) *Deep Ecology and World Religions: New Essays on Sacred Ground*. New York: State University of New York Press.

Bergthaller, H., and Mortensen, P. (eds) (2018) *Framing the Environmental Humanities*. Leiden, The Netherlands: Brill.

Berry, E. (2015) *Devoted to Nature: The Religious Roots of American Environmentalism*. Oakland: University of California Press.

Conway, J. K., Keniston, K., and Marx, L. (1999) *Earth, Air, Fire, Water: Humanistic Studies of the Environment*. Cambridge, MA: University of Massachusetts Press.

Coolsaet, B. (2021) *Environmental Justice: Key Issues*. London: Routledge.

DeLoughrey, E., Didur, J., and Carrigan, A. (2015) *Global Ecologies and the Environmental Humanities: Postcolonial Approaches*. 1st ed. New York and Oxford: Routledge.

Elvey, A. (2013) "Rethinking Neighbour Love: A Conversation Between Political Theology and Ecological Ethics," in A. H. Cadwallader and P. L. Trudinger (eds) *Where the Wild Ox Roams: Essays in Honour of Norman C. Habel*. Sheffield: Sheffield University Press.

Fletcher, M.-S., Hamilton, R., Dressler, W., and Palmer, L. (2021) "Indigenous Knowledge and the Shackles of Wilderness," *PNAS* 118(40). www.pnas.org/doi/full/10.1073/pnas.2022218118 (accessed August 1, 2022).

Heise, U. K., Christensen, J., and Niemann, M. (eds) (2017) *The Routledge Companion to the Environmental Humanities*. London: Taylor & Francis Group.

Merchant, C. (1980) *The Death of Nature: Women, Ecology, and the Scientific Revolution*. London: Wildwood.

Newcombe, M. (2023) *Religion, Narrative, and the Environmental Humanities: Bridging the Rhetoric Gap*. London: Routledge, Forthcoming.

O'Gorman, E. et al. (2019) "Teaching the Environmental Humanities: International Perspectives and Practices," *Environmental Humanities* 11(2): 427–60.

Oppermann, S., and Iovino, S. (eds) (2016) *Environmental Humanities: Voices from the Anthropocene*. London: Rowman & Littlefield Publishers.

Plumwood, V. (1993) *Feminism and the Mastery of Nature*. London: Routledge.

Rigby, K. (2019) "Weaving the Environmental Humanities: Australian Strands, Configurations, and Provocations," *Green Letters: Studies in Ecocriticism* 23(1): 5–18.

Schliephake, C. (2020) *The Environmental Humanities and the Ancient World: Questions and Perspectives*. Elements in Environmental Humanities. Cambridge: Cambridge University Press.

Tsing, A. L., Swanson, A. E., Gan, E., and Bubant, N. (2017) *Arts of Living on a Damaged Planet: Ghosts and Monsters of the Anthropocene*. Durham: Duke University Press.

Wells, C. W. (2018) *Environmental Justice in Postwar America: A Documentary Reader*. Seattle: University of Washington Press.

# 3 Ecology

## Context, Interconnectedness, and Complexity

*Whitney A. Bauman, Richard Bohannon, and Kevin J. O'Brien*

### Introduction

Robin Wall Kimmerer is an enrolled member of the Citizen Potawatomi Nation, a plant ecologist, and a prolific writer and expert on the intersections between science, indigeneity, and environmental issues. In her essay "The Sound of Silverbells," she writes about teaching pre-med students in Kentucky, most of whom began her course uninterested in the complexities of plant biology and ecology.

The essay begins with frustration: "Their total disinterest in ecology pained me. To me ecological insight was the music of the spheres, but to them it was just one more requirement" (2013: 216–17). Attempting to expand her students' awareness, Kimmerer took them on a three-day field trip to the Great Smoky Mountains. Teaching them to read the "ecological map" of the land and its vegetation, she laid down in the moss to view the forest from a spider's perspective, and she lamented the signs of warming and degradation in the forest. Noticing her deep passion for the subject, one of the students asked her, "Is this like your religion or something?" (ibid.: 220).

Kimmerer's immediate response was to change the subject, but on the final day of the trip she reconsidered this when the students spontaneously began to sing the Christian hymn, "Amazing Grace." "I knew now that they hadn't missed it all. *Was blind, but now I see*. And they did. And so did I" (ibid.: 221). She argues that the land itself was the real teacher on that trip. The silverbells and the poplars and the bunchberries stirred her students to feel something religious, which they put into Christian terms as the gift of grace. Kimmerer summarizes:

> **BOX 3A**
>
> The earth is so richly endowed that the least we can do in return is to pay attention.
>
> —Robin Wall Kimmerer (2013: 217)

DOI: 10.4324/9781003259466-5

As a plant biologist, Kimmerer taught her students something about the science of ecology, which studies organisms in their living and nonliving contexts. As an indigenous educator, she also taught them what she calls spiritual ecology, which focuses on the importance of respecting and relating to the life of the forest in more than technical terms. As an environmentalist, she offered a moral lesson about the damage industrialized cultures are doing to earth's ecosystems. Each of these perspectives is connected to her identity as an ecologist, which encompasses scientific, cultural, spiritual, and moral ideas.

Like religion, ecology is a big concept, used in many ways in many contexts. In academic settings in the United States, ecology is most often discussed as a scientific discipline that emphasizes the importance of researching living things in their living and nonliving contexts. The insights of scientific ecology are vitally important, and many of the scholars discussed in this chapter are, like Kimmerer, trained scientists. However, our focus here is not on the science of ecology but on a common thread that connects it to many other ways of knowing. We write about ecology as humanistic scholars of religion; from that lens, the following sections will explore the many complications of ecology as an issue of philosophy, history, religion, ethics, justice, and cosmology.

In all these forms, ecology teaches that life must be understood in context: individuals inevitably exist in communities and everything is connected to everything else. This interconnected context is profoundly important for anyone who wants to understand and engage common life in the 21st century, because it is fundamental to the environmental and climate justice movements. But these movements are also informed by the more diverse and controversial conclusions people draw from ecological ideas, and such complexities are just as important as interconnectedness, particularly in discussions of religion and environmentalism.

## The Synthesis of Ecology

The word "ecology" was coined by the German biologist and public intellectual Ernst Haeckel (1834–1919). Insisting that plants and animals do not naturally live in laboratories and so cannot be fully understood there, he called for a new academic field that would study living things in their contexts, attending particularly to the complicated systems of interrelationship that make life possible. He was also among the first thinkers to begin to draw the then-disparate sciences of geology, evolution, chemistry, physics, zoology, embryology, and psychology into conversation, insisting that the natural world can only be understood with an interdisciplinary range of methodologies and perspectives.

Inspired by Darwin's theory of evolution, Haeckel imagined evolution as a "tree of life," and he drew an influential image of each species as a branch of life, with common roots but broadly diverse expressions. For him, the fact that such diverse life could coexist revealed an "economy of nature." Drawing on the Greek root of economics, *oikos*, he named his new science "ecology," which would study, explain, and reflect on the economics of nature.

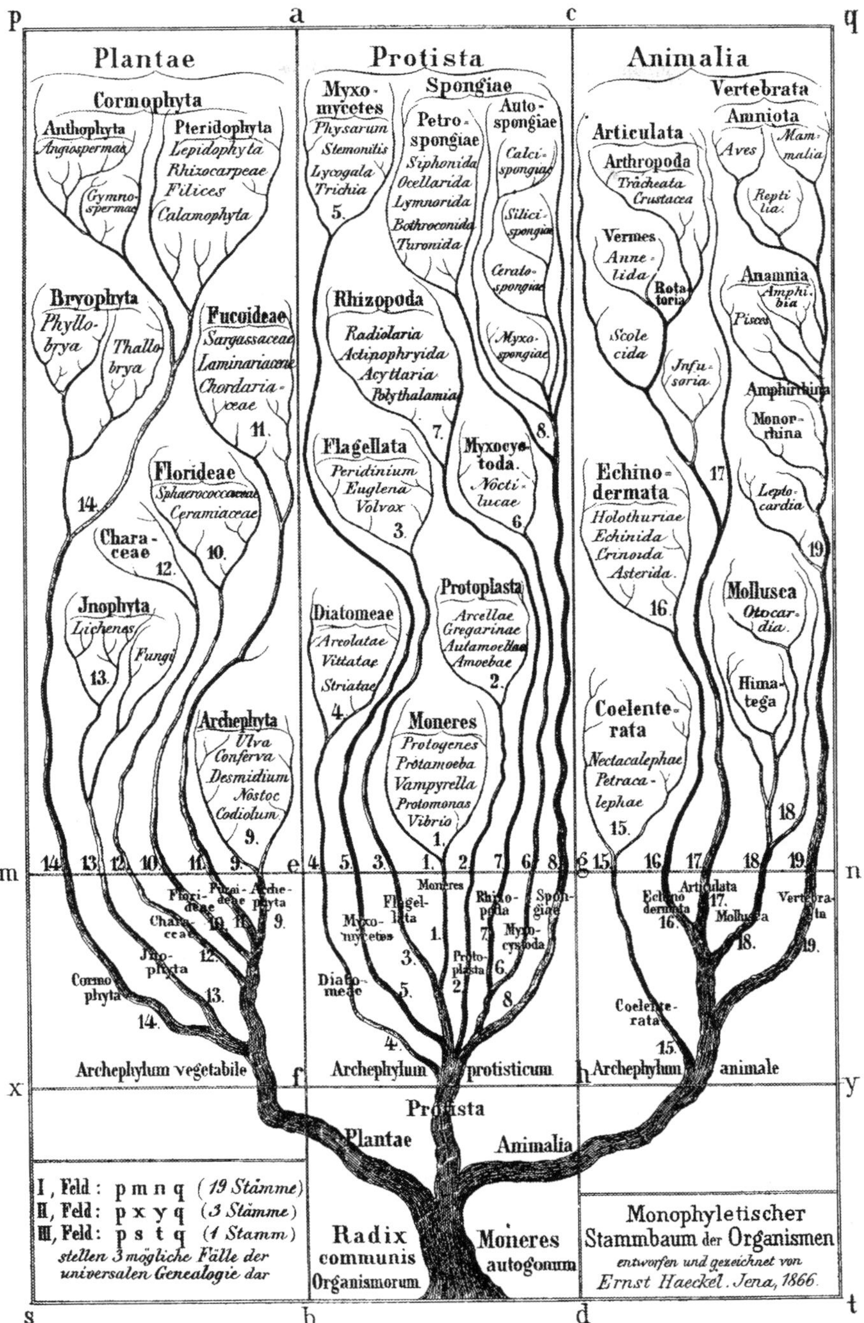


*Figure 3.1* Ernst Haeckel, who coined the word "ecology," is also credited as the first thinker to envision the evolution of species as a "tree of life," which he depicted in this drawing from *The General Morphology of Organisms* (1866). Haeckel's emphasis on the interconnection of species, and to some extent his spiritual beliefs, are reflected in his labeling the trunk of this tree as *radix communis organismorum*, or "the common root of all life."

In addition to being a natural scientist, Haeckel was a philosopher and social theorist. He believed that human beings would live most harmoniously with themselves and the world if they understood everything as part of the "order of nature." He writes:

## BOX 3B

The orderly course of evolution, according to fixed laws, now leads the human spirit through long eons from a primeval chaos to the present "order of the cosmos."

—Ernst Haeckel (1895: 32–3).

Here Haeckel argues that evolution and the complexity of the natural world should transform "the human spirit"; understanding the connection between all forms of life and the basic materials of the cosmos should lead to spiritual and moral as well as scientific insights. So, for Haeckel, ecology was not only about researching and studying natural systems. It was also about cosmic truths and moral imperatives. In creating ecology, he sought a course of study that would inform a broad moral and spiritual worldview.

We use the word "ecology" as one of the key frameworks for this book because we appreciate the way it emphasizes contexts and the importance of diversity. Haeckel's insight that life can only be understood in its interconnected contexts is wise and crucial. His understanding that science and spirituality are connected inspires the field of religion and ecology. His attempt to synthesize biology and cosmology and moral philosophy reflects contemporary conversations about environmental issues. His call to study the "economy of nature" to inform and transform human economies remains instructive in the 21st century as people struggle to imagine, build, and maintain just and sustainable economic structures.

In other ways, though, studying Ernst Haeckel requires caution. While insightful and creative, he was also deeply and troublingly prejudiced. He believed that different races of humans were different species that had evolved at different times, and that "Caucasian, or Mediterranean man (*Homo mediterraneus*)" was superior to all others and had produced "most eminent actors in what is called 'Universal History'" (1914: 429). While such white supremacist ideas were relatively common in Haeckel's cultural context, they are nonetheless inexcusable. He neglected the fact that nature is always interpreted by the person studying it, always filtered through a cultural context. He did not realize how easy it is to read one's own sociocultural location, prejudices, and identities back into the natural world.

Scientists of Haeckel's era, many of whom were white European males from Christian cultures, tended to assume that the natural world would prove their own religions, races, languages, and cultures to be the "most advanced" in the history of evolution. This is a culturally specific version of what is called the anthropic principle: that the entire process of universal expansion and geo-evolution has led up to the pinnacle of certain kinds of *Homo sapiens*. Sadly, many who came after Haeckel continued these ideas, using interpretations of ecological science to justify social Darwinism and racial divisions. His belief that human beings could be cleanly divided into racial groups by science and that those racial groups could be ranked shows the dangers of an ecological project. (For more on the racist assumptions that shape too much ecological and environmental thinking, see Chapter 8.)

In using "ecology" in this chapter and this book, we seek to reject the racism and white supremacy of Haeckel's thinking, and we aim to be more cautious about drawing simplistic connections between natural systems and human cultures. We appreciate that ecological thinking has, since Haeckel, become less interested in ranking "the most eminent" species or group in any context. We hope to be more aware than Haeckel was of the limits of our own knowledge and the importance of complexities and connections between people, cultures, and ecosystems.

With those cautions in mind, though, we remain committed to other aspects of Haeckel's proposal for ecology. The project of synthesizing scientific, cosmological, philosophical, and moral ideas about the interconnections between forms of life remains important and has been continued by many other inspiring thinkers.

### The Social Construction of Ecology

Historian Carolyn Merchant offers a set of tools with which to understand the mixed legacy of Haeckel and other ecologists who make problematic assumptions. In her extensive studies of how European science developed, she shows that early scientists assumed that the world was constructed in a series of hierarchies, with some creatures and beings more important than others. This hierarchical approach explains Haeckel's assumption that one species would be more "eminent" than others.

Merchant also notes that the founders of most Western scientific disciplines were men, who tended to assume that women's ideas were less important and tended to seek evidence in their studies of strict gender roles and the power of males as the norms in the natural world. Their sexism, like their racism, was not a product of careful study but rather of the interpretative lenses they brought to it. They looked for evidence that male Europeans were at the top of a hierarchy, and so they found it.

These ideas are social constructions. Merchant emphasizes:

#### BOX 3C

Concepts of nature and women are historical and social constructions. There are no unchanging "essential" characteristics of sex, gender, or nature. Individuals form concepts about nature and their own relationships to it that draw on the ideas and norms of the society into which they are born, socialized, and educated. People living in a given period construct nature in ways that give meaning to their own lives as elites or ordinary people, men or women, Westerners or Easterners.

—Carolyn Merchant (1990: xvi)

While Ernst Haeckel hoped for a broad and integrative approach that could find common truths in nature, Carolyn Merchant instead emphasizes that people—including scientists and philosophers—are influenced by their times, their contexts, and their assumptions. All truths are constructions, approximations of reality that must be tested and could be wrong.

This argument that knowledge is constructed is commonly associated with postmodernism, which has led many scholars to turn away from "nature." The word is fairly rare in the work of most ecological scientists because it is so broad and imprecise, because it is politically controversial, and because it is increasingly difficult to find any place or creature on earth that is natural in the sense of not being influenced and shaped in some way by human activity. Nature is, in many ways, a human construction.

However, Carolyn Merchant's approach is not to stop talking about nature or ecology but rather to recognize the importance of talking about them with full awareness that they are constructions. This is what feminist philosopher of science Sandra Harding calls "strong objectivity": in order to gain better knowledge of an event, process, or situation, one must also analyze one's own subject-position (2005). While all views of human beings and our relationships to nature are influenced by social contexts, they also help to shape those contexts. As people who want to make the world better, we need to be careful about the language we use, need to be aware of our assumptions, and need to think carefully about the implications of the ideas we share.

Merchant demonstrates this well. After making it clear that all science is socially constructed, she argues that ecological science offers a promising set of ideas about nature and human beings for the 21st century. She emphasizes that the holistic view of ecology resonates with that of traditional and Indigenous cultures, which have historically "succeeded in living in equilibrium with their environments." These holistic ideas, including an emphasis on "cyclical processes," "the interconnectedness of all things, and the assumption that nature is active and alive," resist the hierarchical views of early Western scientists (1990: 293). From this perspective, Haeckel's tree might be replaced with a web or a democratic assembly, in which relationships are horizontal and equal rather than hierarchical.

Arguing that holistic ecology should inform both the environmental movement and the women's movement, Carolyn Merchant's work became influential in ecofeminism and helped to shape philosophy, theology, and social theory that combines gender and ecological analysis. Her work has also influenced thinkers in queer theory and queer ecology and has been supported by ecological analysis that demonstrates a wide range of gender and sexual expressions in the natural world (Roughgarden 2009). (For more on the intersection of religion and ecology with gender and sexuality, see Chapters 5 and 6).

Carolyn Merchant demonstrates that ecology, like religion, is a social construction. Those who make broad and sweeping assumptions about it should be questioned and critiqued. But this is not a dismissal. Ecology is a powerful construction that is uniquely relevant to the challenges of environmental degradation.

**Spiritualities of Ecology**

Any ecology that people can talk and think about is a social construction, and ecological truths shape the ways people understand and relate to the wider world. This means that ecology can have religious and spiritual implications, that it shapes people's relationship to fundamental truths about themselves, their relationships, and wider reality.

Consider, for example, the work of ecologist Nalini Nadkarni. Inspired to study trees in college, Nadkarni went on to graduate study and worked in Costa Rica, where she developed a pioneering technique using mountain climbing equipment to reach, observe, and learn about the previously unstudied canopies of rainforests. Her studies of the small plants and ecosystems that thrive and create soil on the top of trees earned academic acclaim and helped to shape her field.

Nadkarni was also personally moved by her research, finding comfort in the strength of trees and the ways that forest ecosystems support a wide diversity of life across the world. She frames this most broadly as the truth that everyone and everything is connected and part of something larger than themselves, which she thinks of as a religious statement. She writes:

**BOX 3D**

I found spiritual solace and guidance by looking to trees and other representatives of nature. One of the most basic ways to gain—or regain—my sense of self was through meditation and conscious breathing and this, I realized, is also linked to trees. The word spirit is derived from the Latin word, *spirare*, to breath, the same root for spirituality, inspire, and expire. Although trees do not have lungs or gills as animals do, they breathe.

—Nalini Nadkarni (2011: 259).

Nadkarni recognized a parallel between her own religious practice of mindful breathing and tree respiration, so she felt her connection with the wider world more fully.

Here, careful research and analysis of the forest led to deeper truths and mysteries; Nadkarni's measurement of life in tree canopies led her to a deeper respect for the truths and values that cannot be fully measured. She also suggests that her religious background influenced her ecology, writing that her respect for the diversity of life is rooted in the diversity of the home where she grew up. Her father was a Hindu immigrant from India and her mother was raised Orthodox Jewish in Brooklyn; their house prominently featured an ivory statue of Ganesha and a menorah. But, she writes,

> those deep cultural differences my family embodied did not create a conflict. Rather, they fostered something enriching [and] set the stage for the way I have come to view nature—not as consisting of monochromes, but rather

> as comprising many colors and textures, all necessary to creating a complex and resilient whole.
>
> (2011: 253)

This scientific and religious appreciation for diversity has led Nadkarni to speak and write not only for other academics and students but also for religious communities. In that work, she has found that trees are central in many spiritual traditions: the bodhi tree in Buddhism, the tree of life in Christianity, the tree of the knowledge of good and evil in Judaism. While listening to a preacher in a Baptist church, Nadkarni noticed that this group of Christians found solace and guidance comparable to what she had learned: "he and his flock view Jesus the way I view trees, as entities who hold us in their strong limbs and protect us" (2011: 260).

The natural world also matters religiously in similar ways for many key figures in environmental history. Marjory Stoneman Douglas, who was instrumental in the establishment of Everglades National Park, had a particular reverence for the Everglades drawn from her family's Quaker background. Rachel Carson's work on the oceans and in *Silent Spring* drew from Albert Schweitzer's Christian ethic and its "reverence for life." Oceans, rivers, deserts, mountains, and every other ecosystem can teach spiritual as well as scientific lessons. Furthermore, environmentalist causes are advanced when religious people join them. This is why the prominent ecologist and environmentalist E. O. Wilson addressed his book *The Creation: An Appeal to Save Life on Earth* to Christians despite the fact that he himself is an agnostic. He hoped Christians would be inspired to conservation when the appeal was framed respectfully in biblical language (2007). He, like Nalini Nadkarni and Ernst Haeckel, understood that the ways people relate to the world around us is a deeply spiritual issue.

## Ecological Ethics

Other environmentalists use ecological truths to appeal to philosophical and secular ethics rather than religion. Perhaps the most famous example is Aldo Leopold, who was one of the most prominent environmental thinkers of the 20th century. He began his professional life working for the US Forest Service, spending time in Arizona and New Mexico before transitioning to teach wildlife management at the University of Wisconsin. While there, he and his family purchased eighty acres of land that had previously been logged and overgrazed. Leopold put his training to work to learn about and restore the land, recording his reflections in the book *A Sand County Almanac*.

Aldo Leopold's writing is famous in part because he carefully observed the world around him, combining his ecological education with the close attention of someone who loved wildlife and nature. He movingly describes seasonal transitions, the migrations of geese, and the relationships between trout and a stream. His writing is also famous because he used his observations to develop a moral perspective. While most of his contemporaries in forestry thought of wildlife management as a purely economic project that should maximize human use of the natural world, Leopold called for a "land ethic" that treats the non-human world as part of humanity's moral community. He argued that efforts to "conquer" and "control" the land would always fail in the long term and hoped people could learn to cooperate with natural systems.

Perhaps the most famous articulation of Leopold's ethic is his instruction to:

## BOX 3E

Examine each question in terms of what is ethically and esthetically right, as well as what is economically expedient. A thing is right when it tends to preserve the integrity, stability, and beauty of the biotic community. It is wrong when it tends otherwise.

—Aldo Leopold (1966: 240)

Central to Leopold's argument is an insistence that human beings cannot thrive if we relate to the natural world in purely instrumental and economic terms. He begins the essay by citing a scene in the epic poem *The Odyssey* in which the hero kills a dozen of his slaves for having betrayed his household. Leopold notes a contrast in moral responses to this story. An ancient Greek audience, which may have believed that a male master can do what he wants with female slaves, would not be shocked. But a contemporary audience should be appalled because our morality is quite clear that slavery—treating human beings as property rather than members of a community—is categorically wrong. Leopold praises the fact that human beings have expanded our morality and calls for a further expansion that will recognize it is also wrong to treat land and other species as merely economic property.

While Haeckel had sought to study "the economy of nature," Leopold instead emphasized a distinction between ecological ethics and economics. This contrast has remained prominent in environmental debates ever since. Public discourse frequently presents a choice between preserving a species and reducing toxic pollution on one hand or protecting jobs and economic development on the other. This suggests that environmentalism and economics compete in a zero-sum game, only one can win. The same logic is frequently heard in debates about climate change, in which the need to transition away from fossil fuels is balanced against the economic importance of the fossil fuel industry.

However, Leopold and most environmental ethicists who have come after him do not ultimately believe that people must choose between economics and ecology. Instead, they argue that economic systems need to be understood in their context. The human economy is always a subset of natural systems. Human beings can only thrive if the environment is healthy enough to support them. Leopold critiqued the mechanistic and instrumental approach to conservation in his day for making the false assumption "that the economic parts of the biotic clock will function without the uneconomic parts" (1966: 229–30). Instead, he insisted, people must learn that our livelihoods and our thriving depend on the larger natural systems of which we are a part. The land is a community; human beings and our institutions are members of that community.

This embrace of the biotic community is not merely an intellectual enterprise for Leopold. In beginning to understand and appreciate the beauty of ecosystems, he also learned that the wolves and deer and geese and trees and mountains were part of his community and deserved to be considered on their own terms. He began, in other words, to care about the non-human world. And this informed his ethics, as he called on readers to love the ecosystems around them.

This emphasis on care as a motivation to action has also continued in environmental ethics. Consider the ways activists in the 1970s combined photographs of the earth from space with calls to "Love your Mother." Consider the ways anti-logging activists in the 1990s personalized the ancient trees they were trying to protect in order to convince loggers and the public that they matter. Consider the way young climate activists in the 21st century insist that if parents love their children, they will take bold action to mitigate and adapt to a warming world.

### Identity, Ecology, and Justice

Like all other thinkers, Aldo Leopold came from a particular social context, and some of the assumptions and claims he made based on his context should be questioned and challenged. One such assumption is that there is a common "ethic" among human beings and that a singular "land ethic" is needed for human beings moving into the future. A white man of European descent, Leopold paid very little attention to the ethics developed by indigenous communities and non-Western cultures and did not consider that people with less privilege than him might need different kinds of ethics, might have different needs for economic thinking, and might have different opportunities to love and care for pristine biotic communities.

This critique is made powerfully by Lauret Savoy, a geologist, environmental studies professor, and public intellectual. Savoy has African American, European American, and Native American heritage and reflects on the ways her identity and her family's relationships with race and ethnicity shape her approach to environmental issues. It also shaped her relationship to Leopold's land ethic. As a descendant of slaves and someone aware of the profound ways slavery has shaped the history of the US and the world, she writes, "I couldn't understand why in a book so concerned with America's past, the only reference to slavery, to human beings as property, was about ancient Greece." This leads her to a broader critique of the sweeping generalizations in Leopold's writing: "I so feared that his 'we' and 'us' excluded me and other Americans with ancestral roots in Africa, Asia, or Native America" (2015: 33–4).

Savoy also makes a very personal connection with the fact that her father, Willard Savoy, published a book in 1949, the same year *A Sand County Almanac* was released. Savoy's book is a novel, the story of a biracial, light-skinned man who sometimes passes as white, sometimes advocates for civil rights as a proud black man, and seeks to live peacefully with his family from diverse backgrounds. The book's title reflects its main character's difficult relationship with US culture: *Alien Land* (Savoy 1949).

Aldo Leopold never met Willard Savoy, but Savoy's daughter wonders what the famous ecologist could have learned from her father about land and about the limits of the "we" and "us" of the land ethic. She wonders what would become of an "alien land ethic," building an ecological concern for natural systems while also taking seriously different experiences of oppression and privilege arising from different identities.

Lauret Savoy demonstrates that ethics should never be a merely abstract concept. Human behavior is shaped not only by big ideas and moral principles but also by the social structures in which people live and the institutions that structure their daily lives. In far too many cases, people's actions are also shaped by privileges, exclusions, and/or microaggressions based on race, ethnicity, gender, sexuality, ability, and class. No ecological ethics is complete without accounting for these dynamics.

Aldo Leopold assumed that "we" human beings had moved beyond slavery and prejudice and so were ready to take the next step of incorporating the land into our communities. Lauret Savoy suggests that this assumption only made sense from the warped perspective of Leopold's privilege and that his appeal to a universal human identity implicitly excluded the experience of people, like her father, who continue to face racist oppression. The lesson she draws from this is that anyone thinking ecologically should be careful not to focus only on abstractions and ideals and should instead pay attention to the specific lived experiences and behaviors of particular human beings. She writes:

**BOX 3F**

The scope of America's "thinking community" remains narrow. A democratic dream of individual liberties and rights hasn't yet contributed to a "co-ordinated whole"—whether human, biotic, or the land. Danger lies in equating theory with practice, or ideal with committed action, as personal responsibility and respect for others, and for the land, can still be lost to lip service, disingenuous manners, and legislated gestures to an ideal.

—Lauret Savoy (2015: 44)

This caution is vitally important for anyone concerned with ecological and environmental issues. Many environmental activists appeal to ideals of clean environments and waste-free lifestyles while ignoring the ways toxic wastes and garbage are exported to poorer nations. Climate activists from wealthy nations spent decades emphasizing the threats posed to polar bears without mentioning the disproportionate threats faced by poor communities of human beings in coastal and desert climates. Western environmentalists too often appeal to broad principles without learning from the specific ideas of marginalized and Indigenous communities.

Black liberation theologian James Cone made this point well in an influential essay titled "Whose Earth Is It, Anyway?" which critiques most environmental discourse for lacking "a truly radical critique of the culture most responsible for the ecological crisis" and suggests "perhaps whites could learn something of how we got into this ecological mess from those who have been the victims of white supremacy" (2001: 30).

Any approach to ecology that seeks to learn from diversity must learn from the diversity of human communities. As Savoy and Cone insist, this cannot simply be an abstract ideal of collaborative discourse but must take seriously the legacies of colonialism, slavery, and oppression that have separated and harmed some people while privileging others. This is an essential part of ecological ethics, ecological attention, and any intersection between ecology and religion.

## Ecology and Cosmology

Another important thinker at the intersection of race and ecology is Carl Anthony, an architect and urban planner who co-founded the Earth Island Institute's Urban Habitat Program in 1989. Based in the Bay Area of California, this project focused on issues of health, transportation, and leadership with a focus on the poor and racial minorities. It was one of the first explicit environmental justice projects in the United States. While most major environmental organizations were focused exclusively on wildlife and national politics, Anthony sought to build a more sustainable city by partnering with marginalized people.

In his book *The Earth, The City, and the Hidden Narrative of Race*, Anthony argues that the environmental movement needs to connect the industrial technologies that are degrading the earth to their origins in slavery and exploitation. The fossil fuel economy is only possible because of the uncompensated labor of people of color and the stolen resources of non-European cultures:

> From the outset, slavery went absolutely hand in hand with the reckless plundering of ecosystems in the New World. The exploitation of the people and environments of the New World and human beings stolen from Africa created tremendous wealth that was the foundation of the financial power that now runs the world.
>
> (2017: 17)

Thus, he argues, anyone who seeks to change the power structures of the contemporary world needs to struggle against racism and colonialism.

For Carl Anthony, a key resource in that struggle is cosmology, an attention to the long history of the universe and the participation of human beings and our planet in a billion-year-old drama. Learning from Catholic priest Thomas Berry and cosmologist Brian Swimme's book *The Universe Story* (1992), Anthony argues poor and marginalized people can be empowered and energized to deal with their immediate problems when they understand them in the wide context of cosmic history. He writes:

**BOX 3G**

The universe story could be big enough to contain this kind of inclusive reimagining of our relationship with the planet. The old story about how society evolved until we reached the pinnacle of industrial capitalism is disintegrating. The new story is that we are the end product of a process of 13.7 billion years in which the human journey is a small portion of the end. The new story includes the birth of our universe, the formation of Earth, the emergence of the first cell and human evolution, the rise of humanity in Africa, and the great migrations of all Earth's peoples around the globe.

—Carl Anthony (2017: 21)

Anthony's ideas contain the same themes as the other ecological thinkers in this chapter: the interconnectedness of things, the importance of multiple kinds of understanding, and the extension of communities. The difference is the scale: he argues that it is important to understand that the entire cosmos is an interconnected community, that the physics and math required to understand space is also part of ecological knowledge.

Cosmological ecology teaches that every organism on earth is part of a web of connections and relationships because every particle everywhere emerged from the same cosmic birth. Everything in existence is linked by gravitational and physical forces, so nothing is separate and no one is alone. Ecology in this sense is not just about studying the "environments" and "ecosystems" of the earth, but it is also a recognition that every human being is a part of a broader system, a part of the cosmic interplay between matter and energy. This is, indeed, what the famous *Earthrise* image means to so many people: everything we think of in human histories has happened on this tiny planet and in connection with all other life that has ever evolved on the planet.

These facts can inspire both wonder and responsibility. It can be amazing to ponder that the universe has expanded for 14 billion years, the sun formed 4.6 billion years ago, life began evolving on earth 3.7 billion years ago, and our species has existed for about 200,000 years. Each and every one of us came from this cosmic history, we are all part of the drama of our planet, our solar system, and our universe. These amazing facts can also, for some, inspire ethical responsibility: because all things are interconnected, everyone should strive to nurture and support connections, to coexist.

However, these same facts can also inspire despair, and a sense that humanity is ultimately irrelevant. Lisa Sideris writes,

> The vast cosmic scope and sweep of the Universe Story cultivates global—literally, cosmopolitan—sensibilities that have little to do with humans becoming strongly attached to and responsible for their particular environments. From the standpoint of the universe as a whole, the fate—immediate

> or long term—of one particular planet in an obscure corner of an infinite cosmos seems rather inconsequential.
>
> (Sideris 2017: 12)

We're not here to tell you whether you should be enlivened or brought to despair by the Universe Story; Sideris' critique highlights that scientific data does not speak for itself, as science studies scholars such as Bruno Latour (1988) have long pointed out; it is we humans who make sense of it. Our knowledge of the universe, derived from the work of scientists, becomes intelligible when we tell stories to make sense of that knowledge and place ourselves within those stories.

For Carl Anthony, learning about cosmology empowered him in his work as an environmental organizer and executive. Recounting a meeting in which his voice as a black man was not being respected, he writes, "I found myself saying, 'I don't

*Figure 3.2* *Earthrise*, a famous photograph taken by Apollo 8 crewmember Bill Anders in 1968, has become an iconic image in the environmental movement. The picture of Earth from space, with the moon in front, offers cosmological context for all of human history and planetary life.

have to put up with this. I'm the end product of fourteen billion years of evolution.' Everyone stopped and took notice. I was amazed at how good that affirmation made me feel. I discovered that I had a place" (2017: 145).

The cosmological story of the universe offers an unimaginably broad perspective, contextualizing the challenges and experiences of today. It can also demonstrate that no single human perspective should outweigh all others, empowering voices that have been excluded to join conversations about how to participate in this small corner of the cosmos.

## Conclusion: Ecology Inspires Questions

This chapter has quoted seven thinkers who shed important light on ecological topics: Robin Wall Kimmerer, Ernst Haeckel, Carolyn Merchant, Nalini Nadkarni, Aldo Leopold, Lauret Savoy, and Carl Anthony. Each emphasizes an idea that we have argued is foundational to ecological thinking: individual lives must be understood in the context of broader communities. Nothing can be understood well unless we also understand its connections to others. This idea is fundamental to the academic study of religion and ecology and so also fundamental to the chapters in this book.

As important as this common ground is, a more interesting reflection on the seven thinkers discussed here concerns their very different approaches. For example, how possible and appropriate is it to apply the truths one finds in ecological thinking to other people in other cultures? Ernst Haeckel, Aldo Leopold, and Carl Anthony make broad and sweeping claims about ecology, proposing universal truths and pointing the way toward unifying theories of truth and ethics that could bring people together. By contrast, Carolyn Merchant, Nalini Nadkarni, and Lauret Savoy focus on the ways particular experiences shape ecological truths, leaving room for people from different contexts and identities to come to different conclusions. Which approach seems easier? Which one seems more likely to lead to important conclusions? Which seems more relevant to contemporary problems?

Another question concerns the difference between the sources of authority used in ecological thinking. Robin Wall Kimmerer and Nalini Nadkarni draw lessons from particular forests and particular creatures. Carl Anthony and Carolyn Merchant emphasize their careful academic study of scholars and experts in relevant fields. Lauret Savoy and Nalini Nadkarni emphasize what they learned from their family experiences. Are any of these sources less legitimate than the others? Should any be given primacy over the others? Are there important sources of ecological wisdom not represented in this chapter?

Those questions inform a third: What should be the relationship between ecological thinking and social justice? All the thinkers we have cited here assume that there is such a relationship, that the interconnection of ecology has implications for how human beings should live together. But they come at this with different approaches. Aldo Leopold emphasizes that ecological ethics is an extension beyond existing standards of justice, while Robin Wall Kimmerer focuses on lessons about human justice that can be learned from the natural world itself. Lauret

Savoy calls for an ecological theory responsive to the specific injustices inflicted upon Black and Indigenous peoples in the United States, while Carolyn Merchant focuses more on the injustices faced by women in Western cultures. Is one of these approaches to the intersection of justice and ecology more valid? More urgent? More convincing?

Our task in this chapter is not to answer these questions, nor even to help you to conclusively answer them yourself. Rather, the goal here has been to introduce you to the kinds of thinkers and the kinds of thinking that prepare one to think about such questions, recognize their importance, and respect multiple answers. It is great if you have clear answers to these questions about justice, authority, and universality; such clarity can often create the kind of passion that leads to action and organizing. But it is also okay if you do not have answers. It is important, whether you have answers or not, to recognize that smart people who have thought about these issues for years draw different conclusions.

If a key lesson of ecology is about context and interconnection, then it is important to recognize one's own thinking about ecology as something that happens in context, connected to other ideas. Our thinking about this topic, our resonance with some thinkers and rejection of others, is influenced by who we are and where we come from. Much like many different entities, species, organisms, and processes come together to make up a given ecosystem, so multiple perspectives weave together to give us a much richer and colorful overall tapestry of knowledge. When we recognize that there are always multiple interpretations, we can become more open to learning why others from other contexts think differently from ourselves. Such learning is, we think, as important as the grace-filled lessons that Robin Wall Kimmerer and her students found in the Great Smoky Mountains.

## References

Anthony, C. (2017) *The Earth, the City, and the Hidden Narrative of Race*. New York: New Village Press.

Cone, J. (2001) "Whose Earth Is It, Anyway?" in D. Hessel and L. Rasmussen (eds) *Earth Habitat: Eco-Injustice and the Church's Response*. Minneapolis: Fortress Press, 23–32.

Haeckel, E. (1866) *Generelle Morphologie der Organismen*. Berlin: Reimer.

———. (1895) *Monism as Connecting Religion and Science: The Confession of Faith of a Man of Science*, trans. J. Gilchrist. London: Adam and Charles Black.

——— (1914) *The History of Creation*. 6th ed. New York: D. Appleton and Company.

Harding, S. (2005) "Rethinking Standpoint Epistemology: What Is 'Strong Objectivity'?" in A. Cudd and R. Andreasen (eds) *Feminist Theory: A Philosophical Anthology*. Oxford: Blackwell.

Kimmerer, R. W. (2013) *Braiding Sweetgrass: Indigenous Wisdom, Scientific Knowledge, and the Teachings of Plants*. Minneapolis: Milkweed Editions.

Latour, B. (1988) *The Pasteurization of France*, trans. A. Sheridan and J. Law. Cambridge, MA: Harvard University Press.

Leopold, A. (1966 [1949]) *A Sand County Almanac, with Essays on Conservation from Round River*. New York: Oxford University Press.

Merchant, C. (1990 [1980]) *The Death of Nature: Women, Ecology, and the Scientific Revolution*. San Francisco: HarperCollins.

Nadkarni, N. (2011). *The Colors of Nature: Culture, Identity, and the Natural World*, eds. A. Deming and L. Savoy. Minneapolis: Milkweed Editions, 251–62.

Roughgarden, J. (2009) *Evolution's Rainbow: Diversity, Gender, and Sexuality in Nature and People*. Oakland: University of California Press.

Savoy, L. (2015) *Trace: Memory, History, Race, and the American Landscape*. Berkeley: Counterpoint Press.

Savoy, W. (1949) *Alien Land*. New York: New American Library.

Sideris, L. (2017) *Consecrating Science: Wonder, Knowledge, and the Natural World*. Oakland, CA: University of California Press.

Swimme, B., and Berry, T. (1992) *The Universe Story: From the Primordial Flaring Forth to the Ecozoic Era—A Celebration of the Unfolding of the Cosmos*. San Francisco: HarperCollins.

Wilson, E. O. (2007) *The Creation: An Appeal to Save Life on Earth*. New York: Norton.

## For Further Reading

Adams, C. J. (ed) (1993) *Ecofeminism and the Sacred*. New York: Continuum.

Cronon, W. (ed) (1995) *Uncommon Ground: Toward Reinventing Nature*. New York: W.W. Norton & Co.

Latour, B. (2004) *The Politics of Nature: How to Bring the Sciences into Democracy*. Cambridge: Harvard University Press.

Mitchell, S. (2018) *Sacred Instructions: Indigenous Wisdom for Living Spirit-Based Change*. Berkeley: North Atlantic Books.

Nixon, R. (2011) *Slow Violence and the Environmentalism of the Poor*. Cambridge, MA: Harvard University Press.

Worster, D. (1994) *Nature's Economy: A History of Ecological Ideas*. New York: Cambridge University Press.

# Part II

# Intersectional Locations

# 4 Taking Indigeneity Seriously

*Dana Lloyd*

## Introduction

What makes a person indigenous? Is indigeneity a biological fact? A legal one? Is it about culture? Or politics? And why should scholars of religion and ecology care about indigeneity and about who is Indigenous?

Indigeneity is a global term of solidarity, connecting peoples around the world who have struggled against colonization—Native Americans, First Nations, Aboriginals, Pacific Islanders, and others.

> Who gets to be "indigenous" is typically measured through historical continuity. Language, cultural forms of association in traditional communities, common ancestry with original occupants of lands, and occupation of ancestral lands are some of the ways that historical continuity is established, but as Native studies scholars have shown, proving historical continuity requires adjudication at state, federal, and global levels.
>
> (Teves, Smith, and Raheja 2015: 111)

This means that indigeneity is often understood as relationship to land, indeed, spiritual relationship to land, which is one possible reason for scholars of religion and ecology to be interested in indigeneity.

But indigeneity is about more than this and also about less than this. For example, because Indigenous peoples have often been violently removed from their ancestral lands, relocated to cities, or confined in reservations by settler states, we should not romanticize indigeneity as an unsevered attachment to land. We cannot talk about indigeneity without talking about settler colonialism and genocide, about racialization and marginalization. But we should also, when talking about indigeneity, talk about survivance and about sovereignty. And we will, shortly.

Indigeneity is a contested term, and while it is meant to create solidarity across cultures, nations, and ethnic identities, it can also exclude and erase. What it means to understand indigeneity legally, what it means to understand it culturally, and what it means to understand it politically are often different things. In the US, the federal government may say it recognizes as Indigenous (as Native American or, as federal law still calls them, "American Indian") only those who are enrolled

DOI: 10.4324/9781003259466-7

in a "tribe" (another term used by the US government, which some today find offensive, preferring the term "nation"). Specific Indigenous nations can determine their own rules about membership. Many use what is known as "blood quantum," accepting as members, or citizens, only those who have a certain amount of "Indian blood" or ancestry (for example, one has a one-quarter blood quantum if one of her four grandparents is of exclusively Native American ancestry and her other three grandparents are not Native). But blood quantum (or its successor, which is popular today, DNA) does not really specify belonging to any specific tribal nation, just a vague, general identification as Indian, or Native, or Indigenous. Scholars such as Kim Tallbear (2013) (Sisseton Wahpeton Oyate) and Adrienne Keene (2018) (Cherokee) have criticized the racialized understanding of indigeneity as blood quantum or DNA and pointed out some of its absurd results: Should an Indigenous person find out a potential date's blood quantum in advance, to determine whether their future children would be able to enroll in their tribe? How can tribes determine the status of children of same-sex couples?

Other Indigenous nations do not have any blood quantum standards but require members to be a direct descendant of a tribal member, be a permanent resident of the reservation, or prove some cultural knowledge and community participation. All of these definitions are problematic in one way or another. As Eva Marie Garroutte (Cherokee) ironically asks, "what if my grandma eats big macs?" (2003: 61). In Canada, the Cowessess First Nation has undermined the legal definition of "Indian" in the Indian Act by acknowledging kinship relations to members who have not been federally recognized or who have lived in urban areas, away from the reserve (Innes 2013).

I live and work in Philadelphia, on Lenni Lenape land, and I write about Yurok struggles for sovereignty in Northern California. But I grew up in Tel Aviv, and my understanding of indigeneity and of settler colonialism is always in relation to the specificity of Palestine/Israel. Therefore, my work needs to be accountable to Lenape, Yurok, and Palestinian peoples. I keep questioning my positionality as a white, non-Indigenous woman who writes and teaches about indigeneity. I do not have a good answer yet, but I do think that the work of understanding indigeneity and of fighting against settler colonialism is—should be—the responsibility of white settlers.

What I would like to think about in this chapter is what scholars of religion and ecology can learn from Indigenous studies. This is a complicated question because what I do not want religion and ecology scholars—including myself—to do is to engage in colonialist knowledge extraction and "borrow" theories and methods from Indigenous scholars (Liboiron 2021). However, I do want indigeneity to change how we do our work—how we think, write, and teach—and how we live in the world. What does it mean to take indigeneity seriously when thinking about religion and ecology? In other words, what indigeneity calls us to consider is how to study religion and ecology on stolen land.

Perhaps the first thing we all ought to do is write what religious studies scholar Natalie Avalos (Chicana of Mexican Indigenous descent) calls a decolonial autobiography. Here is how she describes the assignment she gives her students:

> Think about the land that you were born into. Imagine the land itself has many layers—what is its history? Who were its first inhabitants or peoples? Or even the many inhabitants that coexisted there? What is its colonial history? What is your position in relation to this colonial history? How do you and your family fit in this picture? When did they arrive to this land (if known)? From where? Where do you live now? What is this place's history? What is your relationship to the colonial relations of power in this land?
>
> (Avalos 2018)

I imagine one receives different essays when assigning it in different institutions—public universities, predominantly white ones, tribal colleges and universities, historically Black colleges and universities, or religious institutions—but Avalos' point is that we all have some relationships to some lands and that reflecting on these relationships is important to how we learn about indigeneity (or perhaps to how we learn anything on stolen land).

**BOX 4A**

How does your own decolonial autobiography affect your understanding of religion and ecology?

### Thinking About Indigeneity in Religion and Ecology

So how can taking indigeneity seriously change how we think about religion and ecology? I will start by recounting some things that I learned from thinking about indigeneity. First and foremost, the scholarly work I do is not decolonial. Following Tuck and Yang's (2012) now-famous phrase "decolonization is not a metaphor," we should refer as decolonial only to giving back stolen land. In this sense, we cannot decolonize our syllabi, our classrooms, or our conferences. Max Liboiron (Métis) uses "anticolonial" when talking about their lab practices, and I strive to do anticolonial work in my scholarship and in my teaching, but I also want to acknowledge that I often fail and that my scholarship and teaching take place in a settler-colonial setting, no matter how I do them. This does not mean I should not keep trying.

Secondly, we should consider marking the identity of scholars we cite. What does that mean? It means that if we believe that Indigenous identity is place-based, then Indigenous scholarship is also rooted in specific places. Therefore, it is significant that a scholar writes as Cherokee, or Cree, or aboriginal. Liboiron critiques the practice of only marking Indigenous scholars in this way as naturalizing and neutralizing whiteness, and so they mark non-Indigenous scholars as well, and they base their marking on scholars' self-identification, which means that sometimes a scholar is identified as "unmarked."

Having to tell readers where a specific scholar I cite is from means that I have to find out lots of different things. If I am committed to this practice, I cannot cite an author just assuming that they are Indigenous (or just assuming that they are not

Indigenous). I have to know what their tribal affiliation is, and then I need to decide whether to mark them through the official anglicized name of their tribal nation or to use their language (for example, do I refer to Vine Deloria, Jr., a prominent Native American scholar, as Standing Rock Sioux or as Lakota?) I also need to learn how to spell and pronounce these names. You may have noticed that I cited Teves, Smith, and Raheja at the beginning of this essay and did not mention anything about their identity. Stephanie Nohelani Teves is Kānaka Maoli, or Native Hawaiian, and Michelle H. Raheja is of Seneca descent. Andrea Smith used to identify as Cherokee, but the Cherokee Nation has contested this identification, which has caused many scholars to decide not to cite her work anymore, arguing even if her work has been considered smart and important, one cannot separate the scholarship from the scholar and we should not support someone who has pretended to be Indigenous by citing her work (Lakota historian Philip Deloria [1998] called it "playing Indian"). Others disagree and say that if the work is useful, we should use it. Whatever we decide to do in a given case, taking indigeneity seriously means that we should know these things, care about them, and make (sometimes hard) decisions.

There are other ethical questions that come with taking indigeneity seriously in scholarship on religion and ecology. As I am a non-Indigenous scholar, my work is not and will never be Indigenous. I do not and cannot attempt to speak for the Yurok people even if my research and writing are *about* them. Actually, I do not think my research and writing are *about* the Yurok Nation. I said earlier that it is, but let me be more specific. I just finished writing a book about a legal case in which the US Supreme Court has said that it was constitutional for the US government to destroy land that is sacred to the Yurok, Karuk, and Tolowa Nations and is located in a national forest. This does not mean that my work is *on* or *about* Yurok, Karuk, or Tolowa peoples. However, taking indigeneity seriously means I must know their side of the story; I need to try to understand what it means that this land is sacred to them and how they have responded to this devastating court ruling.

Actually, taking indigeneity seriously means that, following Eve Tuck (Unangax̂), I do not want to write about this ruling as devastating. In an open letter to scholars (2009), Tuck acknowledges that scholarship that focuses on damage and oppression means well, as it is intended to hold states and majority groups accountable and to promote a discourse on reparation, but she argues that the unintended consequence of such focus is perpetuating a one-dimensional image of a marginalized group as hopeless and depleted. This is why I say that even as indigeneity calls us to think about genocide and settler colonialism in our work on religion and ecology, it also calls us to think of Indigenous sovereignty.

In my own work, it is also important that I know about Alfred Kroeber, the infamous Berkeley anthropologist who studied California Indigenous peoples in early and mid-20th century. Kroeber's work depicted the Indigenous peoples of Northern California as "primitive" and "vanishing"; he collected and studied the remains of Indigenous ancestors, which was then just unethical and today is illegal, and he displayed a Yahi man as a living exhibition at the Berkeley Museum as "the last wild Indian." The man, whom Kroeber named "Ishi," lived in the museum for a few years, until his death from tuberculosis in 1916, and then Kroeber sent his body for autopsy, against his explicit wishes to be cremated and buried without autopsy. Given what I know about Kroeber, I should have no expectation that Yurok people share any knowledge with me, even if I think that taking indigeneity seriously means I need to know their side of the story when I write about that legal case in which they were involved. Taking indigeneity seriously requires me to know about—and respect—ethnographic refusal (Simpson 2014).

## Theoretical Frameworks

My main argument in this chapter is that to take indigeneity seriously means certain theoretical frameworks should guide our thinking about religion and ecology. These frameworks include genocide, settler colonialism, and Indigenous sovereignty. Thinking within the framework of genocide might mean that we ask how to apply this category, coined in Europe after World War Two, to the North American context (Alvarez 2015; Dunbar-Ortiz and Gilio-Whitaker 2016: 58–66). While some scholars find the concept of genocide useless in this context (either because it is anachronistic or because it is too legalistic), others find it fitting to describe at least some episodes in the history of US-Native relations, and they think that it is important to remember the atrocities of the past and that categorizing them as genocide is the appropriate way to remember them. If genocide does apply to the Native American context, what does it mean? Can a Native nation take the US government to an international tribunal to be tried for the latter's crimes against the former? Thinking within the framework of genocide might also mean that we categorize some current phenomena as ecocide and ask how they affect Indigenous peoples around the world (Short 2016). It might mean that we understand blood quantum as "statistical genocide" (Dunbar-Ortiz and Gilio-Whitaker 2016: 79).

As religious studies scholars, we should also think about genocide, at least as an open question, when we think about the beatification of Junipero Serra, founder of the California mission system, which led to forced conversions and significant violence and abuse (Gómez, forthcoming). Genocide should be on our mind when we respond to New Agers who use Sephora's "starter witch kit" (Keene 2018) with little or no attention to the Indigenous traditions that are being co-opted and appropriated by it. Genocide should be on our mind when we read, approvingly, Pope Francis' encyclical *Laudato Si'* (2015) but do not read other papal bulls that legitimized the enslavement and murder of Native Americans who were dismissed as pagans.

> **BOX 4B**
>
> In what contexts did you learn about genocide in your life and education to this point? Was the word used about some historical atrocities but not others? Why do you think that might have been?

However, settler colonialism may be an even more appropriate theoretical framework than genocide when thinking about indigeneity. As historian Patrick Wolfe (2006) famously puts it, settler colonialism is a structure, not an event. Tiffany Lethabo King (2019) writes that settler colonialism is "a milieu or active set of relations that we can push on, move around in, and redo from moment to moment" (40). While genocide is also understood as a systemic plan rather than a discrete event, it does refer to a series of events in the past. Settler colonialism is more readily understood as a system, complete with ontology and epistemology, that structures our present. The point is that in settler-colonial contexts—as opposed to other contexts—genocidal events follow what Wolfe called "a logic of elimination": the Native is to be eliminated in order to be replaced by settlers (recall Deloria's "playing Indian"). Settlers' goal is to dispossess Indigenous peoples from their lands so that settlers can gain ownership of these lands. This is the point that the theoretical framework of genocide misses when applied to the Native American context. The framework of settler colonialism also helps us to see that while it is easy to criticize the Global North's obsession with development, growth, capital, and accumulation, the supposedly opposite desire to preserve nature also follows a colonialist logic. As Liboiron reminds us, not only pollution but also recycling assumes access to Indigenous land (more on this shortly).

But settler colonialism is not enough. Following Tuck's call to stay away from damage-centered scholarship, I propose that taking indigeneity seriously means taking Indigenous sovereignty seriously. Therefore, when religion and ecology scholars think of various struggles to protect, for example, Native American sacred sites, we should strive to understand them as struggles to protect—first and foremost—Indigenous sovereignty (McNally 2020).

However, the idea of Indigenous sovereignty has been critiqued by Indigenous and non-Indigenous scholars: Kahnawà:ke Mohawk scholar Taiaiake Alfred (2002) argues that sovereignty is not an appropriate political objective for Indigenous peoples, as the concept itself is essentially Western and has served as a tool in colonizing Indigenous peoples. Political theorist Joan Cocks (2014) agrees and asks about "the tendency of those oppressed by sovereign power to make counter-sovereignty bids to save themselves" (9). What does it look like to take seriously both Indigenous sovereignty and its critiques? In the context of studying religion and ecology, it might mean simply that we center Indigenous knowledge rather than settler-colonial knowledge, as religious studies scholar Jennifer Graber (2022) has done with the Kiowa Feather Dance (which the US government called the Ghost Dance). Religious studies scholar Sarah Dees (2021) and Cherokee philosopher Brian Burkhart (2020) point out the public significance of centering Native knowledge and history in the practice of naming places such as mountains and lakes.

In what follows, I demonstrate what I think it looks like to take indigeneity seriously in scholarship on religion and ecology by looking at one issue that is of interest to scholars of religion and ecology—wilderness preservation—through the theoretical lenses of genocide, settler colonialism, and Indigenous sovereignty.

**BOX 4C**

Are the theoretical frameworks of genocide, settler colonialism, and Indigenous sovereignty compatible with each other? Does one seem more compelling than the others?

### The Coloniality of Wilderness

Wilderness is an important American idea with spiritual significance, but it also brings to mind the doctrines of *terra nullius* and Christian discovery, two doctrines that have served to justify the conquest of many lands in North America and elsewhere. By designating an area as wilderness, we define it as pristine—it has not been touched by human beings—thus erasing Indigenous existence in and impact on the area before its "discovery" by Europe. As the Wilderness Act of 1964 declares, lands designated as wilderness are

> an area of undeveloped Federal land retaining its primeval character and influence, without permanent improvements or human habitation, which is protected and managed so as to preserve its natural conditions and which (1) generally appears to have been affected primarily by the forces of nature, with the imprint of man's work substantially unnoticeable; (2) has outstanding opportunities for solitude or a primitive and unconfined type of recreation; . . . and (4) may also contain ecological, geological, or other features of scientific, educational, scenic, or historical value.
>
> (Wilderness Act, 2(c))

According to legal scholar John Copeland Nagle (2005), the supporters of the enactment of the Wilderness Act wanted to promote spiritual values. Wilderness leaves the land as it was created by God, it provides us with the opportunity to encounter God, be in solitude, and experience spiritual renewal. Yet the Wilderness Act itself fails to note the spiritual values of wilderness. Geographer Linda H. Graber (1974) reminds us that wilderness is not necessary for the enjoyment of outdoor recreation or for the preservation of wildlife habitat. Perhaps what she is saying is that the secular justifications for wilderness preservation are not convincing. "Whether we realize it or not," she concludes, "an influential portion of the American public treats wilderness as sacred space" (10).

Representative Morris Udall, sponsor of the Wilderness Act, echoed religious sentiments when he said that "[t]here ought to be a few places left in the world left the way the Almighty made them" (Nagle, 958). John Muir (1993) found in Alaska the "perfectly natural effect of simple and appreciable manifestations of the presence of God" (30). Roderick Nash (2001) generalized this idea when he wrote that "wilderness symbolized divinity" (280). Henry David Thoreau (1862) famously proclaimed that "in Wildness is the preservation of the World" (665). Indeed, wilderness is central in the Hebrew Bible. For example, most of the Pentateuch takes place in the desert, where the Israelites wander for forty years before reaching (and conquering) the Promised Land. These stories, which are highly influential in American political thought in particular and in settler-colonial thought more generally, portray wilderness as sacred and development as secular, or even sinful. For example, Moses' successful attempt to produce water from a rock in the book of Numbers is punished harshly; because of Moses' attempt to "develop" the wilderness, he is banned from entering the Promised Land.

**BOX 4D**

Are there "wilderness" areas in your local community or elsewhere that are important to you? What do you know about how those areas came to be thought of as "wild" and how they are protected from development? Are peoples indigenous to the region part of the decisions made about those areas?

Designating areas as wilderness has, historically, meant dispossessing Indigenous peoples from their lands. So the idea of wilderness has very real, material consequences, contributing to the system and patterns of genocide discussed earlier.

Kānaka Maoli food studies scholar Hi'ilei Julia Kawehipuaakahaopulani Hobart (2019) writes about the role a discourse on emptiness played in the Thirty Meter Telescope (TMT) controversy on the Mauna Kea in Hawai'i. She writes that "much of Maunakea's development, from earliest Western contact to the present day, has been predicated on an idea of its emptiness" (30). Discourses of absence and emptiness, she continues, "have systematically produced the Mauna as a place without humans, spirituality, nation, or even atmosphere" (31). Imposing "Western spatial imaginaries" of emptiness upon Indigenous geographies has justified development projects from uranium mines and nuclear test sites to pipeline construction (30). So Native Hawai'ians have resisted the TMT specifically and Western colonialism more broadly by appealing to the life of the land in which Native people share and participate.

Anishinaabe jurist John Borrows (2019) examines the role that the doctrine of *terra nullius* played in the case of *Tsilhqot'in Nation v. British Columbia* (2014), where the central question was whether, at the time of discovery, the Tsilhqot'in Nation's social organization was of a sufficiently high level to establish aboriginal title. Supposedly, if the Tsilhqot'in Nation was too nomadic, or not self-governing, then the territory to which they claim aboriginal rights had been legally vacant.

> Social organization can be a synonym for self-government. When a nation organizes itself over an entire territory and controls land, makes decisions about its use, and excludes others in accordance with its laws, we should be clear about what we are saying—such a nation governs itself.
>
> (98)

The settler-colonial question here is not "How do the Tsilhquot'in people understand their relationship to this place?" but it is, instead, "Does their relationship to the place fit a Western standard of ownership?"

This approach fits the system of settler colonialism, removing Native peoples and perspectives in order to make room for settlers. Even though Native peoples had lived as sovereign before European arrival in the Americas, their existence and the marks they have left on the land have been erased. "Landscapes understood to be natural are . . . understood not only to be untouched but also to be waiting for civilizing instruments to develop them, as if that is their inevitable fate: a virgin prairie ready for the plow," writes historian Frieda Knobloch (1996: 2).

However, wilderness preservation is also not inherently good. Métis historian Mark David Spence (2000) reminds us that wilderness preservation went hand in hand with Native dispossession. Environmental historian William Cronon (1995) critiqued the idea of wilderness as a pure manifestation of the sublime as concealing its roots in 19th-century frontier ideology, and validating a long history of dispossession and conquest. In other words, both development and preservation have worked as tools for settler-colonial dispossession. Perhaps the conclusion is that environmental discourse is useless to Indigenous peoples altogether. As Vine Deloria, Jr. (1992) writes, "Inherent in the very definition of 'wilderness' is contained the gulf between the understandings of the two cultures. Indians do not see the natural world as a wilderness" (281). "Preserving" wilderness does not mean returning it to relationship with Native peoples, and so it does not contribute to Indigenous sovereignty.

Imagining land as wilderness goes hand in hand with imagining its inhabitants as primitive, childish, and savage. As Chief Justice John Marshall put it in *Johnson v. M'Intosh* (1823),

> The tribes of Indians inhabiting this country were fierce savages, whose occupation was war, and whose subsistence was drawn chiefly from the forest. To leave them in possession of their country, was to leave the country a wilderness; to govern them as a distinct people, was impossible, because they were as brave and as high spirited as they were fierce, and were ready to repel by arms every attempt on their independence.
>
> (590)

But as Native American studies scholar Dina Gilio-Whitaker (Colville Confederated Tribes) points out, there is a paradox inherent to how the US has thought about Indigenous peoples and wilderness: "The virgin wilderness construct presupposes a landscape unadulterated by human intervention, which imagined the Indigenous inhabitants incapable of (or unwilling to) alter their environments. At the same time, paradoxically, it implied a landscape largely devoid of human presence" (2019: 39). This inherent contradiction has to do with a historical ambivalence of European settlers toward Indigenous peoples. On one hand, they desired to be like the Indigenous people they encountered—free and authentic—and on the other hand, they needed to extirpate them. "Virgin wilderness narratives are a way to discursively eliminate Indigenous peoples from the land as a form of erasure or extirpation" (97, footnote 11).

Ecologist Ramachandra Guha's (1989) postcolonial critique of deep ecology and wilderness preservation acknowledges that the shift from an anthropocentric approach to a biocentric approach to the environment is welcome both in religious discourse and in scientific discourse. However, the idea that only the environment's integrity, not human needs, should guide any intervention in nature is unacceptable, according to Guha. Indeed, the idea of wilderness is "positively harmful" when applied to the developing world (72). In countries such as India, Guha tells us, the setting aside of wilderness areas has resulted in a direct transfer of resources from the poor to the rich. Designated wilderness areas are managed for the benefit of tourists and the needs of the locals are never considered. In the US itself, "the function of wilderness is to provide a temporary antidote to modern civilization . . . for most Americans it is perfectly consistent to drive a thousand miles to spend a holiday in a national park" (79).

Ojibwe author David Truer's (2021) writing about the national park system demonstrates what it looks like to think of wilderness preservation through the lenses of genocide, settler colonialism, and Indigenous sovereignty. He reminds us that members of the California State militia, the first white men to have laid eyes on Yosemite in 1851, had gone there "to kill Indians." "By the time the militia's campaign ended," he writes, "many of the Miwok who survived had been driven from Yosemite, their homeland for millennia, and forced onto reservations." But the story he tells does not end with genocide and the creation of national parks.

> In some respects, ours is an era of Native resurgence. For all we have suffered, there remain 574 federally recognized tribes in the United States. When the first national parks were created at the end of the 19th century, only about 250,000 Native people were left in the U.S. Now there are more than 5 million Native Americans throughout the country.

At the same time, the national parks are not doing so well, and the park system is struggling to guarantee their future. Truer calls for the return of the national parks to their original, Indigenous inhabitants so that they can manage them: "That's something Indians are good at: pushing ahead while bringing the past along with us. We may be able to chart a better way forward." This is one part of the #LandBack movement, which is about much more than the national parks. It is about restoring languages, ceremony, medicine, and kinship relations. It is about Indigenous sovereignty.

**BOX 4E**

Given the critiques of wilderness recounted in this section, do you agree that preservation is just as harmful as development? If so, what can we do about it? How would returning those lands to the Indigenous peoples from whom they were taken lead to a better future? Can scholarship on religion and ecology support the #LandBack project? Would such support move toward decolonizing rather than merely anticolonial work?

**Case Study: Oak Flat**

Chi'chil Bildagoteel, known in English as Oak Flat, is the place where Ga'an (guardians or messengers between Apache peoples and the Creator, Usen) reside. It is a 6.7-square-mile stretch of land within what is currently managed by the US federal government as Tonto National Forest, east of Phoenix, Arizona. Since 2014, a proposed copper mine has threatened to permanently alter the area through an underground mining technique that would cause the earth to sink, up to 1,115 feet deep and almost 2 miles across (Smith 2022). Apache Stronghold, a grassroots organization, has challenged the proposed mining plan in court, arguing that destroying their sacred sites would infringe on their free exercise of religion, a right promised to them by the First Amendment to the US Constitution, the American Indian Religious Freedom Act (1978), and the Religious Freedom Restoration Act (1993).

Because of how US law works, this case is controlled by precedent from 1988 (*Lyng v. NICPA*), where the US Supreme Court declared constitutional a plan to build a road and log trees in the High Country in northern California, an area sacred to the Yurok, Karuk, and Tolowa peoples, which has been managed by the federal government as the Six Rivers National Forest. Forty years after the *Lyng* case was tried in court, the Apache peoples are arguing that their case is different from the High Country, even though the cases sound very similar, and that even though the court failed to protect the High Country from development, it should protect Oak Flat. The main difference between the cases is that the Yurok, Karuk, and Tolowa relied on the religion clauses of the First Amendment to the US Constitution and on the American Indian Religious Freedom Act—a law that has been declared to have "no teeth"—whereas the Apache have the Religious Freedom Restoration Act, which is supposed to bypass the *Lyng* precedent.

More substantially, the Apache argue that because Oak Flat would be utterly destroyed by the mining, no religious exercise at this place would be possible at all. In the case of the High Country, the court said that building a logging road through the sacred area would not prohibit any religious exercise, that the place would still be accessible—indeed, even more accessible—to Yurok, Karuk, and Tolowa people who want to use the place for religious purposes. The Oak Flat case is different because the place as they know it will not exist anymore if it is mined.

The Ninth Circuit Court of Appeals rejected their claim, justifying their decision by saying that the Apache only recently revived their ceremonial use of Oak Flat, and therefore, destroying this place does not pose a substantial burden on their free exercise of religion. Religious studies scholar Michael McNally (2023) argues this justification is factually wrong, but what I would like to point out is that even if it is factually correct, reading this case through the theoretical lens of settler colonialism would help us see that if Apache ceremonial life in the area had been suppressed until recently, we should look to the settler state as culprit. Indeed, we should wonder how Chi'chil Bildagoteel has become part of the Tonto Forest rather than an Apache reservation.

The land transfer is conditioned on a successful environmental review, and so at the time of this writing, there is still a chance that Oak Flat will be protected for environmental reasons. However, unless Apache Stronghold takes the case to the Supreme Court and wins, Oak Flat will not be protected as a sacred place.

### *Discussion Questions*

1. How do the theoretical lenses of genocide, settler colonialism, and Indigenous sovereignty help us to think about the Oak Flat case? Is one of these theories more useful than the others? In what way? Would such a theoretical framework be helpful to Apache Stronghold in court? For example, is it possible to argue that the destruction of the landscape, including the Ga'an, is genocidal, because the Ga'an are members of the Apache peoples? Given the frameworks of settler colonialism and Indigenous sovereignty, is it reasonable to expect a settler court to rule in favor of Apache Stronghold?
2. How can environmentalists, religious leaders, and religious studies scholars support Apache Stronghold in this struggle to protect Oak Flat? Should they even try to do so?
3. What would be the implications of protecting Oak Flat environmentally? What are the implications of protecting it explicitly as sacred?

## References

Alfred, T. (2002) "Sovereignty," in P. J. Deloria and N. Salisbury (eds) *A Companion to American Indian History*. Malden: Blackwell.

Alvarez, A. (2015) *Native America and the Question of Genocide*. Lanham, MD: Rowman and Littlefield.

*American Indian Religious Freedom Act* (1978) 42 U.S.C. § 1996.

*Apache Stronghold v. United States*, No. CV-21-0050, 2021 WL 535525, at *1 (D. Ariz. February 12, 2021).

Avalos, N. (2018) "Decolonial Approaches to the Study of Religion: Teaching Native American and Indigenous Religious Traditions," *Religious Studies News*, November 5, https://rsn.aarweb.org/spotlight-on/teaching/anti-racism/decolonial-approaches (accessed December 12, 2022).

Borrows, J. (2019) *Law's Indigenous Ethics*. Toronto: University of Toronto Press.

Burkhart, B. (2020) "Indigenizing Philosophy through the Land: On the Nature of the Concept," *Political Theology Network*, July 2, https://politicaltheology.com/indigenizing-philosophy-through-the-land-on-the-nature-of-the-concept/ (accessed December 9, 2022).

Cocks, J. (2014) *On Sovereignty and Other Political Delusions*. New York: Bloomsbury.

Cronon, W. (1995) "The Problem with Wilderness," in W. Cronon (ed) *Uncommon Ground: Toward Reinventing Nature*. New York: W. W. Norton.

Dees, S. (2021) "US Landmarks Bearing Racist and Colonial References are Renamed to Reflect Indigenous Values," *The Conversation*, April 26, https://theconversation.com/us-landmarks-bearing-racist-and-colonial-references-are-renamed-to-reflect-indigenous-values-157850 (accessed December 12, 2022).

Deloria, P. J. (1998) *Playing Indian*. New Haven, CT: Yale University Press.

Deloria, V. (1992) "Trouble in High Places: Erosion of American Indian Rights to Religious Freedom in the United States," in M. A. Jaimes (ed) *The State of Native America: Genocide, Colonization, and Resistance*. Boston: South End Press, 267–90.

Dunbar-Ortiz, R., and Gilio-Whitaker, D. (2016) *"All the Real Indians Died Off" and 20 Other Myths About Native Americans*. Boston, MA: Beacon Press.

Francis, P. (2015) *Laudato si'*. Vatican City: Vatican Press.

Garroutte, E. M. (2003) *Real Indians: Identity and the Survival of Native America*. Berkeley: University of California Press.

Gilio-Whitaker, D. (2019) *As Long as Grass Grows: The Indigenous Fight for Environmental Justice, from Colonization to Standing Rock*. Boston: Beacon Press.

Gómez A. (2023) " 'We Survived This': California Missions, Colonialism, and Indigenous Belonging," *Political Theology*, forthcoming.

Graber, J. (2022) " 'They Call It Ghost Dance . . . But It's Feather Dance': Indigenous Histories in the Study of Religion and US Empire," in T. Wenger and S. A. Johnson (eds) *Religion and US Empire*. New York: New York University Press.

Graber, L. H. (1974) *Wilderness as Sacred Space*. Washington, DC: The Association of American Geographers.

Guha, R. (1989) "Radical American Environmentalism and Wilderness Preservation: A Third World Critique," *Environmental Ethics* 11(1): 71–83.

Hobart, H. J. K. (2019) "At Home on the Mauna: Ecological Violence and Fantasies of Terra Nullius on Maunakea's Summit," *Native American and Indigenous Studies* 6(2): 30–50.

Innes, R. A. (2013) *Elder Brother and the Law of the People: Contemporary Kinship and Cowessess First Nation*. Winnipeg: University of Manitoba Press.

*Johnson v. M'Intosh* (1823) 21 U.S. (8 Wheat.) 543.

Keene, A. (2018) "Love in the Time of Blood Quantum," in K. Ratteree and N. Hill (eds) *The Great Vanishing Act: Blood Quantum and the Future of Native Nations*. Golden, CO: Fulcrum Publishing.

King, T. L. (2019) *The Black Shoals: Offshore Formations of Black and Native Studies*. Durham, NC: Duke University Press.

Knobloch, F. (1996) *The Culture of Wilderness: Agriculture as Colonization in the American West*. Chappell Hill, NC: University of North Carolina Press.

Liboiron, M. (2021) *Pollution Is Colonialism*. Durham, NC: Duke University Press.

*Lyng v. Northwest Indian Cemetery Protective Association* (1988) 485 U.S. 439.

McNally, M. D. (2020) *Defend the Sacred: Native American Religious Freedom Beyond the First Amendment*. Princeton, NJ: Princeton University Press.

———. (2023) "The Sacred and the Profaned: Protection of Native American Sacred Places That Are Already Desecrated," *California Law Review* 111: 395–464.

Muir, J. (1993) *Letters from Alaska*. Madison: University of Wisconsin Press.

Nagle, J. C. (2005) "The Spiritual Values of Wilderness," *Environmental Law* 35: 955–1003.

Nash, R. F. (2001) *Wilderness in the American Mind*. New Haven: Yale University Press.

*Religious Freedom Restoration Act* (1993) 42 U.S.C. §§ 2000bb-2000bb4.

Short, D. (2016) *Redefining Genocide: Settler Colonialism, Social Death and Ecocide*. New York: Zed Books.

Simpson, A. (2014) *Mohawk Interruptus: Political Life Across the Borders of Settler States*. Durham, NC: Duke University Press.

Smith, A. (2022) "At Oak Flat, Courts and Politicians Fail Tribes," *High Country News*, July 26, www.hcn.org/articles/indigenous-affairs-justice-at-oak-flat-courts-and-politicians-fail-tribes (accessed December 12, 2022).

Spence, M. D. (2000) *Dispossessing the Wilderness: Indian Removal and the Making of the National Parks*. New York: Oxford University Press.
TallBear, K. (2013) *Native American DNA: Tribal Belonging and the False Promise of Genetic Science*. Minneapolis: University of Minnesota Press.
Teves, S. N., Smith, A., and Raheja, M. H. (eds) (2015) *Native Studies Keywords*. Tucson: University of Arizona Press.
Thoreau, H. D. (1862) "Walking," *Atlantic Monthly* 9: 657–74.
Truer, D. (2021) "Return the National Parks to the Tribes," *The Atlantic*, April 12, www.theatlantic.com/magazine/archive/2021/05/return-the-national-parks-to-the-tribes/618395/ (accessed December 9, 2022).
*Tsilhqot'in Nation v. British Columbia* (2014) 2 SCR 256.
Tuck, E. (2009) "Suspending Damage: A Letter to Communities," *Harvard Education Review* 79(3): 409–27.
Tuck, E., and Yang, K. W. (2012) "Decolonization Is Not a Metaphor," *Decolonization: Indigeneity, Education & Society* 1: 1–40.
*Wilderness Act* (1964) Public Law 88–577 (16 U.S.C. 1131–1136).
Wolfe, P. (2006) "Settler Colonialism and the Elimination of the Native," *Journal of Genocide Research* 8(4): 387–409.

## Further Reading

Deloria, V. (1973) *God Is Red: A Native View of Religion*. Golden, CO: Fulcrum Publishing.
LaDuke, W. (2015) *Recovering the Sacred: The Power of Naming and Claiming*. Chicago: Haymarket Books.
McLeod, C. (2001) *In the Light of Reverence*. Oley, PA: Sacred Land Film Project (documentary film).
O'Brien, S. C., and Talamantez, I. (2020) *Religion and Culture in Native America*. Lanham, MD: Rowman and Littlefield.
Simpson, L. (2021) *As We Have Always Done: Indigenous Freedom Through Radical Resistance*. Minneapolis: University of Minnesota Press.

# 5 Gender

*Amanda M. Nichols*

## Introduction

"Gender is a social construct."[1] As a student in the humanities and social sciences, this is one of the first dictums you will learn. But what does it mean? And why does it matter?

The answer to these questions is elusive, yet gender, as a construct, is ubiquitous. Gender informs every layer of the world that modern humans have constructed for themselves. It is embedded within our histories, our religious traditions, and our relationships with the non-human natural world. It pervades our politics, geographies, economies, and industries. It is suffused in literature, popular culture, social media, and our favorite pastimes.

The term "gender," as I use it here, will refer to the various meanings that modern society attaches to individuals based on the ways that they look, act, dress, and perform. Gender is often confused with biological sex (the chromosomes that individuals are born with)[2] and with sexual orientation (how individuals perceive themselves in relation to the individuals they are attracted to). Gender also tends to be defined in binary terms (masculine and feminine) which precludes recognition of non-binary identities (e.g., agender, transgender, and genderqueer).[3] Gendered constructs (e.g., boys like trucks while girls like dolls; women are emotional while men are rational) are learned and reinforced through socialization. These categories and the ways that they define how individuals interact with and relate to one another and their various environs are not static: they are constantly renegotiated, learned and unlearned, made and remade.

Today, gender matters because it informs the ways that individuals can and do engage in their world. In our climate insecure present, different bodies bear the brunt of environmental burdens in different ways. The persistence of gendered stereotypes exacerbates these burdens. To begin to shift the ways that we, as a society, think about gender, we must first learn about its history—about where it came from, the ways that it informs our institutions, beliefs, and social practices, and the ways that it continues to effect individuals and groups.

DOI: 10.4324/9781003259466-8

> **BOX 5A**
>
> What are some common gendered constructs that you are already aware of that are widely used and accepted in our society today? How have gendered constructs or stereotypes affected you? Have they influenced the ways that you interact with other people or the various environments that you inhabit?

## Gender and Religion: A Brief History

Religion has contributed to the formation of certain ideologies, or accepted systems of ideas and beliefs, about gender. These ideologies have become so entrenched within our societal and cultural belief systems that they are, in many cases, difficult to perceive. Informed by patriarchal (male-centered) worldviews that privilege men over women and over the rest of the biological world, ideologies often perpetuate the marginalization of certain individuals and groups. This privileging is based on an understood system of hierarchical dualisms whereby categories of identity are conceptually divided into two parts, where one is considered the "ideal" and the other is considered "lesser" (e.g., male/female, human/animal, white/black, rich/poor, heterosexual/homosexual, able-bodied/disabled, cisgender[4]/transgender).

Patriarchal worldviews are so deeply embedded within our cultures and societies that they have become part of what Michel Foucault (1975) called our "regimes of truth." These regimes of truth influence the ways that power is established and negotiated within society. They tend to be widely accepted forms of social and/or scientific knowledge about the way the world "is" that operate in society as (largely) uncontested truths. They are reproduced and perpetuated in different ways throughout society. They also function in specific ways to establish and maintain power for a particular group of people (generally middle- or upper-class, heterosexual, cisgender, white men).

Depictions of a hierarchical ordering of existence can be traced back to at least the late 5th century BCE in the work of Plato. The Western Abrahamic traditions (Judaism, Christianity, and Islam) have been particularly culpable in disseminating such patriarchal worldviews. Illustrations of this ordering, known as the great chain of being, delineate humans (and men in particular) as inferior only to the angels (depicted on the second level) and God (who is at the pinnacle). Humans are followed in the hierarchical structure by the animals (in order of level, birds, then fish, and then "beasts" [or land mammals]), and then by the earth, or land, at the very bottom.

This hierarchical model is apparent, albeit to different degrees and with some variations, in the creation stories described in the religious texts of the Abrahamic traditions (the Jewish Torah, the Christian Bible, and the Islamic Qur'an). A number of passages can be cited as evidence for this hierarchical ordering of existence including, most often, those found in the book of Genesis. Though their exact translations vary, the common interpretations of some of these passages are rendered in the following examples: In Genesis 1:27, God is said to have created man in his own image (i.e., *imago dei*). Later, in Genesis 2:22, God creates woman from the rib of man, "for man." Genesis 1:26 says that man was created to "rule over," or "have dominion over," "the fish of the sea and the birds of the air, over the livestock, and over all the earth itself and every creature that crawls upon it." Genesis 1:28 goes on to say that after God created both man and woman, he commanded them to "be fruitful and multiply, and fill the earth and subdue it."

Scholars in a variety of fields, including environmental history and religious and gender studies, argue that these hierarchical ideologies have informed our patriarchal worldviews and have been used to justify omission, marginalization, silencing, and violence directed at women, minorities, non-human animals, and the earth. Philosophers and theologians have detailed the pervasiveness of exclusions based on gender and linked these omissions directly to patriarchal religious worldviews. Omissions based on gender have also been prominent in the field of religion and many scholars, including Simone de Beauvoir (1949), Michel Foucault (1978), and Carolyn Merchant (1980), have written in detail about the relationships between patriarchal worldviews, institutions, and cultural practices. Ideologies about gender, they showed, are continuously reproduced as cultural myths in society.

**BOX 5B**

What are some other ways that you can think of that patriarchal ideologies are reproduced in society? Think about the power dynamics in these examples. Who stands to benefit and in what ways might they do so?

Scholars in the field of environmental history have also shown that patriarchal religious worldviews have shaped the ways that people think about and interact with the environment. In his now well-known essay "The Historical Roots of our Ecologic Crisis," Lynn White Jr. (1967), for instance, argued that the root of the modern ecological crisis can be found in medieval Christianity. White showed that the anthropocentric (human-centered) worldview promoted in Western Christianity established a hierarchical dualism between humans (and man in particular) and the non-human natural world. This separation, White argued, asserted human dominance over nature and justified the exploitation of nature as a decree mandated by God (1967: 1205). White was also critical of scientific and technological innovations including agricultural machines that enabled humans to produce and harvest a surplus of food and led to the Industrial Revolution. This development, he argued, changed humans' relationship to the land from "part of nature" to "exploiter of nature" (White 1967: 1205). White warned that the ecological crisis would worsen "until we reject the Christian axiom that nature has no reason for existence, save to serve man" (1967: 1207).

North American environmental historians have also detailed the ways that religious worldviews influenced individuals' moral perspectives and broader social attitudes about nature. These worldviews, they argued, have informed the ways that people engage with the natural world. Moreover, they are often reified in and perpetuated by secular and religious institutions and cultural practices. Informed by their work, many other scholars in the field have critically examined the relationships between humans, patriarchal religious presuppositions, and environmental practices.

> **BOX 5C**
>
> How do patriarchal ideologies inform the groups or communities that you participate in? What hierarchical dualisms can you identify present within these groups? In what ways do you think these ideologies and dualisms inform the ways that people relate to and interact with one another?

### Gender in Political and Social Movements

In the late 18th and early 19th centuries, socio-political movements focused on establishing equality between men and women began. Though they have changed over time, these movements have persisted and are still ongoing. Today, they are collectively referred to as the feminist movement. Scholars have identified four distinct "waves" of this movement, which they differentiate based on the primary social and political aims of the time. Though feminist critiques of society had been made well before the 19th century,[5] they were not widely known or socially adopted in the West.

From the late 18th century, however, women throughout the Western world organized around the shared mission of securing voting, property, and education rights equal to those held by men. This first wave of the movement was considered successful in many ways, but foremost because it ignited widespread social and political debate about gender inequalities that eventually facilitated legal change.

The first wave of the feminist movement was not without problems, however. It is now widely recognized that the successes of first-wave feminism were also exclusionary in some ways: they only applied to white women and, in most cases, only to those in the middle and upper classes. Though these successes went a long way toward helping white women gain some equality through legal autonomy, they also exacerbated other hierarchical dualisms, including and especially divisions between those of different ethnic backgrounds and in different social classes.

Beginning in the 1960s with the rise of second-wave feminism, scholars and activists began to problematize discrimination and call out absences based on gender in historical narratives, in modern academic discourses, and in society. Second-wave feminism focused on a broader range of issues related to inequality between the sexes, including domestic relationships, reproductive rights, and women's sexuality.

In her 1963 book *The Feminine Mystique*, which is now considered one of many catalysts for the second wave of the feminist movement, Betty Friedan problematized social conventions related to women's domesticity. Friedan documented a prevalent social phenomenon that arose during the 1950s among middle-class white women in the United States which she termed the "problem that had no name." In the United States, women entered the workforce during World War II as a means of sustaining the economy while men were away at war. When the men returned, however, many women were forced out of the workplace and relegated back to the domestic sphere. The problem, as Friedan identified it, was a widespread sense of dissatisfaction among women who were no longer satisfied solely by their domestic roles within the nuclear family.[6] Patriarchal social customs of the time, however, dictated that women were primarily restricted to the domestic sphere. Moreover, prevailing cultural myths about gendered norms established a set of specific roles for women, which they were supposed to desire and be satisfied by (i.e., being a wife, mother, and homemaker). Second-wave feminism instigated widespread rejection of these norms and triggered major societal changes as women began to enter the workforce in droves.

Second-wave feminism is also known for its critiques on discriminations based on sexual orientation and ethnicity, which are discussed in more detail in the following chapters. Activists, academics, feminists of color, and lesbian feminists helped to expand the discourses of second-wave feminism, shifting the central focus from injustices based solely on gender to include injustices based on sexism, racism, classism, and homophobia. They showed how patriarchal ideologies have enabled hierarchical dualisms related to ethnicity (white/black) and sexuality (heterosexual/homosexual), just as they have dualisms related to gender. Moreover, they linked these ideologies to Western monotheistic religious views, which have perpetuated certain norms around heterosexuality as the morally correct form of attraction (see also Bauman 2023, this volume).

Political lesbianism emerged as part of second-wave feminism as a rejection to heteronormativity in the movement and in society more broadly. Feminist poet Adrianne Rich, for instance, wrote in detail about the ways lesbianism is perceived in society. She questioned ideological presuppositions about "compulsory heterosexuality" or the idea that "heterosexuality is presumed to be the 'sexual preference' of 'most women'" (Rich 1980: 633). The contributions of second-wave feminism helped to dramatically shift the ways that we think about gender and the ways that it has been used in society.

The third wave of the feminist movement closely followed the second, building on concerns about gender inequality and incorporating discussions about the ways sexuality and ethnicity exacerbate gender disparities. Beginning in the early 1990s, third-wave feminism is distinct because of its focus on "intersectionality." Coined by Kimberlé Williams Crenshaw in her 1989 article "Demarginalizing the Intersection of Race and Sex," intersectionality refers to the ways that ethnicity and sexuality (and other factors) combine with gender to create compounded forms of oppression. Crenshaw writes, for instance, that

> Black women are sometimes excluded from feminist theory and antiracist policy discourse because both are predicated on a discrete set of experiences that often does not accurately reflect the interaction of race and gender. These problems of exclusion cannot be solved simply by including Black women

> within an already established analytic structure. Because the intersectional experience is greater than the sum of racism and sexism, any analysis that does not take intersectionality into account cannot sufficiently address the particular manner in which Black women are subordinated.
>
> (Crenshaw 1989: 140)

A number of feminist authors, including Patricia Hill Collins (2000), bell hooks (2000 [1984]), and Audre Lorde (1984), have detailed the ways that thinking about intersectionality can help us to better understand different types of violence and discrimination enacted against women. In particular, Lorde (1984) emphasized that acknowledging these differences helps us to think about and understand the lived experiences of individuals and the ways that compounded oppressions impact them in different ways. By not doing so, she argued, we preclude the formation of productive solidarities within and across groups (Lorde 1984).

One of the most important contributions to third-wave feminism was made by philosopher Judith Butler. In their[7] 1990 book, *Gender Trouble*, Butler complicated notions of gender by arguing that all gender is performance. According to Butler, there is no distinguishable universal identity that exists behind any gender construct (e.g., "woman" or "man"). Rather, individuals reenact or "perform" commonly accepted gendered tropes in the ways that they dress, act, emote, interact with, and relate to others. This is important, Butler argued, because it means that any individual can actively choose how they perform their gender. Butler called for individuals to "trouble" commonly accepted gendered tropes through the ways they perform gender in society. *Gender Trouble* also made waves in the feminist movement, however, because Butler argued that biological sex, like gender, is a constructed category and therefore another product of a dualistic patriarchal worldview. Because all individuals, despite their biological sex, perform their identities through a set of culturally constructed gendered tropes, biological sex is only made meaningful through gendered performance. Therefore, they said, biological sex as a distinct category does not exist without the category of gender and is, thus, also constructed by patriarchal cultural discourses. Butler's work has been influential in feminist theory and is regarded as one of the foundations of the field of queer theory, which began in the 1990s.

The fourth wave of the feminist movement began in the early 2010s and carries on the work of the previous waves, in that it attempts to dispel gendered stereotypes and cultural norms informed by patriarchal religious worldviews. The primary difference in fourth-wave feminism is that it uses online digital media as a platform to promote feminist ideas and women's empowerment. The fourth wave is also distinct in that it is constituted by concerns about not only gender equality but also equity, which takes seriously the history of social disadvantages experienced by certain groups and aims to rectify them. Moreover, it further expands discussions of intersectionality started by third-wave feminists to think about historically marginalized groups ranging from single mothers to indigenous populations and the differently (mentally and physically) abled, among many others.

The fourth wave has also been marked by discussions about trans rights. Importantly, these conversations have increased public awareness about problems related to access of public facilities based on gender identification. They have also precipitated concrete social change in that, increasingly, access to gender-neutral or gender-inclusive spaces are being made available in shared public spaces. Another important distinction of the fourth wave of the feminist movement is its breadth. The use of social media in particular has enabled individuals to share their stories at a previously unprecedented rate. This has become an important method of spreading public awareness about gender-related abuse and violence, including and especially about sexual harassment and sexual assault.

**BOX 5D**

Today, more people are becoming aware of and embracing non-binary gender identities than ever before. What impacts do you think this will have on the ways your community thinks and talks about gender? Do you think this will impact the ways that people mobilize around shared causes in the future? What problems or limitations might they encounter along the way?

### Ecological Feminism: Where Gender and Nature Intersect

Ecological feminism, or ecofeminism, is an offshoot of feminism that connects the subjugation of women to human dominance over and exploitation of the non-human natural world. Ecofeminism, a term first introduced by Françoise d'Eaubonne in 1974, holds that patriarchal worldviews that have privileged men over women in society are also responsible for perpetuating hierarchical dualisms that depict humans as superior to non-human organisms and the earth.

One of the earliest contributors to ecofeminism was Carolyn Merchant, who critiqued the modern mechanistic worldviews and the scientific revolution for contributing to ideologies that objectify and subjugate women in her book *The Death of Nature* (1980). Later, in *Earthcare* (1996), Merchant detailed the ways that women have historically been connected to nature and the environment in cultural narratives. She problematized these connections and argued that they allow for violence against both women and the earth. Indian environmental activist and scholar Vandana Shiva, however, wrote persuasively in *Staying Alive* (1988) that women who participate in subsistence economies have unique and deep understandings of natural process. Gender differences matter, she argued, because women in these communities have special relationships with the earth that contribute to a holistic understanding of their environments.

In general, ecofeminism argues that patriarchal worldviews link women to the earth and feminize nature by using terms like "mother earth" or "mother nature" or anthropomorphizing nature as feminine.[8] Some ecofeminists have even critiqued environmental justice discourses for linking environmental exploitation to the language of "rape of virgin land." Other ecofeminists have also related the exploitation of women to that of non-human animals. In her 1990 book *The Sexual Politics of Meat*, Carol Adams linked the oppression of women and the exploitation of non-human animals by showing the ways women are portrayed as hypersexualized "pieces of meat." Drawing on the work of these scholars, I have shown the ways that women continue to be related to nature, the earth, and non-human animals in popular culture through the use of commercial advertisements (Nichols 2021a). These ads function in religion resembling ways in pop culture, I argued, to continue a culture of violence that subjugates women and the earth. Scholars Lori Gruen and Greta Gaard have linked patriarchal worldviews and oppressions based on gender to the marginalization and oppression of individuals based on their ethnicity, class, sexuality, ability, and species (see, e.g., Gaard 1993; Gaard and Gruen 1993).

Today, there are multiple branches of ecofeminism that vary in their critiques of gendered discourses and their approaches to imagining a feminist form of environmentalism. The three most well-recognized branches include cultural, liberal, and socialist ecofeminist perspectives. Cultural ecofeminists tend to be those who understand women and men as essentially different in the ways that they act and relate. Liberal ecofeminists advocate for equality between men and women in society. Socialist ecofeminists critique capitalism for perpetuating dualisms (including those between humans and nature and between men and women) through gendered divisions of labor and human accumulation of resources for profit.

Though ecofeminist contributions are important for the ways that we think about the intersections of religion, gender, and the environment, it is also important to recognize that they are limited. Ecofeminism has been critiqued as "essentialist" and for reinforcing patriarchal dominance in the ways that it relates women and people of color to the natural world. Proponents of ecofeminism are also often critiqued for the strict dichotomies they draw between men and women and between nature and culture, among others. This dualistic worldview is understood as being counterintuitive to the inclusion of non-binary individuals and for forming false distinctions between human beings and the other-than-human natural world. Val Plumwood argued, for instance, that "forms of oppression from both present and past have left their traces in western culture as a network of dualisms, and the logical structure of dualism forms a major bias between forms of oppression" (Plumwood 1993: 203). Importantly, Plumwood's book *Feminism and the Mastery of Nature* stands as one of the most important contributions to the field of ecofeminism.

Another challenge to ecofeminism has been that, in addition to being simplistically portrayed as merely opposite to men, women are often depicted as a collective, homogeneous group. But "women" cannot be so easily categorized, nor can they be presumed to share the same ideas or experiences as other women. In "Is Female to Male as Nature is to Culture," cultural anthropologist Sherry Ortner argued that the experience of "women" is not one cohesive and identifiable thing but that the "actual treatment of women and their relative power and contribution vary enormously from culture to culture, and over different periods in the history of particular cultural traditions" (Ortner 1972: 5). This is important because lumping women together as a cohesive group with a shared identity can minimize and even erase the lived experiences and unique contributions of individuals.

## BOX 5E

What examples can you think of from popular culture that equate women with nature or personify nature as feminine that you are aware of? How are these depictions empowering? How are they problematic?

### Gender in the Field of Religion and Nature

A number of important contributions have been made to the discussion of gender within the subfield of religion and nature. These contributions look critically at the intersections of patriarchal worldviews, gender, and environmental practices and help us think about the ways religion, gender, and environmentalism are connected to one another.

Sarah Pike, for instance, investigated the ways that second-wave feminism shaped New Age and neopagan religions in North America (2004). These groups, she argued, believe that changing individual preconceptions about gender is a necessary precondition to broader social transformation that reconsiders the ways that "gender" has been historically constructed and thought about. In *At Home in Nature*, Rebecca Kneale Gould (2005) detailed the practice of homesteading and showed how it produced "competing identities" for those who practiced this simple style of living with the land because divisions of labor did not always align with traditional gendered stereotypes. Sarah McFarland Taylor explored the effects of environmental and social justice movements on women's congregations in *Green Sisters* (2007). She showed how these movements opened up important pathways for nuns, in particular, to call into question widely accepted forms of power and authority, as well as gendered stereotypes and the dominant cultural narratives that perpetuate them (Taylor 2007: 30).

Some critical approaches that engage ecofeminism have also been proffered that fall within the religion and nature discourse. Heather Eaton took a critical approach to ecofeminism in *Introducing Ecofeminist Theologies* (2005) and showed how certain common themes (such as the association of women and nature) developed historically. She also detailed the strengths and limitations of these claims for the ecofeminist agenda. Other scholars have criticized the lack of critical engagement with gender analysis beyond ecofeminism in the field of religion and nature. In her article "Has Ecofeminism Cornered the Market?" Tovis Page (2007) argued that there has been a "near exclusive emphasis" on ecofeminism in the field. Despite its usefulness in critiquing androcentric worldviews, the approach is limited, she said, because it primarily focuses on Western religious traditions and fails to consider the ways that other worldviews have shaped gendered constructs in other times and places (Page 2007: 293, 300–3). Later, in 2011, Page expanded on this critique and argued that many contributions in the field fail to approach gender from a critical frame of analysis.

A number of recent contributions in the field of religion and nature have also helped to facilitate a shift in the ways that we are thinking about gender in current socio-political contexts. The *Journal for the Study of Religion, Nature and Culture*

(*JSRNC*), for instance, has published articles on special issues titled "Engendering Nature" (Nichols and Berendt 2021) and "Ambiguous Legacies: Contested Futures" (Gould and Powell 2022), which include contributions that showed the ways that gendered discourses have been, and continue to be, used in popular and academic discourses.

## Case Study: From Bikinis to Bombs: Gender and the Nuclear Debate

In 1946, French designer Louis Réard debuted what would later become a staple in women's swimwear fashion: the bikini. Unlike other two-piece swimsuits that came before it, the bikini showed the wearers' navel—an audacious fashion decision for the time. The design was so controversial, in fact, that the Catholic Church "formally decreed" the bikini "sinful" (Le Zotte 2015). What is most striking about the bikini, however, is not how much skin it showed, but rather where the name came from.

Between 1946 and 1958, the United States government conducted a series of nuclear tests in the Marshall Islands, a chain of small islands located to the northeast of Australia in the Pacific Ocean. The first such test took place on July 1, 1946, when a nuclear bomb was detonated above a target fleet stationed just off the coast of Bikini Atoll. When he unveiled the bikini only four days later, Réard claimed that the design "was sure to be as explosive as the U.S. military tests" (Le Zotte 2015).

Examples of the ways that gender intersects with religion and environmentalism proliferate in the history of the nuclear debate. Since the beginning of the Manhattan Project in 1942, the development of nuclear technologies has been couched in gendered binarism. The male scientists who were tasked with developing the first nuclear weapon, code-named Trinity, were said to wield destructive, "godlike" power. In the aftermath of the Trinity detonation, Robert J. Oppenheimer, the father of the atomic bomb and leader of the Manhattan Project, famously quoted the Hindu god Vishnu in the Bhagavad-Gita when he said, "Now, I am become Death, the destroyer of worlds." Code names for nuclear operations and weapons tended to be stereotypically masculine and included Fat Man and Little Boy, the atomic bombs dropped respectively on Hiroshima and Nagasaki in August 1945.

Moreover, much of the discussion around the development of nuclear technologies that engages women has been focused on the idea of the nuclear family. Mary Ann Schofield has written at length about the gender dynamics that were present in Los Alamos, New Mexico, where the Manhattan Project was based. Among other things, she noted that "Lost Alamos did not welcome women, 'normal' society, or family life" (Schofield 2009: 68). However, nuclear technology did come "packaged as a sleek and attractive electrical good," John Wills has shown, strategically advertised so that women would "welcome the atom into their homes" and "reap the benefits of man's work" (2006: 82).

Analogously, women's resistance to nuclear technologies has, in many cases, misrepresented and trivialized their concerns, which have often been framed as motivated *solely* by issues appertaining to the domestic sphere (i.e., the health and well-being of children and future generations). This portrayal does not accurately represent the breadth of women's understanding of, concerns about, or resistance to the development of nuclear technologies. Moreover, it enables the perpetuation of the hegemonic patriarchal assumptions in which nuclear technologies were developed. In some protest groups, however, including the Greenham Common Women's Peace Camp in England and the Mothers for Peace organization based in San Luis Obispo, California, women strategically employed their identity and experience as "mothers" to help legitimate their cause. Today, we might choose to understand this as an act of "reclaiming." Women used the word "mothers," which has traditionally been employed to describe their role as caretakers confined predominately within the domestic sphere, subversively to warrant their presence in traditionally male-dominated spaces.

We must not forget, however, that the term "mothers" may also be exclusionary in some ways: among other things, it may not allow space for women who are childless by choice, women unable to have children, lesbian women, trans women, and/or gender non-binary individuals with or without children. Presuppositions about gender also exacerbate environmental justice concerns by obscuring the ways that compounded disadvantages affect individuals and communities. Traci Brynne Voyles evidenced this in her book *Wastelanding: Legacies of Uranium Mining in Navajo Country*, when she wrote that "imposing Western gender dichotomies through colonial economic development policies forecloses (in fact, colonizes) indigenous notions of gender . . . [and] ignore[s] and subvert[s] queer history, culture, life, and sexualities (often violently)" (2015: 133).

As Whitney A. Bauman and Heather Eaton wrote in the previous edition of this collection, "bodies matter" because they "shape how we experience the world" (2017: 56). In the ongoing global debate about nuclear disarmament, this point is especially relevant. By analyzing data from radiation survivors in Hiroshima and Nagasaki, biologist Mary Olson showed that ionizing radiation has a disproportionately greater impact on the bodies of individuals identified as biologically female (those with two X chromosomes) than on bodies identified as biologically male (those with one X and one Y chromosome) (2011). Yet "safe" levels of radiation exposure are still evaluated on a model developed in 1974 called "reference man." This model, Olson said, is "based on the average adult male 'height, age, weight . . . lifestyle, average temperature, [and] it specifies that he is white'" (interview with Mary Olson). The model does not take into account how biological differences might exacerbate the risks associated with radiation exposure. Moreover, it fails entirely to consider environmental and other compounding risk factors (ethnicity, age, economic status, geographic location, etc.) that cause radiation to affect different bodies differently.

The gendered binarism that framed the early nuclear discourse persists. At the time of this writing, the risk of intercontinental nuclear weapons exchange is higher than at any other point since the Cold War.

Rising sea levels caused by anthropogenic climate change pose an increasing threat to high-level nuclear waste interim storage sites around the world. Nuclear radiation poses a significant risk not just to humans but to the health and stability of our ecological systems. As we engage in the present and look to the future, it is important to remember that different bodies (human and non-human) will bear the brunt of these environmental burdens differently.

### *Discussion Questions*

1. Much like the bikini, which was once thought of as extreme and controversial, the use of nuclear technologies has now become mainstream. How does the widespread cultural adoption of inventions and technologies like these perpetuate gendered stereotypes? Why is this important?
2. Look around you. What items around you do people in your society use every day? Think about your appliances or cell phone, the car you drive, the shampoo you use, or the clothes you wear. How have the histories of these everyday items been informed by patriarchal ideologies? How are these items advertised, marketed, and sold? In what ways are common everyday items gendered?
3. In some modern environmental and social movements, women have found that leveraging "motherhood" can be a valuable tool for resistance. However, we rarely see "fatherhood" mobilized in a similar way. What does this suggest about the intersections of religion, gender, and the environment in our society today?

## Notes

1 Much of the content in this chapter has been adapted from material originally written for my PhD dissertation (Nichols 2021b).
2 Simone de Beauvoir (1949) was the first to differentiate between biological sex and gender as a socially constructed category. This is an important distinction because some individuals identify as a gender that does not align with their biological sex.
3 The term "agender" refers to an individual who does not identify as any gender, while transgender refers to an individual whose gender identity is different than their biological sex. Genderqueer is a term used by individuals who do not identify within the gender binary (male/female) and may see themselves outside of that binary or as somewhere in between.
4 Cisgender refers to an individual whose gender or the way that they identify corresponds with their biological sex.
5 Simone de Beauvoir (1949) identified feminist critiques dating back to the 15th century. It is reasonable to think that there may have been others before this time, though there is a dearth of historical records available to support this claim.
6 Nuclear family refers to the core group of members that make up a family unit and traditionally includes two parents and their dependent children. It is important to note that the term has historically been understood and used to refer to those families that have heterosexual parents (one male and one female) but now includes family units with same sex parents.
7 "Their" is a gender neutral pronoun used to refer to an individual who does not identify within the gender binary of male/female.
8 References to "mother nature" and "mother earth" are prolific in popular culture. Conservation International, for instance, in their short film series *Nature is Speaking* voiced Julia Roberts as Mother Earth (2014; www.youtube.com/watch?v=WmVLcj-XKnM).

Another example is the Disney movie *Moana* (2016), where nature is personified through the goddess and mother island Te Fiti, who is depicted as both a vengeful, wrathful, and destructive force as well as a benevolent bringer of life.

## References


Adams, C. (2010 [1990]) *The Sexual Politics of Meat: A Feminist Vegetarian Critical Theory*. New York: Bloomsbury.

Bauman, W., and Eaton, H. (2017) "Gender and Queer Studies," in W. A. Bauman, R. Bohannon, and K. J. O'Brien (eds) *Grounding Religion: A Field Guide to the Study of Religion and Ecology*. London and New York: Routledge, 56–71.

Butler, J. (1990) *Gender Trouble: Feminism and the Subversion of Identity*. New York: Routledge.

Collins, P. H. (2000) "Gender, Black Feminism, and Black Political Economy," *Annals of the American Academy of Political and Social Science* 568(1): 41–53. https://doi.org/10.1177/000271620056800105

Crenshaw, K. (1989) "Demarginalizing the Intersection of Race and Sex: A Black Feminist Critique of Antidiscrimination Doctrine, Feminist Theory and Antiracist Politics," *The University of Chicago Legal Forum* Article 8: 139–67.

de Beauvoir, S. (2011 [1949]) *The Second Sex,* trans. C. Borde and S. Malovany-Chevallier. New York: Vintage Books.

d'Eaubonne, F. (2020 [1974]) *Le Féminisme ou la Mort*. Paris: Le Passager Clandestin.

Eaton, H. (2005) *Introducing Ecofeminist Theologies*. London and New York: T & T Clark International.

Foucault, M. (1978) *The History of Sexuality: An Introduction*, trans. R. Hurley. New York: Pantheon Books.

———. (1995 [1975]) *Discipline and Punish: The Birth of the Prison*, trans. A. Sheridan. New York: Vintage Books.

Friedan, B. (1963) *The Feminine Mystique*. New York: W. W. Norton & Company.

Gaard, G. (ed) (1993) *Ecofeminism: Women, Animals, Nature*. Philadelphia: Temple University Press.

Gaard, G., and Gruen, L. (1993) "Ecofeminism: Toward Global Justice and Planetary Health," *Society and Nature* 2(1): 1–35. https://genderandsecurity.org/projects-resources/research/ecofeminism-toward-global-justice-and-planetary-health

Gould, R. K. (2005) *At Home in Nature: Modern Homesteading and Spiritual Practice in America*. Berkeley and Los Angeles: University of California Press.

Gould, R. K., and Powell, R. C. (eds) (2022) "Ambiguous Legacies: Contested Futures (Special Issue)," *Journal for the Study of Religion, Nature and Culture* 16(3): 337–434.

hooks, b. (2000 [1984]) *Feminist Theory: From Margin to Center*. 2nd ed. Cambridge, MA: South End Press.

Le Zotte, J. (2015) "How the Summer of Atomic Bomb Testing Turned the Bikini into a Phenomenon," *Smithsonian Magazine*, May 21, www.smithsonianmag.com/smithsonian-institution/how-wake-testing-atomic-bomb-bikini-became-thing-180955346/

Lorde, A. (1984) *Sister Outsider: Essays and Speeches*. Berkeley: Crossing Press.

Merchant, C. (1980) *The Death of Nature: Women, Ecology, and the Scientific Revolution*. New York: HaperCollins Publishers.

———. (1996) *Earthcare: Women and the Environment*. Abingdon and New York: Routledge.

*Moana*. (2016) Dir. R. Clements and J. Musker. Burbank, CA: Walt Disney Studios Motion Pictures.

Nichols, A. M. (2021a) "Converting the Masses: Advertising Nature and Gender in the Post #MeToo Movement Era," *Journal for the Study of Religion, Nature and Culture* 15(1): 83–113. https://doi.org/10.1558/jsrnc.39591

———. (2021b) *Women on the Edge of Time: Grief and Power in the Nuclear Age*. Ph.D. Dissertation, University of Florida, Gainesville.

Nichols, A. M., and Berendt, T. (2021) "Special Issue: Engendering Nature," *Journal for the Study of Religion, Nature and Culture* 15(1): 1–142. https://journal.equinoxpub.com/JSRNC/issue/view/1975

Olson, M. (2011) *Atomic Radiation Is More Harmful to Women*. Nuclear Information Resource Services. *Nuclear Monitor* 736(6192). http://nirs.org/wp-content/uploads/radiation/radhealth/radiationwomen.pdf

Ortner, S. B. (1972) "Is Female to Male as Nature Is to Culture?" *Feminist Studies* 1(2): 5–31.

Page, T. (2007) "Has Ecofeminism Cornered the Market? Gender Analysis in the Study of Religion, Nature, and Culture," *Journal for the Study of Religion, Nature and Culture* 1(3): 293–319. https://doi.org/10.1558/jsrnc.v1i3.293

———. (2011) "Feminist, Gender, and Sexuality Studies in Religion and Ecology," in W. A. Bauman, W. R. Bohannon II, and K. J. O'Brien (eds) *Grounding Religion: A Field Guide to the Study of Religion and Ecology*. Eugene, OR: Pickwick Publications.

Pike, S. M. (2004) *New Age and Neopagan Religions in America*. New York: Columbia University Press.

Plumwood, V. (1993) *Feminism and the Mastery of Nature*. London and New York: Routledge.

Rich, A. (1980) "Compulsory Heterosexuality and Lesbian Existence," *Journal of Women in Culture and Society* 5(4): 631–60. https://doi.org/10.1353/jowh.2003.0079

Schofield, M. A. (2009) "Lost Almost and Caught between the Fences: The Women of Los Alamos, 1943–1945 and Later," in G. Kurt Piehlr and B. Rosemary Mariner (eds) *The Atomic Bomb and American Society: New Perspectives*. Knoxville, TN: University of Tenessee Press, 65–88.

Shiva, V. (1988) *Staying Alive: Women, Ecology, and Development*. London: Zed Books.

Taylor, S. M. (2007) *Green Sisters: A Spiritual Ecology*. Cambridge, MA: Harvard University Press.

Voyles, T. (2015) *Wastelanding: Legacies of Uranium Mining in Navajo Country*. Minneapolis, MN: University of Minnesota Press.

White, L. Jr. (1967) "The Historical Roots of Our Ecologic Crisis," *Science* 155(3767): 1203–7.

Wills, J. (2006) *Conservation Fallout: Nuclear Protest at Diablo Canyon*. Reno, NV: University of Nevada Press.

## Further Reading

Adams, C. (2014) "Why a Pig? A Reclining Nude Reveals the Intersections of Race, Sex, Slavery, and Species," in C. Adams and L. Gruen (eds) *Ecofeminism: Feminist Intersections with Other Animals and the Earth*. New York: Bloomsbury, 208–24.

Butler, J. (2004) *Undoing Gender*. New York and London: Routledge.

Crist, E. (2013) "Ecocide and the Extinction of Animal Minds," in M. Beckoff (ed) *Ignoring Nature No More: The Case for Compassionate Conservation*. Chicago: University of Chicago Press, 45–62.

Merchant, C. (2014) "Ecofeminism and Feminist Theory," in M. Boylan (ed) *Environmental Ethics*. Malden, MA: Wiley Blackwell, 59–63.

Plumwood, V. (1993) *Feminism and the Mastery of Nature*. London and New York: Routledge.

Warren, K. (2014) "The Power and Promise of Ecological Feminism," in M. Boylan (ed) *Environmental Ethics*. Malden, MA: Wiley Blackwell, 64–70.

# 6 Sexuality and Queer Studies

*Whitney A. Bauman*

The connections between sexuality, queer studies, and religion and ecology may not be immediately obvious.[1] However, when we take into account the co-construction of concepts such as sex, gender, sexuality and nature, the connections begin to come into focus. As many feminists and other critical theorists have argued, the hetero-patriarchal structure that privileges male, white, able-bodied, wealthy bodies over others and that tends to privilege Western ways of knowing over others is the same structure that places humans above the rest of the natural world. In other words, the descending hierarchy of value, or "great chain of being," that moves from an ultimate reality/god to some males, to some females, to other males and females (poor and of color), then to animals and the earth is also tied to a heterosexual gender/sex binary: cis male and cis female. There is, within this hierarchical ordering, an assumed "compulsory heterosexuality" (Rich 1994).

As Greta Gaard and others have pointed out, the discourses that maintain this hetero-patriarchal structure are contradictory. On the one hand, those individuals thought to be "deviant" are more "like animals" that give into their "base desires." This implies that being less like animals and more reasonable and/or godly is somehow better. On the other hand, proponents of this hetero-patriarchal structure argue that being "queer" is "unnatural," implicitly suggesting that being more "like nature" is better (Gaard 1997). So both religious discourses and discourses about "nature," are tied up in maintaining white, heterosexual-patriarchy.

Many studying sexuality and queer studies would argue that upsetting any part of the racist, hetero-patriarchal structure, helps to challenge the system in ways that might lead to more just human-human relations and more eco-friendly human-earth relations (Halberstam 2011). This chapter, then, explores various authors and ideas that "queer" concepts of nature, and others that "queer" concepts of religion. Queer here does not just have to do with gender and sexuality. Rather, it means to blur boundaries of our categories and to point out the porous nature of all reality and particularly bodies that make up the planetary community. It means to point out the co-constructed, historical-cultural-biological nature of all human concepts and ideas. In conclusion, we will look at a case study based on the so-called "Ecosexual Manifesto." Developed by Annie Sprinkle and Beth Stephens, the ecosexual movement is meant to queer the boundaries between humans and the rest of the natural world. It demonstrates some of the different ways we (Western, nature-estranged)

DOI: 10.4324/9781003259466-9

humans might embody a queer spirituality/religiosity and understanding of human-earth relations.

Throughout the chapter, I argue that unless boundaries between humans and the rest of the natural world are queered, sexist, hetero-sexist, racist, and ableist worlds will continue to be the norm (Ko 2019). First, however, let us start with a brief introduction to what, exactly, queer studies is.

## Queer Studies: A Brief Intro

Bodies matter. Bodies shape how we experience the world, as do the ways certain bodies are privileged in different cultures and societies just by virtue of certain features of those bodies. One's race, class, ability, gender, sex, and sexuality all shape the ways in which one's body develops and grows. Historically, systems that privilege maleness, whiteness, able-bodiedness, and heteronormativity have been dubbed "patriarchal." One goal of queer studies is to show that both religious traditions and the more-than-human natural world reveal a spectrum of experiences of sex, gender, and sexuality. Such an understanding helps us to critique the hierarchies and dualisms found in patriarchy.

Gender and sexual dimorphism (the idea that only male or female are options) and its corresponding heteronormativity (the idea that heterosexuality is the norm) are so strong in especially monotheistic cultures that even early botanists/biologists read these dualisms into the rest of the natural world. Linnaeus describes plants as "families" with a male father, female mother, and offspring (Schiebinger 1993: 11–39). Even today, many doctors and scientists operate on such binaries: for example, despite the fact that as many as 1 in 1,000 children are born intersex, and despite the fact that the rest of the natural world has a spectrum of genders, sexes, and sexualities, too many medical professionals label people who do not fit into "male" or "female" categories as somehow problematic. The general practice by US physicians today is still to make a choice, along with the parents of the child, between male or female when a child is born intersex. This is an example of how bodies are materially constructed through historical-cultural concepts. The public debates and arguments about gender-affirming therapies and surgeries, particularly in the United States, are another bit of evidence of the ongoing power of heteronormative ideas of gender, sex, and sexuality.

Queer studies, following theorists such as Michel Foucault and Judith Butler, argues that sex, gender, and sexuality are all constructed over time through religious, philosophical, cultural, scientific, and other discourses. In other words, there is no essential reason why women and men should act, dress, and behave in certain ways; rather, these behaviors are constructed differently by different humans over time. What is "natural" and "normal" are ever-changing and co-constructed categories. Though some queer thinkers have been charged with complete constructivism—the idea that nature is *only* a construction of human culture and language—most would not go this far. Again, as Judith Butler argues in *Bodies That Matter*, nature and our embodiments also co-construct the world (Butler 1993).

**BOX 6A**

Are there ideas about gender and sexuality about which you think differently from your parents or grandparents? If so, how do you explain these differences, and what caused them? If not, what do you think explains the continuity of these ideas?

Indeed, believing that nature is completely constructed would maintain a divide between humans and the rest of the natural world. Opposing this, most queer theorists argue that nature, like religion, is a category that changes over time and that all categories—human, animal, plant, technology, male, female, straight, gay, and so on—are fluid and interconnected (Butler 1993). Our categories never match up directly with the way that the world really is, because both our categories and our realities are fluid. Life itself is in constant flux and processes of exchange.

For example, think about the ways different dogs and cats experience the world. It depends partly on how they are embodied (large, small, long hair, short hair, etc.). It also depends on their interactions with humans, whether they are indoor or outdoor, domestic or wild. There is no single experience of cat-ness or dog-ness. Lions, tigers, leopards, and tabby cats probably have radically different experiences of the world, though they are the same biological family. The same is true of wolves, coyotes, and wire-haired dachshunds. And then there are hyenas, a different species and family from both dogs and cats but sharing some of the phenotypic similarities to both cats and dogs. And yet a wild lion in a sub-Saharan savannah probably has more common experiences with a wild hyena there than with the cat in my house. The point is that our categories do not capture a complicated world in constant flux, in which bodies-in-relationship evolve into ever new forms of embodied life. Thus, we might argue that nature is a lot "queerer" than meets the eye and that the categories we use to make sense of it are never as solid as we tend to think.

In the human world, Butler makes this point by arguing that categories such as gender, sex, and sexuality are performative rather than essential. This means that we are thrown into socio-biological scripts, and we perform our identities according to those scripts. We never perform them perfectly, however, and because of that, there are abjections, leftovers, or parts of subjects that get "left out" of a given performance. Some people who appear biologically male do not perform "masculinity" as it has been defined by the culture, for example, or some people who perform "femininity" feel no sexual attraction to males. If enough of these abjections build up over time, then the political will to co-create a shift increases, leading to a paradigm shift in the ways the culture thinks about gender, sex, and sexuality, among other identity markers (Butler 1993).

The scripts that are co-constructed over time to tell us what it means, among other things, to be "male" and "female," have inputs from many different sources including religious ones. This poses questions about religion and religious ideas that emerge from specific contexts and return to effect the embodiments of those contexts in different ways.

### Religion, Sexuality, and Queer Studies

Just as the patriarchal hierarchy has specific places for women in the ordering of the world, it also dictates precise ways in which men and women should relate to each other. Heteronormativity, the idea that being born heterosexual is both the norm and "natural," has been a significant part of many religious traditions, in particular monotheistic ones. Some queer studies scholars of Christian, Jewish, and Islamic texts, however, have argued that readings of holy texts that see only gender dimorphism, sexual dimorphism, and heteronormativity are anachronistic. In the story of the garden of Eden, for instance, Adam begins as a genderless/sexless mud creature, made from the *adamah* (dirt). In this story, the original human is neither male nor female. The female Eve was made to be a companion species, not as subordinate to the male Adam (Trible 1978). Other scholars have pointed out the various sexualities, genders, and sexes that are found throughout texts and commentaries of these traditions (Boisvert and Daniel-Hughes 2017).

> **BOX 6B**
>
> Are there religious texts, traditions, or practices, that you frequently hear brought up in discussions about gender, sex, and sexuality in your community? Are there other texts, traditions, or practices (religious or otherwise) that you think should be included in these conversations more often?

In Christian contexts, heteronormativity must be understood in the context of teachings that advocate celibacy. In the New Testament letters of Paul, in the Catholic priesthood, and in monastic traditions across Christian history, one can find arguments that the most faithful path is to forego sex entirely. The ideal form of being in the world is the celibate form, suggesting that there is something wrong or imperfect with sex itself. For much of Christian history and still in some Christian traditions, priests are exclusively male and cannot marry. Nor is this unique to Christianity: monastic traditions of Buddhism and Jainism also see celibacy as part of the spiritual path toward enlightenment, or at least as a way of avoiding some of the traps of desire. Heteronormativity, then, is at most "second best" to this celibate form of life. This connects to the dualistic thinking discussed earlier: if the body and its passions are inferior to dispassionate rationality and the spirit, then it makes sense to instruct religious people to distance themselves from physical desire.

Of course, celibacy is not universally valued in religious traditions. In Islam, Judaism, Protestant and Orthodox Christianity, and many Hindu traditions, sex is accepted for priests and all others. Indeed, in some traditions of Hinduism the body is part of the spiritual practice (e.g., yoga and tantric practices). However, even in these latter traditions, the assumed sex is usually understood to be heterosexuality, and sex is usually understood as ideally oriented toward procreation (Ruether 1983: 100).

But like everything else, religions are fluid and constructed, never monolithic. So it should be no surprise that there are all manners of exceptions to the dominant stance toward heteronormativity in religious traditions. For example, there are many records of same-sex relations within Buddhist and Christian monastic life. Indeed, if one felt no desire for the opposite sex centuries ago, what better way to avoid the life of procreation than to become a monk or nun in a community of people who are all the same sex?

Furthermore, most Indigenous American, African, Asian, Middle Eastern, and South Asian cultures have or had understandings of humanity that include multiple genders and sexes. "Third Genders" or "Third Spirits" were often revered by communities as spiritual leaders and/or healers (Wilhelm 2003). These traditions have challenged the normativity of heterosexuality and gender/sex binarism for centuries. These ideas are important resources for contemporary movements that challenge heteronormative religions or work to adapt more welcoming practices and beliefs that are open to different expressions of sex and sexuality.

Like all other species, human beings are internally diverse, in our sexual expressions as in every other aspect of our lives. Religions that seek to reduce this diversity—to limit the possibilities of human becoming with narrow historical concepts that have been handed down by cultures, languages, and traditions—will be continually challenged.

Finally, most extant religious traditions start with a queering of dominant ways of understanding community and living together as human beings. Moses rejected slavery and argued for a new life in community, queering the hierarchy into which he had been born. Jesus urged his disciples to leave their families behind and start new ones that are neither male nor female, Gentile nor Jew, queering the social order around him. The Buddha rejected the extremes of poverty and affluence for a middle path that understands the entangled web of which we are all a part and which we all affect, queering inherited notions of power and enlightenment. Indigenous trickster figures queer every aspect of life, blurring the boundaries between living and dead, male and female, humans and animals to point out that all things are interrelated and entangled, nothing fits neatly into our tiny human concepts. These and other motifs of religious traditions may aid in a queer interpretation of human beings and nature as well.

## Nature Is Queer

Gender and sex binaries and heteronormativity are challenged not only by queer approaches to religion and religious studies but also by queer understandings of the rest of the natural world. In her book *Evolution's Rainbow*, Joan Roughgarden highlights the multiplicity of sexualities within and between organisms and species and the ways in which heteronormative assumptions have been read into the evolutionary record and the natural world (Roughgarden 2004). She also notes that cooperation is at least as important as competition in understanding the evolution of life on the planet. Competition and survival of the fittest are often discussed as the "basic" dynamics of nature. But this is not the only case. Think of all the various organisms, bacteria, and plants and animals that must come together to make a single organism's life viable on this planet. Even our own bodies are made up of their own complex ecosystems that scientists are now referring to as microbiomes. These organisms are better understood as cooperating, not competing.

Such cooperation is not just on the ecological and biological levels but on the geological and climatic levels as well. The natural world is deeply relational, interdependent, and always entangled, from the quantum level to the cosmic. Scientific understandings of nature that focus on reduction and categorization miss some of the messy "entangled bank" of the natural world.

Many queer theorists argue that if human beings are entangled with a natural world in which there are a variety of sexes and genders, then human cultures should not be limited or narrow. Magnus Hirschfeld founded the Institute for Sexuality Studies in Berlin, Germany, at the end of the 19th century in order to explore this dynamic. At the Institute, researchers explored and encouraged homosexuality, bisexuality, transgender identities, and other identities that challenged heteronormativity and the gender/sex binary. These identities were understood and accepted as part of the spectrum of embodied reality. Hirschfeld saw this research as a clear extension of evolutionary theory: the loosing of species distinctions based on created forms of life also loosed the "normative" male and female types. The fluidly cooperative aspects of the natural world suggested to him that there could be no single "ideal" male, female, or human.

This should be understood as an important scientific revolution. Copernicus and Galileo challenged the idea of a fixed creation centered around the Earth. Darwin challenged the idea of a fixed natural order centered around human life. Hirschfeld and others realized that evolutionary change challenges fixed forms of male/female, human/animal, animal/plant, and so on. This resulted in the opening up to a plurality of ways of being in the world: ways of living that already existed but were not recognized or supported by heteropatriarchal discourses.

Ernst Haeckel, the father of modern ecology and a promoter of evolutionary theory throughout Europe, agreed with and supported Hirschfeld's institute. Changing ideas about nature—that humans evolve from and with the rest of the natural world—led to changes in understandings of humans and their relationship to the rest of the natural world. One conclusion is that there is no compulsory gender/sex binarism and heterosexuality in nature. Nothing we see around us is fixed by an ultimate form or god; rather, identities co-evolve and emerge out of an ongoing and open process. Life manifests in a spectrum of embodiments (Hirschfeld 1914).

The basic insight that nature is much queerer than we first imagined is the basis for a growing body of literature around queer ecology. The spectrum of sexes and sexuality that exist in the planetary community is just one component of this emerging discourse. Another important part is the blurring of the boundaries between humans, animals, plants, minerals, and even technology—all are part of the entanglement of the planetary community and any given individual embodiment (Morton 2013).

## BOX 6C

Queer theory critiques ideas that sexuality should be determined by what is "natural." And yet queer theory also seeks to learn from the diversity of sex, gender, and sexuality within the natural world. Does the tension between these approaches seem to you like a contradiction? What can be learned from it?

Karan Barad, for instance, explores the implications of these queering ideas at the quantum level, focusing on subatomic reality and noting that all of the world is, most basically, made up of relationships rather than distinct objects. Everything that exists consists of networks and systems of actants co-acting on one another (Barad 2007). She argues that this "distributed agency" challenges the idea that there is a stable and fixed "nature." Other physicists and cosmologists have argued that since we base most of our knowledge upon the 5% of the visible universe, the other 95% being made up of dark energy (around 70%) and dark matter (around 25%), it would be the ultimate hubris to conflate knowledge of reality with the way the world "really" is (NASA). From these perspectives, the contemporary sciences of evolution, ecology, physics, and cosmology (among others) lead us to wonder about and marvel at nature rather than control the world around us as if we humans (some humans at least) are managers of all other life on the planet.

### Challenging Anthropocentrism with Queer Eyes

If we can queer understandings of what it means to be human from religious, scientific, and philosophical/theoretical perspectives of "nature" and what is "natural," then we can begin to loosen the foundations of the systems and structures of patriarchy. We might begin to live in ways that validate and support the plurality of emerging life within the planetary community. From a queer perspective, whether hierarchical views of life that interpret the world as a series of binary opposites were ever useful, they are certainly now obsolete. Once these seams of the patriarchal garment are unraveled, it is clear that cultural norms about gender and sexuality are constructions, open to remaking and reimagining. Most important for this chapter is that challenges to sex and gender binaries and to heteronormativity are intimately tied to challenging the dividing line that separates humans from the rest of the natural world. From a queer perspective, our ideas of nature will inevitably challenge simple ideas of human identity and sexuality, and vice versa. Once we begin to challenge any of these loci, the others become entangled in the process.

In one of the earliest texts on the intersection between religion, sexuality, sex, gender, and environmentalism, Daniel Spencer emphasizes the ways that better understanding human bodies also helps people to understand other earth bodies (Spencer 1996). Opening up our desire beyond the confines of heteronormative expression means that we can also challenge other confines, "queering" the divide between humans and animals or humans and the rest of the natural world. David Abram makes this point by noting that gravity is at heart the original form of eros or attraction:

> Gravity—the mutual attraction between our body and the earth—is the deep source of that more conscious delirium that draws us toward the presence of another person. Like the felt magnetism between two lovers, or between a mother and her child, the powerful attraction between the body and the earth offers sustenance and physical replenishment when it is consummated in contact.
>
> (Abram 2010: 27)

Our bodies are the primary ways through which we relate to one another and the rest of the planetary community. Such relationships cannot be confined to one form of expression; any attempt to do so is yet another way to keep people "locked in" to the patriarchal hierarchy of values and its binary system for organizing the world.

Queering understandings of what it means to be male, female, human, plant, mineral, animal, organic, and machine means recognizing that such designations are abstractions that only partially capture the ever-shifting and evolving relationships that constitute our daily planetary lives. If cultural ideas of sex, gender, and sexuality are keeping us from opening to multiple ways of being and becoming in the world, then queer theory challenges religious, scientific, and philosophical discourses to pay more attention to the multiplicity of planetary embodiments throughout human histories.[2]

Ways of thinking that fall under the umbrella of the so-called new materialisms and other understandings of nature that we might refer to as "queer" challenge the sharp distinctions between various organisms. They remind us again that the "natural" world is radically interrelated and dynamic.[3] This is, indeed, what Darwin observed in his *Origin of Species*: species are merely a category that we use to understand the world; in reality, strict dividing lines between species do not exist (Hogue 2008). Species are always embedded in ecosystems, and individual lives within those species depend on viruses, water, air, and countless other species of life. Whatever else "nature" is, it is not a fixed category that can be understood accurately from the human perspective. Nature is always in flux and interactive.

On the one hand, queer understandings of nature challenge the divide between humans and other plants and animals. Humans are also comprised of their relationships with the rest of the natural world. These relationships are also active and always fluctuating and in turn challenge the fixed categories of what it means to be "human" or "dog" or "chimpanzee" or "tree." As the philosophers Gilles Deleuze and Felix Guattari note, all human beings are assemblages of plant, animal, and mineral (Deleuze and Guattari 1987).

On the other hand, queer understandings of nature also challenge the lines between organism and machine and between life and non-life. As feminist philosopher of science Donna Haraway says, we are all cyborgs: assemblages of organisms, languages, ideas, and technologies (Haraway 1991). Human ideas and technologies—our languages, our mathematics, our inventions—transform both the world and our subjective experience of it. The fossil-fueled and digital machines we use daily increasingly define us. In this sense we are always and already cyborgs, or organic machines.

**BOX 6D**

How does the idea of the natural world and human culture as constructed, fluid, and changeable feel to you? Is it confusing? Scary? Liberating? Exhausting? Why do you think you have this reaction?

Two lessons are worth emphasizing from these observations. First, our categories for describing nature are interpretive rather than descriptive and should never be confused with the ultimate reality of the interrelated and ever-changing worlds in which we live. As Timothy Morton notes,

> Queer ecology requires a vocabulary envisioning this liquid life. I propose that life-forms constitute a mesh, a nontotalizable, open-ended concatenation of interrelations that blur and confound boundaries at practically any level: between species, between the living and the nonliving, between organism and environment.
>
> (Morton 2010: 275)

A second implication of "queering" nature, is that it trips up human exceptionalism and social oppressions that rely on dualistic distinctions such as humans/animals, culture/nature, and what is "natural" or "unnatural." In disassembling our understandings of nature, we are freed to see the world more queerly, as more complex, dynamic, and entangled. We can perceive multiple connections with other organisms and entities that are not possible under patriarchal and other static readings of nature.

In fact, the very idea of a stable nature may be the cause of many of our ecological and social ills. Nature is often defined as something that is not human, outside of culture. Nature is idealized. Some suggest that nature can save human cultures and societies if we would just "listen" more. The problem here is that any "nature" we might listen to is always and already constructed, conditioned by the cultural assumptions of the one seeking to listen. Treating nature as if it is a universal that can be understood from outside of culture not only reifies a particular understanding of reality but also reifies certain social and political relations among humans and between humans and the rest of the natural world. To be sure, the new materialisms and queer understandings of "nature" are also interpretations, but at least they are interpretations that recognize the reality that all understandings of nature involve hermeneutics and that political and economic systems build up around understandings of what "nature" and "culture" are.

For these reasons, political ecologists like Bruno Latour seek to get rid of the concepts of "nature" and "culture" all together, arguing that both should be understood as already and always co-constitutive of any given collective in the world (Latour 2004). In other words, the planetary community is an entanglement of various actants, which come together and organize in specific ways, but which are dynamic and interactive and never beyond the realm of co-construction. There is no "natural," but there are better and worse ways that the planetary community can co-become. Latour, for instance, argues that we should think of nature as a critical zone, two kilometers above and below the ground, in which all life we know of exists. From this perspective, he argues, humans have much to learn from termites, who have evolved to thrive within this critical zone. (Latour 2021).

Nature, in the last analysis, is much queerer than we thought. Everything we think we know is, too. So people must always come together to decide again and again what types of worlds we want to co-create and take responsibility for these co-creations. From a queer perspective, the important work is ensuring that new co-creations that take into account those entities left out of any given planetary construction. Those who were previously degraded, left out, and excluded have the most to contribute to a new construction. The process of co-construction, collecting, re-attuning, deconstructing, and co-constructing again continues ad infinitum.

## Case Study: The Ecosexual Manifesto

Annie Sprinkle and her partner, Beth Stephens, have been encouraging and embracing erotic desires for nature for decades. They have also been staging protests against mountain top removal and deforestation. Sometimes these protests involve holding wedding ceremonies in which the two of them or other self-identified ecosexuals get married to mountains, forests, rivers, and trees. More recently, they codified their own thoughts about what ecosexuality is in their "Ecosexual Manifesto." Throughout their work, they argue for a new type of sexuality that finds romantic love with the entire planet and the individuals therein.

Sprinkle and Stephens argue that this romantic love is at the heart of a new type of romanticism, one that understands our bodies as intimately connected with other bodies on the evolving planet. According to them, ecosexual is not exclusive identity, so one can identify as LGBTQIA+ or even heterosexual and still be ecosexual. It only requires an opening up to the principles laid out in their manifesto. The five points of the manifesto are as follows:

1. We are the ecosexuals. The Earth is our lover.
2. We make love with the Earth. We are aquaphiles, terraphiles, pyrophiles, and aerophiles.
3. We are a rapidly growing global community of ecosexuals.
4. We are ecosex activists. We will save the mountains, waters, and skies by any means necessary, especially through love, joy, and our powers of seduction.
5. Ecosexual is an identity. For some of us, being ecosexual is our primary (sexual) identity, whereas for others it is not. Ecosexuals can be GLBTQI, heterosexual, asexual, and/or Other.

You can read the full manifesto here: https://sprinklestephens.ucsc.edu/research-writing/ecosex-manifesto.

Sprinkle and Stephens also made a film about ecosexuality called *Goodbye Gauley Mountain: An Eco-sexual Love Story* (available on Netflix, iTunes, and perhaps in your library). Read or listen to the manifesto through the provided link and try to watch the film if you are able. As you are reading/watching, take note of the feelings that emerge: What was challenging? What seemed "right" or "wrong" in terms of your gut reactions and why? If queer theory is correct about the co-construction of identities, these co-constructions happen over time through habits, thoughts, ideas, and behaviors that shape us at pre-conscious emotional and affective levels. Therefore, we have to examine the "why" of our feelings in order to discern what motivates them, which historical and personal circumstances influence us. After you have reflected on your own feelings about the film, have a discussion with others who have done the same and think about how ecosexuality challenges heteronormative patriarchy and how it might challenge some religious ideas about what it means to be human in relationship to the rest of the planetary community.

### *Discussion Questions*

1. What is your initial, personal reaction to the idea of "ecosexual" as an identity and an approach to activism? Why do you think you have that reaction?
2. In what types of political actions and protests do you think the rituals Annie Sprinkle and Beth Stephens have created might have a positive impact? In what types of actions would they not help? Why?
3. What does it mean for you to "love" a non-human animal, or a plant, or a place? How is that different from or the same as what you see in the ecosexuality movement?
4. What might it mean to think of your entire body as a site of *eros*, or love and engagement with the world around you (not necessarily sexually)?

## Notes

1 This is a significantly modified version of the chapter in *Grounding Religion*, 2nd ed. co-written with Heather Eaton.
2 Our "planetary" bodies refer to the ways we are bound up ecologically and evolutionary with all other earth bodies. (See, e.g., Bauman 2014).
3 The new materialisms refer to a group of thinking about all of life—energy/matter, body/mind, technology/nature—in an interrelated, immanent, and non-dualistic way. (See, e.g., Bennett 2010).

## Works Cited

Abram, D. (2010) *Becoming Animal: An Earthly Cosmology*. New York: Vintage.
Barad, K. (2007) *Meeting the Universe Halfway: Quantum Physics and the Entanglement of Matter and Meaning*. Durham, NC: Duke University Press.
Bauman, W. (2014) *Religion and Ecology: Developing a Planetary Ethic*. New York: Columbia University Press.
Bennett, J. (2010) *Vibrant Matter: A Political Ecology of Things*. Durham, NC: Duke University Press.
Boisvert, D., and Daniel-Hughes, C. (2017) *The Bloomsbury Reader in Gender, Religion, and Sexuality*. Oxford, UK: Bloomsbury.
Butler, J. (1993) *Bodies That Matter: On the Discursive Limits of Sex*. New York: Routledge.
Christ, C. (1997) *Rebirth of the Goddess: Finding Meaning in Feminist Spirituality*. New York: Routledge.
Daly, M. (1973) *Beyond God the Father: Toward a Philosophy of Women's Liberation*. Boston, MA: Beacon Press.
Deleuze, G., and Guattari, F. (1987) *A Thousand Plateaus: Capitalism and Schizophrenia*. Minneapolis, MN: University of Minnesota Press.

Eaton, H. (2005) *Introducing Ecofeminist Theologies*. New York: T&T Clark.
Gaard, G. (1997) "Toward a Queer Ecofeminism," *Hypatia* 12(1): 114–37.
Halberstam, J. (2011) *The Queer Art of Failure*. Durham, NC: Duke University Press.
Haraway, D. (1991) *Simians, Cyborgs and Women: The Reinvention of Nature*. New York: Routledge.
Hirschfeld, M. (1914) "Ernst Haeckel und Die Sexualwissenschaft," in H. Schmidt (ed) *Was Wir Ernst Haeckel Verdanken, Zweiter Band*. Leipzig, Germany: Verlag Unesma.
Hogue, M. (2008) *The Tangled Bank: Toward an Ecotheological Ethics of Responsible Participation*. Eugene, OR: Wipf & Stock.
Keller, C. (2003) *Face of the Deep: A Theology of Becoming*. New York: Routledge.
Ko, A. (2019) *Racism as Zoological Witchcraft: A Guide to Getting Out*. Brooklyn, NY: Lantern Books.
Latour, B. (2004) *Politics of Nature: How to Bring the Sciences into Democracy*. Cambridge, MA: Harvard University Press.
———. (2021) *After Lockdown: A Metamorphosis*. Cambridge, UK: Polity Press.
Merchant, C. (1980) *The Death of Nature: Women, Ecology and the Scientific Revolution*. New York: HarperCollins.
———. (2005) *Radical Ecology: The Search for a Physical World*. 2nd ed. New York: Routledge.
Morton, T. (2013) *Hyperobjects: Philosophy and Ecology After the End of the World*. Minneapolis, MN: University of Minnesota Press.
———. (2010) "Queer Ecology," *PMLA* 125(2): 273–82, March.
NASA. "Dark Energy, Dark Matter," https://science.nasa.gov/astrophysics/focus-areas/what-is-dark-energy (accessed January 19, 2023).
Plumwood, V. (2002) *Environmental Culture: The Ecological Crisis of Reason*. New York: Routledge.
Rich, A. (1994) "Compulsory Heterosexuality and Lesbian Existence," in A. M. Jaggar (ed) *Living with Contradictions: Controversies in Feminist Social Ethics*. New York: Routledge.
Roughgarden, J. (2004) *Evolution's Rainbow: Diversity, Gender, and Sexuality in Nature and People*. Berkeley, CA: University of California Press.
Ruether, R. R. (1992). *Gaia and God: An Ecofeminist Theology of Earth Healing*. New York: HarperCollins.
———. (1983) *Sexism and God Talk: Toward a Feminist Theology*. Boston, MA: Beacon Press.
Schiebinger, L. (1993) *Nature's Body: Gender in the Making of Modern Science*. Boston, MA: Beacon Press.
Spencer, D. (1996) *Gay and Gaia: Ethics, Ecology and the Erotic*. Cleveland, OH: Pilgrim Press.
Trible, P. (1978) *God and the Rhetoric of Sexuality*. Minneapolis, MN: Fortress Press.
Wilhelm, A. D. (2003) *Tritiya-Prakriti: People of the Third Sex: Understanding Homosexuality, Transgender Identity, and Intersex Conditions Through Hinduism*. Philadelphia, PA: Xlibris Publications.

## Further Reading

Bauman, W. (ed) (2018) *Meaningful Flesh: Reflections on Religion and Nature for a Queer Planet*. Earth, Milky Way: Punctum Books.
Hoel, N., Wilcox, M., and Wilson, L. (2021) *Religion, the Body, and Sexuality: An Introduction*. New York: Routledge.

Sandilands, C. M., and Erickson, B. (2010) *Queer Ecologies: Sex, Nature, Politics, Desire*. Bloomington, IN: Indiana University Press.

Sprinkle, A., Stephens, B., and Kelin, J. (2021) *Assuming the Ecosexual Position: Earth as Lover*. Minneapolis, MN: University of Minnesota Press.

Stenmark, L., and Bauman, W. (eds) (2018) *Unsettling Science and Religion: Contributions and Questions from Queer Studies*. Lanham, MD: Lexington Books.

Sturgeon, N. (2009) *Environmentalism in Popular Culture: Gender, Race, Sexuality, and the Politics of the Natural*. Tuscon, AZ: University of Arizona Press.

# 7 The Poor of the Earth

*Miguel A. De La Torre*

This chapter focuses on the intersection of ecological degradation, specifically that caused by global warming, and the world's minoritized, specifically those who are poor and of color. All too often, such a focus would incorporate a class analysis component. But discussion of "class" usually relies on Eurocentric concepts rooted in the writings of thinkers like Max Weber, Barrington Moore, or Karl Marx. To discuss class is to assume a Eurocentric worldview and impose this way of gazing upon the world's population. Rather than beginning any discussion of the intersection of environmental degradation and the poor upon Eurocentric notions of class, this chapter instead focuses on the poor themselves and their worldviews.

We begin with the obvious, the earth is on fire! Regardless of what actions we decide to implement, irreversible climate change has already occurred. The best we can hope for is slowing down its devastating effects. And yet the warming of our planet is met by some with more economic privilege and conservative views as a hoax, and if temperatures are rising, they raise doubt by suggesting that it is not necessarily caused by human actions. Whatever legislative action should be considered cannot negatively impact the profit margins of corporations, the so-called job creators. Meanwhile, many on the left, while having a better grasp of the existential threat faced by humanity, still fail to comprehend who is most impacted. The inhabitants of planet Earth are not equally affected. Regardless of the rhetoric, we really are not all "in this together." The poor of the earth are more susceptible to the consequences of a warming planet. The poor of the land, forced to work under a blistering sun for daily bread, lack the luxury of air conditioning, let alone reliable electricity. Droughts, which wither crops, usher in famine, which disproportionately impacts them due to the lack of means required to horde the earth's resources.

Take Guatemala as an example. The increase in temperatures since the 1960s by 1.8°C has reduced needed rainfall for staple crops like corn and beans. It is estimated that because of global warming, these crops will decrease about 14% by 2050, impacting famine and causing migration to the north in the form of environmental refugees. The irony is that the Central American country minimally contributes to greenhouse gases, emitting only 1.1 tons annually per person (compared to the US's 16.5 tons per person). And yet Guatemalans unduly suffer the brunt of global warming's consequences.[1] And just as non-Europeans throughout the world

DOI: 10.4324/9781003259466-10

face greater consequences from global warming, so too do communities of color in the US.

When a heat wave hits the States, health risks are not evenly distributed. According to an eleven-state study conducted by the National Oceanic and Atmospheric Administration, neighborhoods that are poor and of color experience temperatures up to 20 degrees hotter than predominately white neighborhoods due to historical redlining practices (associated with federal mortgage appraisal policy). Ninety-four percent of formerly redlined areas—which mostly remained low-income communities of color—are exposed to higher temperatures.[2] Juanita Cruz-Perez, a Latina living in the low-income San Antonio neighborhood of the Westside, who could not afford to turn on her air-conditioning as temperatures reached triple digits said it best: "When you are poor, the sun finds you."[3]

During summer months, when high temperatures intersect with air pollution, pregnant African American women have a greater likelihood of birthing premature children who are underweight or stillborn as compared to Euro-Americans (Bekkar et al. 2020: 4). When Texas was hit with a winter storm in 2021, four million low-income residents of color were the first to experience rolling blackouts, the first to endure burst pipes when temperatures dipped, and the last to see power and plumbing restored. The lack of middle-class resources needed to flee to safety (i.e., Cancún) endangered their lives.[4]

### Environmental Colonialism

The richest 10% of the world's population is responsible for half of global carbon emissions; meanwhile, the poorest 50% only produce 10% (Conceição 2020: 121). The twenty richest countries are responsible for three-quarters of the world's emissions.[5] Rather than working collectively to reduce the threat of climate change, these wealthy nations spend billions to limit their own risks, specifically the effects of drought and rising sea levels. Those located farthest from the equator, specifically the industrial countries of the Global North who made their exploitative wealth off the backs of the Global South, are most responsible for the warming climate. And yet they will be least affected. Rather than safeguarding the planet for all its inhabitants (not just some humans), a coordinated effort continues to dismantle environmental protection policies. These policies have led to significant increases in greenhouse gas emission and thousands of deaths each year, primarily among the poor, most of whom are from non-European origins. These deaths are mainly due to the health impacts of poor air quality.[6]

> **BOX 7A**
>
> Does the fact that rich countries and rich people contribute so much more than poorer peoples to climate change surprise you? Does it concern you? What do you imagine could change to reverse this trend?

Seeking profits at the expense of sustainability creates a moral failing exasperated by the reluctance of the global wealthy to prevent future ecological damage. Because the poor of the Global South and the poor within industrial nations in the Global North relegated to communities of color are the ones most impacted by ecological degradation, profiteers of industries negatively impacting the planet spend millions to create doubt, dismissing climate change as a hoax. Executives like Robert E. Murray of Murray Energy, for example, spent a million dollars to cast doubt on human-made climate change.[7]

During US President Donald Trump's four years in office, some 112 environmental rules relegating clean air, water, wildlife, and toxic chemicals were reversed.[8] Forty-one scientists, many of whom were appointed by Trump to serve on the Scientific Advisory Board of the Environmental Protection Agency, signed a letter warning that these regulatory changes were ignoring scientific data and evidence.[9] Twenty key officials placed in charge of environmental policy in his administration came from careers in the oil, gas, coal, chemical, and agriculture industries. Three of them had served in state governments establishing records of resisting environmental regulations. At least four had ties to Koch Industries, which has spent millions to defeat clean energy measures.[10] And yet, in a world where nay is yay, then-President Trump, a climate change denier, provided a list of "alternative facts" dislodged from reality to portray his administration's record as exhibiting "America's environmental leadership."[11]

That the poor suffer more due to the consequences of global warming is not a coincidence, nor should it be surprising. Colonialism, a global venture which seeks to profit at the expense of the poor, determines how much pollution is economically acceptable, a formula embraced by both Eurocentric conservatives and liberals. This is best illustrated by Lawrence Summers, a Democrat who worked as the chief economist for the World Bank during the early '90s.[12] Among his responsibilities was the supervision of all the institution's publications, including the *World Development Report*. In one of the publications which he oversaw, the topic of "dirty industries" was discussed. In response, Summers wrote a private memo to six highly placed colleagues. Unfortunately for him, the private memo was eventually leaked to the press. He wrote,

> Just between you and me, shouldn't the World Bank be encouraging more migration of the dirty industries to LDCs (Less Developed Countries)? . . . The measure of the costs of health impairing pollution depends on the foregone earnings from increased morbidity and mortality. From this point of view a given amount of health impairing pollution should be done in the country with the lowest cost, which will be the country with the lowest wages. I think the economic logic behind dumping a load of toxic waste in the lowest wage country is impeccable and we should face up to that. . . . I've always thought that underpopulated countries in Africa are vastly underpolluted, their air quality is probably vastly inefficiently low compared to Los Angeles or Mexico City.
>
> (George and Sabelli 1994: 98–100)

Summers argued that "a load of toxic waste" dumped in a rich country (code language for white population) would cause illness and death to high-wage earners. According to Summers, a forty-year-old with a $20,000 per year of potential earnings who has an estimated twenty-five more years of productivity will contribute $500,000 to the global economy. But if the "load of toxic waste" were instead dumped in a poor country (code language for non-European) with a $360 GNP and life expectancy averaging fifty-five years, the contribution of such a worker to the global economy would be a measly $5,400 (ibid.). This logic, treating people as commodities, suggests that those from Eurocentric origins possess greater economic value than the global poor. The sanctity of life becomes replaced with the sanctity of profits. "Dumping" pollutants on poor countries perpetuates a colonializing formula that links the domination of the earth and the domination of the indigenous inhabitants.

**BOX 7B**

Do most environmental messages that you encounter in your daily life include connections between the fate of the earth and the fate of poor, marginalized, and indigenous peoples? Why do you think that is?

We can witness the implementation of a colonialist's economic worldview in places like Savar, Bangladesh, where a toxic stench arises from their waterways due to the dumping of garment factories' wastewater. The second largest global source of water pollution is textile dyeing, responsible for one-fifth of all industrial water pollution and a tenth of all carbon emissions.[13] Bangladesh is, after China, the second largest garment manufacturing hub in the world, exporting in 2019 some $34 billion worth of garments (Koopman et al. 2020: 101). These factories, producers of cheap clothes for Western department stores like Wal-Mart, JC Penney, and H&M, are ecologically devastating the area so Americans can wear affordable and colorful fashion. Food supplies are threatened as rice paddies become inundated with toxic wastewater, fish stocks are decimated, coconut trees have stopped producing coconuts, and smaller waterways are now filled with sand and garbage. Dumping a load of toxins on poor nations results in the killing of the river, poisoning of the soil, and devastating the entire environment.[14] The situation is so bad that the children of garment workers attending Genda Government Primary School report dizziness and lightheadedness. They often retch during class, making learning impossible. Because Bangladesh is vulnerable to global climate change, millions could be displaced as crop yields significantly drop with the onslaught of changing weather patterns and rising sea levels (ibid.).

### Profiting at the Expense of the Poor

With the election of Joe Biden in 2020, a false hope arose that he would overturn much of the damage set in place during the Trump years. And while the enactment of the 2022 Inflation Reduction Act is promising at the time of this writing, it may not be enough to overcome the political hold neoliberal industrial polluters has on the US government. Unfortunately, more damning than Trump's environmental policies are the federal judges put in place to secure the interest of global economic producers. From 1997 to 2017, two of America's richest men, David and Charles Koch, gave more than $6 million to the Federalist Society, a nonprofit institute that recruits conservative and libertarian judges. They underwrote junkets for judges to Florida beachfront properties and Utah ski resorts so they could attend seminars on the importance of capitalist market forces in society.

The Koch brothers have always been interested in capturing the Supreme Court because of the pivotal role it plays determining corporate regulatory power. Through the organization Americans for Prosperity, they unleashed a grassroot army of volunteers to ensure the appointment of then-President Trump's nominees to the federal court. A once-in-a-lifetime opportunity existed to "flip" the Supreme Court and change its ideological balance. Americans for Prosperity undertook the national campaigns to ensure the appointments of Neil Gorsuch and Brett Kavanaugh. On Kavanaugh alone, they spent about "seven figures."[15]

Since the 1984 *Chevron v. Natural Resources Defense Council* decision, the court applied what came to be known as the "Chevron deference," which allowed government agencies to interpret the law enacted by Congress whenever said law appeared ambiguous. This allowed government agencies—like the Environmental Protection Agency (EPA)—to establish and implement complex regulations upon corporations not necessarily explicit in the laws established by Congress. Using this principle, the EPA threatened the profit margins of Koch Industries, a multinational corporation (worth $115 billion in revenue in 2020), which—among other ventures—engaged in the manufacturing, refining, and distribution of petroleum.

Once a MAGA Supreme Court was established with the nomination of Amy Coney Barrett, thanks in part to Koch's political and financial influence, the favor was returned within a year with *West Virginia v. EPA*, which weakened the 1984 decision. EPA was now powerless to act in addressing climate change whenever clear congressional authorization was lacking. The decision immediately struck down an EPA plan to reduce carbon emissions from power plants. The Supreme Court ruling could have made it difficult, if not impossible, for the US to achieve the goal set by the Paris Agreement to significantly reduce greenhouse gases by 2030. While language to reverse the decision was included in the Inflation Reduction Act, we still wonder if this reverses the trend or simply provides a reprieve. Regardless, not since the early 20th century has the Supreme Court struck down such a wide assortment of federal regulations on corporations, truly insuring a return to a laissez-faire generated economy detrimental to the poor's daily existence.

**BOX 7C**

Are there local political trends in your community that, like this discussion of the US Supreme Court, demonstrate the influence of wealth on environmental and other policies?

Economic inequality feeds into political inequality as the wealthy few pour riches into political campaigns to elect politicians more committed to protecting and securing the financial interests of a small elite class than the public good. This obscene concentration of wealth in a few hands conservatively contributes to the deaths of at least 21,300 people each day due to hunger, lack of healthcare access, and gender-based violence (Ahmed et al. 2022: 12–13). The twenty richest billionaires are also responsible for emitting, on average, eight thousand times more carbon into the environment than the billion poorest people on the planet (ibid.: 7, 13, 22). It is conservatively estimated that by 2030, some 231,000 people will die each year due to climate change in poor countries.

## The Intersection of Environmental Racism and Poverty

To be poor and a non-Euro-American means being exposed to greater death-causing pollutants. A growing body of evidence suggests that race, ethnicity, and the economic level of a neighborhood are the most significant variables determining where commercial, industrial, and military hazardous waste sites will be located. Consider the three North Carolina countries that are predominantly Black, Native, and Latinx. These counties were already home to most of the state's industrial hog operations. But between 2012 and 2020, some thirty million turkeys and chickens were added to the equation—increasing their numbers by 36% (compared to a 17% increase which occurred over the same time throughout the rest of the state). To the 4.4 billion gallons of liquefied waste produced annually by the hog population was added one million tons of waste from the fowl. These pits of liquid manure and urine, many unlined, foul air quality and seep into the water supply after rain.[16]

The race and ethnicity of those who are poor is the most significant predicator where the commercial hazardous waste facilities are located. Blacks are 75% more likely than other Americans to live in areas situated near hazardous waste facilities (Fleischman and Franklin 2017: 6). Regardless of African Americans' income levels, they are subjected to higher levels of air pollution than Euro-Americans, breathing 1.5 times more sooty pollution emitted from burning fossil fuel. Exposure to polluted air, as we know, is linked to lung disease, heart disease, premature death, and now COVID-19.[17] Womanist ethicist Emilie Townes argues that the sustained impact of toxic waste on the lives of people of color who, because of poverty, are relegated to live on ecologically hazardous lands is akin to a contemporary version of lynching an entire people (1995: 55).

The US military is another major contributor to climate change, and its ecological damage equals a hundred countries combined.[18] It also plays a role in endangering the poor, especially those relegated to indigenous communities. Of the 651 nuclear weapons or devices exploded on the US mainland, all occurred on Native American territories (Seager 1993: 63), most of which on the lands of the Shoshone nation (LaDuke 1993: 99). Uranium, necessary in developing atomic weapons, is mainly mined on Navajo territory. And while most uranium mines in the United States have been abandoned, they still emit high levels of radioactive gases. A main ingredient of uranium mining's solid waste is radium-226, which remains radioactive for some sixteen thousand years (ibid.: 99, 102). This explains why Navajo teenagers have a rate of organ cancer seventeen times the national average (Hamilton 1993: 71).

The impact of pollution upon the poor was exasperated by the 2020 pandemic. But instead of considering the intersection between race/ethnicity, poverty, pollution, and the spread of the coronavirus, medical doctor and Ohio State Senator Stephen Huffmann dismissed the disproportionate COVID-19-related deaths of Blacks and Latinxs during the first year of the pandemic by wondering, "Could it just be that African-Americans or the colored population do not wash their hands as well as other groups or wear a mask or do not socially distance themselves? Could that be the explanation of why the higher incidence?"[19] Latinxs—part of what Huffman called "the colored population"—did not disproportionately die from the virus at higher rates because they were dirtier than Euro-Americans; they died because they were poor. Poverty forces Latinxs to live in neighborhoods that have higher instances of pollution, making them more vulnerable to the effects of the virus.

Consider the predominately poor Latinx neighborhood of Globeville in Denver, Colorado. Its residents experience higher hospitalization rates (2.9 per 1,000) than the predominately Euro-American neighborhood of Country Club (0.3 per 1,000) located just six miles south. During the coronavirus pandemic, to be Latinx in Denver meant being twice as likely as Euro-American counterparts to be hospitalized for the virus. Becoming infected and dying was not due to the air Latinxs breathe. Globeville air is dirtier than that inhaled by whites. In fact, the Globeville zip code (80216) has been designated as the most polluted zip code in the United States! Air quality monitoring conducted over five years prior to the 2020 pandemic showed Globeville's air quality (or lack thereof) repeatedly exceeded EPA's safety limits.[20] Because a correlation exists between air pollution and the susceptibility of contracting COVID-19, areas where the poor live, often comprising people of color, due to institutionalized racism and economic deprivation, intensified the probability of contracting COVID-19. A Harvard 2020 study confirmed that small increases in long-term exposure to air pollution was responsible for major increases in COVID-19 death rates (Wu et al. 2020: 1).

**BOX 7D**

Did you experience and/or notice inequalities in vulnerability and access to medical care during the pandemic? How might those trends relate to other environmental and health issues?

Comparing the environmental quality of life of poor neighborhoods (usually of color) to Euro-American communities reveals prevalent environmental racism. Globeville becomes a prime example of Lawrence Summers' enunciation of the neoliberal economic position on this issue when he worked at the World Bank. He may have argued that "promoting development is the best way to protect the environment" (George and Sabelli 1994: 170); however, the poor of the world—including the residents of Globeville who experienced "a load of toxic waste" dumped upon them—might beg to differ.

## Decentering Man

While all of humanity faced a deadly global virus in 2020, the earth continues to face its own virus: a Eurocentric neoliberal worldview. The economic formula that reduces the planet, its resources, and all creatures dependent upon it to a commodity is an existential threat to humanity and, more importantly, to the planet. Eurocentrism must be rejected if any hope exists for the survival of humanity. This worldview created a Eurocentric theological perspective where the main concern is the relationship between humans and their Deity, followed by, to a lesser degree, relationships among humans. When we consider the religion undergirding the colonial project—a certain interpretation of Christianity—the emphasis remains on a heavenly abode with little connection to or understanding of a collective or communal spirituality linked to the land. The earth, after all, will be destroyed to make way for the reign of God.

The problem is the way in which some interpret the biblical call for "man" to have dominion over the earth. Such a Western Eurocentric way of understanding creation is damning for the poor, and as such requires rejection. "Man" is centered within the biblical story, waiting for some ethereal eternal home. The ultimate goal for the Christian believer is to reside with their God in heaven, making this planet but a place of sojourn, which simply prepares them for their celestial destiny. If the earth is reduced to a stepping-stone, then its neglect is at best ignored, at worse encouraged. The greatest threat to the environment is a Eurocentric Christian theology that joyfully anticipates "the end of time." This eschatological view welcomes the destruction of the earth because it indicates the second coming of Jesus. At that time, he will rapture (remove from the earth) the faithful who are destined to be saved from the tribulation (earth's devastation). Why worry about the environment when, in the twinkling of an eye, the great late planet Earth will end in a conflagration?

In contrast, most indigenous worldviews from Africa and the Americas maintain a sacred respect for earth, where the earth and all inhabitants are not a possession or some "thing" to dominate or own. Consider the words of Smohalla of the Wanapum:

> You ask me to plow the ground. Shall I take a knife and tear my mother's bosom? Then when I die she will not take me to her bosom to rest. You ask me you dig for stone. Shall I dig under her skin for bones? Then when I die I cannot enter her body to be born again. You ask me to cut grass and make hay and sell it, and be rich like white men. How dare I cut off my mother's hair.
>
> (1896: 721)

Such respect is absent from many Western Christian groups who perceive of a God who said, "Let us make man[21] in our image, after our likeness: and let them have *dominion* over the fish of the sea, and the fowl of the air, and over the cattle, and over all the earth, and over every creeping thing that creepeth upon the earth" (Gen. 1:26, KJV). For them, the earth is a thing to which man has dominion, possession, and ownership. The earth is given to be used, and because man is the center of creation, for the benefit and sake of man it is to be misused and abused if need be. This traditional understanding of "man" (which means cisgender males) is ordained by their God to rule over creation. Man (not those who are cisgender females), occupying the pinnacle of creation, created in the very image of God, continues to be a foundational Eurocentric religious worldview. Consider the words of Pope John Paul II, who claimed, "Everything in creation is ordered to man and everything is made subject to him" (1995: 61).

Wilderness, unproductive land, or virgin land awaits the seed of man to inseminate progress and civilization. Domination and domestication assume the profitability of land. Those who may live on the land are defined as uncivilized for they have failed to make the land productive and profitable. Land subjugation and the subjugation of the original inhabitants are based on the same Eurocentric neoliberal economic worldview. No longer are humans to live in harmony with nature but are expected to reign over nature. Hence, an incongruency exists between two worldviews. One calls for dominion over the fish of the sea, the fowl of the air, the cattle of the land, and every creeping thing. The other treats humans as but one species among many. When man is the center of the created order, the environment becomes an unlimited storehouse of raw materials for man to use in whatever way he sees fit. Often, these resources are sacrificed in the neoliberal quest of economic growth. Turning the earth to a profit-generating center makes the bottom line more important than the earth itself. But what if the purpose of the earth is not to turn a profit? What if man is not the reason or purpose of the earth's existence?

According to indigenous Americans' worldviews, within the circle of creation all are equal in value to the Creator. Osage thinker George "Tink" Tinker explains, "A chief is not valued above the people; nor are two-legged valued above the animal nations, the birds, or even trees and rocks" (1994: 126). Humans, just one aspect of creation, must balance their needs within the world which requires preserving for one's descendants who will live "seven generations from now." Appropriating from the earth requires reciprocating. Taking from the plentifulness of creation requires returning to it so as to maintain balance (Kidwell et al. 2001: 33).

Commodifying the earth and its resources for profit at the expense of those on the margins of Eurocentric power and privilege is unsustainable. Because the earth's resources are not everlasting, proper stewardship is essential to maintain and sustain harmonious relationship with nature, as with other humans. Abusing the environment for profit creates pollution, lowers life expectancy for the disenfranchised, and is a major source of many illnesses and diseases for those living close to the environmental degradation, usually those who are poor and of color. The exploitation of the earth's resources is interconnected with the exploitation of the poor who are marginalized. To discuss the plight of one requires considering the other. Brazilian liberation theologian Leonardo Boff highlighted this link when he connected the very "cry of the earth" with the "cry of the poor." For him, the same worldview that justifies the institutionalized violence responsible for the exploitation and subjugation of the poor also justifies abuse and devastation of the earth (1997: xi).

An important link exists between the oppression of the poor and the oppression of nature. Consider the words of Alice Walker:

> Earth itself has become the n*gg*r of the world. It is perceived, ironically, as other, as alien, evil, and threatening by those who are finding they cannot draw a healthful breath without its cooperation. While the Earth is poisoned, everything it supports is poisoned. While the earth is enslaved, none of us is free. While the Earth is a "n*gg*r," it has no choice but to think of us all as Wasichus [Lakota term for Euro-Americans]. While it is "treated like dirt," so are we.
>
> (1981: 147)

To seek the liberation of the planet requires understanding the intersection of the disenfranchisement of the poor and the devastation of the earth. Any attempt to move toward environmental justice must incorporate the perspective of those most impacted, the poor of the earth.

**BOX 7E**

How does your own social, economic, political, and religious context orient you to understand environmental problems? Have you worked to change that understanding in any way?

Often when Euro-Americans discuss environmental justice, they fail to elucidate the interconnectedness between the oppression of the earth and the oppression of the poor. The privileged do not reside in the toxic and infested neighborhoods to which the poor are relegated. So they fail to connect poverty, race, and ethnicity with the ecologically hazardous places where the poor live. Karen Baker-Fletcher captures this disconnect when she writes,

> There is a tendency among middle-class eco-feminist and mainstream eco-theologians to enjoy the privilege of extensive international travel which informs their spirituality. Such a privilege enables them to have the luxury of providing a global analysis. In contrast, there are many within the U.S. environmental justice movement who would find it a luxury to leave their own neighborhoods. This is the cause of a credibility gap between theologians in the academy and the grassroots from which liberation spirituality emerges.
>
> (2004: 125–6)

The failure of Euro-American environmentalists to seriously consider the role of poverty limits their understanding of climate change. If environmental justice is the goal, then those environmentalists benefitting from class privilege cannot continue to ignore the role poverty, racism, and ethnic discrimination plays. Failure of the Euro-American environmental justice movement to consider these intersections consigns those on the margins to greater ecological health risks, thwarting development of a holistic approach for the liberation of the earth and all the species which find life therein.

## Case Study and Questions: Earth as a Living Spiritual Entity

What we call Earth is alive, and on it depends all life—not just the lives of humans who drink its water, breathe its air, and eat what its trees produce but also all living creatures that swim in the water, fly through the air, and roam among the trees, and just as important, the water, air, and trees themselves. It is worth reflecting on how it can change our perspectives to view the entirety of the planet, our home, as alive.

This material earth that Eurocentric Christian neoliberal thought has reduced to a commodity—the soil and water, the rocks and mountains, the plant and trees, the air and storms—are due agency and respect. Why? Because these elements are alive with their own spirit, their own temperament, their own aspirations, they have their own rights to exist and flourish.

Consider, for example, water. Among the Taos Pueblo community, their earliest ancestors are believed to have emerged from the waters of Ba Whyea (Blue Lake). Into these waters the dead will return, becoming spirits that merge with the cloud people known as kachinas, who are rain-bringing Pueblo Indian spirits. Aztec cosmology, from what would become Central America, venerate Chalchiuhtlicue (She of the Jade Skirt), the goddess of rivers, lakes, streams, and other fresh waters, who is associated with fertility and brings forth maize, the life source of the people. She is the wife (or sister) to Tlaloc, the god of rain. The Yellow River in China, one of the world's major water arteries, is believed to be the greedy, unpredictable, and destructive deity Hebo, while the sacred Ganges River of India, the holiest of all Hindu rivers, is synonymous with the goddess Gaṅgā. Prior to Christianity, even European indigenous people recognized water's sacredness. The Celts of Ireland knew the river Boyne as the goddess Boann, the Welsh understood Llyr to be god of the sea, and the Gauls identified the river Seine with the goddess Sequana.

Stones are also alive and cry out the praises of creation. The Yoruba people of present-day Nigeria maintain that when the orishas (quasi-deities) left the earth to return to the spiritual domain, they left their *ashé* (cosmic energy) embedded in the rocks and stones. One can learn to hear the stones' *ashé* cry out, important when communicating with the orishas. Stones can also be malevolent. Take for example the Iroquois of modern-day New York. They understand Tawiscara (associated with Flint), grandson to the mother goddess Sky Woman, to be a powerful creator driven to constantly do terrible things. Tawiscara, disliking his twin brother, refused to wait to be born and instead cut his way out of his mother's womb, resulting in her death. Since then, he compulsively brings harm to humanity.

Earth-based worldviews that understand water and rocks as living entities due respect are rooted in the terrestrial abode of their ancestors, meaning that the planet's preservation cannot be taken for granted. Indigenous worldviews maintain a sacred respect for creation, a respect historically abused by Western religions like Christianity that gaze toward the heavens as the focus of their faith. Terrestrially focused worldviews instead require living in harmony with the planet, which is alive and has its own spirit, along with all creatures that are dependent on the planet. Neither people, nor animals, nor land, nor rivers, nor rocks, nor air can be reduced to a monetary value. The elements that compose the earth are not to be domesticated, sold, enslaved, abused, or mistreated. To do so creates pollution, lowers life expectancy, accelerates the extinction of species, and becomes the source of illnesses and diseases for the poor. Once the earth is stripped of its spiritual entity and reduced to a commodity to be sold to the highest bidder, it can be manipulated to economically benefit a global minority at the expense of the global majority relegated to poverty.

### *Discussion Questions*

1. Should anyone be understood to "own" land, water, rocks, minerals, and air? Is the ownership of land and its resources akin to slavery? While such a hierarchy has been proven harmful to the earth, what other groups are affected? What is the connection between the land and the poor of the earth?
2. What does it mean for water or rocks to have life? To have a spirit? How can living spirits such as these be respected and protected?
3. What would Christianity look like if it focused on a terrestrial-based worldview? How might the biblical text be reinterpreted from such a different social location?
4. Who benefits by maintaining the earth-dominating Euro-Christian religion and a neoliberal economic global structure? Who suffers? Can we imagine what such a new world based on respect for the living earth would look like?

## Notes

1 Somini Sengupta, "As Earth Heats Up, Inequity Boils Over," *New York Times*, August 8, 2020.
2 "NOAA and Communities to Map Heat Inequities in 11 States," *National Oceanic and Atmospheric Administration*, www.noaa.gov/media-release/noaa-and-communities-to-map-heat-inequities-in-11-states (accessed May 7, 2022).
3 Edgar Sandoval, "Poor in Texas and Helpless Against Heat," *New York Times*, July 27, 2022.
4 Alexa Ura and Juan Pablo Garnham, "Already Hit Hard by Pandemic, Black and Hispanic Communities Suffer the Blows of an Unforgiving Winter Storm," *The Texas Tribune*, February 19, 2021.
5 Somini Sengupta, "U.N. Report Says Rise in Emissions is Still Alarming," *New York Times*, November 27, 2019.
6 Nadja Popovich, Livia Albeck-Ripka and Kendra Pierre-Louis, "The Trump Administration Rolled Back More Than 100 Environmental Rules. Here's the Full List," *New York Times*, January 20, 2021.

7 Lisa Friedman, "Despite Debt, Coal Executive Spent Big on Climate Denial," *New York Times*, December 18, 2019.
8 Nadja Popovich, Albeck-Ripka and Kendra Pierre-Louis, "The Trump Administration is Reversing Nearly 100 Environmental Rules. Here's the Full List," *New York Times*, October 15, 2020.
9 Coral Davenport and Lisa Friedman, "E.P.A. Policies Scorn Science, Panel Reports," *New York Times*, January 1, 2020.
10 Lisa Friedman and Claire O'Neill, "Who Controls Trump's Environmental Policy?" *New York Times*, January 24, 2020.
11 Katie Rogers and Coral Davenport, "In Speech, Trump Portrays U.S. As a Leader on the Environment," *New York Times*, July 9, 2019.
12 Lawrence H. Summers was the World Bank's chief economist and vice president for development economics from 1990 until 1993. When he left the World Bank, he serves as undersecretary of the US Treasury Department during the Clinton administration—eventually serving as his secretary of the Treasury from 1999 until 2001. Afterwards, from 2001 to 2006, he served as the president of Harvard University. President Obama, in 2009, appointed him to serve as the director of the White House National Economic Council. In short, he is not some right-wring climate denier.
13 Helen Reagan, "Asian Rivers are Turning Black. And Our Colorful Closets are to Blame," *CNN*, September 28, 2020.
14 Julhas Alam and Martha Mendoza, "Toxic Tanneries Forced to Move Pollute New Bangladesh Site," *Associated Press*, July 6, 2018; and Jim Yardley, "Bangladesh Pollution, Told in Colors and Smells," *New York Times*, July 15, 2013.
15 Christopher Leonard, "A Koch Brother's Big Bet on Judge Barrett," *New York Times*, October 13, 2020.
16 Sarah Graddy, Ellen Simon, and Soren Rundquist, "Exposing Fields of Filth: Factory Farms Disproportionately Threaten Black, Latino and Native American North Carolinians," *Environmental Working Group*, 2020, www.ewg.org/interactive-maps/2020-fields-of-filth/.
17 Linda Villarosa, "Pollution Is Killing Black Americans. This Community Fought Back," *New York Times*, July 28, 2020.
18 Benjamin Neimark, Oliver Belcher, and Patrick Bigger, "The U.S. Military Is a Bigger Polluter Than More Than 100 Countries Combined," *Quartz*, June 28, 2019.
19 Trip Gabriel, "Ohio Lawmaker Asks Racist Question about Black People and Hand-Washing," *New York Times*, June 11, 2020.
20 Katie Weis, "Denver Hispanics Neighborhoods with Higher COVID-19 Hospitalization Rates also Have Higher Air Pollution Levels Than White Neighborhoods," *CBS Denver*, August 6, 2020.
21 Most English Bibles translated the Hebrew word *hā'ādām* (literally "the *adam*") as "man," a male-gendered individual, as opposed to the Hebrew word *'iššāh*, which is translated as "woman." But the word *adam* can also be a reference to a proper name, as in the case of Adam, the partner of Eve. And finally, *adam* can be translated as "humanity."

## References

Ahmed, N. et al. (2022) *Inequality Kills: The Unparalleled Action Needed to Combat Unprecedented Inequality in the Wake of COVID-19*. Oxford: Oxfam International.

Baker-Fletcher, K. (2004) "Spirituality," in M. De La Torre (ed) *Handbook of U.S. Theologies of Liberation*. St. Louis: Chalice Press.

Bekkar, B., Pacheco, S., Basu, R., and DeNicola, N. (2020) "Association of Air Pollution and Heat Exposure with Preterm Birth, Low Birth Weight, and Stillbirth in the US," *Journal of the American Medical Association* 3(6): 1–13.

Boff, L. (1997) *Cry of the Earth, Cry of the Poor*, trans. P. Berryman. Maryknoll: Orbis Books.

Conceição, P. (2020) *Human Development Report 2020: The Next Frontier—Human Development and the Anthropocene*. New York: United Nations Development Program.

Fleischman, L., and Franklin, M. (2017) *Fumes Across the Fence-Line: The Health Impacts of Air Pollution from Oil & Gas Facilities on African American Communities*. Baltimore: National Association for the Advancement of Colored People.

George, S., and Sabelli, F. (1994) *Faith and Credit: The World Bank's Secular Empire*. Boulder, CO: Westview Press.

Hamilton, C. (1993) "Environmental Consequences of Urban Growth and Blight," in R. Hofrichter (ed) *Toxic Struggles: The Theory and Practice of Environmental Justice*. Philadelphia: New Society Publishers.

John Paul II. (1995) *The Gospel of Life*. New York: Random House.

Kidwell, C. S., Noley, H., and Tinker, G. (2001) *A Native American Theology*. Maryknoll: Orbis Books.

Koopman, R. et al. (2020) *World Trade Statistical Review 2020*. Geneva: World Trade Organization.

LaDuke, W. (1993) "A Society Based on Conquest Cannot Be Sustained: Native Peoples and the Environmental Crises," in R. Hofrichter (ed) *Toxic Struggles: The Theory and Practice of Environmental Justice*. Philadelphia: New Society Publishers.

Seager, J. (1993) "Creating a Culture of Destruction: Gender, Militarism, and the Environment," In R. Hofrichter (ed) *Toxic Struggles: The Theory and Practice of Environmental Justice*. Philadelphia: New Society Publishers.

Smohalla of the Wanapum. Quoted in James Mooney (1896) "The Ghost-Dance Religion and the Sioux Outbreak of 1890," in J. W. Powell (dir) *Fourteenth Annual Report of the Bureau of Ethnology to the Secretary of the Smithsonian Institution 1892–93, Part 2*. Washington, DC: Government Printing Office.

Tinker, G. (1994) "Spirituality, Native American Personhood, Sovereignty and Solidarity," in K. C. Abraham and B. Mbuy-Beya (eds) *Spirituality of the Third World: A Cry for Life*. Maryknoll, NY: Orbis Books.

Townes, E. (1995) *In a Blaze of Glory: Womanist Spirituality as Social Witness*. Nashville: Abingdon Press.

Walker, A. (1981) *Living by the Word*. San Diego: Harcourt Brace & Company.

Wu, X. et al. (2020) *Exposure to Air Pollution and COVID-19 Mortality in the United States: A Nationwide Cross-Section Study*. Boston: Harvard Department of Biostatistics, Chan School of Public Health.

## Further Reading

Agyeman, J. et al. (eds) (2009) *Speaking for Ourselves: Environmental Justice in Canada*. Vancouver, BC: UBC Press.

Bannon, B. (2016) *Nature and Experience: Phenomenology and the Environment*. Lanham, MD: Rowman & Littlefield.

Bullard, R., Johnson, G., and Torres, A. (2011) *Environmental Health and Racial Equity in the United States: Building Environmentally Just, Sustainable, and Livable Communities*. Washington, DC: American Public Health Association.

Byrne, J., Glover, L., and Martinez, C. (eds) (2017) *Environmental Justice*. New York: Routledge Press.

De La Torre, M. (2021) *Gonna Trouble the Water: EcoJustice, Water, and Environmental Racism*. Cleveland: The Pilgrim Press.

———. (2022) *Shifting Climates Shifting People*. Cleveland: The Pilgrim Press.

Harris, M. (2017) *Ecowomanism: African American Women and Earth-Honoring Faiths*. Maryknoll: Orbis Books.

Radford Ruether, R. (1996) *Women Healing Earth: Third World Women on Ecology, Feminism, and Religion*. Maryknoll: Orbis Books.

Ray, S. J. (2013) *The Ecological Other: Environmental Exclusion in American Culture*. Tucson: University of Arizona Press.

# 8 Race

*Carol Wayne White*

## Introduction

Race is an essential part of the human experience in the contemporary world, as individuals and institutions use it (along with ethnicity) to identify select differences among people as well as shared experiences. While race is often difficult to describe and its meaning has changed over time, there are important sociological perspectives that I employ in this chapter. Moreover, I suggest that one effective way of addressing race within the paradigm of ecology and religion is through the lens of religious naturalism, an umbrella term for a variety of theoretical perspectives that share the common conviction that nature is ultimate or that nothing transcends nature. Departing from traditional forms of religiosity, these perspectives either reject or reinterpret traditional concepts (e.g., God or supernaturalism), and they build on current developments in the sciences and humanities to conceptualize the category of the human, its ethical orientations, aesthetic appreciations, and forms of religious valuing. Specifically, religious naturalism conceptualizes humans as relational, natural processes, and it encourages us to enact new values and behaviors with each other and with the more-than-human worlds that are an integral part of existence.

As a capacious ecological worldview, religious naturalism also promotes justice for myriad nature, a term for the diverse forms, processes, and functions of matter, including human life, that exist and constitute reality. Accordingly, religious naturalism increases our awareness of the important issues at stake when conjoining ecology and race. It exposes a binary logic that has helped justify forms of environmental racism affecting communities of color, and it increases our awareness of subtle forms of anthropocentricism in our ecological discourses, which retain problematic views of the more-than-human worlds as "other." In short, religious naturalism has the potential to move beyond this problematic binary logic and the widespread colonization of nature.

In the first section, I introduce Val Plumwood's analysis of the logic of colonization (Plumwood 1993), which deepens our understanding of an influential, early modern binary construction (nature-culture) that divided reality into spheres of lesser-greater value. I explore how this binary logic was further extended with the development and presence of white supremacy in the Euro-American context. For example, dominant cultural norms and practices strengthened by this binary logic

DOI: 10.4324/9781003259466-11

viewed the humanity of US blacks and other ethnic and racial groups as closer to nature and not as important as that of white Euro-Americans. I also draw on recent theoretical insights that demonstrate white supremacy as a further extension of this binary logic, providing fuller understandings of key terms, such as nature, race, ethnicity, racism, and the construction of whiteness.

In the next major section, I respond to these historical and conceptual problems by introducing religious naturalism as an ecological religious framework that helps to address both white supremacy and problematic conceptions of the human-nature continuum. This demonstrates religious naturalism's efficacy in reconfiguring human animals' relation to land, to other forms of sentient life, and indeed, to each other. I also discuss how race has been featured in recent ecological perspectives, specifically examining religious naturalism's response to the racialization of nature. While the specific examples I offer are primarily from African American history, I also make references and connections to other racial and ethnic groups.

Following these conceptual explorations, I offer in the third section a brief discussion of some ethical implications of religious naturalism as an ecological religious worldview. I suggest it can bring diverse groups together that share a common goal of both enriching human-human relationships and transforming humans' relationality with the more-than-human worlds of which we are a part.

## Colonization of Myriad Nature and the Nature-Culture Binary Logic

In *Feminism and the Mastery of Nature*, Val Plumwood synthesizes ecological critiques of human domination of nature with various critiques of hegemonic social relations to identify what she calls the logic of colonization. This logic operates within the structure of one's relationships to the other (as evinced in accounts of oppression such as sexism, racism, and colonialism) as a hierarchical dualism. As Plumwood explains, this structural dualism exemplifies a standpoint of mastery that "results from a certain kind of denied dependency on a subordinated other" (Plumwood 1993: 41). The colonized (or subordinated others) are appropriated and incorporated into the selfhood and culture of the master, and their agency is denied or minimized. What results is a dualistic structural formation that shapes both identities. Plumwood's analysis unveils an instrumentalist reasoning operative in the logic of colonization that re-situates inherently mutually interdependent, reciprocal entities into relationships dominated by precarity.

As Kate Rigby summarizes in her illuminating assessment of the value of Plumwood's ecopolitical orientation, key features of hierarchical dualism include "backgrounding" the independent interests and agency of the subordinate group and the denial of dependence upon their services on the part of the dominant one, the refusal to recognize any similarities between the dominant and subordinate groups in favor of a "hyperseparated" construction of their differences ("radical exclusion"), the definition of the subordinate group in terms of lack vis-à-vis the valued traits of the dominant one ("incorporation"), a disregard for differences among members of the subordinate group ("homogenisation"), and the accordance of value to them primarily or exclusively as a means to an end ("instrumentalism") (Rigby 2020: 3).

In *The Death of Nature*, Carolyn Merchant has also provided important historical examples of the hierarchical dualism Plumwood theorizes, drawing important parallels between early modern European views of nature and cultural perceptions of various groups, including women, indigenous peoples, and Africans. In works of literature and artistic representations, influential writers and thinkers of the 16th and 17th centuries imposed a nature/culture dichotomy or dualism, which assumed the superiority of human culture to nature (Merchant 1980: 143). Merchant notes that an older organicism, where humans felt some form of intrinsic kinship with other natural processes, was eventually passed over in favor of a utilitarian approach to natural processes that emphasized humans' distinction from and superiority to them. This new dominant ethos led many prominent thinkers, with a wide range of emphases, to distinguish active, creative human culture from inert, brute environment.

Merchant focuses primarily on the gender implications of this binary differentiation, examining its role in justifying a hierarchical order of nature where women were situated below men and their physiological functions of reproduction, nurturing, and childrearing were viewed closer to nature and less important in the functioning of culture. She argues,

> At the root of the identification of women and animality with a lower form of human life lies the distinction between nature and culture fundamental to humanistic disciplines such as history, literature, and anthropology, which accept that distinction as an unquestioned assumption.
>
> (Merchant 1980: 143)

Merchant's study also sheds light on an ideology of dualism that operated as an integral component of Western European cultural imperialism and expansion: the purported "civilized" races of Europe identified and distinguished their own normative humanity over and against other groups they encountered in the Americas, Asia, and Africa. As an extension of the nature-culture dichotomy, racialized notions of differentiation helped to justify the West's colonization and exploitation of various groups, leading to such disparaging views as savage Indians and morally or intellectually inferior blacks (Merchant 1980: 132, 144). Similar derogatory racial differentiations are found in the 19th-century observations of Percival Lowell, the famous American astronomer and businessman who traveled extensively in Japan. In *The Soul of the Far East* (1888), Lowell writes,

> As for Far Orientals, they are not of those who will survive. . . . If these people continue in their old course, their early career is closed. Just as surely as morning passes into afternoon, so surely are these races of the Far East, if unchanged, destined to disappear before the advancing nations of the West.
>
> (Lowell 1888: 225–6)

These historical examples serve as early indicators of the social construction of Euro-American "whiteness" as a system of representation and cultural value based on differentiations of superiority and inferiority. As African philosopher Emmanuel Eze has persuasively argued, Enlightenment reasoning provided an ideal intellectual basis for establishing and legitimating the hegemony of the West over other peoples and traditions Europeans encountered in Asia, Africa, and the Americas (Eze 1996: 5). Traditions, values, and folk practices, often associated with groups and identities radically different from or not easily compatible with Enlightenment ideals, were often viewed suspiciously and assigned lowly positions on the hierarchy of value, beneath the required level of cognition or scientificity (White 2016: 22). In some cases, as with the earlier gender example, dominant groups also attempted to legitimate their position via a set of beliefs that explains or justifies some actual or potential social arrangement.

These historical practices reveal specific ways race has become a key method of identification in the contemporary world. As many scholars have noted, ever since white Europeans began colonizing populations of color elsewhere in the world, race has served as the "premier source of human identity" (Smedley 1998: 690). While in the past theorists had developed categories of race based on various geographic regions or skin tones, the German physician, zoologist, and anthropologist Johann Friedrich Blumenbach (1752–1840) introduced one of the famous groupings by studying human skulls. Accordingly, Blumenbach divided humans into five races:

- Caucasian or White race: people of European, Middle Eastern, and North African origin
- Ethiopian or Black race: people of sub-Saharan Africans origin (sometimes spelled Aethiopian)
- Malayan or Brown race: people of Southeast Asian origin and Pacific Islanders
- Mongolian or Yellow race: people of all East Asian and some Central Asian origin
- American or Red race: people of North American origin or American Indians (MacCord 2014)

Current scholarship resolutely challenges these categories. Race is now commonly viewed as a social construction used primarily to describe an individual's appearance or superficial physical characteristics, such as skin color, that a particular society considers significant. Accordingly, racial typologies like Blumenbach's have become outdated.[1]

Like race, the meaning of the term "ethnicity" has also changed over time. Although commonly used interchangeably with race, ethnicity is now properly understood as describing cultural factors such as nationality, culture, ancestry, language, and religious traditions and beliefs. Individuals may also self-identify or be associated with ethnicities in complex or even contradictory ways. For example, ethnic groups such as Irish, Italian American, Russian, Jewish, and Serbian might be included in the "White" racial category. Such historical and scholarly understandings of race and ethnicity are helpful when understanding the development and rise of modern capitalism and its connections to slavery, the processes of colonialism in modernism, globalization, and the widening disparity of social and economic inequalities (Embrick et al. 2015).

Within the growing field of critical race theory (CRT), race and ethnicity are imbued with theoretical complexity and examined in the context of power structures based on notions of white supremacy and white privilege (Crenshaw 1989; Crenshaw and Gotando 1996; Valdes et al. 2002). At its inception, CRT emerged from legal scholars' awareness of the machinations of racial categories in perpetuating and reinforcing the marginalization of select groups perceived as nonwhites. As CRT scholars note, however, race is mistakenly used to describe and "explain" genetic traits such as skin color, eye color, hair color, bone/jaw structure, and so on.

At the same time, CRT scholarship shows that even though terms like "blackness" and "whiteness" are constructions, they take on meanings that apply to certain groups of people in such a way that it becomes difficult to think of those people without certain affectively charged associations. Thus, the blackness and whiteness of individuals and groups are regarded by a racist culture—which takes too seriously the associations adhering to these terms, as their essential features—as, in fact, material, biological features of these individuals and groups (White 2016: 23). Race and racism have therefore become central concepts in understanding the complex of social relations derived from perceived identity differences in US history. In recent years, CRT has extended a study of these terms with other forms of subordination, as in the work of Chicano critical theorists applying the inextricable layers of racialization subordination based on gender, class, immigration status, surname, phenotype, accent, and sexuality (Dixson and Roussau 2006: 171). Additionally, race as a social construction has been specifically aligned with the idea of whiteness as a normative category for establishing a group's humanity (Delgado and Stefanic 2012).

**BOX 8A**

Why does it matter that "race" is a socially constructed category? Can you provide examples of the construction of race from your own experiences? Do you understand yourself as part of a racial group or ethnic community? Why or why not?

One of the earliest academic formulations of structural racism was offered by Manning Marable, who defined it as "a system of ignorance, exploitation, and power used to oppress African-Americans, Latinos, Asians, Pacific Americans, American Indians and other people on the basis of ethnicity, culture, mannerisms, and color" (Delgado and Stefanic 2012). Manning's formative definition emphatically shifted the discussion of race and racism from a problematic and limited black-white discourse to one that includes multiple identities, voices, and experiences. He also offered a fuller, astute notion of "race" operative in racism:

> When we talk about race, we don't mean a biological or genetic category, but rather, a way of interpreting differences between people which creates

> or reinforces inequalities among them. In other words, "race" is an unequal relationship between social groups, represented by the privileged access to power and resources by one group over another. Race is socially constructed, created (and recreated) by how people are perceived and treated in the normal actions of everyday life.
>
> (Marable 2001: 6)

Embedded in this definition are the crucial points made earlier by Merchant about nature and gender: one group believes itself to be superior and has the material, ideological, and institutional power to implement behaviors and establish a hierarchy of social order that adversely affects large groups of individuals perceived to be different. Laura Pulido presents a similar, fairly robust conception of race and its role in social formation, describing race's pervasive and hegemonic presence, its "multiscalar nature, and its multiple forms of existence, including ideas, words, actions, and structures" (Pulido 2000: 15).

For those currently engaged in assessing the construction of whiteness and its role in perpetuating various social injustices, these theoretical and historical perspectives on structural racism are crucial. As Tammerie Day has suggested, white thinkers are ethically charged to both identify and resist the subtle, nuanced, and even explicit ways the construction of whiteness operates to advance specific social, economic, ethical, and political agendas:

> Whiteness has been used throughout US history to divide and manipulate, to exclude or include persons of particular ethnicities or classes. Irish, German, Italian, and Jewish peoples all have experienced variable treatment depending on whether elite whites needed to include or exclude them.
>
> (Day 2012: 45)

## Religious Naturalism: Conjoining Ecology, Race, and Religion

A central point in this chapter is that the forms of cultural imperialism and racism supporting the Euro-American construction of whiteness evolved from the nature-culture dichotomy described by Merchant. As well, much of American literature has been founded on the underlying assumption of the superiority of human culture to nature (Merchant 1980: 144). Addressing the fuller complexities of this binary logic may require readers to explore anew the very categories of nature and culture as organizing concepts in our various humanistic discourses. These insights are especially relevant when considering race within the paradigm of ecology and religion. Important questions arise: Is it possible to integrate concerns for race and ecology in ways that depart from this entrapment of binary thinking? Can we avoid re-inscribing what Plumwood describes as pernicious forms of the logic of colonization while endorsing justice for all aspects of nature, including human nature? Religious naturalism can help us address both questions with its conceptions of myriad nature and the material, relational human. Religious naturalism specifically reframes humans as natural processes in relationship with other forms of nature and affirms the inherent value of the "more-than-human world(s)" of which humans are a part. As such, religious naturalism has the potential to address in creative ways the familiar human-nature binary that has perpetuated the various "isms" targeted by critical race theorists, eco-justice advocates, feminists, queer scholars, postcolonial critics, and social justice activists of all persuasions.

Religious naturalists draw on two fundamental convictions: (1) the sense of nature's richness, spectacular complexity, and fertility and (2) the recognition that nature is the only realm in which people live out their lives. Within the context of ecology and religion, this means that any truths humans are ever going to discover, and any meaning in life, are revealed within natural reality. This religious view expressly rejects any suggestion of the supernatural; there is nothing that transcends the natural world.

## BOX 8B

Donald Crosby summarizes the prominent status of nature in religious naturalism:

> Nature requires no explanation beyond itself. It always has existed and always will exist in some shape or form. Its constituents, principles, laws, and relations are the sole reality. This reality takes on new traits and possibilities as it evolves inexorably through time. Human beings are integral parts of nature, and they are natural beings through and through. They, like all living beings, are outcomes of biological evolution. They are embodied beings whose mental or spiritual aspect is not something separate from their bodies but a function of their bodily nature. There is no realm of the supernatural and no supernatural being or beings residing in such a realm.
>
> (Cosby 2008: ix–x)

What is appealing about this view of nature? What is limiting? What other views of nature do you find support for in the contemporary world?

Nature itself becomes a focal point for gauging our human desires, dreams, and possibilities, for assessing what can emerge from the past. Religious naturalism reflects meaningfully on the emergence of matter (and especially life) starting with the big bang, promoting views of myriad nature as complex processes of becoming.[2] Its fundamental conception of humans as natural processes intrinsically connected to other natural processes helps to blur the arbitrary ontological lines that human animals have erected between ourselves, other species, and natural processes.

One portrayal of human beings in religious naturalism is of star-born, earth-formed creatures endowed by evolutionary processes to seek reproductive fitness under the guidance of biological, psychological, and cultural systems that have been selected for their utility in mediating adaptive behaviors (Rue 2005: 77). Humans maximize their chances for reproductive fitness by managing the complexity of these systems in ways that are conducive to the simultaneous achievement of personal wholeness and social coherence. This suggests that our humanity is not a given but rather an achievement. Consider that from a strictly biological perspective, humans are organisms that have slowly evolved by a process of natural selection from earlier primates. From one generation to another, the species that is alive now has gradually adapted to changing environments so that it could continue to survive. Our animality, from this perspective, is living under the influence of genes, instincts, and emotions, with the prime directive to survive and procreate. Yet this minimalist approach fails to consider our own personal experience of what it is like to be an experiencing human being. Becoming human, or actualizing ourselves as human beings, emerges out of an awareness and desire to be more than a conglomeration of pulsating cells. Our humanity is not reducible to organizational patterns or processes dominated by brain structures, nor by DNA, diet, behavior, and the environment. Human animals become human destinies when we posit fundamental questions of value, meaning, and purpose to our existence. Our coming to be human destinies is structured by a crucial question: How do we come to terms with life?

**BOX 8C**

Why do you think most US citizens are reluctant to see themselves as part of myriad nature? What role might traditional views of religion play in this refusal? How does religious naturalism challenge ideas about religion and nature that are common in your own community?

Appreciating humans as one distinct biotic form emerging from and participating in a series of evolutionary processes that constitute the diversity of life has monumental religious implications. First, sacrality is a specific affirmation and appreciation of that which is fundamentally important in life: relational nature. Humans are interconnected parts of nature and our sacrality is a given part of nature's richness, spectacular complexity, and beauty. Additionally, we enact our humanity in seeking and finding community with others and with otherness. This is a simple value that religious discourse has advanced and reiterated again and again. Ursula Goodenough observes,

> We have throughout the ages sought connection with higher powers in the sky or beneath the earth, or with ancestors in some other realm. We have also sought, and found, religious fellowship with one another. And now we realize that we are connected to all creatures. Not just in food chains or ecological equilibria. We share a common ancestor. We share genes for receptors and cell cycles and signal-transduction cascades. We share evolutionary constraints and possibilities. We are connected all the way down.
>
> (Goodenough 1998: 73)

Finally, humanity's inextricable interconnectedness with all that is becomes one starting point for applying "meaning and value" to its existence, for coming to terms with life. Becoming human, in this sense, is acknowledging, embracing, and enacting this fundamental material interconnectedness in ways that transform us and others. With its persistence of placing humans within a wider ecological framework, religious naturalism inspires the conception of the human as an emergent, interconnected life-form amid spectacular biotic diversity. Our humanity emerges, or transformation unfolds, only to the extent that human animals recognize and value our constitutive, embodied, material relationality. In doing so, humans learn anew who and what we might become as we enact our relationality with other natural processes.

## Religious Naturalism and the Racialization of Nature

In light of these theoretical convictions, religious naturalism underscores a thorny, important issue that has been acutely recounted in feminist, liberationist, and postcolonial critiques: the traditional exclusivity of the category of the "human" itself. Their persuasive critiques stress that the normative human subject has been primarily conceptualized as and associated with the lived experiences of white males of European descent, into whose ranks African Americans and other minoritarian subjects have not traditionally been admitted. With this understood, the "racialization of nature" that is unique to North America's dominant environmental narratives becomes obvious. This term aptly describes certain racialized groups' experiences of nature that were adversely affected by the "institutions, legislation, and the social mores and beliefs of the dominant culture" (Finney 2014: 35).

This development reveals another pernicious dimension of the culture-nature dichotomy introduced earlier, disclosing a " 'legacy of making people of color signify the natural' as a prelude to exploitation of nonwhite peoples and the natural environment" (Finney 2014: 38). As Paul Outka states, "whites viewed black people as part of the natural world, and then proceeded to treat them with the same mixture of contempt, false reverence, and real exploitation that also marks American environmental history" (Outka 2008: 3). Here, a fuller, complex rendering of the US environmental narrative emerges in which some of the earliest specific conservation and preservation initiatives to protect "pristine nature" led by John Muir and Gifford Pinchot can be juxtaposed to other legislative acts that prohibited select racial groups, who were deemed closer to nature.

Dianne Glave's *Rooted in the Earth* (2010) brings in another dimension of the racialization of nature and the complexities that arise when conjoining race and ecology. She unearths an unexamined (and important) aspect of American environmental history by challenging an influential stereotype of African Americans as divorced from environmental and ecological concerns. Countering this assumption, she reconstructs a historical narrative of African Americans offering a range of attitudes, activities, and perspectives based on their experiences with land and other natural processes. She writes, "From ancient Africa to the modern-day United States, people of African descent have continued the legacy of their relationship with the land" (Glave 2010:

3). On the one hand, as Glave argues, the creation of African Americans' connection to nature was initially set within a context of trauma and violence, illustrative of the crisis of exile and alienation experienced by Africans taken from their native lands to American shores, which hinged on the critical "middle passage" (Glave 2010: 4). Additionally, the mass migrations of African Americans to northern urban cities after slavery, a process that continued into the 1970s, distanced them from the rural experiences of their parents and grandparents, who lived and worked in fields, gardens, and woods. In summarizing this dimension of the legacy, Glave observes,

> Scorn, distaste, and fear of nature became the emotional legacy of a people who had been kidnapped from their homelands and forced to make the long journey across the Atlantic Ocean to pick cotton and prime tobacco for often violent and abusive masters.
>
> (Glave 2010: 5)

On the other hand, Glave identifies a conscious environmentalism as one key strand of this African American legacy, associated with such notable figures as George Washington Carver, Ned Cobb, and Thomas Monroe Campbell (Glave 2010: 6). These early pioneers engaged in preservation and conservation efforts that showed an intimacy with the land; their land ethics sought to avoid extreme exploitation and mere instrumentalism. For instance, Carver, a paradigmatic figure and leader of the Tuskegee Experiment Station, championed recycling and waste control, lectured on horticulture at leading universities, and wrote numerous pamphlets explaining to farmers how improved techniques could raise their standard of living.

**BOX 8D**

According to George Washington Carver,

> Unkindness to anything means an injustice done to that thing. If I am unkind to you I do you an injustice, or wrong you in some way. On the other hand, if I try to assist you in every way that I can to make a better citizen and in every way to do my very best for you I am kind. The above principles apply with equal force to soil.
>
> (Glave 2010: 7)

In which ways does this principle from Carver both fit into and depart from the key tenets of religious naturalism?

In light of these divergent experiences, Glave raises an important question: What makes the environmental experiences of African Americans distinctive? Unlike their freed (white) counterparts, she notes, enslaved people did not simply discover wilderness; rather, they actively sought healing, kinship, resources, escape, refuge, and salvation in the land. Associating this relationship with a lack of ownership leads Glave to posit a different model for understanding blacks' complex historical relationship to nature and land (Glave 2010: 8). A superficial grasp of this model of relationality, she suggests, has helped perpetuate the current, dominant assumption that African Americans are not keen on environmental concerns.

Following the lead of Merchant, we must continue to ask whether our socially conscious ecological views are still couched in the predictable binary of a dynamic human culture and passive natural environment. While it is crucial to demonstrate white supremacy's role in maintaining the invisibility and marginalization of African Americans and other groups in mainstream environmental discourse, people of color (and all people) must also be vigilant in contesting the popular (and problematic) view of nature that constitutes much of US history. This is a narrative that overestimates human animals' autonomy, positioning us outside of complex, myriad nature and rendering invisible our inextricable connections. As shown by Glave's examples, more-than-human nature is still accorded value according to its usefulness to racialized humans or if it mirrors what we value in ourselves. Additionally, as Carver's example suggests and as found in the responses of some religious traditions, the notion of humans being honorable stewards makes humans' ethical relation to nature a matter of our generosity.

Religious naturalism aids us in confronting these complex and thorny issues. On the one hand, as a model of ecological discourse, religious naturalism's reconstruction of the human addresses the tyrannical presence of white supremacy, as well as its concomitant "isms" that have denied black (and other marginalized) subjects their rightful claims to enacting and actualizing their humanity in different ways. On the other hand, religious naturalism's retrieval of the human thwarts the aims of traditional humanisms that have positioned our species outside of myriad nature and eclipsed the interrelatedness of all natural processes. In short, the primary conception of human nature that religious naturalism evokes is ontologically enmeshed and entangled with other forms of natural life.

> **BOX 8E**
>
> Ideas of "humanity" that radically distinguish our species from all others can clearly harm not only the world beyond humanity but also human beings who are dismissed as "more" natural and so "less" human. Are there any similar dangers to the naturalistic idea that being human is fundamentally about being connected and enmeshed with all other forms of natural life?

### Promises of Religious Naturalism: Ethical Considerations

The basic conception of the human as an emergent, interconnected life-form amid spectacular biotic diversity has far-reaching ethical implications within the context of ecology and religion. First, as we have seen, religious naturalism contributes to an intellectual legacy that seeks to overcome the deficient conceptions of myriad nature couched in problematic binary constructions. Not only does it present human beings as biotic forms emerging from evolutionary processes sharing a deep homology with other sentient beings, but it also emphasizes humans valuing such connection. Accordingly, while challenging racially constructed views that have persistently placed blacks and other "racialized groups" outside of the circle of humanity, religious naturalism also rejects a view of our humanity solely as an individualistic phenomenon. Some type of communal ontology is implied. A crucial lesson here is that notwithstanding the cultural and national differences and specificities we construct, humans are all genetically connected and part of a greater whole. Any harm done to another sentient life is essentially harm done to us. In this religious worldview, we celebrate relational selves that can resist solipsistic tendencies and egoistic impulses; there are no isolated individuals standing over against the fields of interaction. Put another way, we are constitutionally relational and inevitably entangled in temporal becoming.

Religious naturalism also contributes to new aesthetic-ethical paradigms for living, experiencing, and seeing differently as relational, material beings. Robin Wall Kimmerer's work is very helpful here. As both a scientist—a bryologist, or an expert in moss—and cultural preserver of the wisdom of the Citizen Potawatomi Nation, Kimmerer conjoins elegant narratives of human perspectives with more-than-human ones that accentuate new ways of speaking and listening. As our knowledge about plant life unfolds, she contends, so must human vocabulary and imaginations change and expand. Kimmerer provides a lucid example of this marriage of poetic, indigenous wisdom with Western scientific wisdom when speaking of the nature of gifting or, better yet, of the gifting of nature from the vantage point of her cultural heritage. Using strawberries as an example, she speaks of a worldview in which there is a relational quality of receiving and reciprocating between and among various actors. For example, when elaborating on the "gift" of berries, she states,

> The plant has in fact been up all night assembling little packets of sugar and seeds and fragrance and color, because when it does so its evolutionary fitness is increased. When it is successful in enticing an animal such as me to disperse its fruit, its genes for making yumminess are passed on to ensuing generations with a higher frequency than those of the plant whose berries were inferior. . . . What I mean of course is that our human relationship with strawberries is transformed by our choice of perspective. It is human perception that makes the world a gift. When we view the world this way, strawberries and humans alike are transformed.
>
> (Kimmerer 2013: 30)

In Kimmerer's work, one experiences a sense of wonder and humility that honors intelligence in all kinds of life. Her insights accentuate the keen sensibilities of religious naturalism, expanding our perspectives on just how entangled our human capacities are with other forms of nature.

Kimmerer's scientific and cultural insights reflect a key epistemological notion in religious naturalism known as metaphysical perspectivism, which holds that the world has a plurality of entities, each with its own individuality, particularity of expression, and distinctive perspective on everything else. Crosby writes,

> All the elemental particles, atoms, molecules, compounds, inorganic and organic entities and combinations of those entities, including human beings and their histories, cultures, and societies, and all of the actions, reactions, functions, qualities, and traits of these particular things and their relations are included. No two perspectives or systems of them are exactly alike.
>
> (Crosby 2008: 67–8)

That humans' perspectives are *included* with and influenced by the perspectives of other existents in the universe, I suggest, compels humans to reflect further and creatively on how we become our humanity. Honoring our radical relatedness entails a constant yearning to achieving our humanity—a task that can never be completed in an unfolding, mysterious universe. Such mystery destabilizes our sense of knowing in the pursuit of classifying and organizing the profound mystery of nature's profound alterity. Metaphysical perspectivism thus sheds light on the notion of humans dwelling differently, encouraging us to be more attentive to how we are experiencing the strange, relational worlds of which we are always constituted. In this sense, religious naturalism challenges us to consider how other life forces, bodies, and modes of being—infinitely multiplied—share in the capacious entangled web of life and the shifting, ontological orderings that are a part of myriad nature.

With its notion of metaphysical perspectivism, religious naturalism promotes a sense of the irrefutable interconnectedness of all life. This religious orientation reminds humans that within our particular realms of activity and capacities of influence, we have a responsibility to act in ways that promote the flourishing of all life.

## Case Study: Environmental Justice Communities and the Anticipation of Religious Naturalism

As featured in popular culture, the US environmental movement can seem to be a favorite cause of affluent white Americans who consume organic foods, contribute to causes devoted to the fate of extinct animals, and vacation in eco-villages in Costa Rica. In this dominant environmental narrative, the lives, interests, and well-being of communities of color are seldom mentioned or acknowledged. As environmental justice advocates have shown, however, the "human" populations most often affected by environmental degradation are both communities of color and those that are economically disadvantaged. Residents of these "environmental justice communities" often live in neighborhoods surrounded by freeways and industrial facilities or in small towns without clean drinking water or sidewalks. They are often excluded from public investments.

Environmental justice communities also do not experience pollution from just one source, nor are their lives affected by one type of facility or pollutant. Instead, their communities are routinely chosen to host an array of facilities that spawn adverse ecological effects. Accordingly, they often cope with a range of health issues, exacerbated by numerous factors alongside environmental policy: poverty, unemployment, education, access to political power, and more. These communities are experiencing environmental racism, a pernicious extension of the various forms of racism and economic injustices encountered in American life.

It is important to note that communities of color have not been passively indifferent to the various forms of environmental assaults in their neighborhoods outlined earlier; nor have they lacked a critical ecological consciousness that might contribute to the range of issues addressed by the US environmental movement. Dating back to the early 1960s, Latino farm workers led by Cesar Chavez fought for workplace rights, including protection from harmful pesticides in the farm fields of California's San Joaquin Valley. In 1967, African American students in Houston opposed a city garbage dump in their community that had killed two neighborhood kids. West Harlem residents in 1968 also fought unsuccessfully against the siting of a sewage treatment plant in their community.

One paradigmatic illustration of an environmental community resisting the racial implications of environmental degradation also occurred in 1982 in Warren County, North Carolina. This small rural African American community protested the dumping of six thousand truckloads of soil laced with toxic polychlorinated biphenyls (PCBs) into a newly constructed hazardous waste landfill. The dump trucks first rolled into Warren County in mid-September. Residents and their allies met the trucks in protest, insisting that PCBs might leak into drinking water supplies despite reassurances from state leaders. With bodies sprawled on roads leading into the landfill, community members engaged in nonviolent street protests. They also held marches and other forms of protest in the following six weeks. More than five hundred people were arrested—the first arrests in US history over the siting of a landfill. Although the community members of Warren County ultimately lost that specific battle—the toxic waste was eventually deposited in the landfill—their cries were not in vain. The struggle to protect their lives, their children, and their homes from the dangers of toxic waste materials garnered national media attention, heralding the advent of the environmental justice grassroots movement.

In the years since the unfolding drama in Warren County, environmental justice communities across the US have built coalitions of various racial and ethnic groups (primarily African Americans, Latinos, Asians, Pacific Islanders, and Native Americans) to develop multifaceted forms of resistance to environmental racism, as well as more recent problems associated with the climate crisis. For example, the California Justice Alliance (CJA) is a contemporary example of communities of color considering how racial dynamics are also implicated in addressing climate justice. As is the typical scenario in environmental racism in general, climate change disproportionally affects low-income communities and communities of color in the US and across the globe. Too often, communities of color bear the burden of dirty fossil fuels and are the ones that will be hit first and worst by climate change. In response, the CJA seeks to put equity at the center of the climate debate to ensure that environmental justice is a priority in climate policy. It calls for communities of color to play a central leadership role in climate policies to ensure the most vulnerable communities are not left behind (https://caleja.org/what-we-do/climatejustice).

In making crucial connections among problems that are often perceived as isolated, environmental justice communities anticipate the aims of religious naturalism. With its capacious cosmology, religious naturalism strengthens the case for addressing ecological degradation and climate justice. Its theoretical and ethical claims alert us to the dangers of isolationist agendas that environmental justice advocates apparently resist (Cole and Foster 2001: 10–14). For example, the environmental justice movement demonstrates religious naturalism's sense of the irrefutable interconnectedness of all life when it concurrently advocates against the depletion of natural resources; challenges the policies that both create land polluted by landfills, oil refineries, and nuclear-waste repositories and force poor racial and ethnic communities to live near these sites; and fights for referendums that preserve the delicate ecosystems supporting whales and dolphins. As these efforts suggest, religious naturalists and environmental justice advocates share a general maxim: harm done to any one sector of natural processes, inclusive of human organisms, is harm done to all.

Inspired by the claims of religious naturalism, a more robust environmental justice movement intentionally challenges and unmasks subtle binary differentiations that ground the most recent variations of the nature-culture continuum represented by these grassroots movements. Honoring all materiality, religious naturalism compels us to cast aside problematic bifurcations of racial and ethnic terms that often result in an us-versus-them mentality. With such a naturalist worldview, we can better identify and resist the ill effects of white supremacy on all of us, resisting its power in determining how certain racial and ethnic bodies are treated. We can also detect and challenge the subtle processes of the racialization of nature endemic to American environmental history. These important ecological values are ones that social justice advocates can extend to enact important ethical, political, economic, and social changes in American life.

Religious naturalism compels us onward in these struggles, as we continuously expand our views of nature, including human nature, and refuse to be distracted by the various entrapments of the binary logic outlined earlier. One possible future emerging from these efforts is a transformed sphere of existence, where humans make a claim on life and honor, to the best of our ability, our inextricable relationality with each other and with the more-than-human words that constitute our being here.

### *Discussion Questions*

1. In which ways do you see the binary logic discussed in the essay reflected in this brief account of environmental injustice and the communities that resist it?
2. How might religious naturalism contribute to the ongoing environmental justice struggle? How might such commitment be different from that established by more traditional or otherworldly religious traditions?

3. In the previous quote, George Washington Carver insists that good citizenship means kindness toward other people and the soil. How could that ideal be brought into a dispute about the siting of toxic waste? What does "kindness" look like when toxic substances must be disposed of?

## Notes

1 In biological studies, "races" are associated with genetically distinct populations within the same species; they typically have relatively minor morphological and genetic differences. Although all humans belong to the same species (*Homo sapiens*), and even to the same subspecies (*Homo sapiens sapiens*), there are small genetic variations across the globe that engender diverse physical appearances, such as variations in skin color. Although humans are sometimes divided into races, the morphological variation between races is not indicative of major differences in DNA. For example, recent genetic studies show skin color may drastically change in as few as a hundred generations, spanning 2,500 years, as a result of environmental influences. Furthermore, the DNA of two humans chosen at random generally varies by less than 0.1%. This is less genetic variation than other types of hominids (such as chimpanzees and orangutans), leading some scientists to describe all humans as belonging to the same race—the human race.

2 This brief section is adapted from my fuller discussion in Chapter 2 of *Black Lives and Sacred Humanity* (White 2016).

## Works Cited


Cole, L., and Foster, S. (2001) *From the Ground Up: Environmental Racism and the Rise of the Environmental Justice Movement*. New York: New York University Press.

Crenshaw, K. (1989) "Demarginizing the Intersection of Race and Sex: A Black Feminist Critique of Antidiscrimination Doctrine, Feminist Theory and Antiracist Politics," *University of Chicago Legal Forum* 139–67.

Crenshaw, K., and Gotando, N. (eds) (1996) *Critical Race Theory: The Key Writings That Formed the Movement*. New York: New Press.

Crosby, D. (2008) *Living With Ambiguity: Religious Naturalism and the Menace of Evil*. Albany: State University Press of New York.

Day, T. (2012) *Constructing Solidarity for a Liberative Ethic: Anti-Racism, Action, and Justice*. London: Palgrave Macmillan.

Delgado, R., and Stefanic, J. (2012) *Critical Race Theory: An Introduction*. 2nd ed. New York: New York University Press.

Dixson, A. D., and Roussau, C. K. (eds) (2006) *Critical Race Theory in Education: All God's Children Got a Song*. New York: Routledge.

Embrick, D., Burnsma, D., and Nanney, M. (2015) "On Moving Forward," *Sociology of Race and Ethnicity* 1(2): 205–8.

Eze, E. (ed) (1996) *Race and the Enlightenment*. Malden, MA: Blackwell Publishers.

Glave, D. (2010) *Rooted in the Earth: Reclaiming the African American Environmental Heritage*. Chicago: Chicago Review Press.

Finney, C. (2014) *Black Faces, White Spaces: Reimagining the Relationship of African Americans to the Great Outdoors*. Chapel Hill, NC: The University of North Carolina Press.

Goodenough, U. (1998) *The Sacred Depths of Nature*. New York: Oxford University Press.

Kimmerer, R. W. (2013) *Braiding Sweetgrass: Indigenous Wisdom, Scientific Knowledge, and the Teachings of Plants*. Minneapolis: Milkweed Editions.

Lowell, P. (1888) *Soul of the Far East*. Boston and New York: Houghton, Mifflin and Company.

MacCord, K. (2014) "Johann Friedrich Blumenbach (1752–1840)," *Embryo Project Encyclopedia* (2014-01-22). ISSN: 1940-5030 http://embryo.asu.edu/handle/10776/7512 (accessed August 2022).

Marable, M. (2001) "Structural Racism and American Democracy: Historical and Theoretical Perspectives," *Souls* 3(1): 6–24.

Merchant, C. (1980) *The Death of Nature: Women, Ecology and the Scientific Revolution*. New York: HarperCollins Publishers.

Outka, P. (2008) *Race and Nature: From Transcendence to the Harlem Renaissance*. New York: Palgrave Macmillan.

Plumwood, V. (1993) *Feminism and the Mastery of Nature*. New York: Routledge.

Pulido, L. (2000) "Rethinking Environmental Racism: White Privilege and Urban Development in Southern California," *Annals of the Association of American Geographers* 90(1): 12–40.

Rigby, K. (2020) *Reclaiming Romanticism: Towards and Ecopoetics of Decolonization*. New York: Bloomsbury.

Rue, L. (2005) *Religion Is Not About God: How Spiritual Traditions Nurture Our Biological Nature and What to Expect When They Fail*. Piscataway, NJ: Rutgers University Press.

Smedley, A. (1998) " 'Race' and the Construction of Human Identity," *American Anthropologist* 100(3): 690–702.

Valdes, F., Harris, A., and McCristal Culp, J. (2002) *Crossroads, Directions and a New Critical Race Theory*. Philadelphia: Temple University Press.

White, C. W. (2016) *Black Lives and Sacred Humanity: Toward an African American Religious Naturalism*. New York: Fordham University Press.

## Further Reading

Bullard, R., Mohair, P., Saha, R., and Wright, B. "Toxic Wastes and Race at Twenty: 1987–2007: A Report Prepared for the United Church of Christ Justice & Witness Ministries," www.nrdc.org/sites/default/files/toxic-wastes-and-race-at-twenty-1987-2007.pdf (accessed December 6, 2015).

Cole, L., and Foster, S. (2001) *From the Ground Up: Environmental Racism and the Rise of the Environmental Justice Movement*. New York: New York University Press.

Crosby, D. (2013) *The Thou of Nature: Religious Naturalism and Reverence for Sentient Life*. Albany: State University of University Press.

Hogue, M. (2010) *The Promises of Religious Naturalism*. Lanham, MD: Rowman & Littlefield.

Stone, J. A. (2008) *Religious Naturalism Today: The Rebirth of a Forgotten Alternative*. Albany: State University of New York Press.

Westra, L., and Lawson, B. E. (2001) *Faces of Environmental Racism: Confronting Issues of Global Justice*. Lanham: Rowman & Littlefield Publishers.

# 9 Disability

*Lisa D. Powell*

Disability as an academic discipline emerged along with the disability activism of the mid to late 20th century. As the civil rights movement gained ground in the 1960s, people within the disability community likewise organized against the injustices enacted against people with impairments. Not only were buildings and public transport inaccessible to many, so too were education and employment opportunities. The early movement for disability rights achieved numerous legislative advances in the United States, including the Architectural Barriers Act of 1968, the Rehabilitation Act of 1973, and the Education for All Handicapped Children Act of 1975. Yet despite the passing of these federal laws, not all needed protections were enacted and many of those that were enacted were not enforced.

So in 1977, after the federal government delayed signing all sections of the Rehabilitation Act into law, the disability community organized an extended sit-in at the headquarters for the US Department of Health, Education, and Welfare in San Francisco. This powerful protest for the rights of people with disabilities, called the 540 Sit-in, lasted for 26 days. It was but one of the many protests and acts of civil disobedience, such as the Capital Crawl of 1990, that led to the eventual passing of the Americans with Disabilities Act in 1990. This landmark legislation remains an important watershed, although most disability activists argue that it does not go far enough. Critical disability perspectives on numerous academic disciplines, policy, and public life have expanded in the decades since and continue to challenge the ableist systems and assumptions prominent in Western society.

Historically, people with disabilities have been looked at with pity or fear and treated in dehumanizing ways: sterilized, institutionalized, and hidden out of sight. Religious discourses and practices have often reflected these dismissive attitudes toward people with disabilities: positioning them as bodies worthy of charity and pity, exemplars of innocence, or symbols of God's power to heal. Christian theology has even considered the very existence of people with non-typical bodies or minds to be a result of sin entering the world rather than identifying differences of body-minds as an integral part of the diversity of God's creation. One of the first theologians to push back against this tendency in Christian theology was Nancy Eiesland, who developed a liberation theology from the perspective of disability (1994).

DOI: 10.4324/9781003259466-12

Disability studies typically differentiates between "impairment" and "disability." "Impairment" refers to one's particular embodiment, and can include physiological, sensory, neurological, mental, and intellectual difference. "Disability" refers to the socially constructed barriers and stigmas applied to that impairment or "as the way impairment is turned into deficiency or obstacle as a consequence of the way that society is organized socially, politically, and also environmentally" (Taylor 2019). Using a wheelchair to move from one place to another is not itself disabling. A lack of ramps, wide door frames, and elevators that can accommodate a wheelchair, though, is disabling. Having limited use of one's arms is not itself disabling, except as society stigmatizes the use of other body parts, such as the feet or the mouth, to complete tasks typically done with hands.

This distinction is often associated with what is called the social model of disability, which focuses on the injustice associated with the way society limits access and constructs barriers to the full participation of people with disabilities in society and public spaces. The social model is also known for its celebration of disability as one form of human diversity. This is a contrast with the medical model, which is critiqued for positioning impairments as something to be fixed and for imposing an expectation that bodies and minds look, act, and/or function according to socially determined norms. Disability activism and scholarship challenge this notion of normativity and point out that "normal" abilities tend to be those associated with White, hetero-cisgendered, able-bodied males, against whom all other bodies are measured, deviance determined, and value ascribed.

## BOX 9A

Why do you think the distinction between impairment and disability is important to people with impairments? Why would it be important to disability activists?

### Eco-Ableism

Unfortunately, the rhetoric and priorities of the climate movement and groups associated with environmental protection have too often worked within dominant standards of normativity and so conflict with the concerns and needs of people with disabilities. This environmentalist tendency to disregard the lives of people with disabilities is termed eco-ableism. In what follows, we will consider (1) how the lives and needs of people with disabilities are ignored in the ableist lens of some environmentalist campaigns and attitudes, (2) how eco-ableism frames access for people with disabilities as harming an otherwise pristine natural landscape while presenting non-disabled access to nature as unobtrusive, and (3) how campaigns to stop pollution often harness ableist fear of disability to motivate action. In conclusion, we will consider a case study of pollution to an aquifer in southern Tucson that resulted in many disabilities and chronic illnesses among the community in the region, and consider how one scholar, whose congenital impairments were a result of this contaminated water, is framing ecological harm as disablement.

***Eco-Ableism in the Environmental Movement***

The ableism in some iterations of the environmental movement was exposed in November 2021 at the Twenty-Sixth United Nations Climate Change Conference of the Parties (COP26), where world leaders met to discuss global climate policy. The meeting venue was not wheelchair-accessible, barring the Israeli Energy Minister Karine Elharrar from attending the first day of discussions.

Eco-ableism is also evident in the recent push to limit the availability of plastic straws. This movement was ignited in 2011 by a nine-year-old boy in Vermont who was moved by stories of plastic particles in the ocean and stories of sea turtles choked or harmed by straws in their habitats. He convinced a café in his hometown to ask people if they want a straw instead of automatically giving them. This quickly developed into a campaign to “Be Straw Free.” Bans on single-use plastic straws sprang up in numerous cities across the US, and some companies stopped making them available in their restaurants and stores. The situation was often framed to consumers and patrons to suggest a simple binary: you could want a straw, or you could care about sea turtles.

However, it is not that simple for millions of people with disabilities. Bendable plastic straws were invented to help people in the hospital stay hydrated, and they assist people with a range of disabilities who in many cases cannot take fluids independently without them. Reusable straws are not necessarily a simple answer; they are difficult to clean, especially for those with impaired dexterity, which is one of the reasons many require the straw in the first place. Most reusable straws are also inflexible, which can pose a danger to people with disabilities. In 2018, a woman in England was impaled and killed by falling on a metal straw in her cup.

Outright bans punish people with disabilities. Framing the issue as “if you choose to use a plastic straw then you don’t care about the planet” is unjust for people who need those straws to take in essential liquids. Eliminating plastic straws will not make a dent in the magnitude of ecological destruction, but it makes life much harder for many people with disabilities. This is not to suggest efforts to reduce single-use plastic use should be stopped as inherently ableist but that the voices, expertise, and lived experiences of people with disabilities should be included in the decision-making process.

**BOX 9B**

Do you think it would be possible for environmentalists to campaign against plastic waste and discourage unnecessary usage of straws without risking eco-ableist stigmatization and endangering people with disabilities? What might such a campaign look like?

The blanket straw ban in some cities is a classic example of the neglect of the voices and needs of people with disabilities. Such a ban would not have happened if people with disabilities had been consulted. This is the dynamic that gave rise to the slogan of the disability rights movement: “Nothing about us, without us.” If a policy is going to directly impact the lives of people with disabilities, then people with disabilities need to be involved in developing it. Jewish ethicist Julia Watts Belser notes that people with disabilities are often neglected in the ways dominant culture understands and responds to disasters. She studies the stories of impaired people who drowned when Hurricane Katrina hit New Orleans in 2005 because no accessible public transportation was available to get them out of the city. Bringing these stories into conversation with biblical and rabbinic accounts of disasters, Belser observes that the death of a person with disabilities is not just a tragedy but also reflects a set of political choices that seems to suggest that the lives of certain people do not matter. Belser calls the deaths of people with disabilities in New Orleans a "devastating indictment of the price of social inequality and ableism" (2015: 63).

### *Access to the Natural World*

Another form of eco-ableism can be seen in the way some conservationists view access for people with disabilities to be particularly intrusive and disruptive, even suggesting that the wilderness is not a place for people with disabilities. Rhetoric and attitudes around the wilderness and the "adventure" associated with the great outdoors is at times explicitly ableist.

One example of this attitude is described by Alison Kafer, who reflects on nature lovers' outcries against accessible trails and boat launches. She writes that "in their view increasing disability access and protecting the environment are irreconcilable. But the fact that it is often only disability access that comes under such interrogation suggests an act of ableist forgetting." The access needed by most people, non-disabled included, requires an alteration of the landscape, an intrusion of machinery and tools to cut trails, clear trail heads, and more. Yet interventions that allow people to walk to natural sites "are seen as natural [while] wheelchair-accessible trails are seen as unnatural" (Kafer 2017: 216).

Kafer, who uses a wheelchair, recounts her visit to a wildlife refuge in Rhode Island, where she learned that the local community was outraged over efforts to make trails wheelchair-accessible. The complaint was against the materials used (in this case crushed asphalt) and the noise anticipated with trails accessible to wheelchairs. Of course, there were no restrictions on cell phones, children, large groups, or dogs, all of which can also create noise on trails and potentially scare off birds—it was specifically the potential wheelchairs that disturbed the community.

Another example comes from complaints made about a group of disabled and non-disabled hikers who made the trek to a newly accessible cabin in the White Mountains. Other hikers complained that the group took up too much room on the trail and assumed that the wheelchairs harmed the terrain. *The New York Times* published a letter to the editor about the occasion that called the wheelchair hikers "selfish" because of the damage they would do to the trails. Even more upsetting, it seems, was the very fact that this backcountry cabin was made accessible to people with disabilities through the addition of a ramp. One reporter asked "why people in wheelchairs could drag themselves up the trail and not drag themselves up the steps to the hut" (Kafer 2017: 216). But those steps themselves are an accommodation, a fact that is not noticed simply because it is an accommodation provided to people who move in ways deemed "normal" and therefore worthy of accommodation.

Kafer uses these as examples of "how nondisabled access is made invisible while disabled access is made hypervisible" (Kafer 2017: 215). It is only when bodies considered atypical seek access that accommodation is treated as excessive or unnatural. Says Kafer, "The sooner we recognize that all trails are built interventions on the landscape," created to gain access, the sooner we can begin the work of accommodating more bodies, making every trail as accessible as possible (Kafer 2017: 222).

Certain trails will never be accessible to all people; they cannot be and should not be, for some people aren't in the condition to hike certain terrains or to certain elevations. Not all trails are safe for every type of body, including the non-disabled. Disability access is not a demand that everything be accessible to every one. It is instead a demand that everything be made be as accessible as is reasonable and appropriate for that ecosystem. This should not be too hard to sell since widespread accommodation is generally better for everyone. Boardwalks, for example, not only provide access—for those with mobility impairments, for the elderly, for those hiking with children—but also protect fragile terrain below from traffic and better encourage people to remain on the trail.

A final example of this form of ableism comes from an ad campaign placed by Nike in *Backpacker* magazine for a trail-running shoe called the Air Dri-Goat. Along with a picture of the shoe was the following text:

> You're probably asking yourself, "How can a trail running shoe with an outer sole designed like a goat's hoof help me avoid compressing my spinal cord into a Slinky on the side of some unsuspecting conifer, thereby rendering me a drooling, misshapen non-extreme-trail-running husk of my former self, forced to roam the earth in a motorized wheelchair with my name, embossed on one of those cute little license plates you get at carnivals or state fairs, fastened to the back?" To that we answer, hey, have you ever seen a mountain goat (even an extreme mountain goat) careen out of control into the side of tree? Didn't think so.
>
> (Kafer 2017: 207)

**BOX 9C**

What ableist rhetoric do you see in the text of the Nike advertisement? What connections do you see between the ways this text treats people with disabilities and the way it treats non-human animals?

The previous examples seem obviously offensive and inexcusable, blatant demonstrations of eco-ableism as they position disabled bodies as a foil to bodies worthy of access to nature and outdoor exploration, mocking and pitying impaired bodies as incapable of experiencing the wilderness. They depict disabled bodies as not belonging to cultures of outdoor recreation or of nature-loving witness.

They portray nature itself as inherently inhospitable to atypical bodies yet assume that it should be accessible to more typical bodies. This erases the fact that access to nature is constructed through trails carved out of mountain sides, parking lots paved at trailheads, cabins erected, and stairs positioned for the access and convenience of those with typical bodies. The wilderness has been shaped, changed, and adapted to create the parks and preserves these conservationists are so passionate to remain untouched from broader access.

### *Environmental Action and Ableist Rhetoric*

Eli Clare's memoir *Exile and Pride* stands as a witness against the dominant ableist adventure narrative. Clare recounts growing up in the Pacific Northwest and weaves together the clear cutting of its forests and overfishing of its waters with his experience as a queer person with cerebral palsy. He has walked from LA to DC, has "backpacked solo in the South Appalachians, along Lake Superior, on beaches at Point Reyes," and has "slogged" his way "over Cottonwood pass and down South Monitors Dunes" (Clare 2015: 4). In his 2017 book *Brilliant Imperfection*, Clare demonstrates how much of the rhetoric of ecological justice relies on ableism.

He traces the relationship between the body and ecosystems, and between healing discourses and restoration efforts. He links the devastation wrought by ecological monocultures to the drive within White Western settler colonialism to create a human monoculture, which opposes both the diversity of ecosystems and of embodied human experiences. Farming and forestry practices that fragment ecosystems to produce monocultures for harvesting extract resources with an eye on production and efficiency without care for the diversity upon which life depends. So, too, the colonizing impulse attempts to extinguish spiritualities and cultures that honor nature and humanity's symbiotic relationship within it—the same drive that simultaneously devalues bodies that do not perform for economic expansion.

Clare asks, "How do we witness, name, and resist the injustice that reshape and damage all kinds of body-minds—plants and animal, organic, and inorganic, nonhuman and human—while not equating disability with injustice?" (Clare 2017: 56). How do we talk about the impact of environmental pollution and not frame the lives of those impaired as the most dreaded consequence of pollution? Or how can we advocate for environmental justice without exploiting ableist fear of disability as the motivator for change?

Clare recounts a conversation with a friend whose disability was acquired in utero because of military dumping near her childhood home, which leached into the groundwater. The work of this friend, renowned artist and animal activist Sunaura Taylor, will be featured in the case study at the end of this chapter. She uses a power wheelchair, has limited use of her arms and hands, and paints with her mouth. Clare describes her struggle to express her "hatred for military dumping without feeding the assumption that [her] body is bad, wrong, and unnatural" (Clare 2017: 56). Clare reminds us that disabled bodies are positioned as cautionary tales used in arguments against drunk driving, drug use, air pollution, lead paint, asbestos, vaccines, and on and on, all relying on the symbolic use of people disabled because of these actions and substances. Campaigns elicit images of people in wheelchairs because of a drunk driver, children with learning disabilities because of lead contamination, and people with asthma and cancer because of pollution. All of these images of people with impairment or illness are deployed to warn people, suggesting that living a life in such a condition is a dreaded consequence. How should people who live with these impairments interpret these images? For Sunaura Taylor, it is possible to denounce environmental pollution, like that which produced her disability, without communicating that she does not value her body as it is. Clare reports that she arrived at the slogan "I hate the military and love my body" (2017: 56).

Environmental organizations regularly launch campaigns intentionally leveraging ableism to mobilize people to act for environmental causes, relying on an assumed fear of disability to spur change. Because it is framed in this way, the pollution itself is not targeted as the injustice; instead, attention is focused on the impairment that results from pollution. Thus, impaired bodies serve as the symbol of injustice.

One example is the Get the Lead Out campaign, which seeks to motivate people to act for the removal of lead from public water supplies (particularly in schools) by leveraging disability fear. The campaign in essence asks, "You don't want your kids to have learning disabilities or a lowered IQ? To not grow as tall as they could be? To have a hearing impairment? Then write your legislator, write your school board, get the lead out!" Though this is a paraphrased statement of the campaign literature, it accurately reflects the gist of the messaging. The resources on the website, sample advocacy letters, tweets, and so on, all refer to the way lead impacts how children learn, grow, and behave. Rudolph Reyes II, a Latino religious ethicist who identifies as neurodivergent, puts it bluntly, "The ecological disgust of a disabled body is assumed and leveraged to combat water pollution" (Reyes 2021: 91).

Is the impairment itself the injustice to be eliminated or is it the pollution? If we look closely at the Get the Lead Out campaign's argument, it frames the problem not as pollution but as children developing disabilities. Lead should be removed not because it is inherently bad but because disability is bad. Reyes recognizes that the nuance of this dilemma can be challenging for the non-disabled to understand. Dominant culture is saturated in ableism, simply assuming that disability is obviously to be avoided. But this sounds different to people who are impaired, who are disabled by societal prejudice, who have already been exposed to lead or other pollutants. To such people, campaigns like Get the Lead Out can seem to suggest that they themselves are a problem.

## Threading the Needle

It is not easy to critique pollution while not dismissing those who have been impaired by it. But disabled environmental activists argue that the work of threading this needle is essential. Clare calls on readers to acknowledge "the connections between disability, chronic illness, and injustice while also holding on to the inherent value of disabled and chronically ill people" (2017: 62).

Reyes explains, "I am not arguing that we should not witness and name the slow violence done to children through water pollution, but rather reframe the narrative where disability is not the center of these acts of witnessing and naming injustice" (2021: 91).

Reyes also points out that the Get the Lead Out campaign is "an example of eco-ableism that obscures environmental racism" (Reyes 2021: 91). The most famous case of lead in drinking water of course, is Flint, Michigan, where over 60% of the population is Black or Brown (according to the 2018 census). Disabled people of color have higher rates of poverty, incarceration, arrests, and use of force by police officers than people of color who are not disabled, and much higher rates than Whites with or without disabilities. Being or becoming a disabled person of color compounds the injustices and oppressions already faced.

This intersection of injustice where race, class, environmental pollution, and ableism come together is also important to Eli Clare's work. Clare describes a Sierra Club campaign titled Beyond Coal. One ad shows the belly of a pregnant woman captioned "This little bundle of joy is now a reservoir of mercury." And in fine print, "Mercury pollution from our nation's coal-burning power plants is harming pregnant women and their unborn children. Mercury is a powerful neurotoxin that can damage the brain and nervous system—causing developmental problems and learning disabilities." Another Beyond Coal image is of a boy puffing on an inhaler. Again, the image of a chronically ill human is deployed as a motivator to stop the destruction of the ecosystem.

The Sierra Club here tries to persuade people that coal plants need to be shut down by using human disability as a terrifying consequence of environmental destruction. Birth defects and learning disabilities become symbols of environmental damage. Clare writes, "This strategy works because it taps into ableism. It assumes that viewers will automatically understand disability . . . as tragedy in need of prevention and eradication, and in turn that these tragedies will persuade us to join the struggle." He says, "By bluntly leveraging ableism, the ads conflate justice with the eradication of disability" (2017: 56). Such simplistic representations of disability cause harm in a number of ways. (1) People's different ways of learning, and ways of living with conditions deemed birth defects, simply serve as "proofs of injustice" and thus act to deny the rich and complicated lived realities of people with disabilities. (2) It frames disability solely as damage located within individuals "while disregarding the damage caused by ableism" (2017: 56). Disability here is a defect in a body-mind, unrelated to the systems and structures that marginalize people with impairments. (3) It avoids addressing the racism and classism behind the toxic pollution. Sierra Club's campaign, for example, should not locate the injustice in disability, but neither should it only identify coal burning and extracting fossil fuels as injustice without noting the complex web of intersecting oppressions at work here, including systems that force poor people and people of color to live and work near environmental destruction and toxic waste. It is not disability that must be eradicated, but injustices against the people with disabilities, the poor, people of color, and whole ecosystems.

So what is the injustice in these cases? Is it just that we need to get lead and mercury out of the water because children there may not grow as tall, may develop learning disabilities, and may become hard of hearing (injustice as disability)? Is the injustice ableist cultures and educational systems that do not accommodate a range of physical and intellectual abilities and learning modalities (injustice as ableism)? Is it the white supremacy that pushes pollution and toxic sites specifically to areas of concentrated communities of color (injustice as racism)? Is it the water pollution that damages all matters of life, organic and inorganic (environmental injustice)? Can we motivate people to change behavior for the sake of the non-human, non-animal, for the biological matter considered not cute enough for a campaign or deemed insignificant by society when they are vital to healthy ecosystems? We must simultaneously shift our cultural valuations to recognize that human diversity is vital to healthy communities.

**BOX 9D**

Can you think of other rhetoric in environmental efforts, from your community or beyond, that frame the problem in a way that excludes or objectifies people? Can you imagine ways to reframe campaigns so that they instead capture the multifaceted injustices of environmental degradation?

Christian theologians and ethicists also face this challenge of "threading the needle." Many seek to affirm that body diversity is a beautiful part of God's creation that should be celebrated, including the range of impairment and ability that arise naturally in the world. This approach often comes by way of seeing impairment, illness, and pain as a natural part of God's creation, not a result of sin entering the world. However, many find that such naturalization of impairment hides the human causes of much disability worldwide, both the physical cause of the impairment through war, violence, pollution, and malnourishment, for example, and the social cause of much of the suffering associated with the impairment (Betcher 2014). It is beneficial for the lives of people with disabilities when churches come to understand differing bodies and minds as offering rich and valuable contributions to communities. But such affirmation must also be joined with specific action to end discrimination against people with disabilities, to rectify social inequities that produce disablement, and to support the needs of people with disabilities and their caregivers.

The work remains to confront injustices brought against all people, the injustice against life on this planet, plant and animal, human and non-human. But how we frame that advocacy matters. So the question for all environmentalists should be "how do [we] support movements for ecological justice without supporting ableist ideologies?" (Reyes 2021: 87). How do we frame calls to action against environmental abuses that do not cast impaired bodies as tragic fates? How do we mobilize people in an ableist culture to act without harnessing, and thus empowering, their disgust at disability as motivation? Or drawing again from Clare, how can we "witness, name, and resist the injustice that reshape and damage" all kinds of body-minds while affirming the inherent worth of that diversity?

## Case Study

In recent research, Sunaura Taylor traces the history of the aquifer in south Tucson and the military waste dumping above it that leached into the water of the community, including that of her childhood home. The pollution came from the Hughes Aircraft Plant, which manufactured parts for aircraft and missiles initially used against North Korea. In 1952, the plant began disposing chemicals in the environment, including trichlorethylene (TCE), which was used to degrease planes and clean missiles and was dumped into a large pit with no liner. Taylor explains,

> As the contamination spread underground into the aquifer and then into neighborhood wells, the TCE plume, as it eventually came to be known, reached out 10 square miles from south to north and a mile and a half east to west.
>
> (2019)

These chemicals entered the municipal and private wells across southern Tucson, where the population was largely Mexican American, and into portions of the Tohono O'odham nation land. Taylor describes a situation where chemicals, developed for weapons to kill and disable Korean citizens, were also killing and disabling residents of Arizona. Her research sits at the intersection of environmental racism, imperialism, eco-justice, and disability.

People in these neighborhoods began to notice their plants dying when they watered them. Their pets and farm animals got sick. And then the people themselves grew ill from the water they drank and used for cooking and bathing. Many were diagnosed with cancers, brain tumors, and chronic illnesses. Babies were stillborn and others were born with congenital heart impairments or other disabilities.

The community members organized, forming Tucsonans for a Clean Environment, which became one of the first environmental justice movements in the US. They demanded to be heard by city officials but were initially dismissed as "hysterical Hispanic housewives." Spokespeople from the Pima County Health Department and the Hughes Aircraft Company declared that the illnesses were not the result of pollution but rather came from a predisposition to sickness in these populations, which were "genetically disadvantaged." Officials also suggested that poor diets and lifestyle were to blame, even telling residents during one meeting that they were getting sick "because of the chilies and beans they ate" (Taylor 2021). Despite these racist dismissals, the citizens did not give up and successfully demonstrated that their water was toxic because of the plant and its waste lagoon. By the mid-1980s, the Tucson Water Department shut down wells with more than 920 times the EPA's allowable levels of TCE. Thanks to the tireless organizing of the community, investigative journalism by local reporters, and major litigation, they secured a state-of-the-art water treatment facility and won a quarter of a million dollars for a healthcare clinic to focus on TCE-related health concerns in their community.

Tracing the history of this aquifer and community, Taylor argues that we need a language of "ecological disablement" to communicate "the webs of disability that are created spatially, temporally, and across species boundaries when ecosystems are contaminated, depleted, and profoundly altered" (Taylor 2019). She explains, "Disabled ecologies are the material and cultural ways in which disability is manifested and produced among human and nonhuman entities" (Taylor 2021).

Disability in environmental discourse is typically used in two ways: (1) as a warning that human disability is a result of pollution that draws on ableist fear of impairment or (2) as a metaphor for damage to ecosystems, which is ubiquitous in environmentalist writing. Taylor provides evidence for disability and health used metaphorically by a range of scholarly and popular authors including Bill McKibben, Anna Tsing, Bruno Latour, and Naomi Klein. Ecological risk assessment, for example, measures the "impairment" of an ecosystem, and the Environmental Protection Agency (EPA) defines "impairment" as "a detrimental effect on the biological integrity of a water body caused by an impact that prevents attainment of the designated use" (www.epa.gov/tmdl). The EPA tracks these "impaired waterbodies" and the plans to mitigate the pollution that has resulted in impairment. Of particular interest in this example, is the utility of the water as it relates to its identification as "impaired." When a waterbody cannot be used for the purposed intended due to the biological impact of pollution, it is deemed "impaired." Taylor identifies an important connection here as she makes her case for the proposed: "ecological disablement." The waterbody is measured based whether or not it can "attain" its "designated use," a framing familiar to those with disabilities. People are deemed disabled by society because they do not produce capital, or they do not work with the expected efficiency within the economic system. So, too, waters are deemed impaired based on the impact of pollution on their utility.

Taylor certainly recognizes a tension between this vocabulary and the position of disability activism. Comparing impairment to ecological damage could have the effect of enforcing the medical model of disability that views an impairment as something requiring an intervention, a fix, or a cure. Like the campaigns mentioned earlier, arguing that nature is "impaired" could end up feeding the assumption that anything not serving dominant needs must be repaired. Taylor recognizes this danger but finds it a useful frame nonetheless.

Disability justice offers something important to the climate movement because it includes both the material reality of the body and the socio-cultural indexing of that body. In both the disability movement and the movement for environmental justice, the socio-cultural valuation of bodies matters—both for how society responds and cares for different embodiments and how society responds to the ecological distress of particular ecosystems. Just as disability justice interrogates the ways society values and devalues bodies, environmental justice should interrogate the ways society deems ecosystems worthy or unworthy. Which ecosystems are seen as worth treating, restoring, and saving? By whom? Some areas of the planet are given up as sacrificial zones for toxic waste, their land and life abandoned as not worth saving. These places tend to be in the most economically impoverished nations and neighborhoods, the most likely to be populated by Black and Brown peoples. Taylor explains, "Ableist ecologies would have us accept 'sacrifice zones' ('permanently impaired' environments in historical expendable communities) of people and lands and animals as the price to be paid for our modern pleasures" (2021).

The community in southern Tucson was treated as a sacrifice zone. The land, water, and systems that sustain life there were disabled, and people were sickened. But although the human community learned not to drink the water, they did not abandon it. Instead, they continued to advocate for its protection and restoration. Taylor says,

> Although residents . . . often do associate the groundwater with death, the aquifer itself has been treated with care and kinship for more than three decades. Even though south-siders have not drunk from its waters since the mid-1980s, organizers and community members have stuck with it. They have not abandoned it.
>
> (Taylor 2021)

She likens this political-relational model to indigenous ways of knowing and being in relationship with ancestral lands and the animals and non-animal life that reside and flow there:

> Indigenous epistemologies have long understood the environment as kin, or even as an extension of one's body. Native scholars and communities often relate to nature not as separate from human culture, but as family that can be maimed and made ill. For example, when asked how Native people can reclaim relationships to homeland in urban spaces when land or water is too polluted to swim in or eat from, Leanne Simpson, a Michi Saagiig Nishnaabeg scholar, writer, and artist, has this to say: "You do not abandon your mother when she is sick. You do not abandon the land because it is contaminated or encroached upon."
>
> (Taylor 2019)

We must not determine worthiness of bodies—human, non-human, organic, or inorganic—based on utility. Instead, value resides in the kinship, the relationship we have with one another, including the river, the land, and the ecosystems within which we reside.

### *Discussion Questions*

1. How does Taylor's language of "ecological endangerment" help to frame what was done to the aquifer in south Tucson? What other frames can you imagine being used to understand this situation which would highlight different aspects?
2. Do you know of other "sacrifice zones," ecosystems and communities that are commonly accepted to be more polluted than others? Who speaks for and stands up for them?

3. Much of the work trying to motivate change in the climate movement is ultimately about the impact of climate change on the human species. Does shifting the conversation to "disabled ecologies" alter perceptions of non-human life and ecosystems? Does it make it more possible to recognize kinship beyond one species? Does this approach humanize ecosystems in a way that is just another form of anthropocentrism?

## References

Belser, J. W. (2015) "Disability and the Social Politics of 'Natural Disaster': Towards a Jewish Feminist Ethics of Disaster Tales," *Worldviews* 19: 51–68.

Betcher, S. (2014) *Spirit and the Obligation of Social Flesh: A Secular Theology for the Global City*. New York: Fordham University Press.

Clare, E. (2015) *Exile and Pride: Disability, Queerness, and Liberation*. Durham: Duke University Press.

———. (2017) *Brilliant Imperfection: Grappling with Cure*. Durham: Duke University Press.

Eiesland, N. (1994) *The Disabled God: Toward a Liberatory Theology of Disability*. Nashville: Abingdon Press.

Kafer, A. (2017) "Bodies of Nature: The Environmental Politics of Disability," in S. Jaquette Ray and J. Sibara (eds) *Disability Studies and the Environmental Humanities: Toward an Eco-Crip Theory*. Lincoln: University of Nebraska Press.

Reyes, R. (2021) "Beyond the Prophetic Temptation of Ecological Disgust," in M. A. De La Torre (ed) *Gonna Trouble the Water: Ecojustice, Water, and Environmental Racism*. Cleveland, OH: Pilgrim Press.

Taylor, S. (2019) "Disabled Ecologies: Living with Impaired Landscapes," talk given at University of Berkley March, Transcript, https://belonging.berkeley.edu/video-sunaura-taylor-disabled-ecologies-living-impaired-landscapes (accessed September 22, 2022).

———. (2021) "Age of Disability: On Living Well With Impaired Landscapes," *Orion Magazine*, Winter, November 9, p. 202, https://orionmagazine.org/article/age-of-disability/ (accessed September 22, 2022).

## Further Reading

Betcher, S. (2015) "The Picture of Health: 'Nature' at the Intersection of Disability, Religion and Ecology," *Worldviews* 19: 9–33.

Butler, L., Wolf-Fordham, S., and Rehr, R. (2022) "Building a More Inclusive Climate Movement: Climate Change and Disabilities," *Journal of Environmental Health* 84(9): 34–6.

Ray, S. J. (2013) *The Ecological Other: Environmental Exclusion in American Culture*. Tucson: University of Arizona Press.

# 10 Privilege and Power

*Laura M. Hartman and Kevin J. O'Brien*

## Introduction: Defining Privilege

"Membership has its privileges."

This was the slogan of the American Express credit card in the 1990s. In exchange for a membership fee, credit card holders had access to certain rewards. The campaign assumed that a privilege comes from voluntary membership: it's something you might opt into, or buy into, to get perks. Privilege, in this view, is a nicer seat on the airplane or access to a fancy resort. Privileges are not essentials; they are add-ons and luxuries.

Recent movements for justice use the word privilege in a very different way. The Movement for Black Lives, for example, emphasizes that "white privilege" means that people who look and are treated as white in the Western world are less likely to be arrested, incarcerated, injured, or killed by government authorities. Privilege here is not a luxury; it is far more basic and essential. White people have the privilege of living in a system that assumes their lives matter and their freedoms deserve protection. In protest, activists argue that safety should not function as a privilege, granted only to some. It should be a right, freely and fully belonging to all.

In this chapter, we use the term "privilege" in both senses: privilege includes luxuries, and it includes basic rights. We draw our definition from Ijeoma Oluo: "Privilege, in a social justice context, is an advantage or set of advantages that you have that others do not" (2018: 59). Privilege includes the status of not having to pay shipping from an online retailer. It includes having stairways and chairs built with your size, body type, and abilities in mind. It includes being able to vote and having political leaders who are responsive to your input. It includes living in a culture that treats you as though your life matters. All of these are advantages that some people have but others do not, so all are privileges.

Some privileges are earned. If you get extra fries because you work at the restaurant or extra pay for taking on a challenging task at the factory, it is reasonable to say that you deserve it. Other privileges are unearned. It is hard to say that anyone deserves to be treated with deference or trust because of their gender, sexuality, race, or who their parents are. Such privileges are inherent in identities that are largely not chosen, based on what social scientists call "dominant group membership" (Sanders and Mahalingam 2012: 112). We live in cultures that are not only

DOI: 10.4324/9781003259466-13

unequal—some people have privileges that others do not—but also unjust—some of those privileges are distributed without regard to who deserves them.

As you read this chapter, we hope you will think about the distribution of physical, social, and cultural advantages in your own context and how they came about. We also hope you will think about which privileges seem unjust and which, if any, seem justified. Part of this work also includes self-reflection, ensuring that you are aware of your own privileges. This might be the most important part of studying this topic because, as we will argue in the next section, privilege comes with power and with the responsibility to use that power.

## Recognizing Our Privilege

The classic stories of Buddhism teach that the prince Siddhartha Gautama spent the first decades of his life in a palace separating him from the suffering of the world. Ashvagosha's *Deeds of the Buddha* describes Gautama's early lodgings as "palaces like celestial mansions brought to earth, as white as the clouds of autumn and comfortable in all seasons," in which "the prince spent his time listening to refined music performed by lovely maidens." Eventually, though, he became curious and convinced his charioteer to show him what life was like beyond his palace walls. He was shocked by what he saw, particularly by the signs of sickness, age, and death. For the first time in his life, he saw people suffering. Once he had seen this, Siddhartha's luxurious home "felt as if it were empty," and he realized he was living in a false world. Aware that his privilege was limiting him, Prince Gautama gave it up, left the palaces, and went into the woods to meditate. He later achieved enlightenment and became the Buddha (de Bary 1969: 60–4).

There are many lessons to be drawn from such a story. One is about systems that try to hide people from others' suffering and therefore from apprehending their own privilege. Such systems, the story teaches, are dishonest and limit growth and maturation. Another lesson is that people tend to be unaware of their privilege until they see the world from a new perspective.

Sometimes activist movements and diversity trainings ask people to "check" or "unpack" their privilege. Siddhartha did this by recognizing he lived in a small and shielded world that denied the reality of suffering. The rest of us can do it by examining our identities and memberships and honestly accounting for the advantages they offer. A famous example of this is the influential article "White Privilege: Unpacking the Invisible Knapsack," in which Peggy McIntosh, a white woman, imagined her white privilege as "an invisible package of unearned assets which I can count on cashing in each day, but about which I was 'meant' to remain oblivious." McIntosh articulated twenty-one such privileges in her 1989 essay, and many thinkers have since expanded the list (1989: 10).

The authors of this chapter have significant privileges. We are and appear white, speak English in mid-Atlantic accents, identify as the genders that most people assume when they see us, and are descended from European colonizers. So we have significant advantages in the United States, where we live and have citizenship. We each received extensive education early in life that provided a path to reliable middle-class incomes. Our bodies and minds work in ways that our culture deems "normal" and do not require explanation or accommodations in most settings.

Neither of us has always recognized our privileges. Indeed, when we were young, we were unaware of most of the advantages we enjoyed. In some cases, like Siddhartha, we were prevented from understanding our privilege by the systems around us. Kevin grew up in Atlanta, Georgia in the 1980s and was taught that racism was a thing of the past, that equality had been achieved and white people no longer had unearned advantages. This was not true then, and it is not true now. But he needed to gain perspective by moving away from his hometown and getting to know nonwhite colleagues and friends before he could understand that his racial identity comes with privilege. On a similar note, Laura was raised assuming that gender discrimination was a thing of the past; it was not until college that she read influential essays that convinced her the work of feminism is far from over. We also both suspect that we have other important privileges of which we are still not fully aware, and we continue to work to learn more about the world and other people's experiences.

We want to cautiously suggest that you, reader, are also privileged; you also have advantages not everyone shares. You may not be as privileged as we are, and you may have identities and characteristics that pose real challenges in your cultural context. But perhaps other chapters in this book have helped you to recognize some privilege you enjoy based on your race, ethnicity, gender, sexuality, class, or ability. It is also possible that you have privilege in subtler ways. If you have the right to vote, or a private vehicle, or relatives who would loan you money or offer emotional comfort in a time of need, you have advantages that not everyone shares. The fact that you are reading these words suggests that you benefit at least from an education and enough time to learn from a textbook. These may not feel like privileges, but they are, as evidenced by the fact that those without them often work hard to give their children a chance for them.

It is also possible to suggest that those of us who live in relatively stable climate conditions have something we might call "climate privilege." People who live in floodplains that have filled with water, or forests that have burned, or growing deserts suffer and are often forced to involuntarily seek new homes. Those of us who have not had to move, have not lost relatives to extreme weather, and do not fear multiple seasons each year have advantages that not everyone shares. Unfortunately, the number of people with such privilege is likely to keep shrinking. The IPCC predicts that even the lowest possible levels of warming will "cause unavoidable increases in multiple climate hazards and present multiple risks to ecosystems and humans" (IPCC 2022: 13). Extreme weather will become more widespread and common as average temperatures and sea levels increase.

If you have significant privilege that you have not really thought about before, acknowledging it might stir up emotions. It is normal, for example, to feel angry and defensive. It is also normal to feel skeptical, understandable if your initial response to the preceding paragraphs was to note the areas in which you are not privileged. It is also normal to feel distracted, perhaps by thinking about other people who have more privileges than you. The ways in which you are marginalized are valid and matter enormously. But it is also important to recognize and accept when you have privileges.

> **BOX 10A**
>
> What are two or three areas of your life in which you experience significant privilege, where you have advantages that not everyone shares? When did you become aware of those advantages, and how?

Acknowledging privilege allows us to engage it with curiosity, to recognize things about the world that we have not seen before. If you are descended from colonizers, accepting that fact can help you to begin humbly learning about the cultures and people indigenous to the place where you live. If you have never thought about your literacy as a privilege before, acknowledging it might help you to notice systems around you that would be difficult to navigate if you could not read the dominant language of your area. If the notion of climate privilege is new to you, that is a good reason to read more about climate change (including in the next chapter of this book).

It is also common to feel some level of guilt about privilege, to feel like one has done something wrong. In most cases, though, privilege comes from large systems that existed before we were born. No one chooses their racial or gender identity, and none of us built the cultural, linguistic, and educational systems that shaped our young lives. You did not decide to live in a culture that privileges certain identities, certain kinds of education, and certain types of resources. There is nothing wrong with having been born white, male, heterosexual, neurotypical, traditionally able-bodied, or wealthy. So it is generally not useful to take on individual blame or guilt for privileges.

However, privilege comes with responsibility. Once we understand that we have advantages that others do not, we are responsible for deciding what to do about it. And since privileges are created by and impact systems, a large portion of that responsibility is about working for systemic change.

### Using the Power of Privilege

Anyone who has privilege has power. When privileges are not earned and are not distributed justly, privileged people should use that power to benefit those with fewer advantages.

Your privileges give you agency. This might be direct and obvious. If you are an enfranchised citizen, then you have the power to vote and to shape your nation and your locality. This is power that children, non-citizens, and others do not have. If you are a white person in a place where the police and other civic authorities treat white people with respect, then you have the power to safely monitor the creation and enforcement of laws.

Other forms of power might be subtler or less direct. In places where women are more threatened by aggression and violence from strangers, men gain power by simply not needing to worry while walking down the street alone. In societies where there is subtle discrimination against queer people in the workplace, straight people gain power by simply not spending as much energy protecting their rights or advocating for themselves. In physical structures built with stairs, people with ambulatory legs gain power by being able to travel freely through the most direct routes while others are denied access or forced to use an entrance around the back that leads to an unreliable elevator.

Some ways of using the power inherent in privilege are fairly modest. Cisgendered people can make a point of sharing their pronouns and encourage others to do the same so that the process is normalized and trans people do not feel singled out. Men who tend to have their voices heard in meetings can remain quiet or use their power to amplify and give credit to the voices of others who are less respected. Able-bodied and neurotypical people can use some of the energy and time saved by the structures that work for them to learn about, and advocate for, more inclusive design.

**BOX 10B**

Consider an area where you do not feel advantaged, where others have significantly more privilege than you. What would you like people with those privileges to do with their power? What do you think prevents them from doing so?

Another approach to privilege involves choosing not to use it, in order to change social structures. Rather than simply advocating for good public transit, a person with a car can give up that privilege and choose to support and ride the bus. People with access to a wide range of foods from around the world can choose to eat more locally and lower on the food chain to preserve resources for others and for future generations.

Other ways of surrendering privilege are more radical and can produce more substantial and systemic change. For example, Christian ethicist and Baptist minister Jennifer Harvey argues that white people who understand the evils of racism need to "surrender" their whiteness in order to resist the system of white supremacy. Of course, this does not mean that anyone can choose not to be white. Indeed, Harvey argues that white people have the responsibility to "admit, acknowledge, name, repent, and otherwise own" the privileges that come from their racial identity. But she says that the next step is "endlessly and actively refusing to be white." This means rejecting, working against, challenging, and disrupting the systems that give white people advantages (2014: 190). "Refusing to be white" means resisting rather than enjoying the privileges that come from whiteness. In other words, Harvey asks white people to recognize their privilege and then to surrender it as much as possible by working against the system that created it.

Another example of surrendering privilege was discussed earlier. Siddhartha Gautama, recognizing that life in his palace had cut him off from reality, surrendered his class and economic privilege by giving up his possessions. In most interpretations of this story, surrendering wealth increased Buddha's spiritual understanding and allowed him to inspire and teach others. Many religions have traditions of this kind of voluntary poverty, with prominent monastic orders in Buddhism and Christianity and traditions of renunciation among leaders in some sects of Hinduism and Islam.

Most of these traditions are careful not to valorize or celebrate the poverty that those without privilege are born and forced into. Instead, they lift up the virtue of voluntary renunciation, of declining possessions or luxuries when one has the privilege and the option to do so. Not everyone can or should give up all their possessions, but most everyone can at least learn something from those who do, and those with luxuries can also consider whether the world would be better off if we had less.

It is important to note that in the examples just discussed, privileged people are not asked to use or give up their privilege as an act of charity that only benefits others. Rather, surrendering wealth and working against white supremacy are understood to be good for the privileged person. The Buddha taught that material possessions cannot lead to true happiness, and that at least some people will be happier if they live without wealth. Jennifer Harvey and other antiracist activists teach that white people are limited by white supremacy and will be better off if they struggle against the systems that have given them advantages at the cost of the common good. In these views, surrendering privilege and working against unjust advantages benefit everyone, including the privileged.

## Worldview Privilege

Given this book's focus, it is important to discuss the ways certain ideas, traditions, and faith communities are privileged. We call this "worldview privilege," which refers to advantages given to any system of ideas that explain the world or to those who ascribe to a certain worldview.

This kind of privilege is often explicitly religious. For example, Lutheran Christianity is privileged as a state religion in Denmark, Iceland, and Norway. This provides some material advantages to Lutheran churches and their members. It also gives primacy to Lutheran ideas and practices in public discussions and rituals. In Morocco, Algeria, Libya, and Egypt, Islam is the state religion, which gives Muslim leaders significant political influence and cultural power. All of these countries have diverse populations, with people from different faiths and some people practicing no religion at all, but the ideas and members of certain religions are privileged (Pew Research Center 2017).

Religion can also be privileged in places without state religions. Most European countries and countries that were colonized by Europe are officially secular, but Christianity is frequently still assumed as a cultural norm. Christian holidays structure commonly accepted calendars and Christian practices are broadly accepted.

In these places, Muslims who worship together on Fridays are more likely to need special accommodations at their workplaces than Christians who worship together on Sundays or Saturdays. Hindus and Sikhs who want to celebrate Diwali with friends and neighbors are more likely to need to explain the holiday than Christians who want to celebrate Christmas.

**BOX 10C**

What religious identities (if any) are privileged in the political systems you most actively participate in? If religious beliefs and groups influence politics where you live, do you think that influence is mostly beneficial or harmful? Why?

Worldview privilege is not only about religion, though. Any time a set of assumptions about the world is given power, a worldview is being privileged. And not all worldviews are religious.

Since the Enlightenment, most universities have been designed to privilege a worldview that focuses on rationality and scientific pursuits. This worldview assumes that natural phenomena can be rationally explained, that experiments and models can predict the behavior of systems, and that educating people to think for themselves frees them. These ideas are at the foundation of most universities and do not need to be defended the way ideas based on faith or tradition do. As university professors ourselves, the authors of this chapter embrace this worldview. We believe that communities are healthy when they privilege rational and scientific thinking. But we nevertheless see the importance of naming the worldview and the fact that it is privileged at our institutions.

Another powerful set of assumptions in the contemporary world is market capitalism, which has grown from an economic system into a worldview. Capitalism teaches that human beings are self-interested by nature and that the invisible hand of the market coordinates self-interested actions in ways that benefit everyone. It assumes that the most important relationships between people are economic and that value can be determined by markets. It also assumes that human enterprises are healthiest when they are growing and expanding.

Philosopher David Loy argues that this view of the world should be understood as "the most successful religion of all time, winning more converts more quickly than any previous belief system or value-system in human history" (1997: 276). He argues that most people in the capitalist system assume that its ideas are true, that they privilege these ideas and the people who align themselves to them. While we prefer the broader term "worldview" to what Loy calls "religion," we agree with him that capitalism has become a belief system widely accepted and rarely questioned.

Imagine, for example, going to a city council meeting and hearing an argument about what to do with a local forest. One person, influenced by the worldview of capitalism, argues that the land should be sold to a builder to provide revenue and economic development. Another, influenced by a different worldview, argues that the trees have inherent value and should be left undisturbed no matter how much money it costs. In most places, the first voice would be judged as logical and practical, while the second (although logical and practical to the person espousing it) would seem revolutionary and idealist. This suggests that the capitalist worldview is privileged.

The first task of understanding the privilege of any worldview is to recognize it. Do you live in a community that embraces the worldview of capitalism? Is it assumed that rich people should have power, that success can be measured in wealth, and that economic growth is a necessary good? If so, it is worth naming the fact that the worldview of capitalism is being privileged.

**BOX 10D**

Among communities you are involved in, which ones seem to privilege market capitalism and the beliefs listed in this section? What communities privilege other worldviews over capitalism?

The next step is to consider what should be done about this privilege. After recognizing that one lives in a culture that values market capitalism, one might dedicate time to succeeding within it. This means training for a well-paying job, budgeting carefully, and achieving economic wealth. In the worldview of capitalism, wealth is power. Such power can allow one to help the poor, protect the environment, defend democracy, or engage in any other project deemed worthwhile. This is the path of Andrew Carnegie, Dolly Parton, the effective altruism movement, and many others who have pursued the privileges of market capitalism and tried to use their wealth to benefit the world.

An alternative approach is to work against the privilege of capitalism, to rebel against the system. Some have done so by publicly surrendering their wealth. The Catholic saint Francis of Assisi famously renounced his merchant father before beginning his religious ministry in the 12th century. A more contemporary example is the organization Resource Generation, which organizes young people who inherit wealth to give away some or all of what they have with the explicitly anticapitalist goal of "equitable distribution of wealth, land, and power" (https://resourcegeneration.org). This represents a surrendering of capital in the hopes of diminishing its power, moving toward a world that privileges wealth and market capitalist ideas less.

It is vital to understand which worldviews are privileged in any given community, to name the big ideas that are assumed to be true and "common sense," and to understand how this came to be. It is also important to know that other worldviews *could* be privileged. Many human societies throughout history have not prioritized market economics as the best or only way to understand people and relationships. Universities can be structured to privilege faith over science. Capitalism and rationality enjoy privilege in our contemporary contexts, but whether they should continue to do so is a question that requires careful thought.

## Environmental Privilege

In a book about the environment, it is also important to consider environmental privileges. If you can easily access clean water and healthy food, if you live near parks, and/or if you can easily travel to see and enjoy wild animals, you have advantages that not everyone shares.

The reality of environmental injustice (which you can read more about in Chapter 15) reveals that benefits and burdens are not fairly distributed. Human social inequalities manifest in the environments where we live. From Cancer Alley on the Gulf Coast to climate refugees fleeing rising seas, those who are disadvantaged in other areas of life also tend to suffer heavier burdens from environmental degradation. Conversely, those who benefit from despoiling the land are more likely to live far away from the impacts of these destructive practices. This is environmental privilege.

Some have argued that environmentalism itself is inherently privileged, that those who are struggling to put food on the table while working low-paying jobs do not have time or energy to worry about preserving a threatened forest in some wilderness. There's truth to this sentiment, but only if we define environmental concern in terms of faraway wild places. Marginalized people may not always have the ability to visit a national park, but they also cannot ignore imminent threats to their lives in the form of air pollution, toxic exposure, wildfires, hurricanes, and other environmental effects. Some marginalized communities live in places that are treated as "wilderness," and have to defend their right to remain in and a part of the ecosystems there.

Having the option to *not* be concerned with environmental issues is a sign of privilege. The privileged can buy air conditioners when temperatures rise, eat organic food when mainstream agriculture uses too many harmful chemicals, or move to a new home when pollution increases. The privileged live in systems that assume they own and have the right to the places where they live.

Denying the reality and gravity of climate change may be the pinnacle of environmental privilege. To say that global warming is not a significant problem as extreme weather events increase is to rely on one's advantages to stay safe as others are threatened. We can only believe that climate change is someone else's problem and that we will be safe if we live in systems that shelter us from the consequences of environmental degradation.

It is also an expression of privilege to say that climate change is so serious and so catastrophic that nothing can be done. Such a statement refuses to acknowledge that people have ways of fighting back against climate disruption and ways of helping those displaced and threatened by it. Those who attest to despair over climate change often believe, deep down, that their privilege will protect them. Mary Anaïse Heglar writes that "doomer dudes" in the climate sphere are "almost always white men because only white men can afford to be lazy enough to quit . . . *on themselves*" (Heglar 2019). Lives hang in the balance with every fraction of a degree warmer or cooler; to give up or to say it is too late is to renounce responsibility and to retreat into privilege.

Worldview privilege is at play in environmental privilege as well. For example, consider the phenomenon of car culture: an assumption, particularly widespread in North America, that car usage is a prerequisite to participation in society. This worldview is manifested in highway and city plans that are made to promote cars at the expense of other modes of transportation.

Cars, even electric ones, have a high environmental cost. They require considerable resources and release substantial greenhouse gasses. The assumption that spaces should be built to make driving easier creates urban and suburban sprawl, gobbling up green spaces and paving over the good earth. In the United States, cars kill thirty thousand to forty thousand people per year and untold millions of animals, but we barely even register the carnage because we assume that the costs of car travel are "normal" and "inevitable."

It can be a struggle to think outside of the worldview of car ownership. For many people in North America, it just seems normal to hop in a car any time you want to go somewhere or to value your sixteenth birthday (getting a driver's license) more than your eighteenth (getting to vote). Those who seek a shift away from cars—transit, bike, and pedestrian advocates—are widely dismissed or marginalized. The built environment of most North American cities (as well as many other parts of the world) now requires the use of a car to get around efficiently and safely; the car-centric worldview has literally shaped the streets and neighborhoods around us. Adhering to the worldview of car culture blinds people to the privileges it confers on some users (those who have cars and can drive) and robs from others (those who do not or cannot). Car culture also blinds us to other possibilities, to the fact that most people in the world today and most people for all of human history have gotten around just fine without cars.

As the example of car culture reveals, privilege plays out in the environmental sphere in multiple ways. Recognizing it and analyzing it are prerequisites to doing something about it—working together to use whatever privileges we have in pursuit of a better and more just world.

## Responsibility and Community

In summary, privilege is real; we live in systems that give some people advantages over others. Privilege can shelter privileged people from reality, like Siddhartha in his palace. Privilege is frequently unjust because advantages are not all distributed equally or according to desert. And yet privilege comes with power because those given advantages have the capacity to resist or change the systems in which we all live.

Almost everyone has privilege in some areas of their lives, and this chapter has suggested that this entails responsibility. The first responsibility is to admit it. People who refuse to see their own privileges are frustrating at best, and can frequently be dangerous to those who do not share their status. It is important, therefore, to become aware of our privileges.

Such awareness allows us to consider how we can constructively use or surrender our privilege. It also helps us to realize that we are part of and related to a larger community. White people who are unaware of their racial privilege can rarely form meaningful and deep relationships with people of color because they fail to recognize the different ways people of color have to function in public spaces. Men who do not notice their gendered privilege tend to also not notice the struggles of the women and non-binary people they know. Recognizing privilege makes it possible to learn from and be part of a wider community.

> **BOX 10E**
>
> Are there people who do not share your privileges and identities who you would like to better understand? What keeps you from getting to know such people or from learning about them?

People with cars who recognize this as a privilege can make the decision to sometimes forego it and take public transportation. In doing so, they will meet people they would not otherwise encounter and get to know aspects of their town or city they had never seen before. This makes them better equipped as voters, drivers, and citizens.

People whose belief system is privileged in their communities—such as Christians at a Christian school and capitalists in a capitalist society—can recognize that not everyone around them shares their ideas and can work to become more open and aware. They can ask better questions about how others understand the world and can expand their own understanding of what is and what could be. This may not lead to fundamental changes in anyone's worldview, but it certainly creates the possibility of more genuine communication.

No one has so much privilege and power that they could solve all the world's problems. So no one is responsible for doing that by themselves. But everyone who has privilege is responsible for recognizing what they have and using or surrendering it in a constructive way. The larger our communities are, the more people with whom we can be in conversation about the world and the systems that shape our privileges. The more people we are in conversation with, the more we understand. Honest, humble awareness of privilege makes community more possible.

## Case Study

Have you ever been called, or called someone else, a "tree hugger"?

The history of this term is worth understanding. It begins in India in the late 1400s, a time of increasing population, severe drought, and concomitant environmental degradation. In Rajasthan, a semi-arid area of northwestern India, Guru Jambhesvara arose as a spiritual leader with religious practices that drew on both Hinduism and Islam. He had a close relationship to the environment, digging wells, constructing reservoirs, and planting tens of thousands of trees (Chapple 2011: 340). For centuries since, the Bishnoi tradition he founded has included twenty-nine spiritual rules, of which "eight are about conserving and protecting the animals and trees" (339–40).

In 1730, a crisis arose in Bishnoi territory.

> The ruler of Jodhpur, Maharaj Abhay Singh, ordered the cutting of khejari trees in Khejadali, a nearby Bishnoi village. Amrita Devi, a local woman, noticed this violation of the Bishnoi code, and asked them to stop. When the woodsmen refused, she hugged the trees. The men carried on with their work and cut her down as well, killing her and eventually 362 other villagers.
>
> (Chapple 2011: 340)

These 18th-century "tree huggers" put their bodies on the line in an effort to save the trees, and in doing so they created a legacy of protest.

In the 1970s, inspired partly by the Bishnoi martyrs, another movement arose in Uttarakhand, in the north of India among the forested slopes of the Himalayan Mountains. They named their movement "Chipko," which means "to embrace," and they used their bodies to protest logging and the destruction of their forests. The primary organizers behind Chipko were women who lived in small villages and appreciated the value of the forests as sources of clean water, forage, and fodder. Through their activism, they sought to convince powerful economic and political forces to preserve rather than harvest the trees (Shiva and Bandyopadhyay 1986). They challenged the worldview that suggested profit was more important than the integrity of the forest environment and the communities living within it.

Vandana Shiva, an influential activist and environmental thinker, is originally from Uttarakhand. In the 1970s, she was a graduate student in Canada, but she spent summers and breaks helping the nascent Chipko movement in her area. The frontline activists knew more than Shiva about the forests. But, Shiva writes, she had "training in two languages . . . of domination": English and science. She used the privileges that came from her education to help the Chipko movement ban logging by publishing English-language reports full of data that helped convince powerful people of the truths that frontline communities already knew (Mauro and Shiva 2013). Ultimately, they were successful thanks to the hard work of both frontline activists and influential scholars and leaders.

Another example of hugging trees comes from the practice of tree sitting, in which activists climb into a tree and stay there in shelters so high that they would die if the tree was cut down. Probably the most famous tree sitter is Julia Butterfly Hill, who in the 1990s spent 738 days living in Luna, a 1,500-year-old California redwood tree. She came down only when the Pacific Lumber Company agreed to protect the tree and its surrounding area.

Hill, an educated and charismatic young white woman, was supported by an extensive community, many from the organization Earth First!. They saw to it that she had food, water, supplies, and ample opportunities to broadcast her message of forest conservation. While living in Luna, Hill undertook multiple photoshoots and interviews and even delivered speeches by cell phone. Her experience in the tree was extremely challenging, but it was made easier by the many privileges she enjoyed. She surrendered the privilege of living a "normal" life on the ground in order to leverage various social privileges—her identities, her charisma, her support network—to amplify her message (Hill 2000). Her strategic use of privileges, both deployed and sacrificed, allowed her to speak for the trees.

The 18th-century Bishnoi martyrs did not have similar privileges, and they were unsuccessful in their attempt to protect their forest. However, their sacrifice had extensive effects on the environmental worldview of northwest India, where activists still cite their example and the sacredness of the forests. Scholar Christopher Chapple notes that, to this day, the areas of India that have been, and still are, occupied by members of the Bishnoi community show greater biodiversity of animals and trees than other regions (2011: 340–1).

### *Discussion Questions*

1. What privileges are most central in the Bishnoi martyr example? In the Chipko case? In Julia Butterfly Hill's tree sit?
2. Based on Vandana Shiva's example, could you use your education to help people who are struggling to preserve their environment? What other privileges could you use?
3. What limits do you see in the work of Julia Butterfly Hill and Vandana Shiva? How might someone critique their efforts or find flaws in their approaches?
4. Have you ever considered sacrificing a privilege for an environmental cause? What would you be willing to give up and under what circumstances?

## References

Chapple, C. (2011) "Religious Environmentalism: Thomas Berry, the Bishnoi, and Satish Kumar," *Dialog: A Journal of Theology* 50(4): 336–43.

De Bary, W. (1969) *The Buddhist Tradition: In India, China, and Japan*. New York: Knopf.

Harvey, J. (2014) *Dear White Christians: For Those Still Longing for Racial Reconciliation*. Grand Rapids: Eerdmans.

Heglar, M. A. (2019) "Home Is Always Worth It," *Medium*, https://medium.com/@maryheglar/home-is-always-worth-it-d2821634dcd9

Hill, J. B. (2000) *The Legacy of Luna*. San Francisco: Harper.

Intergovernmental Panel on Climate Change (IPCC). (2022) "Summary for Policymakers," in *Climate Change 2022: Impacts, Adaptation, and Vulnerability*. New York: Cambridge University Press.

Loy, D. (1997) "The Religion of the Market," *Journal of the American Academy of Religion* 65(2): 275–90.

Mauro, I., and Shiva, V. (2013) "A Conversation with Vandana Shiva—Question 3—Treehugging and the Chipko Movement," *YouTube*, www.youtube.com/watch?v=i3EDEqr7haU

McIntosh, P. (1989) "White Privilege: Unpacking the Invisible Knapsack," *Peace and Freedom Magazine*, July–August, pp. 10–12.

Oluo, I. (2018) *So You Want to Talk About Race*. New York: Seal Press.

Pew Research Center. (2017) "Many Countries Favor Specific Religions, Officially or Unofficially," www.pewresearch.org/religion/2017/10/03/many-countries-favor-specific-religions-officially-or-unofficially/ (accessed June 28, 2022).

Sanders, M., and Mahalingam, R. (2012) "Under the Radar: The Role of Invisible Discourse in Understanding Class-Based Privilege," *Journal of Social Issues* 112–27.
Shiva, V., and Bandyopadhyay, J. (1986) "The Evolution, Structure, and Impact of the Chipko Movement," *Mountain Research and Development* 6(2): 133–42.

## For Further Reading

Belser, J. W. (2013) "Privilege and Disaster: Toward a Jewish Feminist Ethics of Climate Silence and Environmental Unknowing," *Journal of the Society of Christian Ethics* 34(1): 83–101.
Daly, H., and Cobb, J. Jr. (1994) *For the Common Good: Redirecting the Economy Toward Community, the Environment, and a Sustainable Future*. Boston: Beacon Press.
Moe-Lobeda, C. (2016) "Climate Change as Climate Debt: Forging a Just Future," *Journal of the Society of Christian Ethics* 36(1): 27–49.
Powers, R. (2018) *The Overstory: A Novel*. New York: W.W. Norton & Co.
Williams, J. (2021) *Climate Change is Racist: Race, Privilege, and the Struggle for Climate Justice*. London: Icon Books.

# Part III

# Issues

# 11 Climate Change

*Laurel Kearns*

The opening ceremony of the 2016 Olympics took tens of millions of viewers by surprise when it included a segment on global warming in the opening video montage. Sobering animated graphs showed how each year is getting hotter and sea levels are rising. This was quite a departure from the usual Olympic opening ceremony focused on celebrating the history and culture of the host nation; that was certainly there, but it was also about the future of Brazil and every other nation on the planet. It demonstrated the urgent need to get citizens across the globe to recognize the threats of climate change and to embrace the changes needed to slow down the rise in the average temperature on earth. Amid the global goodwill, international cooperation, and comradery of the Olympics, Brazil reminded everyone that the same was needed to fight climate change. And yet, by 2018, Brazil had elected an anti-environmental president, and so had the US. Aware of such complexity and continuing changes in how climate change is culturally understood, this chapter explores the diversity of religious responses to it.

Global warming, climate change, global weather weirding, planetary ecosystem shift—even how to name it could be debated. If one says global warming—an accurate description of the year after year of record higher average temperatures—skeptics and deniers point to unusually cold winters in an attempt to dismiss the rest of the evidence. Hence, many use the term "climate change," indicating that what we are seeing is changing weather systems and climatic instability: increased heat, warming oceans, rising water levels, and increasing desertification. All result from higher amounts of greenhouse gas—including carbon dioxide ($CO_2$), nitrous oxide, and methane—that trap heat in the atmosphere. Simply put, these gases are affecting the planet's temperature regulation. But the phrase climate change is also preferred by skeptics and deniers who argue that, because the earth's climate is always changing, contemporary examples are not necessarily anthropogenic or human-caused. Other leaders sometimes use phrases like "global weather weirding" or "global scorching" to remind people of the unpredictability of the phenomenon, which includes severe flooding in some places and temperatures soaring above 54°C (130°F) in others. Many now talk about the climate crisis, climate emergency, climate catastrophe, and climate justice.

DOI: 10.4324/9781003259466-15

Whatever the term, over 99% of peer-reviewed scientific publications on the subject agree that human-induced climate change is real and already happening across the world (Lynas et al. 2021). How global leaders and citizens respond to the climate crisis will determine how much the average global temperature rises in the future. Yet despite the large degree of scientific consensus on anthropogenic climate change, the existence and urgency of climate change are still debated and challenged in some countries, in some political parties, and in some religious groups. This is partly due to a failure to understand many facets of the issue, it is partly due to ideological and material interests, and it is partly due to a widespread desire to avoid thinking or talking about the issue at all.

There is no easy way to approach the topic of climate change; it is too large and too potentially catastrophic. Ethicist Daniel McGuire, however, puts it bluntly: "If present trends continue, we won't." Nor will many species. Religious ethicists ask "Who dies first? Who is sacrificed first?" and answer with troubling trends at the intersections of race, class, indigeneity, gender, and disabilities. We are already seeing structural inequalities in the ways global climate refugees are treated.

Almost daily, news headlines mention some new aspect of climate-related planetary change: ice melting, coral bleaching, monstrous storms, floods, drought, fires, and natural disasters around the globe. As of this writing, 2020 and 2016 have tied as the hottest years since global average temperatures began to be recorded, and most observers predict even hotter weather very soon. In many locales across the globe, 2023 was a year of record temperatures and record flooding. It may be tempting to sink into denial, disbelief, or despair, to dismiss the issue as too big or too out in the future. But such inattention and inaction only make matters worse.

So protesters frequently gather in national capitals, at United Nations (UN) summits, and at the headquarters of fossil fuel companies. Perhaps the biggest global protest involved over a million around the globe on September 21, 2014, the eve of the opening of the UN Summit on Climate Change in New York City. Between three hundred thousand to four hundred thousand people marched in New York, the worldwide total was closer to a million. Representatives of indigenous communities marched in front, followed by members of other "frontline" communities who will be impacted first and worst by climate change. They were joined by unions and profession-based groups, NGOs, students, faith groups, environmental organizations, and so on (Harper 2016). The marchers were a vibrant display of human diversity—young and old of all races, ethnicities, identities, religions, and geographical locales—and included some who marched as representatives of the more-than-human world.

Spurred on by such protests, after more than two decades of attempts, the members of the UN agreed to a global climate accord two years later in Paris. Although few countries have fully met their commitments since, and although commitments to aid poorer countries seeking to adapt to a changing world are the most neglected, as of this writing the Paris Accords still forms the basis of ongoing global negotiations.

Climate politics and climate protests are influenced by and include faith traditions and many people motivated by religion or spirituality. For example, consider the influential Standing Rock protests of 2016, in which the Lakota and Dakota people of the area sought to protect their sacred lands and waters from the Dakota Access Pipeline. They were supported by clergy from a range of religions, along with representatives from over 200 other indigenous groups, activists from other movements, and thousands of military veterans to protest the pipeline. After a lengthy stand-off, the protesters were forcibly and often violently removed by police and the pipeline was built. However, the actions and witness of the Water Protectors and their supporters raised global awareness about the risks that fossil fuel development poses to Indigenous rights, human health, ecosystems, and social justice. This inspired many other protests to keep fossil fuels in the ground.

Divestment is another strategy. On college campuses and outside corporate board meetings and banks across the globe, people have organized to stop endowments from supporting the extraction of fossil fuels. Over $40.5 trillion by over 1550 institutions have been divested (divestmentdatabase.org). Here, too, religion plays an important role: as of January 2023, over 549 faith-based institutions have divested from fossil fuels (Stand.Earth 2021).

Other protests include efforts to stop mountaintop mining for coal, end drilling for oil/petroleum, outlaw fracking for gas and oil, and block transportation of these fuels. Young people across the world joined Greta Thunberg's protests starting in 2018, and many continue to strike from school to advocate for political action or organize large scale Fridays for Future Youth Climate Strikes. Still others work at changing the source and consumption of food and energy on campuses because of their significant climate emissions impact, with Meatless Mondays and Trayless Tuesdays and commitments to support renewable energy and vegan, organic, and locally or ethically produced food or to avoid palm oil.

**BOX 11A**

What responses to climate change are you aware of? Within your own community, can you think of ways to cut down on the burning of fossil fuels and other activities that lead to the emitting of carbon dioxide, methane, and nitrous oxide, the three biggest culprits?

### What Exactly Is Anthropocentric Global Warming?

Scientific evidence is clear: average global temperatures have risen significantly as the result of human-produced greenhouse gases which remain in the atmosphere and trap more of the sun's heat on the planet. Although some greenhouse gases such as carbon dioxide and methane occur naturally, industrial human activity significantly increases their concentration enough to have a measurable and growing impact on the climate. The production and emission of these gases have skyrocketed with increased industrialization, and so pre-existing carbon sinks—soil, plants, oceans—cannot keep up. And in a feedback loop, higher temperatures and fires mean that more plants die and release $CO_{2,}$ while warmer water absorbs less $CO_2$.

Higher temperatures have many impacts. The Arctic and Antarctic ice sheets and glaciers around the world are melting at higher rates, which results in rising sea levels, decreased heat reflection, and changed patterns of seasonal water flows. The increased water vapor in some areas and desertification in others shifts and stalls weather patterns that were once far more predictable. This often results in increased drought, alarming and prolonged heat waves and huge wildfires, as well as extreme storms and precipitation. The frequency and severity of such events is increasing. As climate scientist Katharine Hayhoe puts it, "climate change is supersizing many of our weather events, making them stronger, longer, and more damaging. It's loading our weather dice against us" (Hayhoe 2021: 99). While some use particular events, like an unexpected snowstorm, to argue against the trend, Hayhoe also offers an emphatic reminder: "weather is not climate." She describes the difference by relating climate—the global overall pattern—to a forest, while any particular weather event, which are more local and momentary, is just a single tree (Hayhoe n.d.).

Climate change is not a singular event, it does not occur over just one year, and indeed, the weather pattern of any single year is not the focus. Rather, climate change is the cumulative effect of emissions that have steadily increased since the Industrial Revolution. This has resulted in a hockey stick pattern—a relatively flat slope that begins to rise and shoots exponentially upward over the last century—on a myriad of graphs depicting rising temperatures, glacial melting, ocean acidification, and emissions. We can also see changes in the rate that the permafrost is thawing, spring plant bloom dates, shifting animal habitat and migratory patterns, coral bleaching, and the spread of insect-borne diseases into areas that no longer have long enough, or cold enough, winters to keep mosquitoes or ticks from thriving.

## The Role of Ideas

If the science of climate change is so clear and the threat so great, why has there been so much hesitation, indeed opposition, in so many places to take the problem seriously and develop responses? The answers help to reveal the importance of philosophical and religious studies for any discussion of climate because hesitation comes in part from the ways people act on beliefs and ideas rooted in religious systems and are best understood by the kind of study of ideas and practices that defines religious studies. Resistance to climate action can be traced to political and economic ideologies that have been constructed and reinforced by religious worldviews and affiliations.

### *Misinterpreting the Precautionary Principle*

It has taken a lot of time and effort to convince religious and political leaders that climate change is real and happening. Although some organizations like the World Council of Churches were quick to address it when the issue became increasingly clear in the late 1980s, many others still remain unconvinced that immediate and comprehensive action must be taken. Despite an overwhelming scientific consensus, well-funded and well-organized global campaigns have encouraged delays.

For instance, beginning in the late 1970s scientists for the oil giant Exxon knew of the connection between fossil fuels and global warming, but Exxon nevertheless used marketing and influence to sow doubt and fund denial efforts. The same tactics were used by other fossil fuel and extractive corporations.

At the core of these arguments was generally a suggestion that nothing should be done about climate change as long as there are any doubts about the trends and the implications of proposed solutions. This echoes the famous playbook of the tobacco industry, which also found that casting doubt on the science, even if about small details, was enough to stymie action for decades (Oreskes and Conway 2011).

Those arguments for delay are one interpretation of the precautionary principle, which says action should not be taken when science is uncertain. This principle has been popular among environmentalists who sought to slow the production or distribution of potentially toxic chemicals, insisting that in the absence of certainty about the health impacts of new products, they should not be released. Climate skeptics applied that principle in a new way, arguing that human actions—in this case the burning of fossil fuels and other activities that release climate-changing gases—should not be halted without absolute certainty of the implications and impacts.

But delay is costly. Not doing anything to slow climate change means continuing actions and decisions that exacerbate warming and extreme weather events far into the future. In other words, delaying action on climate change is the opposite of the precautionary principle's intention to prevent harm. On the other hand, cutting greenhouse emissions not only contributes to a more stable climate but also decreases air pollution, reducing harm to both current and future generations of humans and animals. So some climate activists suggest that the precautionary principle should be applied to the extraction of fossil fuels, which should not be allowed because it cannot be proven to be safe.

### *Flight, Fright, or Fight*

The complex results of planetary warming are hard to fathom. The global dimension of climate change and its relatively slow unfolding make it hard to feel the urgency that many activists believe is necessary.

As humans evolved, we depended on a fright, flight, or fight response. We are hard-wired, so to speak, to respond to immediate threats that require extraordinary responses. So a flood in our home inspires immediate action. But the knowledge that floods will become more likely for people in other places and times is less likely to stir an emotional response. So, many people agree intellectually that climate change matters but still do not feel it an immediate enough threat to inspire any kind of action. Polls show that the majority of people think climate change will affect others or future generations but not themselves (Leiserowitz et al. 2022). And perhaps as a result, they are reluctant to talk about it with others.

But the threat of climate change is immediate, it is already happening. Reminders of this can be found in low-lying islands around the world, in drought-stricken and expanding deserts, in forests devastated by growing wildfires. We are already seeing climate refugees forced from coastal areas because of rising sea levels, while others flee years of drought or the salinization of lands due to powerful hurricane/cyclone driven waters. These immediate threats demand an immediate response to the global problem of climate change, but even the political leaders who care about the issue tend to focus more on rescue and recovery rather than preparing for the extreme events, or preventing the harm in the first place.

**BOX 11B**

How are various aspects of climate change affecting your community? Do you ever talk about it with others? Does it seem like an immediate problem where you live? If so, what are people/institutions doing? If not, what do you think it would take to make it so? What do you think it would take to convince more people to react with urgency?

***"You Go First"***

In a complicated geopolitical context, it is also challenging to determine which nations and who within each country should be the most responsible to do something about climate change and pay for it. For example, powerful people in the US have argued that unless China, Russia, India, and other large nations agree to halt or slow their emissions, the US should not have to make any economic sacrifices. This neglects the fact that droughts and floods and food production are already heavily impacting economies around the world, including in the US. Other countries argue the same thing about their own economies and frequently point out that since the US is responsible for a disproportionate amount of past and present emissions, no one should have to change until the US does. Others point to rapid deforestation in countries like Canada, Brazil, and Indonesia as the "real" root of the problem or pin responsibility on corporate interests rather than nation-states. Further, the carbon footprint of a nation or a corporation or a community is complex; responsibility for greenhouse gases does not always conform to political borders. China's and India's economies, for example, are fueled in part by the production of goods for sale in wealthier countries, where consumers eagerly buy cheaper items (including solar panels) made in places with weaker pollution regulations, labor laws, and enforcement (Ivanova et al. 2015). China's or India's emissions, although they could be regulated and prevented, are thus in part attributable to consumers around the world.

Unfortunately, these complexities lead many to take no action at all. As long as others can be blamed, most countries and corporations and people are unwilling to take responsibility for making needed changes.

However, some countries have been willing to go first, working hard to reduce energy consumption while supporting renewable energy production. Denmark, Germany, Spain, England, Costa Rica, and Singapore, for example, have hit fossil-free milestones by reducing consumption while producing energy in ways that do not contribute as much to climate change. These countries recognize that the continued impacts of a warming climate, mentioned earlier, as well as the harm from fossil fuel spills, leaks, and contaminated ground and waters, have significant economic costs, frequently higher than those of taking action.

### *Jobs and the Economy*

A recurring refrain against action on behalf of the climate has been the fear that anything to help natural ecosystems will inevitably degrade economic systems, negatively impacting markets and cutting jobs. At the first Earth Summit in Rio de Janeiro in 1992, then-President George H. W. Bush named the limit of his willingness to take significant action by saying, "The American way of life is not up for negotiation. Period." (2008). This framing by politicians continues, and in the US, it is often used to imply that environmentalists are un-American.

These arguments, sometimes made by religious leaders, assume both that economic success is an unquestionable good and that responses to climate change are inherently destructive to the health of the economy (Kearns 2011). Some climate activists argue against the second assumption by pointing out that climate action can be consistent with capitalism. They point to extremely successful business people who seem to agree, like the founder of Patagonia Yvon Chouinard, who transferred the $3 billion company to a nonprofit and trust fund dedicated to fighting climate change (Gelles 2022). They cite economists who argue that reasonable responses to climate problems can actually grow the economy and create new opportunities. This thinking informed the most expansive climate action ever taken in the US at the time of this writing, the Inflation Reduction Act of 2022. By putting money into technological development, creating incentives, and seeking to expand renewable energy usage without penalizing fossil fuels, this law seeks to respond to climate change without negative impacts on the economy as a whole or any sector within it.

Other climate activists point out that the continued government subsidizing of fossil fuels prolongs their consumption and impacts. They suggest that the mounting costs of climate change, and the gross injustices of the ways its impacts are currently distributed may require a fundamental restructuring or rethinking of capitalism. This calls into question the first assumption named earlier, that economic growth is always a good thing. Is it possible that, because human economies depend completely on natural ecosystems, there must be limits to economic growth?

## BOX 11C

Public arguments about responses to climate change are often about economics: Many who advocate phasing out fossil fuels and quickly adapting to renewable technologies point out that this will in fact increase jobs, wealth, and production. On the other hand, many who oppose such action do so because they are convinced that increased unemployment/poverty and decreased profits will inevitably follow. Which side of this debate do you favor, and why? What other aspects of the issue need to be considered? What kinds of evidence and/or experts might change your mind?

### *Denial/Disbelief*

Despite overwhelming scientific consensus, some still deny the reality of anthropogenic climate change. In the US, some presidential, gubernatorial, and congressional candidates and politicians still proudly declare that climate change is a lie. When pressed as to how they can dismiss the facts, they cite a few denialists with scientific degrees, despite the fact that those experts are generally not well-respected by other climate scientists, nor are their publications peer-reviewed (Oreskesand Conway 2011). In 2016, the United States elected a president who consistently called climate change a "hoax" and reneged on the US participation in the Paris Climate Accords. The same year, Australia elected a prime minister who dismissed the science on climate change as "absolute crap" and ordered the firing or reassignment of hundreds of government-employed scientists involved in climate research. While both men have, as of this writing, been replaced by leaders who take climate change more seriously, denial of the problem continues and is still supported and influenced by the global political power of the fossil fuel and agribusiness industries (dos Santos and Kearns 2023).

Climate denial is also embraced by conservative elements of the three Abrahamic religious traditions—Judaism, Christianity, and Islam (Alper 2022). Some argue that their omnipotent God would never allow a climate catastrophe and that "belief" in climate change is a heresy against orthodox doctrine. But reducing science to a matter of belief, treating it like theology, is a categorical mistake. For scientists, a theory is not a question of belief but an explanation of observable facts.

### *Competing Issues*

Since the impacts of climate change seem far off or far away to many people, some people do not advocate for or take action because they are focused on other issues: a growing wealth gap, poverty, economic growth, political tensions, racial/ethnic tensions and violence, refugees, growing nationalism and militarism, threats of terrorism, shifting patterns of viruses (such as COVID-19) or insect-borne diseases (such as Zika or West Nile), and weather-related disasters. For example, while most people in the US consistently say they are concerned about climate change and want more action, very few rate it as the most pressing or important issue facing the nation (Pew 2022).

By contrast, faith communities and leaders that take climate change seriously frequently argue that climate change is inseparably linked to other justice issues, noting that the fates of poor, marginalized, and indigenous peoples are particularly interconnected with the global climate, as well as that of future generations. The 2015 papal encyclical *Laudato Si'*: *Care for our Common Home*, in its presentation of "integral ecology," argues that responding to global warming will involve also addressing a host of other societal problems. A 2020 rabbinic letter on the climate crisis calls for governments to "legislate a swift and massive program that intertwines ecological sanity and social justice, as they were intertwined in the biblical practice of Shmita/Sabbatical/Seventh Year." Similar concern for the poor and the harm to those most affected is also found in other religious statements, such as the Islamic, Buddhist, and Hindu Declarations on Global Climate Change (FORE 2022). These statements do not just focus on harm to humans, but each articulates their religious values for caring for the ecosystems and creatures that co-inhabit the planet and are threatened.

## Framing Climate Change

So far, we have discussed various mindsets that may hinder people from grasping the reality and impact of climate change and thus hinder any action. Many scholars and scientists, including Hayhoe (2021), have been hard at work figuring out how to change this and what communications strategies will best move people beyond skepticism or inaction. It is clear that just presenting the science has not persuaded enough citizens and politicians to act (Callison 2013; Marshall 2016; Nisbet 2009). Estimates are that while only 12% of the US population fully denies anthropogenic climate change, only about 33% of Americans frequently talk with others about the issue (Leiserowitz et al. 2022).

Matthew Nisbet's work is particularly helpful for understanding how important it is to consider how the issue of climate change is framed in communications. He explains that "frames are interpretive storylines that set a specific train of thought in motion, communicating why an issue might be a problem, who or what might be responsible for it, and what should be done about it." Frames are an important part of social movement messaging, providing cues and shortcuts that depend on the reader/listener to fill in the blanks and complete the picture. In "Communicating Climate Change: Why Frames Matter for Public Engagement," Nisbet analyzes eight main frames that have been used in science-related policy debates. There are variations within each frame, and frames may be presented in a way that is for, neutral with, or against an issue. For instance, frames that emphasize "Social Progress," "Economic Competitiveness," "Scientific Certainty/Uncertainty," and a "Pandora's Box of Catastrophe" are used by both sides of the climate "debate" (2009).

Of course, even referring to the discussion about climate change as a debate is, itself, a frame. When the existence of climate change is presented as an argument between two legitimate points of view, it may appear that each side is equally worthy of consideration. However, in the case of climate change, this is a false balance—if the "debate" is between climate scientists and skeptics, then one side represents an overwhelming majority of research and the other represents a small and marginal faction. Comedian John Oliver demonstrated this by inviting one hundred scientists to "debate" the topic, with ninety-six joining Bill Nye the Science Guy and two joining the climate skeptic.

Three other frames, "Public Accountability and Governance," "Conflict and Strategy," and a "Middle Way" are also helpful in understanding debates over public policy related to climate change. Just as with the uncertainty frame, the conflict frame can be used to shift attention from the issue to whoever is labelled the "enemy" or opponent. Some form of "middle way" is often a default, but this has meant that incremental changes have not kept up with the rising production of greenhouse gas emissions and, with that, rising temperatures, melting ice, and so on.

**BOX 11D**

Michael Nisbet articulates eight frames for discussions of climate change: "Social Progress," "Economic Competitiveness," "Scientific Certainty/ Uncertainty," "Pandora's Box of Catastrophe," "Public Accountability and Governance," "Conflict and Strategy," "the Middle Way," and "Morality and Justice." In discussions of the issue that you have encountered, which frame(s) has been dominant? How can you tell? Are there other frames, such as concern for "future generations" that you have heard?

Nisbet argues that a "Morality and Justice" frame is needed in scientific debates but is often overlooked because science proclaims itself to be "value-free." An important distinction needs to be made here: scientific data is indeed value-neutral, but values shape what scientists choose to study and how results are then acted upon. This is a clear place where religions enter into discussions of climate change policy. Pope Francis made this point in *Laudato Si'*:

> [W]e have to realize that a true ecological approach always becomes a social approach; it must integrate questions of justice in debates on the environment, so as to hear both the cry of the earth and the cry of the poor.
> (2015: 49)

If justice is valued, then a variety of the biophysical and social sciences should study the disproportionate impacts of climate change on those with the least ability to respond, while politicians across the world should prioritize the actions necessary to curtail changes in the climate and listen to those most hurt by it.

In addition, religious and moral traditions teach that non-human creatures should also be cared for and treated with justice. This is another value that is very relevant to any debate about climate change. Biodiversity scientists tell us that species are going extinct at a rate unknown in geologic history as their habitats disappear or shift due to changing weather patterns.

Religious arguments for action to curb global warming can bring the morality and justice frame that Nisbet advocates to debates that have previously focused on science and economics. Religious traditions help people to think about the bigger picture, a longer time continuum, a scale that goes beyond their individual lives.

Of course, it is also important to note the diversity of religious traditions. Not all religious teachings will fit into any single frame, and there are many religious motivations for climate action on behalf of human beings and other creatures. Building on a study of which frames work across faiths (Marshall 2016), we might consider six religious frames for climate action:

1. **Earth as Gift**: Every religious tradition has an explanation for how the world came to be, the value of that world, and gratitude for the gifts of life, such as air, water, and food. This understanding of gift and gratitude, as well as human responsibility for its care, can be an essential basis for motivating action. The "Islamic Declaration on Global Climate Change" quotes the Qur'an 55:10: "[Allah] laid out the earth for all living creatures" (FORE 2022).
2. **Order, Balance, or Harmony in Nature**: Some traditions recognize a sense of balance in nature, and so caution against human disruptions of such balance. For example, the *Hindu Declaration on Climate Change* states, "Climate change is a stark symptom of the deeper problem of humanity living out of balance with what Bhūmi Devi, our shared planet, can renewably provide" (FORE 2022). The growing understanding of the evolution of the universe is another common source for a cosmology that emphasizes the structure and balance of the universe, in which humanity is understood as one part of a much bigger cosmos (Swimme and Tucker 2014).
3. **Immanent Sacred or Divine**: Most religions recognize the awe and deep connection that humans feel with the rest of nature (Faith for Earth 2020). For some, this deep sense of connection is a recognition of the presence of the divine and/or the sacredness of the Earth. Many who feel this deep sense of connection have left institutional forms of religious traditions, while others have worked to demonstrate this recognition of the sacred in their traditions.

   Most indigenous religious traditions emphasize the sacredness of the world around them, as the 2015 *Indigenous Elders and Medicine Peoples Council Statement* to the UN declares, "We recognize our umbilical connection to Mother Earth and understand that she is the source of life, not a resource to be exploited" (FORE 2022). From this perspective, the earth cannot be owned; its integrity must be respected. Many who come from other religious and cultural traditions have embraced these aspects of indigenous traditions and worked to undo the demotion of nature to merely a resource. Such borrowing is not without problems, as it can become cultural appropriation that ignores meaning and context, especially if it does not recognize the injustices inflicted upon indigenous communities.
4. **Care for Others**: Religious ethics can contain strong motivations for individual action that is designed to benefit others: the poor, the neighbor, the stranger, future generations, all creatures. This frame recognizes that global warming is a moral challenge and that individuals cannot sit back and wait for someone else to act first. Instead, people must recognize how their actions add up to collective impact. In some traditions, this perspective is cultivated with an attention to the "common good" or as Pope Francis' 2015 papal encyclical *Laudato Si'* puts it, "Care for our Common Home" (FORE 2022). The 2015 *The Time to Act is Now: A Buddhist Declaration on Climate Change* reminds practitioners "that we are

violating the first precept—'do not harm living beings'—on the largest possible scale" (FORE 2022).

5. **Sin and Karma**: Part of the motivation to act can come from the recognition that climate change and the failure to act to stop it align with traditional religious understandings of bad behavior, whether these are understood through the lens of sin, karma, or conscience. The Ecumenical Patriarch Bartholomew of Constantinople and the Eastern Orthodox Church summed this up nicely in his 1997 statement: "For human beings . . . to destroy the biological diversity of God's creation; for human beings to degrade the integrity of the earth by causing changes in its climate, by stripping the earth of its natural forests or destroying its wetlands; for human beings to contaminate the earth's waters, its land, its air, and its life—these are sins" (quoted in Francis 2015: 8).
6. **Lament and Hope**: At the same time, recognizing the cumulative impacts of our human actions can easily lead to despair and overwhelming grief. Religions have traditions of responding to these emotions. Laments are ways of expressing feelings that can acknowledge the bad that has been done but also make good futures possible. Many religious traditions and rituals offer ways to think about hope or action, even when things seem bad (Fredericks 2021).

## BOX 11E

Which of these religious frames—gift, order and balance, immanent sacred, care for others, sin and karma, or lament and hope—would most likely motivate you to act? Which one would most likely motivate other members of your family? Could thinking about frames help you to talk to others about the urgency of acting on climate change? Evangelical scientist Katherine Hayhoe (2021) recommends starting by talking about something you have in common.

### The Gap Between Belief and Action

The last two sections focused on ideas, beliefs, and ethics, but everyone knows that it is often easy to point out the disjuncture between beliefs and actions. Members of a faith group may believe the same thing but decide to act on it quite differently. Or they may say they believe one thing and yet act in a contrary or hypocritical way. Thus, in addition to beliefs, it is important to acknowledge the impact of religious actions and actors, whether individuals or institutions, in creating change. Religious people and religious communities impact the climate directly through what they do as well as what they believe.

For example, most religious traditions have ethics of restraint to curb excess consumption, greed, and waste. One aspect of this are dietary codes: some forbid eating certain kinds of meat, or encourage adherents to fast or take special care of certain religious foods. Various Indigenous, Jewish, and Muslim food ethics concern the care and slaughter of animals to be eaten. Many Hindu and Buddhist traditions encourage vegetarianism. When lived out, these teachings reduce the emissions related to food animal production or the way land is used (see the next chapter for more on religious food practices).

Religious institutions can also reduce energy (and more general) consumption or change what kind of electricity they use. For example, many Sikh gudwaras, Hindu ashrams, Buddhist temples, Muslim mosques, Jewish synagogues, and Christian churches have installed solar panels or purchased renewable energy. This frequently inspires individuals to do the same, both inside and outside of their own congregation. In this way, religious groups can act as something that social movement theorists call "movement midwives," providing resources, meeting space, communication channels, moral leadership, strategies of action, and individuals linked into networks that often cross geographic, racial, class and other boundaries.

As institutions, religious groups have enormous resources in the lands and buildings that they own. The archived website for the Alliance for Religions and Conservation contains an impressive list of the ways sacred lands and sacred forests are being preserved for the benefit of indigenous communities, wildlife, and the climate (www.arcworld.org). They estimate that 15% of the planet's land surface is considered sacred by, and is often under the care or trust of, religious groups.

It is not just individuals or religious institutions that need to act to slow down climate change; small businesses, corporations, municipalities, educational, health and legal institutions, nonprofits and governments all play key roles, as they can act in ways that individuals cannot. Whatever future human institutions and communities choose in a world of climate change, religious beliefs will influence how people think about what they are doing, religious frames will shape the ways the discussion is conducted, and religious practitioners and communities will be among the actors shaping the world.

## Case Study

When Nobel Peace Prize recipient Dr. Wangari Maathai (1940–2011) started the Green Belt Movement (GBM) in 1977, she had no idea that it would lead to over fifty-one million trees being planted in her home country of Kenya while inspiring similar efforts around the globe. Maathai, working with the National Council of Women in Kenya, started with a simple idea after listening to rural Kenyan women describe the issues that most affected their lives: lack of firewood, lack of good soil to grow crops, and lack of good water. Maathai realized that these could all be traced back to deforestation and the subsequent soil erosion and drying up of streams (greenbeltmovement.org).

A biologist, Wangari Maathai understood that planting trees would help solve the problems. Women would not have to walk as far for firewood, communally owned trees would be less likely to be chopped down, and the growing trees would help improve the soil and reduce heat and evaporation. She also wanted to empower the women and combat poverty, so her vision was for the women to raise the seedlings collectively and plant trees together, receiving payment for their work. Women in local communities took leadership in the care of the trees and growing new ones, making sure that appropriate tree species were raised and that they collectively cared for and benefitted from the trees' growth. Maathai felt this was important for the continued success of the program, emphasizing that solutions came from within the community rather than from outsiders.

Empowerment helped the women involved in GBM to feel they could address the needs of their communities. It connected their need for clean air, water, and food security with their rights and with the basic respect for civic, political, and human rights needed for a democracy. In all, the movement reports that nine hundred thousand women have been involved. As their work became more prominent, it was also increasingly linked to climate change, as the trees they planted absorbed carbon dioxide and combatted changing weather patterns.

Maathai herself was a model of empowerment. She was the daughter of a tenant farmer, who with his wife believed in girls being educated, which was unusual at the time. Maathai won a scholarship to go to college in the US in 1960, and in 1971, she became the first East African woman to receive a PhD. She went on teach at her alma mater, the University of Nairobi, and by the 1980s, she had become a well-known advocate for both women's rights and the protection of valuable Kenyan lands from development. She was beaten and jailed for opposing the destruction of Uhuru, a valuable park in Nairobi. She was also harassed, threatened, and beaten for her GBM work and her opposition to political corruption. Eventually, she was elected to the Kenyan Parliament in 2002, and served as Assistant Minster of the Environment and Natural Resources before going on to even more global positions.

As she worked with GBM and struggled with the political system, Maathai realized that a change in values was needed. Soon the movement began offering workshops and training called Community Empowerment and Education (CEE) seminars aimed at fostering a sense of agency, responsibility, and mutuality. These workshops helped citizens to demand more accountability from political leaders and helped to ensure the protection of valuable forest lands from illegal land grabs and agricultural encroachment.

In *Replenishing the Earth: Spiritual Values for Healing Ourselves and the World*, Maathai lists the necessary values as (1) "love for the environment" that is shown in one's lifestyle, (2) "gratitude and respect for Earth's resources" or "valuing all that the earth gives us", (3) "self-empowerment and self-betterment" or realizing that "the power to change is within you", and (4) "the spirit of service and voluntarism" or a priority on "doing one's part to achieve the common good" (Maathai 2010: 14–15). These values, she argues, are behind the movement's incredible success. They helped to motivate GBM's *mottainai* campaign, to foster the notions of "reduce, reuse, recycle" in Kenya and around the world to cut down on waste and consumption.

Although at first she did not see these values as religious, Maathai came to understand that they were deeply rooted in her own understanding of both her Christian faith and her Kikiyu heritage. Both traditions taught her that the healing of the earth is not separate from the healing of people and their communities. By linking forest ecosystems, women's empowerment, and global climate change, her movement offered resources and energy to combat desertification and droughts.

Maathai's Green Belt Movement inspired the Billion Tree campaign of the United Nations' Environment Program (UNEP), which was launched in 2006. The billion-tree mark was reached in 2007. A few years later, the UN passed the campaign to a youth-led organization called Plant-for-the Planet. By 2021, almost fourteen billion trees had been planted, and the goal had moved to plant a trillion trees (www.trilliontreecampaign.org). While such action could not possibly make up for all impacts of deforestation and climate change, it is an important effort by people working for a better world. It is a fitting tribute to the first environmentalist and first African woman to win a Nobel Peace Prize (in 2004) because, as Maathai writes, "the little things citizens do. That's what will make the difference. My little thing is planting trees." One person can make a difference, especially if they work with others.

#### *Discussion Questions*

1. The Nobel Committee honored Wangari Maathai with its prize for advancing peace. How do you understand the connections she made between women's empowerment, environmental issues, and politics advancing the cause of peace?
2. In addition to tree planting, what other activities do you think could bring communities together, empowering people while also improving their natural environments?
3. Maathai's work crossed scales. It was local (empowering women to plant trees), national (serving in the Kenyan Parliament and working for policy and legal changes), and international (speaking up for global environmental issues and inspiring a United Nations movement). Which of these scales of action is most available to you personally, and at which level do you strive to work in the future? At which scale do you think climate change most needs to be addressed?

### References


Alper, B. (2022) "How Religion Intersects With Americans' Views on the Environment," *Pew Research Center Online*, www.pewresearch.org/religion/2022/11/17/how-religion-intersects-with-americans-views-on-the-environment/

Bush, G. W. (2008) "President Bush Discusses Climate," https://georgewbush-whitehouse.archives.gov/news/releases/2008/04/20080416-6.html

Callison, C. (2013) *How Climate Change Comes to Matter: The Communal Life of Facts*. Durham, NC: Duke University Press.

dos Santos, R. W., and Kearns, L. (2023) "Trojan Horses Facing the Mirror: A Comparison Between Religious Anti-Environmental Movement Organizations in the US and Brazil," *Journal for the Study of Religion, Nature, and Culture*, forthcoming.

FORE. (2022) "Forum on Religion and Ecology," https://fore.yale.edu/Climate-Change/Climate-Change-Statements-World-Religions/

Fredericks, S. (2021) *Environmental Guilt and Shame: Signals of Individual and Collective Responsibility and the Need for Ritual Responses*. New York: Oxford University Press.

Gelles, D. (2022) "The Climate Philanthropists," *New York Times*, September 16.

Harper, F. (2016) "Snapshot of a Movement on the Move: The Paris Climate Talks and Religious Environmentalism," *Journal of Interreligious Studies* 19: 4–13.

Hayhoe, K. (2021) *Saving Us: A Climate Scientist's Case for Hope and Healing in a Divided World*. New York: One Signal Publishers.

Hayhoe, K. (n.d.) "Global Weirding with Katherine Hayhoe," KTTZ.org, https://www.youtube.com/channel/UCi6RkdaEqgRVKi3AzidF4ow. (accessed June 16, 2023).

Ivanova, D., Stadler, K., Steen-Olsen, K., Wood, R., Vita, G., Tukker, A., and Hertwich, E. (2015) "Environmental Impact Assessment of Household Consumption," *Journal of Industrial Ecology* 20: 526–36.

Kearns, L. (2011) "The Role of Religions in Activism," in J. Dryzek, R. Norgaard, and D. Schlosberg (eds) *The Oxford Handbook on Climate Change and Society*. New York: Oxford University Press, 414–28.

Leiserowitz, A., Maibach, E., Rosenthal, S., Kotcher, J., Carman, J., Neyens, L., Myers, T., Goldberg, M., Campbell, E., Lacroix, K., and Marlon, J. (2022) *Climate Change in the American Mind: April, 2022*. New Haven, CT: Yale Program on Climate Change Communication.

Lynas, M., Houlton, B., and Simon, P. (2021) "Greater Than 99% Consensus on Human Caused Climate Change in the Peer-Reviewed Scientific Literature," *Environmental Research Letters* 16(11).

Maathai, W. (2010) *Replenishing the Earth: Spiritual Values for Healing Ourselves and the World*. New York: Doubleday.

Marshall, G. (2016) "Communicating with Religious Communities on Climate Change: Research Overview and Emergent Narratives," *Journal of Interreligious Studies* 19: 1–10.

Nisbet, M. (2009) "Communicating Climate Change: Why Frames Matter for Public Engagement," *Environment: Science and Policy for Sustainable Development* 51(2): 12–23.

Oreskes, N., and Conway, E. (2011) *Merchants of Doubt: How a Handful of Scientists Obscured the Truth on Issues from Tobacco Smoke to Global Warming*. New York: Bloomsbury Press.

Pew Research Center (2022) "Public's Top Priority for 2022: Strengthening the Nation's Economy," *Few Say Religion Shapes Immigration, Environment Views*, www.pewresearch.org/politics/wp-content/uploads/sites/4/2022/02/PP_2022.02.16_2022-Priorities_FINAL.pdf.

Stand.Earth. (2021) "Divest Invest: A Decade of Progress Towards a Just Climate Future," www.stand.earth/divestinvest2021

Swimme, B., and Tucker, M. E. (2014) *Journey of the Universe*. New Haven: Yale University Press.

United Nations Environment Programme and Parliament of the World's Religions (2020). *Faith for Earth: A Call for Action*. Nairobi: UNEP. https://parliamentofreligions.org/climate-action/faith-for-earth-a-call-for-action/

## Further Reading

Conradie, E. M., and Koster, H. P. (2020) *T & T Clark Handbook of Christian Theology and Climate Change*. New York: T&T Clark.

Jenkins, W., Tucker, M., and Grim, J. (2018) *Routledge Handbook of Religion and Ecology*. London: Routledge Press.

O'Brien, K. (Forthcoming) "Religion and Climate Change" in L. Kearns and W. Bauman (eds) *Religion and Nature in North America: An Introduction*. New York: Bloomsbury.

Rasmussen, L. (2013) *Earth Honoring Faith: Religious Ethics in a New Key*. New York: Oxford University Press.

Veldman, R. G., Szasz, A., and Haluza-DeLay, R. (eds) (2014) *How the World's Religions Are Responding to Climate Change: Social Scientific Investigations*. New York: Routledge.

Yusoff, K. (2018) A *Billion Black Anthropocenes or None*. Minneapolis: University of Minnesota Press.

# 12 Animals

## Community Hope and Community Liberation

*Sarah Withrow King*

### Introduction

I was interviewed once by a Christian radio pseudo-shock-jock who wanted to rake me over the coals for my suggestion that Christians—especially those with access and the ability to choose—should care about where their food comes from.

It was not the first time he had interviewed a vegetarian or vegan on his radio show, and he knew all the gory details of factory farming and slaughterhouses in the US. He recited my own talking points to me: gruesome details about the short lives of misery and mutilation for billions of land animals annually destined for nightmarish industrial slaughter lines, lines that move too quickly to ensure that animals are properly stunned before being boiled, skinned, and dismembered.

The suffering of sentient, God-created beings was worth it, he said, if it made food a little cheaper for hungry children.

Another time, talking face-to-face with folks at a Christian music festival, I shared the statistic with one man and his teenaged son that more than seventy billion land animals were farmed and killed for food each year, along with somewhere between one and three trillion sea creatures. The man looked me dead in the eye and said, "And thank God for that."

These and other similar interactions over twenty years of advocacy work have often left me confused, angry, and disheartened. I know I have high expectations, but I just cannot understand why people who follow Jesus Christ—the enfleshed Creator, who was born to a virgin, performed miracle after miracle, astounded expectations of what a Messiah looked like, and *literally conquered death*—are willing to accept such a myopic view of the possibilities of the world. Shouldn't it be possible to liberate animals *and* feed hungry children? Can we not envision something different for ourselves, some way of being and relating with the world, that does not create, as biblical scholar Ellen Davis aptly describes the US food system, "the most death-dealing meat market the world has ever known" (Davis 2009: 97)?

In my activism, I argue that Christians can not only *envision* such a way of being and relating but that we can also *work toward its realization* through our individual and collective acts. I think communities of faith are particularly well-equipped to

DOI: 10.4324/9781003259466-16

participate in this work of thought and practice. And I think it is essential that we do this work now before the crises of climate change, unchecked greed, and systemic racism push us even deeper into a chasm of violence and spiritual poverty.

Because this book is called *Grounding Religion*, and not *Grounding Christianity*, I want to be sure to point out that I approach conversions about animals through the lens of Christianity, and so this chapter will not adequately wrestle with other faiths' views of animals. Friends and colleagues have done wonderful work in this area, including scholars such as David Aftandilian (Native American studies); Barbara Ambrose (Japanese religions); Geoffrey Barstow (Buddhism); Jonathan Crane, Aaron Gross, and Adrienne Krone (Judaism); Sara Tlili (Islam); and Paul Waldau (religious studies and animals). I also encourage readers to look beyond the academy to learn from those who interact with animals directly, including farmers from a variety of religious backgrounds. Randy and Edith Woodley of Eloheh Indigenous Center for Earth Justice, Hisham Moharram of Good Tree Farm of New Egypt, Leah Penniman and the education team at Soul Fire Farm, Tim Van Meter of Seminary Hill Farm, and Sarah Macias of Sister Grove Farm have all been wonderful dialogue partners or teachers to me over the years.

Even within the realm of Christianity, my experience is particular. Most of my work has been with Protestant, Anabaptist, and Evangelical Christians in the US. My social location also impacts my work. I was raised in the United States in Oregon, with economic stability in a suburban neighborhood, on the edge of farmlands. I am of European descent (mostly English, Scottish, and Irish). I enter and hold this conversation with an enormous amount of privilege (a heterosexual, cisgender, neurotypical, English-speaking, White US citizen with a master's degree). There are privileges I do not carry (I am fat, I am a woman, and I live with mental illness). I work at the intersection of academia and activism but come from activist roots and consider myself an advocate, and not an academic.

Twenty years ago, I viewed animal issues in rigid categories, quick to condemn people who came to different conclusions than I did about what was right and what was wrong. I am no longer sure how helpful that approach is to the animals' cause or to our work as humans. So my hope in this chapter is to invite you into a journey, one I have been on for a long time, and one that continues to lead me to surprising people, places, and perceptions.

## Relationships at the Root

I live in Eugene, Oregon, in the Willamette Valley, on the unceded lands of the Chelamela and Kalapuya tribes. In 2019, "An analysis of federal data found Eugene leads the nation in the number of people experiencing homelessness per capita, ahead of both Los Angeles (No. 2) and New York City (No. 3)" (Adams 2022). Every time I leave my home, I encounter a person who is in acute need. Some of the people in need hold signs which say a variation of "anything helps." Some of the people are lying on grass or sidewalks or in building alcoves. Some of the people are walking, talking to themselves, gesturing wildly with their arms and heads. I help when I can, where I can. But I am often guilty of crossing the street to avoid seeing the suffering up close and personal, following in the footsteps of the Priest and the Levite from the Parable of the Good Samaritan.

I visited a local homeless shelter recently, looking for ways to volunteer, to develop relationships with my unhoused neighbors. At one point, the staff member accompanying me said of the ongoing need for laborers: "Look, we live in Eugene. If we see a dog running around in the street, half the city will stop and try to save it. It's not the same with people."

He is not wrong. I cannot count the number of times I have stopped my car, grabbed the leash and treats I keep on hand for emergencies, and tried to convince a confused or frightened pup to trust me. And I cannot count the number of times I have driven by a human being camped on the side of the road, passed out on a bench, or asking for help by holding up a cardboard sign. "I'm unprepared," "I don't have the skills to help," "It might be dangerous," I tell myself, to justify my moral failure.

But why? Why do I act without hesitation to aid the one, but not the other?

I believe part of the reason is that I have been trained, by my culture and my faith, to treat human beings as individuals who should take care of themselves, and this predisposes me to not help other people in need. A part of me quickly assumes that unhoused people did something to "deserve" their fate or that their plight is none of my business. Either way, in this worldview, it is not my responsibility or my role to fix anything for them. So while I feel instinctively that I can and should help a dog running free, for a very long time, I did not have the same reaction to people.

This individualistic approach to other people comes in part from my Christian background. For many of my young adult years, my religious communities emphasized the importance of a personal relationship with God. My individual salvation, and the salvation of other individuals, was a primary focus. Faithfulness was measured in part by one's ability to maintain a consistent and robust regiment of quiet time in Bible study, journaling, and private worship. When we exited this one-on-one communion and turned our view to the broader world, our energy went to maintaining our own personal purity (of word, thought, and deed) and to bringing others into the same kind of life.

**BOX 12A**

Have you been trained to see the world in the individualistic way just described? Has that approach shaped the way you relate to others, and/or the ways others relate to you?

This heavy focus on individualism aligns with a theological anthropology—the way that people relate to and act amid the whole of God's creations—that has been profoundly influenced by White, Euro-American, and colonial interpretations of the Bible. In this worldview, there is a hierarchy of creation, with (certain kinds of) humans at the top. This hierarchy particularly prized "free" and "autonomous" humans, who always tended to be rich enough to meet their own needs in a market system.

This theological anthropology is deeply harmful since

> the core message embedded within colonial Western Christian theological anthropology is that in order to be Christian, one must become "human," and in order to become human, one must become white, and in order to become white, one must accept the hierarchy that protects the image of the heterosexual white male as the image of God on earth, the pinnacle of Creation.
> (Carter 2021: 103)

I am caught in this hierarchy; I might not be at the top of the social ladder, but I am pretty close.

My faith has developed and changed, and as a Christian, I now reject the idea that God sees us only as individuals and wants us focused on personal purity rather than social change. When the image of God is so distorted that only a small segment of the human population is thought to reflect it, we reject the Gospel. We sin (Cone 2010: 99–100).

As I considered why I was so eager to jump out of my car to help a stray dog but unwilling to take similar risks for humans, I struggled to find an answer. It did not *feel* like a racial problem since the vast majority of unhoused folks in Eugene (like the rest of the population) is White. But the reality is that the colonial Western Christianity in which I was raised led me to see some humans as more human and some humans as less human. As such, I have adopted a "judge and jury" attitude, free to condemn some and paternalistically rush to the rescue of others. Rather than be one of a member of God's creation, I put myself in the place of God, with disastrous results (Kidwell et al. 2001: 39–44).

If only I had been paying attention during all my quiet reflection, I might have understood earlier how thoroughly justice was woven into the Gospel: "Woe to you, scribes and Pharisees, hypocrites! For you tithe mint, dill, and cumin, and have neglected the weightier matters of the law: justice and mercy and faith. It is these you ought to have practiced without neglecting the others" (Matthew 23: 23–4, NRSV).

What I am trying to do now is to see myself as one humble member of God's community of creation, to learn from and follow the lead of Indigenous friends like Randy Woodley, who writes, "To our people [Native Americans], being human is a good thing. When we forget our humanity and try to take the place of the Creator is when our actions are really shameful" (Woodley 2012: 69).

Why all this talk about unhoused neighbors, racism, and relationships with other humans in a chapter about "animals"? Because thinking about animal creatures requires us to think about how we view ourselves as human creatures. As religious human creatures, thinking about animal creatures requires us to consider the question: who are we in relation to the sacred (however we understand it), to one another, and to the rest of creation? This is the foundational question upon which our exploration is built.

## BOX 12B

How do you describe your relationship to whatever you consider sacred? To other human beings? To non-human animals? What connections do you see between the way you think about these relationships? Do you see any connections in your everyday life?

### Animals and Ecological Crises

> *Homo sapiens* has rewritten the rules of the game. This single ape species has managed within 70,000 years to change the global ecosystem in radical and unprecedented ways.
>
> (Harari 2017: 73)

The creation accounts shared by the Hebrew and Christian Bibles tell readers that God carefully made all kinds of creatures (Genesis 1–2). Later in the same book, God's care for individual creatures is highlighted as the human Noah builds an ark large enough to fit two of every kind of species (Genesis 6). The psalmists regularly point out God's provision for all sorts of animal species, from goats on a hill to the Leviathan of the sea (e.g., Psalms 50:10–11; 74:12–14; 84:3; 104:10–30). The prophets include animals in their visions of the blessings and curses to come (e.g., Isaiah 11:6–9; 13:21–2; 19:5–8, the Nile will be dried up and "those who fish will mourn"; 30:23–5; and many more). When Jonah gets cranky after God spares Nineveh from destruction, God responds, "And should I not be concerned about Nineveh, that great city, in which there are more than a hundred and twenty thousand persons . . . and also many animals?" (Jonah 4:11). In the Christian New Testament, Jesus compares the love of God to the love of a hen for her chicks (Luke 13:34) and reminds his listeners that God sees every sparrow fall (Matthew 10:29). John's images of cosmic worship portray human and non-human creatures together at the heavenly throne (Revelation 4:6–7).

The God of Christianity cares about all kinds of animals.

The biblical texts also suggest that human beings should care for other animals and that our species' fate is connected to theirs. Take, for instance, Ezekiel 14:13: "Mortal, when a land sins against me by acting faithlessly, and I stretch out my hand against it and break its staff of bread and send famine upon it, and cut off from it human beings, and animals." When Israel shows no faith in God, the psalmist writes that humans and animals alike suffer: "He gave over their cattle to the hail, and their flocks to thunderbolts" (Psalm 78:48). Even Paul's letter to the urban church in Rome points out that

> the creation waits with eager longing for the revealing of the children of God; for the creation was subjected to futility, not of its own will but by the will of the one who subjected it, in hope that the creation itself will be set free from its bondage to decay and will obtain the freedom of the glory of the children

> of God. We know that the whole creation has been groaning in labor pains until now; and not only creation, but we ourselves.
>
> (Romans 8:19–23)

The God of Christianity cares about the whole of creation, including every single creature. All kinds of creatures sing in the choir of creation. All kinds of animals flourish or despair as a result of human behavior, in both the Christian biblical accounts and our present-day realities.

Consider the African forest elephant, the Sumatran rhino, the big blue whale, and the polar bear: creatures each impacted by human-caused changes to their environment, habitat loss, and/or human conflicts. What about the bluefin tuna, the vaquita, or the Yangtze finless porpoise? These water creatures are listed by the World Wildlife Fund as "endangered" or "critically endangered" as a result of commercial fishing operations or overfishing.

As human populations move further and further into (formerly) rural areas, human-animal conflicts increase. As human-caused climate shifts alter ecosystems and disrupt food supplies, animals are forced to venture into human-dominated areas to find provision. Perhaps the poster-animal for climate change ought to be a human instead of a polar bear. Or maybe it should be a chicken.

One particularly disturbing mark of the Anthropocene is the tectonic shift in *who* populates the earth. Yuval Harrari writes,

> The world is populated mainly by humans and their domesticated animals . . . Altogether about 200,000 wild wolves still roam the earth, but there are more than 400 million domesticated dogs. The world contains 40,000 lions compared to 600 million house cats; 900,000 African buffalo versus 1.5 billion domesticated cows; 50 million penguins and 20 billion chickens. Since 1970, despite growing ecological awareness, wildlife populations were halved . . . In 1980 there were 2 billion wild birds in Europe. In 2009 only 1.6 billion were left. In the same year, Europeans raised 1.9 billion chickens for meat and eggs. At present, more than 90 percent of the large animals of the world (i.e., those weighing more than a few pounds) are either humans or domesticated animals.
>
> (Harari 2017: 71–2)

While endangered and vulnerable species are certainly one consequence of human-caused climate change—and a consequence to be mourned—their great disappearance is due in large part to the rapid *increase* of domesticated animals. Most notably: animals used for food. Human's increasing reliance on and consumption of these domesticated/farmed animals has caused seismic shifts in land and water use, increased greenhouse gas emissions and pollution, catalyzed rapid deforestation, decreased crop diversity, consolidated land and power into multinational corporations, and relied on horrific animal cruelty and abusive, racist labor practices to maximize production.

Ellen Davis points out that "beef cattle now consume half the world's wheat, most of its corn (a grain they do not naturally eat), and almost all of its soybeans. In turn, the agriculture industry is the largest consumer of water in North America" (Davis 2009: 99). According to the Food and Agriculture Organization, 59% of the world's arable land is used to feed livestock, either through grazing or feed crop production. Global production of animal foods has tripled in the last fifty years, alongside a rise in extreme chronic hunger. At any given moment, there are about twenty-three billion broiler chickens on earth, and humans consume about sixty-five billion chickens every year (Bennett et al. 2018). A 2008 study found that 70–80% of deforestation of Northern Brazil (the lungs of the earth) was due to expanding cattle operations (Nepstad et al. 2008).

**BOX 12C**

Do you think that the environmental impacts of factory farming get enough attention in public discussions of diet, industry, and climate change? Why or why not?

How much of global greenhouse gas emissions can be attributed to animal agriculture is an ongoing debate; exact figures vary from the unlikely 14.5% in one FAO study to the perhaps-too-large 51% of a Worldwatch Institute paper. In the words of author Jonathan Safran Foer, "We do not know for sure if animal agriculture is *a* leading cause of climate change or *the* leading cause of climate change" (Foer 2019: 96). What we do know, in the words of one climate scientist, is that

> [i]t seems impossible to reverse climate change by capping fossil fuels . . . because the amount of renewable energy infrastructure needed to stop climate change has been estimated by the International Energy Agency to cost at least $53 trillion and take at least twenty years, by which time it's projected to be too late to reverse climate change. In contrast, replacing animal products with alternatives offers a unique dual opportunity to reduce greenhouse gas emissions quickly while freeing up land to enable more trees to capture excess atmospheric carbon in the near term. So replacing animal products with alternatives seems to be the only pragmatic way to reverse climate change before it is too late.
>
> (Foer 2019: 232)

Since "the chief value operative in our industrial food system is monetary, and it is measured by the profit margins of large corporations" (Davis 2009: 23), humans have allowed the growth and expansion of a system that depends on cruelty to function. Human workers suffer in slaughterhouses in which production speed is prioritized over safety. Farm laborers are forced to work in toxic barns, full of gas and particles from tens of thousands of confined animals.

Animals themselves are subject to body mutilations such as tail-docking, beak-trimming, dehorning, and castration—all without painkillers. Mother pigs are confined to crates too small for them to turn around. The short, miserable weeks of a broiler chicken's life are spent in a warehouse reeking of ammonia and dung. Genetic modifications due to consumer preference mean that her breast grows so large that her legs cannot hold her weight and she collapses, her skin burned from the toxic air.

A few moments after giving birth to a calf she has carried for nine months, a dairy cow will wail as that calf is taken from her so that humans can drink her milk and make cheese sticks and Go-Gurt. Industrial fish farms endanger wild fish populations and pollute just as much as dairy and cow farms. Huge fishing trawlers spend months at sea dragging up every living thing, often relying on slave labor to do the nasty work of cleaning and processing dead and dying sea life.

And yet when Christian organizations put together climate action plans, start creation care initiatives in our congregations, or incorporate and grow environmental nonprofits, farmed animals are (usually) nowhere to be found. We push solar panels, energy audits, community gardens, no-mow-May, and electric cars while most barbeques, potlucks, conference buffets, and Christian college cafeterias—at least here in the US—remain an homage to the "standard American diet" of meat, dairy, and eggs from the cheapest possible source.

**BOX 12D**

What experience (if any) do you have interacting with animals who are farmed for food? How have these experiences (or the lack of them) shaped your understanding of food and nutrition? How have these experiences shaped your understanding of environmental issues?

### Partnership in the Reconciliation of all Creation

> To Native Americans, practices are beliefs. In other words, one comes to believe something because one does it.
>
> (Woodley 2012: 96)

What does it mean to live as if God cares about the whole of God's beloved creation? What would it mean for Christians to live as if the words of Paul were true that

> [Christ] is the image of the invisible God, the firstborn of all creation, for in him all things in heaven and on earth were created . . . all things have been created through him and for him. . . . For in him all the fullness of God was pleased to dwell, and through him God was pleased to reconcile to himself all things, whether on earth or in heaven, by making peace through the blood of his cross.
>
> (Colossians 1:15–20, NRSV)

How would the day-to-day actions of Christians change if, as Randy Woodley suggests, "part of our job on earth is to discover what Christ is up to, and to join him in it!" (Woodley 2012: 60). I believe that Christ is reconciling the whole of creation through his life, death, and resurrection. Christ's life offers each of his beloved creatures liberation: liberation from being oppressed and from oppressing, liberation from sin and from sinning, liberation from the bondage to decay. What does such liberation mean for our worship, for the stewardship of whatever little plot of land we find ourselves living or worshiping upon? What does it mean for our grocery shopping? What does it mean for our interactions with insects, pigeons, mice, and bats?

For many years, I believed that the primary solution to animal suffering and the best way to advocate for them was simply to urge individuals to stop killing or otherwise exploiting animals. I believed everyone should be vegan, like me. It has been twenty years since I knowingly bought a personal care product tested on animals, but animal experimentation is still rampant. It has been twenty years since I ate a chicken's breast, but billions of chickens are still killed for food each year. It has been twenty years since I bought leather shoes, but tanneries are still poisoning people the world over.

Individual justice-oriented actions are meaningful and can also improve the health of individuals and their communities. One person deciding to be vegan can be a good thing. But I have learned that it is not *the* answer. Systemic problems require systemic solutions; it is impossible to silo our efforts toward liberation. Just as we are interconnected with one another, so are injustices. We cannot work for the well-being of animals without working for the well-being of *all* God's beloved creations. We must acknowledge how our relationships with other humans are reflected in our relationships with animals.

This means that advocating for just treatment of animals, like advocacy for gender justice, racial justice, economic justice, and so many other issues, will require systemic thinking and thinking change. Such an enormous project can be daunting. But faith communities with conviction to approach environmental, animal, and human justice issues through a lens of liberation can work for non-human creatures in many ways:

1. Include pet food and supplies in food pantries and other community support work.
2. Partner with BIPOC-led projects to help marginalized communities keep and care for their pets (e.g., https://careawo.org/care-centers).
3. Eliminate or drastically reduce the animal products served at community functions. There are many strategies for accomplishing this. Ask people to bring vegan or vegetarian dishes to share. Make catered meals plant-based by default and allow people to opt-in to meat consumption (www.becreaturekind.org/defaultveg).
4. Adopt humane wildlife/pest control practices. Eliminate the use of glue traps and insecticides on community grounds.
5. Conduct a worship service at a local farmed animal or wildlife sanctuary. Tithe money and time to the sanctuary as thanks for the use of their space and the opportunity to learn from them.

6. Ensure Earth Day, Blessings of the Animals, and other creation-focused events include *all* animals and not just the ones that are already socially acceptable to care about.
7. Cultivate the kind of community where attention to non-human creatures is normalized. Ask about people's pets. Share plant-based recipes in the bulletin. Hold a plant-based cooking class. Pray specifically for animals and humans affected by environmental disasters. When spiders or other non-human guests find their way into the sanctuary, escort them outside. Help children in the community see that care for the smallest creature is an important part of our care for one another and our common home.
8. Support the people in your community who are doing work directly with animals (farm and shelter workers, veterinarians, etc.). Ensure that farmers and veterinarians have the mental health support they need for the stresses of their work.
9. Find the farm, field, and slaughterhouse workers in your community and get to know them. Advocate for public policies that support immigrant and migrant laborers and fair labor practices.
10. Make a list of local farms who are trying to exist outside the factory farming system and commit to purchasing food directly from them.
11. Use community spaces (rooftops, window boxes, lawns, and gardens) to grow and share food with people who have limited access to fresh fruits and vegetables.

Randy Woodley helped me think about the Kingdom of God a little differently when he wrote, "Jesus suggests that a new way to live on a daily basis be called the 'kingdom'" (Woodley, 38). Our actions can affirm our connections with others, or they can sever them. Our actions can consolidate power and resources, or they can share them. Our actions can reflect our interdependence, or they can isolate us from that which brings life. My prayer for communities of faith, and for the Christian church specifically, is that we daily press into the promise of the kingdom on earth, as it is in heaven.

## Case Study: Racial Justice and Animal Justice

As this chapter has made clear, it is impossible and inappropriate to distinguish thinking about and treatment of animals from the ways we think about and treat human communities. It is particularly important to recognize the connections between issues of racial justice and issues of animal justice. People in power have frequently justified mistreating people from marginalized racial and ethnic identities by relating them to non-human animals.

The following are three extended quotes from scholars who work at the intersection of animal studies, racial issues, and Christianity. As you read them, think about what it might look like to put their ideas into action: How might taking issues of racism and colonization change the work of those who consider themselves animal advocates? How might taking animal issues seriously change the work of those committed to racial justice and decolonization?

Jeania Ree V. Moore is a scholar of black studies and animal studies, a Methodist deacon, and a writer who had a regular column in the progressive Christian magazine *Sojourners*. In an article titled "Racial Justice and Animal Justice," she writes,

> Black people have long understood as racist the disparate treatment of nonhuman animals and black people. In 1855, Frederick Douglass wrote that, "The bond-woman lives as a slave, and is left to die as a beast; often with fewer attentions than are paid to a favorite horse." One-hundred-sixty years later, Roxane Gay similarly noted the differing reactions to two 2015 killings: Cecil the Lion by an American dentist (worldwide outcry) and Samuel DuBose, a black man, by an American police officer (no such response) . . . This racism carries new urgency in the age of the Anthropocene. As we finally begin to address humans' destructive impact on the world, putting 1 million plant and animal species at risk of extinction, we must also confront how white supremacy harms black and brown people with warped, racist notions of "human being" and false, hierarchical models of creation limiting who is in the circle of care. Like on climate change, evidence abounds.
>
> (Moore 2019: 17)

Christopher Carter is a professor of theology and religious studies at the University of San Diego and an elder in the Methodist Church. He writes explicitly about the resources Christian faith offers for the work of justice in all its forms. In his book *The Spirit of Soul Food: Race, Faith, and Food Justice*, he focuses among other things on the Christian virtue of hospitality:

> What makes Christian hospitality so radical is that it disrupts perceived power dynamics between parties: the poor, the marginalized, and the othered are welcome at the table to sit alongside those who inhabit places of privilege in society. However, I want to suggest that the concept of hospitality be extended to include the nonhuman animals whose marginalization and exploitation have been justified through the same oppressive logic of coloniality. As Christians, we are called to be hospitable to the least of these, and in our current food system, the majority of nonhuman animals are treated as the least—as merely protein units.
>
> (Carter 2021: 133)

Randy Woodley is a professor at George Fox University, a former Baptist pastor, and a Cherokee descendant recognized by the Keetoowah band. He studies and works at the intersection of Christian and Indigenous communities. He and his wife, Edith, created the Eloheh Indigenous Center for Earth Justice to develop a spiritual approach to environmental work. In his book *Shalom and the Community of Creation*, Woodley emphasizes the importance of harmonious communities:

> [Jesus] speaks to us about a new way of living out shalom in the community of creation. My people, and people the world over, understand it as harmony and balance, although it is spoken of with different words among different peoples. The story, our story, is about a party. A Community involving all people and all other parts of creation. The party is demonstrated by carrying out justice and righteousness among our fellow humans and the earth and all her other creatures. The community concerns itself especially with the marginalized and disempowered parts of creation that do not have the voice or the power to speak for themselves. This includes strangers, widows, and orphans. It includes the earth herself, and all of her resources. It includes the remaining indigenous peoples. Shalom in the community of creation—life as God intends it—awaits our embrace."
>
> (Woodley 2012: 165)

***Discussion Questions***

1. What do you find compelling about the idea that racial justice, anticolonialism, and justice for animals should be combined, as these authors suggest? What tensions or challenges might be raised about pursuing such an approach?
2. How do these authors dialogue with Christian ideas? Do you see distinctions in the way they discuss, or do not discuss, their faith?
3. What do you think a Christian church that took these ideas seriously would need to change? How might these points impact sermons and worship services? How might they impact social events and public outreach?
4. What could non-Christians—those from other faith communities and those who are not part of any faith community—learn from these ideas?

## References


Adams, T. (2019) "'We Have a Significant Problem': Eugene Leads US for Homeless Per Capita," *KMTR News*, October 22. https://nbc16.com/news/local/we-have-a-significant-problem-eugene-leads-us-in-per-capita-homelessness (accessed July 8, 2022).

Bennett, C. et al. (2018) "The Broiler Chicken as a Signal of a Human Reconfigured Biosphere," *Royal Society Open Science* 5: 12.

Carter, C. (2021) *The Spirit of Soul Food: Race, Faith, and Food Justice*. Chicago: University of Illinois Press.

Cone, J. (2010) *A Black Theology of Liberation*. 40th Anniversary ed. Maryknoll, NY: Orbis Books.

Davis, E. (2009) *Scripture, Culture, and Agriculture: An Agrarian Reading of the Bible*. New York: Cambridge University Press.

Foer, J. S. (2019) *We Are the Weather: Saving the Planet Begins at Breakfast*. New York: Picador.

Harari, Y. N. (2017) *Homo Deus: A Brief History of Tomorrow*. New York: HarperCollins.

Kidwell, C. S., Noley, H., and Tinker, G. (2001) *A Native American Theology*. Maryknoll, NY: Orbis Books.

Moore, J. R. (2019) "Racial Justice and Animal Justice," *Sojourners*, September–October, pp. 16–17.

Nepstad, D. C. et al. (2008) "Interactions Among Amazon Land Use, Forests and Climate: Prospects for a Near-Term Forest Tipping Point," *Philosophical Transactions of the Royal Society of London Series B, Biological Sciences* 363(1498): 1737–46.

Woodley, R. (2012) *Shalom and the Community of Creation: An Indigenous Vision*. Grand Rapids: Eerdmans.

## Further Resources

### *Texts*

Bauckham, R. (2009) *Living with Other Creatures: Green Exegesis and Theology*. Waco, TX: Baylor University Press.

Camosy, C. (2013) *For Love of Animals: Christian Ethics, Consistent Action*. Cincinnati, OH: Franciscan Media.

Clough, D. L. (2012) *On Animals Volume 1: Systematic Theology*. London: T&T Clark International.

———. (2019) *On Animals Volume 2: Theological Ethics*. London: T&T Clark International.

Copeland, R. L. (2020) *Created Being: Expanding Creedal Christology*. Waco, TX: Baylor University Press.

Crane, J. K. (ed) (2016) *Beastly Morality: Animals As Ethical Agents*. New York: Columbia University Press.

Deane-Drummond, C., Artinian-Kaiser, R., and Clough, D. L. (eds) (2013) *Animals as Religious Subjects: Transdisciplinary Perspectives*. London: Bloomsbury T&T Clark.

Deane-Drummond, C., and Clough, D. L. (eds) (2009) *Creaturely Theology: On God, Humans, and Other Animals*. London: SCM Press.

Deloria Jr., V. (1973) *God Is Red: A Native View of Religion*. Golden, CO: Fulcrum Publishing.

Fernandez, E. (2004) *Reimagining the Human: Theological Anthropology in Response to Systemic Evil*. St. Louis, MO: Chalice Press.

Gilmour, M. (2014) *Eden's Other Residents: The Bible and Animals*. Eugene, OR: Cascade Books.

Gross, A. (2015) *The Question of the Animal and Religion: Theoretical States, Practical Implications*. New York: Columbia University Press.

Gross, A., and Vallely, A. (eds) (2012) *Animals and the Human Imagination: A Companion to Animal Studies*. New York: Columbia University Press.

Gutierrez, G. (1988) *A Theology of Liberation: History, Politics, and Salvation*. Maryknoll, NY: Orbis Books.

Johnson, E. (2014) *Ask the Beasts: Darwin and the God of Love*. London: Bloomsbury Continuum.

King, S. W. (2016a) *Animals Are Not Ours (No, Really They're Not): An Evangelical Animal Liberation Theology*. Eugene, OR: Cascade Books.

———. (2016b) *Vegangelical: How Caring for Animals Can Shape Your Faith*. Grand Rapids, MI: Zondervan.

———. (2019) "The Groaning Creation: Animal Liberation and Evangelical Theology," in M. E. Cannon and A. Smith (eds) *Evangelical Theologies of Liberation and Justice*. Downers Grove, IL: IVP Academic.

Ko, A. (2019) *Racism as Zoological Witchcraft: A Guide to Getting Out*. Brooklyn: Lantern Books.

Ko, A., and Ko, S. (2017) *Aphro-Ism: Essays on Pop Culture, Feminism, and Black Veganism from Two Sisters*. Brooklyn: Lantern Books.
Martin-Schramm, J., Spencer, D. T., and Stivers, L. A. (2015) *Earth Ethics: A Case Method Approach*. Maryknoll, NY: Orbis Books.
Middleton, J. R. (2014) *A New Heaven and a New Earth: Reclaiming Biblical Eschatology*. Grand Rapids, MI: Baker Academic.
———. (2005) *The Liberating Image: The Imago Dei in Genesis 1*. Grand Rapids, MI: Brazos Press.
Moore, S. D. (ed) (2014) *Divinanimality: Animal Theory, Creaturely Theology*. New York: Fordham University Press.
Wennberg, R. (2003) *God, Humans, and Animals: An Invitation to Enlarge Our Moral Universe*. Grand Rapids: Eerdmans.
Yordy, L. (2008) *Green Witness: Ecology, Ethics, and the Kingdom of God*. Eugene, OR: Cascade Books.
York, T. (2015) *The End of Captivity? A Primate's Reflections on Zoos, Conservation, and Christian Ethics*. Eugene, OR: Cascade.
York, T., and Alexis-Baker, A. (eds) (2012) *A Faith Embracing All Creatures: Addressing Commonly Asked Questions About Christian Care for Animals*. Eugene, OR: Cascade.

### *Organizations*

- Animal Interfaith Alliance: https://animal-interfaith-alliance.com
- Companions and Animals for Reform and Equity: https://careawo.org
- CreatureKind: www.becreaturekind.org
- Eloheh Indigenous Center for Earth Justice: www.eloheh.org/the-center-for-earth-justice
- Food Empowerment Project: https://foodispower.org
- Jewish Initiative for Animals: www.jewishinitiativeforanimals.com

# 13 Vegetarianism, Religion, and Food

*Catherine L. Newell*

In 2019, the EAT-*Lancet* Commission released a report on global health, diet, sustainability, and culture. The authors argue that while food systems "have the potential to nurture human health and support environmental sustainability," today they are "currently threatening both." These threats are mounting: "many environmental systems and processes are pushed beyond safe boundaries by food production," which means that "a global transformation of the food system is urgently needed." Consequently, the commission aims to "provide scientific boundaries to reduce environmental degradation caused by food production at all scales." To accomplish this, the commission recommends a diet primarily made up of vegetables, fruits, nuts, seeds, and legumes; eliminating sugars and refined, processed foods; and a drastic reduction of animal products, especially red meat. Essentially, they recommend a (mostly) vegetarian diet. The report notes that

> studies concur that plant-based foods cause fewer adverse environmental effects per unit weight, per serving, per unit of energy, or per protein weight than does animal source foods across various environmental indicators. . . . Vegan and vegetarian diets were associated with the greatest reductions in greenhouse-gas emissions and land use.
>
> (Willett et al. 2019)

In other words, if we want to feed the whole planet without destroying it, we are going to collectively need to rethink our diet—especially raising animals for food.

There are myriad topics we—readers, scholars, and practitioners of various diets and/or religions—could explore under the rubric "religion and food," but in this chapter, we will explore the dietary lifestyle that we will call "vegetarianisms." For the expediency of this chapter and its case study, this term will be inclusive of lacto-ovo-vegetarians (vegetarians who do not eat meat but do eat dairy products and eggs), vegans (who do not consume any animal products, including honey, leather, wool, or products tested on animals), and the general descriptor of "plant-based" (a generalized term that dates back to the origins of vegetarian practices). Specifically, our survey of vegetarianisms will look at their practice as an expression of religious belief, their instrumentalization as a heath practice, their evolution

DOI: 10.4324/9781003259466-17

into a reaction against social and political forces of the 20th century and finally as a form of resistance against pending climate catastrophe. We will end with a case study that asks the question: *should the practice of vegetarianism for environmental reasons be given the same legal protections as the exercise of a religion?*

## The Environmental Consequences of Industrial-Scale Meat Production

This report is just one among many of the last two decades that have warned that global food systems need to change drastically both to feed an expanding population and to curtail climate change. Several meta-analysis studies and in-depth reports have focused particularly on the negative environmental impacts of industrial livestock production, raising animals such as cattle or poultry for their meat or their by-products, like dairy or eggs. The 2006 United Nations report *Livestock's Long Shadow: Environmental Issues and Options* notes that the global livestock sector "has such deep and wide-ranging environmental impacts that it should rank as one of the leading focuses for environmental policy" (Steinfeld 2006). More recently, in 2022 the Intergovernmental Panel on Climate Change (IPCC) warns,

> Climate change is already stressing food and forestry systems, with negative consequences for the livelihoods, food security and nutrition of hundreds of millions of people, especially in low and mid-latitudes . . . The global food system is failing to address food insecurity and malnutrition in an environmentally sustainable way.
>
> (Pörtner 2022)

Across the board, these studies have found that industrial-scale livestock farming negatively affects the planet and contributes to climate change in four important ways: atmospheric pollution, deforestation, freshwater pollution, and biodiversity loss.

Perhaps the most infamous way that livestock agriculture affects the atmosphere is through methane production, particularly from ruminants like cattle (although sheep, goats, and swine also contribute to atmospheric methane). Meat production is one of the largest sources of excess methane in our atmosphere. Like carbon dioxide, methane accentuates the already-problematic greenhouse effect. This means the literal off-gassing of livestock agriculture—the burps and farts of cattle, for example—lingers in the atmosphere, trapping heat in the troposphere for decades. With that in mind, "It is estimated that about 44% of total global methane emissions are from livestock, and that the output is dominated by beef production" (Chai et al. 2019).

In addition to methane production, meat consumption also contributes to deforestation, particularly in the Amazon, which in turn releases sequestered carbon. Unless it is stopped, the clearing of the Amazon rainforest to make farmland for raising beef cattle could "release more than 50 billion tonnes of carbon into the atmosphere in 30 to 50 years" (Schiermeier 2019). It should go without saying that the loss of carbon sinks like the Amazon basin would cause the Earth to warm swiftly and well past the 1.5°C change climate scientists caution is the highest threshold for staving off catastrophic climate disruptions. According to multiple studies, approximately

> 80% of the world's deforestation is related to the food system; and this system is the leading cause of changes in land use and biodiversity loss. Without corrective measures, the environmental impact of the food system could increase by 50–90% in 30 y[ears], reaching levels that are beyond the planetary boundaries.
>
> (Fresán and Sabaté 2019)

Likewise, meat production uses approximately one-third of our global freshwater—water needed to maintain healthy natural ecosystems (Godfray et al. 2018). In addition to the consumption of water by livestock animals (one cow can drink up to thirty-five gallons of water per day) and the water used in the production of their feed (approximately 68% of global agricultural land is used for animal farming and one third of global cropland is used for producing animal feed (Alexander et al. 2016)), local freshwater is often polluted by the alluvial runoff from industrial meat and dairy farms (Graves et al. 2007).

Finally, we now know that livestock production is the "predominant driver of natural habitat loss worldwide" where a "direct cost of land being converted to food production was the loss of nearly one-half of all natural grasslands and the loss of nearly one-third of all natural forests worldwide" (Machovina et al. 2015). Livestock agriculture and its concurrent systems are undeniably "degrading the environment beyond the capacity of natural ecosystems to repair" (Swinburn et al. 2019).

But global demographic changes and the force of culture have made eating meat and consuming animal products not only normal but desirable. In countries experiencing demographic and economic transitions, eating meat has transformed from a rare occurrence to a daily symbol of national prosperity. In China as of 2015, for example, 20% of food consumption by mass was "animal product-based, approximating the global median [with] consumption of animal products . . . on trajectory to reach 30% in 20 years"; in the previous 20 years, the consumption of animal products "increased from 10% to 20% of Chinese diets, and [was] only 5% in 1960. Between 1978 and 2002, China's per capita consumption of meat, milk and eggs increased four-, four-, and eight-fold, respectively" (Machovina et al. 2015; Liu and Diamond 2005). Similar changes are happening elsewhere in Asia, as well as in Africa and India (Bonhommeau et al. 2013). Besides these larger trends, eating meat is often considered both an important part of many food cultures and fundamental to human nature (Hoffman et al. 2013; Rosenfeld and Burrow 2017). Most national cuisines and historical dietary practices include consuming meat and animal products.

**BOX 13A**

Is meat a regular part of your diet? Were you raised eating meat at multiple meals a day? If so, what do you know about when and how meat became integral to the diet of your family of origin?

Despite the ingrained status of meat eating in many modern societies, the negative environmental impacts of meat consumption are overwhelming. As one editorial puts it,

> The emotionally charged debate over the ethical suitability of meat consumption may never reach a conclusion, but it is only comparatively recently that the climate impact of livestock rearing, and the nutritional and health issues caused by meat have become a pressing concern.
>
> (The Lancet 2018)

While the social and emotional costs of going against these powerful historical and economic trends can be difficult, individuals make the choice every single day to be part of a solution by becoming a vegetarian.

### The Entanglement of Religion and Diet

Dietary choices are a useful heuristic—a kind of mental shortcut—for defining religions, because nearly all religions have some kind of dietary rules, including and especially around eating animals. For example, and even though it is not a universally prescribed practice in either faith, various iterations of Hinduism and Buddhism advise eating a vegetarian diet (Walters and Portmess 2001). The Vedas, the world's oldest sacred texts, which date to approximately 1,500 BCE and are foundational to Hindu beliefs and rituals, explore the principle of *ahimsa*—nonviolence against other living beings—and the notion that all living things contain *atman*—a conscious, inner self. These teachings led to the adoption of a vegetarian diet among many Hindus beginning dozens of centuries ago. Considerations of *ahimsa* were also the basis for the Buddha's suggestion to avoid eating animals. Thus, for practitioners of Hinduism and Buddhism, as well as Jainism, *ahimsa* is a motivation for vegetarianism, and prominent traditions in each faith, which understand the consumption of animals slaughtered for food as participating in violence (Waldau and Patton 2006).

Vegetarianism is not generally prescribed in any of the Abrahamic religions, although there are exceptions, and each of the Abrahamic traditions has specific regulations regarding food and animals. Judaism famously has its *kashrut* laws—dietary laws that come directly from the Torah—including very strict directions on the process of raising and slaughtering animals and guidance on which animals should be considered *kosher*, or acceptable to eat. Roman Catholic and Greek Orthodox Christianity require abstention from certain foods throughout the liturgical year; most notably, many practitioners abstain from meat or from all animal products on Fridays (Roman Catholic) or for the duration of the 40 days before Easter (Greek and other Orthodox) to commemorate Jesus' fast in the desert before he began his ministry. Finally, Islam has laws designating some foods *halal*—"lawful" or "permitted"—and other foods *haram*—"forbidden." Like Judaism, Islam has strict dictates on which animals may be eaten for food and how they should be slaughtered. Islam and Judaism share a prohibition on consuming pork, and Islam and several Christian denominations prohibit drinking alcohol (Caballero et al. 2005).

Again, although there are no dietary strictures stating specifically that a meat-free diet is recommended for the full liturgical year, within institutional Abrahamic religions we find instances where practitioners have interpreted scripture or teachings as endorsing a vegetarian or even a vegan diet. Interestingly, however, the reasons for this abstention can be very different (Nath 2010). For example, some Jews and Christians have interpreted God's words in the first chapter of Genesis as endorsing a vegetarian or vegan lifestyle. In Genesis 1:29–30, God says to the newly created humans,

> Behold, I have given you every plant yielding seed that is on the surface of all the earth, and every tree which has fruit yielding seed; it shall be food for you; and to every beast of the earth and to every bird of the sky and to every thing that moves on the earth which has life, I have given every green plant for food; and it was so.

It is only after the Flood that God tells Noah and his family that they may eat the animals they have just saved. Over the centuries, many believers have interpreted this to mean that they are free to eat fruits, vegetables, nuts, and seeds, but not animals.

Other biblical inspiration for a vegetarian or vegan diet comes from the Book of Daniel in the Hebrew scriptures, in which the title prophet declines King Nebuchadnezzar's food and wine, and announces that for ten days he and his friends—who have been taken captive by the king—will only eat legumes or vegetables and drink water, rejecting "the king's meat" (Daniel 1: 12–13). This has been interpreted to show that a diet of vegetables, water, and faith brings superior health and physical strength. The Daniel Fast, as it is marketed today, is an exercise in dietary veganism and the avoidance of refined foods, yeasts, and any drink besides water. This has become a popular trend among Evangelical Protestant Christians seeking weight loss and/or better health (Gregory 2010).

Also in the Christian tradition, Joseph Smith—founder and prophet of the Church of Jesus Christ of Latter-day Saints (also sometimes known as Mormons)—wrote in an 1833 revelation from God titled "The Word of Wisdom" that stimulants (e.g., caffeinated beverages) and alcohol were forbidden. Some have interpreted Smith's included statement that "flesh also of beasts and of the fowls of the air . . . are to be used sparingly [because] it is pleasing unto [God] that they should not be used, only in times of winter, or of cold, or famine" to mean that, in our modern world of plenty, there is no reason to eat animal products at all (Smith et al. 1971). For this reason, many practicing members of the LDS church consider veganism to be a logical extension of the Christian standard for care of the human body.

In sum, vegetarian dietary choices are an important part of some religious practices. For some religious people, abstention from animal products and eating a vegetarian or vegan diet is motivated by care of the body, or care for the soul, or both. While most contemporary discussions of vegetarianism and veganism pay little to no attention to religion, a brief look at the history will reveal that, for many, meat- and animal-product-free lifestyles derive from community-based religious beliefs and practices.

**BOX 13B**

Do you think it is important to distinguish between, on one hand, dietary choices people make for their personal health and preferences and, on the other, dietary choices people make because of long-standing religious and cultural traditions? Why or why not?

### A Brief History of Vegetarianisms and Plant-Based Eating

Some of the earliest known written records in Europe advocating a vegetarian diet date back to religious rituals and practice in ancient Greece. In the 6th century BCE, the followers of the Orphic mysteries banned the use of animals for sacrifice or for eating. Around the same time, taking a more metaphysical perspective, the Greek philosopher and mathematician Pythagoras taught his followers about reincarnation and steered them away from eating animals (Leitzmann 2014). During the Middle Ages and the Renaissance, some, like Luigi Cornaro, reasoned their way into a plant-based diet; the 16th-century Venetian nobleman wrote popular discourses about personal health in which he credited his long life to eschewing animal foods (Cornaro 1768). During the Enlightenment, a few philosophers adopted the "Pythagorean way" and wrote about their vegetarian diets' alignment with their philosophical beliefs.

Nevertheless, before the 19th century, most Europeans were wholly unfamiliar with the vegetarian diet (Preece 2014). Even though meat was not consumed at the levels seen now, for citizens of both agrarian and urban lifestyles—across nearly every continent, for hundreds of years, and with very few exceptions—animal foods were a staple of existence. Despite its historical entanglement with religious practice and connection to philosophical mores, for most of the past 2,000 years, vegetarianism was vanishingly niche in Europe and Asia outside of India's religious vegetarian cultures.

More recently, however, vegetarian diets began to be adopted in the west for a variety of reasons including health concerns, religious notions of redemption, and social reform. Again, even though vegetarianism has been practiced for millennia, it was not until the 19th century that the benefits of a meat-free—or even animal-product-free—lifestyle gradually became known in Europe. Over two hundred years ago in England, for instance, the Bible Christian Church's organizers sincerely believed "that kindness and consideration towards the humble and useful domestic animals was as much a part of the Great Creator's plan as was the divine announcement 'Peace on Earth, good will toward men.'" The church's founder is reported to have said, "If God had meant us to eat meat then it would have come to us in edible form, as is the ripened fruit" (Committee of the B.C.C.M. 2019). When the church's members came to America in 1817, it was to spread the message of Christian redemption along with a lifestyle of vegetarianism and temperance (Metcalfe and Bible-Christian 1840). Fractures within the church's leadership eventually led to a split, but not before its mission profoundly affected the worldview of a freshly minted Presbyterian minister named Sylvester Graham.

Graham's name is familiar today mainly because of his eponymous cracker; this is a shame because his ministry based on vegetarianism for physical and spiritual health was hugely influential for over half a century and his legacy continues even today (Nissenbaum 1980). Graham's philosophy, which he titled the "science of human life," combined contemporary insights on digestive physiology, theories about epidemic disease, and his belief that a vegetarian diet was physically and theologically redemptive (Graham 1833). His prescription for wellness and salvation was fruits, vegetables, and whole-grain bread combined with a prohibition on meat, coffee, tea, spices, and alcohol; this diet became foundational to the practice of vegetarianisms for several decades (Graham 1839). Graham's notions were an inspiration to transcendentalist philosophers like Amos Bronson Alcott and Christian health reformers like Ellen G. White, one of the co-founders of the Seventh-day Adventist Church. Graham's ideas spawned what public health historian Ruth C. Engs (2001) has called a "clean living movement," a period when a health crusade is transformed into a moral obligation in the public consciousness. In early-19th-century America, adopting a meat-free diet for physical and spiritual health became a clean living movement that led to vegetarianism going mainstream (Shprintzen 2013; Iacobbo and Iacobbo 2004).

Vegetarianisms thus arrived in the 20th century associated with religious values and public health campaigns. In addition, starting in the late 19th century, a faction of vegetarians became concerned with what eventually became known as animal welfare, leading to a split in the rapidly growing community of vegetarians over the topics of ethics and cruelty. In particular, the "cornerstone of the arguments for what became known as a vegan diet was always the cruelty, inseparable from the acquisition of dairy products, and the linkage of the meat and dairy industries" (Leneman 1999). The reformer and philosopher Henry Salt, now considered one of the founders of modern veganism, connected animal rights and environmental benefits with the human health of an animal-product-free diet. In 1886, Salt argued that a vegetarian diet that was also free of dairy and eggs was economical, ecologically sound, and humane, stating that there was "a moral advantage" in such a diet (Salt 2021).

While Salt never referred to himself as a vegan, his ideas contributed to the disagreement between lacto-ovo-vegetarians and those who believed in abstaining from all animal products. In 1944, Donald Watson—secretary of the Leicester Vegetarian Society in England—began a campaign insisting that the use of any animal product for food or clothing was unethical; he termed his new way of eating and living "vegan," taking the first three and last two letters from "vegetarian," in order to signify that this new movement was the beginning and the end of vegetarianism (Wright and Adams 2015). With this declaration, the explicitly vegan movement was born.

Throughout the 20th century, vegetarianisms went through various phases of acceptance and popularity, and the various combinations of social, health, and environmental justifications continued to evolve. Health concerns have most often been cited as a motive for the adoption of vegetarian and vegan diets, but over time health became just one of several motivations for such diets (Hopwood et al. 2020). In the 20th century, the causes of animal welfare, ecological concerns, and social justice became conflated in vegetarian practices.

Beginning in the mid-century, both feminists (Adams 2000; Kemmerer 2011) and civil rights activists (Harper 2010; Terry 2014; McQuirter 2010) called attention to the connections between animal rights, health inequities, and environmental injustice. They viewed their vegetarianisms not just as an ethical duty and an exercise in cross-species justice but as a natural outcome of their empathy for other subjugated creatures (Filippi et al. 2010; Hopwood et al. 2020). Finally, the overwhelming evidence that industrial livestock farming is having ruinous effects on the planet has led to environmental philosophy and an accompanying vegetarian diet becoming the basis of a personal lifestyle and moral framework (Foer 2019; Svoboda 2016).

The bottom line for adherents to a vegetarian or vegan diet is conviction, and studies have demonstrated that conviction—the sense that eating a plant-based diet is good for global health, the planet, and/or animal welfare—is the most strongly correlated variable with the duration of the practice (Hoffman et al. 2013). In other words, people who are vegetarian or vegan for reasons that go beyond personal health tend to abstain from eating animals more closely for a longer time. For these practitioners, this is no longer a diet: it is a meaningful way of life (Plante et al. 2019).

## Vegetarianisms as Environmental Practice

With all this as background, we now begin to see the environmental implications of religious and social practices of vegetarianism and veganism. As noted earlier, contemporary vegetarianism and veganism are justified not only by long-standing concerns about human health and animal welfare, but also the dangerous trajectory of climate change. This has led to research arguing that a global reduction in meat and animal-based foods could be the key to transforming our Earth's future. If, for example, a majority of the global population adopted a meat-free or low-meat diet, the evidence suggests that we could reduce emissions by "1.2–2.3 gigatonnes of carbon-dioxide carbon equivalents per year (translating to around 30–60% of the projected 2050 emissions)" while "cropland requirements would be reduced by 450 million to 600 million hectares (about 20–30% of the projected 2050 cropland area [if dietary choices remain unchanged])" (Stehfest 2014). This means that if everyone—from individuals to religious communities to governments—took the EAT-*Lancet* report seriously—supporting vegetarianisms with policy changes, subsidies, and environmental protections—it might be possible to slow climate change, reverse freshwater pollution, and ease pressures on planet-wide biodiversity (Deane-Drummond and Artinian-Kaiser 2018).

**BOX 13C**

Which people, communities, or nations (if any) do you think have particular responsibility to consider adopting more plant-based diets for the sake of the environment? Which people, communities, or nations (if any) do not have such a responsibility?

### A Case Study: Plant-Based Eating as a "Protected Class"

Given vegetarianisms' connection to religion and the solid evidence that a global transformation to a primarily plant-based diet can help protect the planet against the worst effects of climate change, we should take a moment to consider what the stakes of environmental vegetarianism could—and possibly should—be.

In January 2020, a British court ruled that a plaintiff's veganism should be counted as a legally protected class. The plaintiff in the case, Jordi Casamitjana, alleged that he had been fired from his job (which was at—ironically—an animal welfare charity) because he had raised concerns that employee pension funds were invested in companies that used animal testing. The plaintiff claimed he had been fired in retaliation for expressing his concerns that this investment conflicted with both the charity's stated mission and his own deeply held beliefs as a vegan, which for him comprised a moral code. The judge agreed and ruled in the plaintiff's favor, stating that Mr. Casamitjana's veganism met the standards for a protected class under the UK's Equality Act of 2010.

It might not be immediately clear how a set of rules like the Equality Act apply to something as personal as dietary choice. But hopefully this chapter has provided some important food for thought (as it were). Our job in this case study is to reflect on the meaning of this legal ruling in the context of not only the alleged discrimination but also religion.

The Equality Act articulates the rights afforded to "legally protected classes," which is often considered a designation for religious groups. Not just in the UK but also in Canada, the US, and over a quarter of the world's countries, a legally protected class is any group that has been discriminated against based on their race, gender, age, disability, and religion. The UK's Equality Act collates many anti-discrimination laws and regulations, of which religion and strongly held personal beliefs are considered a "protected characteristic," with all those who abide by these characteristics then considered a legally protected class. The act specifies that religion means "any religion," which includes "a lack of religion" and—most significantly for our purposes—"any religious or philosophical belief" (Key Non Parliamentary Papers Government Equalities 2010: Pt. 2, Ch. 1, pg. 3). Thus, it is illegal to discriminate or retaliate against someone who is acting in accordance with a personal religious or philosophical belief, even if those beliefs appear—at least on their surface—to be *only* about food. It was by this standard that the judge found that Mr. Casamitjana's personally held beliefs had been violated.

Casamitjana's lawyers argued that his veganism—his choice to not consume animal product in any form, including as food (meat, dairy, and eggs), clothing (leather or wool), or any product that had been subjected to animal testing—constituted a belief that should be protected by law. So at its most reductive interpretation, by agreeing that Mr. Casamitjana's beliefs met the standard for legal protection by the Equality Act, the judge was effectively ruling that his veganism could be considered a religion.

Given what we have learned about diet's connection to environmental health, the stakes of climate change, and the religious and ethical principles of individuals who abide by some form of vegetarianism, we are prepared to consider the question raised by this judge's ruling: Should the environmental practice of vegetarianism be given the same legal protections as the exercise of a religion?

### *Discussion Questions*

1. Do you think the judge ruled correctly in Mr. Casamitjana's case? Should his veganism—based in his personal philosophical beliefs and moral code—be given the same protective consideration as a religion? Why or why not?
2. Are there other behaviors that are not commonly thought of as "religious" that should be protected using the same standards?
3. What are your feelings on vegetarianisms as a way to combat climate change? Do you think it is a vital environmentalist practice? A useful tool for those who can manage it? A distraction from more important work?

## References

Adams, C. J. (2000) *The Sexual Politics of Meat: A Feminist-Vegetarian Critical Theory*. 10th anniversary ed. New York: Continuum.

Alexander, P., Brown, C., Arneth, A., Finnigan, J., and Rounsevell, M. D. A. (2016) "Human Appropriation of Land for Food: The Role of Diet," *Global Environmental Change* 41: 88–98. https://doi.org/10.1016/j.gloenvcha.2016.09.005

Bonhommeau, S. et al. (2013) "Eating Up the World's Food Web and the Human Trophic Level," *Proceedings of the National Academy of Sciences* 110(51): 20617–20. https://doi.org/10.1073/pnas.1305827110

Caballero, B., Allen, L., and Prentice, A. (2005) *Encyclopedia of Human Nutrition*. Amsterdam: Elsevier Science.

Chai, B. C. et al. (2019) "Which Diet Has the Least Environmental Impact on Our Planet? A Systematic Review of Vegan, Vegetarian and Omnivorous Diets," *Sustainability* 11(15): 4110. https://doi.org/10.3390/su11154110

Committee of the B.C.C.M. (2019) *History of the Philadelphia Bible-Christian Church for the First Century of Its Existence*. Philadelphia, PA: J.B. Lippincott.

Cornaro, L. (1768) *Discourses on a Sober and Temperate Life*. London: Printed for Benjamin White.

Deane-Drummond, C., and Artinian-Kaiser, R. (2018) *Theology and Ecology Across the Disciplines: On Care for Our Common Home*. 1st ed. London: London: T&T Clark.

Engs, R. C. (2001) *Clean Living Movements: American Cycles of Health Reform*. Westport, CT: Praeger.

Filippi, M. et al. (2010) "The Brain Functional Networks Associated to Human and Animal Suffering Differ Among Omnivores, Vegetarians and Vegans," *PLoS One* 5: e10847.

Foer, J. S. (2019) *We Are the Weather: Saving the Planet Begins at Breakfast*. 1st ed. New York: Farrar, Straus and Giroux.

Fresán, U., and Sabaté, J. (2019) "Vegetarian Diets: Planetary Health and Its Alignment with Human Health," *Advances in Nutrition* 10(Supplement_4): S380–8.

Godfray, H. C. J. et. al. (2018) "Meat Consumption, Health, and the Environment," *Science* 361.

Graham, S. (1833) *A Lecture on Epidemic Diseases Generally and Particularly the Spasmodic Cholera: With an Appendix Containing Several Testimonials, Rules of the Graham Boarding House, &c. By Sylvester Graham*. New York: Day.

———. (1839) *Lectures on the Science of Human Life*. 2 vols. Boston: Marsh, Capen, Lyon & Webb.

Graves, A. K., Hagedorn, C., Brooks, A., Hagedorn, R. L., and Martin, E. (2007) "Microbial Source Tracking in a Rural Watershed Dominated by Cattle," *Water Research* 41(16): 3729–39.

Gregory, S. (2010) *The Daniel Fast: Feed Your Soul, Strengthen Your Spirit, and Renew Your Body*. Carol Stream, IL: Tyndale House Publishers.

Harper, A. B. (2010) *Sistah Vegan: Black Female Vegans Speak on Food, Identity, Health, and Society*. New York: Lantern Books.

Hoffman, S. R., Stallings, S. F., Bessinger, R. C., and Brooks, G. T. (2013) "Differences Between Health and Ethical Vegetarians: Strength of Conviction, Nutrition Knowledge, Dietary Restriction, and Duration of Adherence," *Appetite* 65: 139–44.

Hopwood, C. J., Bleidorn, W., Schwaba, T., and Chen, S. (2020) "Health, Environmental, and Animal Rights Motives for Vegetarian Eating," *PloS One* 15(4): e0230609.

Iacobbo, K., and Iacobbo, M. (2004) *Vegetarian America: A History*. Westport, CT: Praeger.

Kemmerer, L. (2011) *Sister Species: Women, Animals and Social Justice*. Urbana: University of Illinois Press.

Key Non Parliamentary Papers Government Equalities, Office. (2010). *Equality Act Impact Assessment: Final version* (Royal Assent). Norwich: Stationery Office Publishers.

The Lancet. (2018) "We Need to Talk About Meat," *The Lancet (British Edition)* 392(10161): 2237.

Leitzmann, C. (2014) "Vegetarian Nutrition: Past, Present, Future," *The American Journal of Clinical Nutrition* 100(suppl_1): 496S–502S.

Leneman, L. (1999) "No Animal Food: The Road to Veganism in Britain, 1909–1944," *Society & Animals* 7(3): 219–28.

Liu, J., and Diamond, J. (2005) "China's Environment in a Globalizing World," *Nature* 435(7046): 1179–86.

Machovina, B., Feeley, K. J., and Ripple, W. J. (2015) "Biodiversity Conservation: The Key Is Reducing Meat Consumption," *Science of the Total Environment* 536: 419–31.

McQuirter, T. L. (2010) *By Any Greens Necessary: A Revolutionary Guide for Black Women Who Want to Eat Great, Get Healthy, Lose Weight, and Look Phat*. Chicago: Lawrence Hill Books.

Metcalfe, W., and Church Bible-Christian. (1840) *Bible Testimony, on Abstinence from the Flesh of Animals as Food: Being an Address Delivered in the Bible-Christian Church, North Third Street, West Kensington, on the Eighth of June 1840: Being the Anniversary of Said Church*. Philadelphia: J. Metcalfe & Co. Printers.

Nath, J. (2010) "'God Is a Vegetarian': The Food, Health and Bio-Spirituality of Hare Krishna, Buddhist and Seventh-Day Adventist Devotees," *Health Sociology Review* 19(3): 356–68.

Nissenbaum, S. (1980) *Sex, Diet, and Debility in Jacksonian America: Sylvester Graham and Health Reform, Contributions in Medical History*. Westport, CT: Greenwood Press.

Plante, C. N., Rosenfeld, D. L., Plante, M., and Reysen, S. (2019) "The Role of Social Identity Motivation in Dietary Attitudes and Behaviors Among Vegetarians," *Appetite* 141: 104307.

Preece, R. (2014) *Sins of the Flesh: A History of Vegetarian Thought*. Vancouver: UBC Press.

Pörtner, H. O. (2022) *Climate Change 2022: Impacts, Adaptation and Vulnerability: Working Group II Contribution to the Sixth Assessment Report of the Intergovernmental Panel on Climate Change*. New York: Cambridge University Press.

Rosenfeld, D. L., and Burrow, A. L. (2017) "The Unified Model of Vegetarian Identity: A Conceptual Framework for Understanding Plant-Based Food Choices," *Appetite* 112: 78–95.

Salt, H. S. (2021) *A Plea for Vegetarianism, and Other Essays; 1886*. Burbank, CA: Creative Media Partners, LLC.

Schiermeier, Q. (2019) "Eat Less Meat: UN Climate-Change Panel Tackles Diets," *Nature (London)* 572(7769): 291–2.

Shprintzen, A. D. (2013) *The Vegetarian Crusade: The Rise of an American Reform Movement, 1817–1921*. Chapel Hill: University of North Carolina Press.

Smith, J., Pratt, O., and Church of Jesus Christ of Latter-Day Saints (1971) *The Doctrine and Covenants, of the Church of Jesus Christ of Latter-Day Saints, Containing the revelations Given to Joseph Smith, Jun., the Prophet, for the Building Up of the Kingdom of God in the Last Days*. Westport, CT: Greenwood Press.

Stehfest, E. (2014) "Food Choices for Health and Planet," *Nature (London)* 515(7528): 501–2.

Steinfeld, H. (2006) *Livestock's Long Shadow: Environmental Issues and Options*, eds. P. Gerber, T. D. Wassenaar, V. Castel, M. Rosales, C. de Haan, and Nations Food and Agriculture Organization of the United and Environment and Development Livestock. Rome: Food and Agriculture Organization of the United Nations.

Svoboda, T. (2016) "Environmental Philosophy as a Way of Life," *Ethics and the Environment* 21(1): 39–60.

Swinburn, B. A. et al. (2019) "The Global Syndemic of Obesity, Undernutrition, and Climate Change: The Lancet Commission Report," *The Lancet (British Edition)* 393(10173): 791–846.

Terry, B. (2014) *Afro-Vegan: Farm-Fresh African, Caribbean & Southern Flavors Remixed*. Berkeley: Ten Speed Press.

Waldau, P., and Patton, K. C. (2006) *A Communion of Subjects: Animals in Religion, Science, and Ethics*. New York: Columbia University Press.

Walters, K. S., and Portmess, L. (2001) *Religious Vegetarianism: From Hesiod to the Dalai Lama*. Albany: State University of New York Press.

Willett, W. et al. (2019) "Food in the Anthropocene: The EAT—Lancet Commission on Healthy Diets from Sustainable Food Systems," *The Lancet (British Edition)* 393(10170): 447–92.

Wright, L., and Adams, C. J. (2015) *The Vegan Studies Project: Food, Animals, and Gender in the Age of Terror*. Athens, GA: University of Georgia Press.

## Further Reading

Carter, C. (2021) *The Spirit of Soul Food: Race, Faith, and Food Justice*. Chicago: University of Illinois Press.

Foer, J. S. (2019) *We Are the Weather: Saving the Planet Begins at Breakfast*. New York: Farrar, Straus and Giroux.

Ko, A., and Ko, S. (2017) *Aphro-Ism: Essays on Pop Culture, Feminism, and Black Veganism from Two Sisters*. New York: Lantern Books.

Preece, R. (2014) *Sins of the Flesh: A History of Vegetarian Thought*. Vancouver: UBC Press.

# 14 Energy

*Terra Schwerin Rowe*

There is a stretch of Highway 287, north of Amarillo, TX, that could easily be seen as something of an energy graveyard. Within a single horizon, one can see nearly the whole range of energy resources from the past two hundred years: trees still dot the landscape alongside a few head of cattle, coal in train cars, oil and natural gas wells, a nuclear plant in the distance, solar panels, and wind turbines in the foreground. Yet, on a closer look one would find that this horizon is not a graveyard but filled with active energy sites: the cattle fattening, the oil well pumping, the coal train chugging, the nuclear plant radiating, the windmill whirring, the solar panels reflecting. In short, this stretch of highway gives a visual representation of what Richard York and Shannon Bell have identified as the false narrative of "energy transition." Over the scope of two hundred years of industrial energy production and consumption York and Bell found that no new "alternative" energy—coal in place of lumber or solar panels in place of fossil fuels—has replaced any previous form of energy. Rather than true energy transitions, each new source has functioned as an addition, expanding the energy available for consumption (York and Bell 2019).

I, for one, long to look at a windmill or solar array and feel hopeful. But Bell and York's study is sobering. Why is it that expanded energy technologies and resources have merely allowed for increasingly energy-intensive lifestyles? Why have none of these new energy "alternatives" ever actually functioned as substitutes that would lead to real change? What would need to happen to break this pattern and actually transition away from energy cultures driving the current climate crisis?

In the 20th century, US Americans became the highest energy consumers in the world. Energy intensive lifestyles in the US tower over even other "developed" nations. By the end of the 20th century US energy consumption was 40% more than Germany, twice as much as Sweden, and three times as much as Japan and Italy (Nye 1999: 6). It does not matter if you are a five-year-old child, a Buddhist monk, or a homeless person. If you live in the United States, you will be consuming significantly more energy than others in the world—"more than double the global average" according to a 2008 MIT study (Gutowski et al. 2008: 2). So a further question is necessary: Why did each of these "alternative energies" intensify energy consumption in certain places and never expand energy access or "trickle

DOI: 10.4324/9781003259466-18

down" to other places that, in the 21st century, still face energy poverty and its severe human and environmental consequences?

Such inequalities and the injustices that arise from them—not least of which is that those who are most likely to suffer energy poverty are also the most likely to suffer the most devastating effects of climate change—evoke profound ethical questions. These are particularly poignant questions for religious traditions that value justice and care for the weak, downtrodden, and vulnerable. Though climate change may finally be receiving broader recognition, it exacerbates challenges that have long been considered by the robust tradition of religious energy ethics (Rowe 2022).

**BOX 14A**

Take a brief energy inventory. Spend five minutes tracing the energy sources and systems you are currently relying on. How far back can you identify where they came from? Do not forget your body, food, and agriculture. Are you aware of justice issues connected to these energy sources?

Even before climate change became a household phrase, the threats of nuclear proliferation and the oil crises of the 1970s spurred North American religious groups to reflect on the ethics of energy production and consumption. Within Christianity, the National Council of Churches began commissioning studies on energy practices and policies as early as 1974 (National Council of Churches of Christ 1974). Amid these studies, Dieter Hessel emerged as a leading figure on religious energy and environmental ethics (Hessel 1979). As a Presbyterian minister and scholar, Hessel helped spur the Presbyterian Church, USA (PCUSA) to adopt a policy statement on environmental issues that addressed energy policy in 1981. The US Conference of Catholic Bishops (1981) also released an early essay, closely followed by the Pontifical Academy of Science's "Mankind and Energy: Needs, Resources, Hopes" (Pontifical Academy of Sciences 1982).

These sources apply key values and religious teachings to energy practices and policies. They assess energy options available, apply guidelines, and articulate norms for making energy decisions on systemic as well as personal levels. Not until the 21st century, though, did serious scholarship begin to emerge that focused on not just applying religious ethics to existing energy practices, but also considering the relationship between religion and energy sciences. In 2010 leading Christian environmental ethicist Larry Rasmussen and professor of combustion Normand Laurendeau organized what they identified as likely the first conference in the US "to consider fully the significant connection between energy and religion" (Rasmussen et al. 2011: 873). Still, conference participants mainly assumed the perspective characteristic of what Bruno Latour calls the "modern constitution," which separates fact and value, science and meaning, and politics and science (Latour 1993). Such thinking leads to an unquestioned assumption that energy sciences and technologies are a given, that they do not produce meaning, are not infused with values, and are morally neutral. In this view, religious folk must reflect and respond to whatever science has rendered.

What has been seriously under-analyzed, then, is the way the concepts, sciences, and technologies of energy have been constructed with key theo-philosophical influences along the way. Looking back at York and Bell's research on the lack of true energy transition over the past two hundred years, one could easily draw defeatist conclusions. But this is not the purpose of their study, which points out that technological solutions cannot be the sole focus of climate mitigation strategies. We also need to look at the cultural influences alongside and within economic systems, values, assumptions, beliefs, and the patterns of living they evoke.

As scholars and proponents of environmental justice have long emphasized, environmental degradation goes hand in hand with social injustices like enslavement, colonialism, and racialized inequalities (Commission for Racial Justice 1987; Cone 2000). When we examine the histories of Western Christian engagements with energy and energy-related concepts, issues of social injustice also come to the foreground, allowing us to better analyze the long histories and entrenched systems informing current energy/climate justice issues. Therefore, if we are to adequately address the imbrications of energy and social injustice, we will need to more fully account for the ways that values, meanings, and even religious beliefs have not merely reflected on energy after the fact but have also informed and infused it from early on, shaping decisions about the directions energy science and technologies would take.

## Energy and Salvation

Though the term "energy" was not popularized in physics until the 19th century with modern thermodynamics, it synthesized ancient and early modern theologies and philosophies, views on the value of work, and understandings of heat. Historians of energy, for example, commonly trace the concept back to the ancient Greek philosopher Aristotle (384–322 BCE) and his neologism, *energeia*. However, some physicists and scholars have emphasized that the idea of energy conservation can be traced even before Aristotle to Parmenides (510–460 BCE) (Lindsay 1976).

Energy conservation would be formalized in the 19th century as the first law of thermodynamics, that energy can be neither created nor destroyed. It may, and likely will, change forms, but energy remains constant. Scholars see anticipations of this idea in ancient Greco-Roman thought, which long emphasized that while human perception of reality often focuses on continual change (plants grow, people die, rivers change course), beneath that flux, something remains constant. While much of Greco-Roman thought has associated this constancy with divinity, the law of energy conservation associated it with energy.

Informed by contemporary thinking, *energeia* is most commonly translated today as "being-at-work" (Sachs 2002: viii). But Aristotle did not think of it this way (Marder 2017). He introduced the term to distinguish between the possession of a capacity (*dunamis*) and the exercise of that capacity (*energeia*). For example, a seeing person's closed eyes would be an example of *dunamis* because they possess the capacity for sight but are not exercising that capacity. When a seeing person opens their eyes, they are exercising their capacity to see, so this would be an example of *energeia*. Along these lines, philosopher David Bradshaw translates Aristotle's *energeia* as the "exercise of a capacity" rather than the more common "being-at-work" (Bradshaw 2004: 3).

Aristotle's distinction between *dunamis* and *energeia* was important to German philosopher Gottfried Leibniz (1646–1716 CE) as he called for a new "science of dynamics." Leibniz distinguished what he identified as *vis mortua* (dead force) and *vis viva* (living force).

Aristotle also directly influenced religious understandings of energy. We have already seen how the idea of energy conservation resonated with a view of unchanging divinity, with each understood as a constant that underlies a surface of change. A similar tendency to align energy concepts with divinity was reinforced in Christianity as early as St. Paul, who regularly employed Aristotle's *energeia* in letters that were incorporated into the *New Testament*. Indeed, Bradshaw demonstrates that St. Paul not only used Aristotle's term but consistently employed it in an "unprecedented" way that proved profoundly influential for later Christian-influenced societies (Bradshaw 2006: 101). While others had applied *energeia* broadly, Paul limited his use of the term to spiritual agents—God, Satan, Christ, angels, or demons. In Philippians 3:21, for example, Paul writes, "[Christ] will transform the body of our humiliation that it may be conformed to the bod of his glory, by the power [*energeia*] that also enables him to make all things subject to himself" (NRSV).

Bradshaw argues that early Christian writers followed this example, and *energeia* became not just an activity or exercise of capacity but specifically an activation attributed to the Judeo-Christian God that led to human fulfillment. That the Pauline letters not only employed the term *energeia* but focused it as a way to talk about divine action and presence—and in particular for human fulfillment as salvation—created a conjunction that would prove influential.

## BOX 14B

Can you think of examples of contemporary energy sources that some people see as "saving" users? How are these claims justified? From what are people being saved?

### Technology, Science, and Salvation

While it is still common to think of religion and science/technology as part of separate, even competing spheres of influence, a closer historical perspective reveals that modern science, technology, and energy emerged with influence from religious values and desires. Historian David Noble, for example, has traced the influence of Christian theologies of creation, fall, and redemption on modern views of what science and technology are, what they mean, and what they should be used for.

Noble emphasizes that through the early Middle Ages, theology attributed value to the mechanical arts, but limited its efficacy to humans in their fallen condition. Later, though, a strain of theology starting with John Scottus Eriugena (800–877 CE), Hugh of St. Victor (1096–1141 CE), and eventually Francis Bacon (1561–1626 CE) and other early proponents of modern science emerged with a different view. The mechanical arts and sciences came to be seen not only as beneficial to humans in their fallen condition but as divinely granted gifts that could help humans regain what had been lost in the fall (Noble 1997). Bacon, for example, asserted in *Novum Organum*, "For man by the fall, lost at once his state of innocence, and his dominion over creation, both of which can be partially recovered even in this life, the first by religion and faith, the second by the arts and sciences" (Bacon 1902: Bk II, aph. 52, 290). Science and technology began to be seen as gifts that could restore humanity to their divinely granted status and thus contribute to religious redemption and fulfillment.

## Energy, Gender, and Human Formation

Aristotle's views on heat also had a lasting influence on science and technology. He theorized that heat moves matter from indeterminate substance to organized and ordered forms. In *Metaphysics* he called this process "concoction" (2002, 7.16, 1040b, 8–10) and explained that it was analogous to what happens when we add rennet to milk, causing unformed liquid to congeal or take on form in the process of making cheese.

For Aristotle, concoction played an essential role throughout biological development and was responsible for sexual differentiation. As feminist critics have pointed out, he viewed male and female characteristics on a continuum such that the male represented the full development of the species (Tuana 1993). The female was consequently defined by a lack or natural deficiency. For Aristotle, the vagina was not a different and distinct biological form but an undeveloped penis. The ovaries, too, were merely under-developed, undescended testicles, and menstrual fluid was merely unconcocted semen. Differences between the sexes, then, were determined by the level of heat available.

In *Generation of Animals*, for example, Aristotle (1942) emphasized,

> It will perhaps be now clearer for what reason one embryo becomes female and another male. For when the first principle does not bear sway and cannot concoct the nourishment through lack of heat nor bring it into its proper form, but is defeated in this respect, then must the material change into its opposite. Now the female is opposite to the male, and that insofar as the one is female and the other male.
>
> (*GA* IV, 1, 766a, 16–22)

Greater amounts of vital heat led to full development of biological forms: everything from differences in sexual organs to full brain development and functioning.

On account of their higher levels of vital heat, Aristotle concluded that males had larger brains with a more developed structure leading to a man's higher capacity for reason and more even temper (*GA* 744a, 25–30).

Aristotle's views had a long and continuing influence on theories of biological development through the influence of Galen of Pergamon (130–210 CE). Galen was a philosopher and physician who remained a leading authority on biological development and medicine in Byzantium for the next fourteen hundred years—and in Western Europe from the 11th century on. Galen continued in the wake of Aristotle's views on the vital role of heat for biological development, including that the female sex represented a lesser developed form. The influence of the view of sex differentiation rooted in heat variance can be seen continuing into medical texts from Ambroise Paré (credited with initiating modern surgery in the 16th century) to 19th century biologists Patrick Geddes and John Arthur Thomson.

In the 19th century, ancient views of heat converged with Leibnitz's proposed science of dynamics to create the modern science of energy, or thermodynamics. Toward the end of the 19th century, Darwinist Herbert Spencer combined evolutionary theory and thermodynamics, merging this long history of sex differentiation based on heat with energy science. Spencer understood the human body as a "closed" energy system and so understood that the amount of energy available in it would decrease over time. This is the second law of thermodynamics, that while energy remains stable (according to the first law of thermodynamics), in closed systems the amount available will degrade or decrease as it changes forms (from mechanical to heat energy, for example). Spencer surmised that the two most vital organ systems in the human body are the brain and the reproductive system and that the two are in competition for energy. He assumed that a female's reproductive system (regardless of pregnancy) required more energy and so impeded her brain's full development.

Based on this theory, women were discouraged from pursuing education in many Western educational systems. Edward Clarke of Harvard medical department, for example, wrote *Sex in Education; Or, A Fair Chance for Girls* (1875), where he argued that a university education would require too much intellectual energy from females, drawing this vital resource away from their reproductive organs and thus limiting their ability to develop fully as women. Consequently, he argued, women should not be allowed to pursue a university education as a way to conserve their energy.

## Energy, Race, and Human Development

When we look at the theological and philosophical ideas that influence understandings of energy, we see repeated examples of scientific claims made about who counts as fully human. Among many early modern thinkers, differences in energy correlated to human development not only in terms of gender but also race. Especially with the emergence of "modern racial science," which developed to defend the institution of slavery, thinkers began to argue that different races had different amounts of energy. In fact, historian Jürgen Osterhammel explains that "the racism of [the 19th century] did not end with skin color: it classified the human 'races' on a scale of potential physical and mental energy" (2015: 658). Anglo races were seen as capable of higher levels of intellectual energy, while Indigenous, African, and Asian races were understood to have energy best suited for manual labor, "base" energy that called for direction and ordering from the more intellectually energetic races.

The same correlation of energy capacity with civilizational development can also be seen in Herbert Spenser's theorization of evolution. He argued that levels of social, civilizational, and human development corresponded to levels of energy available, and he identified a range from "lesser developed" African tribes to the high energy capacities of European races that allowed them to create "more developed" industrial technologies and societies (Spencer, *First Principles*, cited in Daggett 2019: 117–18). Similarly, geologist Charles Lyell assumed a correspondence between energy and societal development. In 1845 he wrote, "it would be visionary to expect that, under any imaginable system this [African] race could at once acquire as much energy, and become as rapidly progressive, as the Anglo-Saxons" (Lyell 1845: 191). Such correlations between high energy, human development, and societal progress have meant that Western societies often interpret energy crises as racial crises.

These connections between energy and development also contributed to the understanding of energy resources and technologies as divine blessings. Coal, for example, was commonly interpreted in the early Industrial Revolution as indicating both divine purpose and racial superiority. In the 19th century, the majority of discovered coal deposits were in Great Britain and the US, and the white citizens of both nations interpreted this as evidence that God had granted the world's most energetic peoples an energy source with which they could raise up all humanity. For example, Barbara Freese cites a quote from a 1856 edition of *Christian Review* celebrating US citizens as

> a race of men energetic and enterprising; fitted by their natural characteristics, by their mental and moral culture, and by their hold on the pure gospel of Jesus Christ, to be leaders in the onward march of humanity, have thrust into their hands, unlooked for and unexpected, a treasure, which if used aright, must secure to them a controlling influence on the affairs of the world.
>
> (Quoted in Freese 2003: 12)

Similar conclusions were drawn about oil, "discovered" first in the US when it was on the brink of Civil War. In this context, oil was believed to be a divine gift, planted at the beginnings of creation but waiting to be uncovered when God's chosen nation needed it the most (Dochuk 2019). Even after the Civil War, early oil was commonly interpreted as redemptive, a savior, and even granted Christ-like characteristics (Rowe 2022).

**BOX 14C**

As these sections have shown, the history of contemporary energy technologies is intertwined with histories of sexism, racism, and colonialism. Should this change the ways people think about or use energy? How?

### Energy Anxiety

The 19th century introduced the double-edged sword of energy. While the first law of thermodynamics conveyed the optimism of an omnipotent divinity who always remained constant, the second law introduced a sense of anxiety at energy continually being lost, going to "waste" if it was not properly employed. According to Cara Daggett, the level of anxiety around energy issues during this period is only matched by the mid-20th century fear of nuclear annihilation and the 21st century energy anxieties sparked by climate change (Daggett 2019: 60).

It is no coincidence, then, that the age of energy science was quickly followed by increased anxieties about energy in bodies and nations. New diagnostic criteria of "fatigue" and energy maladies like neurasthenia emerged at the end of the 19th century. The US conservation movement also has its roots in this context of intensified energy anxieties. Teddy Roosevelt, the US president closely linked to the early conservation movement who would inaugurate the system of national parks, was himself a diagnosed neurasthenic who found treatment in a new religious movement called Muscular Christianity. This form of Protestantism promoted vigorous exercise, including "manly" outdoor activities on the American frontier. For Roosevelt among others, a lack of energy and resource conservation was a matter of what we might now call national security.

But even beyond manhood, what concerned many leaders in Anglo societies was the correspondence of energy and race. It is true, of course, that early conservationists like John Muir were inspired to lobby for national parks and other sustainability measures in response to the encroachment of privatized land, of leveled forests, and a trashed and commodified Niagara Falls. But also functioning here—explicitly in the case of Roosevelt—was the need to conserve in order to ward off weakness sparked by the improper use of energy resources in human bodies and in nations that would, he worried, lead to "race suicide" (qouted in de la Peña 2003, 29).

### The Religion-Energy Science Synthesis

As the previous sections have shown, religion and energy concepts have consistently converged; philosophical and theological ideas, including some deeply destructive and divisive ones, have been informed by and informed the ways energy is understood. If we are going to analyze issues of environmental and social justice as we develop religious energy ethics, it is important to attend to these histories. Religion and energy have long had a relationship of conversation, or perhaps even synthesis.

Another point of connection comes from electricity and magnetism. Historian Ernst Benz has identified a long-standing "electrical theology," in which electricity and magnetism were understood as vehicles of divine agency. Benz argues that the cultural influence of these sciences and technologies was so profound that they initiated a theological shift in the primary metaphors of divinity. Where the sun had been a dominant metaphor of divinity in Greco-Roman theo-philosophy and Mediterranean religious traditions, Benz notes that the 17th and 18th centuries witnessed a profound shift toward more immanent metaphors of divinity consistent with electricity and magnetism (1989).

More recent historians have also highlighted these electrical theologies. Of particular interest in the North American context is their influence on early evangelicalism. Brett Malcom Grainger has written a fascinating alternative history of antebellum evangelicalism and environmentalism. His final chapter is of particular interest here, as it focuses entirely on the variety of electrical theologies that influenced early evangelicals. Grainger notes that evangelicals consistently described their conversion experiences by employing electrical metaphors and electrified affects (2019). In the case of electricity and magnetism, then, this encounter of religion and techno-sciences did not lead to a diminution of religion but produced new forms and expressions of it.

Synthesis is also a better descriptive category for religion and science when we look at the rise of modern energy science. In her genealogy of modern energy, Cara Daggett identifies a functioning "geotheology," informed especially by Scottish Calvinism, which shaped the concepts, ideals, and metaphors employed by early energy scientists. Daggett emphasizes the optimism that accompanied the first law of thermodynamics: the ways it profoundly resonated with a sense of all reality being sustained by a divine force that had the power to give and take life but itself could be neither created nor destroyed (Daggett 2019).

One might expect that the pessimism of the second law of thermodynamics—that energy available to human use is constantly degrading—might have proven challenging from a religious perspective. However, historian Crosbie Smith has demonstrated just the opposite for a small group of influential Scottish energy scientists. William Thomson (ennobled as Lord Kelvin), William Rankine, Peter Guthrie Tait, and James Clerk Maxwell all became leading figures in thermodynamics, and all were evangelicals, concerned with what they perceived to be a rising tide of atheism in society. In particular, they objected to the reigning mechanistic views of natural philosophy and science that interpreted nature as self-sufficient, requiring no divine sustenance or intervention. From this perspective, the second law of thermodynamics seemed to demonstrate that all creation (not just humanity) was subject to a profound degradation consistent with the Calvinist doctrine of depravity. Consequently, Thomson and others felt that in the second law of thermodynamics in particular, they had found scientific verification for their theological view of creation. Contrary to the views of the mechanists, the earth could never sustain itself but was continually in need of divine support and crying out for divine redemption (Smith 1999).

Energy concepts, sciences, and technologies from *energeia* to electricity and thermodynamics have consistently been synthesized with a theological belief in a deity who not only created and continually sustains the world but also planned and provided for its redemption. From electricity to coal, energy resources were regularly interpreted as divine gifts, granted specifically to the energetic nations and races God had chosen to play a larger role in the redemption of the world. These patterns of thought and feeling coalesced around early oil extraction and continue to resonate into the 21st century.

When analyzing and reflecting on why US Americans in particular have been so resistant to mitigating climate change by re-evaluating energy production and consumption, it is important to recognize that this culture has long been invested in a sense that energy leads to and indicates full humanity. Those of us raised in the US have inherited long-standing philosophical, spiritual and theological investments—not just technological, scientific, and infrastructural investments—in an energy intensive culture. Consequently, if US Americans are going to be fully convicted and convinced to enthusiastically explore true alternative energy cultures, merely offering techno-savior energy solutions will not be enough. Alternative modes of divinity, sacrality, and humanity will also need to be explored.

## Case Study

In 1859, near Titusville, PA, "Colonel" Edwin Drake first struck subterranean oil using new methods that proved oil extraction could be a moneymaking proposition. Petroleum had long been collected from the surface of pools and used by Indigenous peoples as a healing ointment. Titusville, though, marked the beginning of drilling for oil, employing technologies used for salt mining, which could extract enough oil for mass consumption. At the time, the primary use for the substance was as an illuminant, taking the place of sperm whale oil, which was becoming less accessible due to overhunting.

Just as with the previous examples of coal and electricity, the predominant reaction of religious folk to the new availability and science of petroleum was synthesis with their existing beliefs. Other resources and technologies like coal, gold, cotton, and railroads had certainly been associated with divine blessing. But oil was particularly prone to religious enchantment (Dochuk 2019; Rowe 2022). It gurgled and gulped, making digestive noises like an animate creature. It came from the ground in starts and stops, seemingly having a mind of its own (Sabin 1999). For some, like Christian Spiritualists and followers of a new religious movement called Harmonialism, oil came to be understood as a medium between spiritual and material realms. In fact, as historian Rochelle Zuck has demonstrated, Christian Spiritualists created their own oil companies like the Chicago Rock Oil Company not primarily to make money but to demonstrate the practical use of religion (Zuck 2014). Once again, in the fight against a rising tide of atheism, energy was employed to support religious faith.

Even more orthodox Christians merged their religious beliefs with oil. Just seven years after the first oil strike in Titusville, Presbyterian pastor Rev. S. J. Eaton published a text, *Petroleum* (1866), about the history of the region and the changes that oil had brought to his parishioners and his home area. Eaton began by placing oil in the scope of a creation narrative:

> Before man was created, the great store-house in the earth's bosom was filled with its minerals, and as the centuries rolled by, in their slow and solemn march, these treasures were gradually brought to light. Not at once did the earth disclose her mighty resources; but just as man needs them, and as they should tend to his own best interests, and the glory of the great Giver.
>
> (60)

Eaton paints a desperate portrait of his county before oil: "hope was just about ready to die out in the hearts of the people" (35) who were facing significant economic hardships. In this context, Eaton concludes,

> It was no mere accidental circumstance that this vegetable deposit was changed to coal and oil nor was it merely a fortuitous event that in these last years these stores of wealth were brought to light. It was the time appointed in the eternal counsels for their appearance. It was the fulfillment of the word of life, that earth should supply abundantly the wants of all the creatures moving upon its surface.
>
> (251–2)

In addition to placing Venango County and oil within the scope of a creation narrative, Eaton also addresses a dampening concern that was already being articulated. Only seven years into a petro-economy, some were already asking: Are we doing this too fast? Are we extracting too much? Will it run out? In a chapter toward the end of the text titled "Permanence of the Supply" Eaton addresses these concerns. He starts with a response of a natural philosopher:

> We have no evidence that the formation of oil has ceased in the regions below. We know that the mighty furnace fires are still kept up, and there is reason to believe that the store of vegetable deposit was at the first ample, and why may we not suppose that the mighty rotors in the rocks below are still key in active operation?
>
> (264)

In the next sentence, Eaton turns abruptly theological: "There is no limit, surely, to Omnipotence" (264). Returning to the mode of natural philosopher, he continues making various arguments based on experience with water wells drying up or coal veins failing. We would not confuse, he reasons, these local cessations with a general conclusion that we have used *all* the world's water or minerals. Change is the constant, he reminds us. Just as some harvests are plentiful and some are meagre, so oil will fluctuate. But it would be a mistake to conclude that no more is being produced in the depths of the earth and that it could all be used up. He concludes these natural philosophical arguments, and the chapter, once again with a theological statement:

> The general result, no doubt, will be that the supply of petroleum will be kept up while there is need of artificial light to carry on the operations of life, whilst any of the purposes to which it is now applied remain to be fulfilled, as until the present organization of society and the world shall have been finally changed. To go upon any other supposition would be to suppose that the course of nature, and the operations of Providence would be changed, and God's wisdom and power cease to be adequate to the supply of the wants of his creatures.
>
> (268)

Eaton has "no doubt" that there will be oil enough for both human needs and desires. As he suggests earlier in the text, the whole experience of Venango County, rescued from its despair, has a message Eaton is eager to preach near and far: "A new lesson has been taught the world, that God's treasures are inexhaustible, and that his hand can never be shortened" (61).

This case study has focused on a text from over a hundred years ago, and scientific understandings of the production and supply of oil have changed considerably. But we should caution against the conclusion that religion and energy interactions have ceased or that oil is now fully disenchanted. Sometimes oil and energy representation still retain a sense of transcendent meaning, salvation, and divine presence even into the 21st century. Take, for example, evangelical E. Calvin Beisner's theological interpretation of oil as an extension of climate denialism in an op-ed for *The Christian Post* (2013).

### *Discussion Questions*

1. What kind of theology is Eaton articulating? What role do humans have in the narrative of creation as he understands it? What are God's primary aims and goals? What role does oil play?
2. Why do you think Eaton so repeatedly connects divine omnipotence with the supply of oil? Given this connection, what would it mean theologically for Eaton to recognize the limits of oil?
3. Where do you see oil and energy in contemporary discourse? What values, religious or otherwise, are reflected in that discourse? What are the social and environmental implications of those values?

## References

Aristotle. (1942) *Generation of Animals: Loeb Classical Library,* trans. J. Henderson. Cambridge, MA: Harvard University Press, 366.

_____. (2002) *Metaphysics*, trans. J. Sachs. Santa Fe: Green Lion Press.

Bacon, F. (1902) *Novum Organum*, ed. J. Devey. New York: P. F. Collier & Son.

Beisner, E. C. (2013) "Fossil Fuels, Enemy or Friend? Divine Design in the Carbon Cycle," *The Christian Post*, October 28, www.christianpost.com/news/fossil-fuels-enemy-or-friend-divine-design-in-the-carbon-cycle.html

Benz, E. (1989) *The Theology of Electricity: On the Encounter and Explanation of Theology and Science in the 17th and 18th Centuries*. Eugene: Pickwick Publications.

Bradshaw, D. (2004) *Aristotle East and West: Metaphysics and the Division of Christendom*. New York: Cambridge University Press.

———. (2006) "The Concept of the Divine Energies," *Philosophy and Theology* 18(1): 93–120.

Clarke, E. H. (1875) *Sex in Education; Or, A Fair Change for Girls*. Boston, MA: James R Osgood and Company.

Commission for Racial Justice. (1987) *Toxic Wastes and Race in the United States: A National Report on the Racial and Socio-Economic characteristics of Communities with Hazardous Waste Sites*. New York: United Church of Christ.

Cone, J. (2000) "Whose Earth Is It Anyway?" *Cross Currents* 50(1–2): 36–46.

Daggett, C. N. (2019) *The Birth of Energy: Fossil Fuels, Thermodynamics, and the Politics of Work*. Durham, NC: Duke University Press.

de la Peña, C. T. (2003) *The Body Electric: How Strange Machines Built the Modern American*. New York: New York University Press.

Dochuk, D. (2019) *Anointed with Oil: How Christianity and Crude Made Modern America*. New York, NY: Basic Books.

Eaton, S. J. M. (1866) *Petroleum: A History of the Oil Region of Venango County, Pennsylvania*. Philadelphia, PA: J.P. Skelly.

Freese, B. (2003) *Coal: A Human History*. Cambridge: Perseus Pub.

Grainger, B. M. (2019) *Church in the Wild: Evangelicals in Antebellum America*. Cambridge: Harvard University Press.

Gutowski, T. et al. (2008) "Environmental Life Style Analysis (ELSA)," International Symposium on Electronics and the Environment, San Francisco.

Hessel, D. (1979) *Energy Ethics: A Christian Response*. New York: Friendship Press.

Latour, B. (1993) *We Have Never Been Modern*. Cambridge: Harvard University Press.

Lindsay, R. B. (1976) *Energy: Historical Development of the Concept*. Stroudsburg, PA: Dowden, Hutchinson and Ross.

Lyell, C. (1845) *Travels in North America, Canada, and Nova Scotia, with Geological Observations*. London: John Murray.

Marder, M. (2017) *Energy Dreams: Of Actuality*. New York: Columbia University Press.

National Council of Churches of Christ. (1974) *National Church Panel on Strip Mining and the Energy Crisis*. New York: Interfaith Center on Corporate Responsibility and the Commission on Religion in Appalachia (NCC).

Noble, D. F. (1997) *The Religion of Technology: The Divinity of Man and the Spirit of Invention*. New York: Alfred A. Knopf.

Nye, D. (1999) *Consuming Power: A Social History of American Energies*. Cambridge, MA: MIT Press.

Osterhammel, J. (2015) *The Transformation of Ute World: A Global History of the Nineteenth Century*, trans. P. Camiller. Princeton, NJ: Princeton University Press.

Pontifical Academy of Sciences. (1982) *Mankind and Energy: Needs, Resources, Hopes*. Amsterdam: Elsevier.

Rasmussen, L., Laurendeau, N., and Solomon, D. (2011) "Introduction to 'The Energy Transition: Religious and Cultural Perspectives'," *Zygon* 46: 872–89.

Rowe, T. S. (2023) *Of Modern Extraction: Experiments in Critical Petro-Theology*. New York: T&T Clark, Bloomsbury.

Sabin, P. (1999) "'A Dive into Nature's Great *Grab-Bag'*: Nature, Gender and Capitalism in the Early Pennsylvania Oil Industry," *Pennsylvania History* 66(4): 472–505.

Sachs, J. (2002) "Introduction," in J. Sachs (trans.) *Aristotle's Nicomachean Ethics*. Newbury: Focus.

Smith, C. (1999) *The Science of Energy: A Cultural History of Energy Physics in Victorian Britain*. Chicago: University of Chicago Press.

Tuana, N. (1993) *The Less Noble Sex: Scientific, Religious, and Philosophical Conceptions of Woman's Nature*. Bloomington: Indiana University Press.

US Catholic Bishops. (1981) *Reflections on the Energy Crisis*. Washington, DC: United States Catholic Conference.

York, R., and Bell, S. (2019) "Energy Transitions or Additions?: Why a Transition from Fossil Fuels Requires More than the Growth of Renewable Energy," *Energy Research and Social Science* 51: 40–3.

Zuck, R. R. (2014) "The Wizard of Oil: Abraham James, the Harmonial Wells, and the Psychometric History of the Oil Industry," In R. Barrett and D. Worden (eds) *Oil Culture*. Minneapolis: University of Minnesota Press, 19–42.

## Further Reading

Daggett, C. N. (2019) *The Birth of Energy: Fossil Fuels, Thermodynamics, and the Politics of Work*. Durham, NC: Duke University Press.

Dochuk, D. (2019) *Anointed with Oil: How Christianity and Crude Made Modern America*. New York, NY: Basic Books.

Frigo, G. (2018) "Energy Ethics: A Literature Review," *Relations* 6: 173–214.

Nye, D. (1999) *Consuming Power: A Social History of American Energies*. Cambridge, MA: MIT Press.

Rowe, T. S. (2023) *Of Modern Extraction: Experiments in Critical Petro-Theology*. New York: T&T Clark, Bloomsbury.

Smith, C. (1999) *The Science of Energy: A Cultural History of Energy Physics in Victorian Britain*. Chicago: University of Chicago Press.

# 15 Justice Otherwise

*Nicole Hoskins*

## Introduction

When the environmental activists from Altgeld Gardens got together, almost every meeting unfolded in the same way, with participants struggling to understand how to get justice for communities plagued by antiblack environmental racism. Many came from or worked in Altgeld, a black housing project in Chicago known as one of the most egregious examples of environmental racism because of city-made water, land, and air pollution.

As the activists presented ideas on one particular day, a woman confidently asserted that the group needed to petition the City of Chicago for a redistribution of resources. For her, the housing project's environmental problems were caused by the city's uneven distribution of environmental burdens to black communities. But after she spoke, she recoiled in disgust remembering how the City constantly insisted that residents prove their worthiness before receiving resources and how, when they were actually granted resources, the City lacked an overall plan and accountability for getting them to their community. Shortly after she realized the limits of her proposed approach, another activist spoke up to suggest the people in Altgeld ought to have a say about what happens in their community. It took only seconds before he backed down, remembering with misgiving that on previous occasions when residents had been included, the City had exploited them to push a political agenda. Plans of action would be drawn up in a collaborative meeting between the activists and the City but then often came to an abrupt halt after an initial photo-op for the press. In short, the activists realized that participatory approaches to justice, as David Pellow argues, are often merely "a step toward a more sophisticated effort at differential inclusion, co-optation, displacement of movement goals, diffusion of grassroots energy, assimilation, and a strengthening of existing power relations" (2018).

The meeting went on like this for the next hour or so, with moments of discovery followed repeatedly by the stark realization that none of the approaches to justice adequately addressed their plight. Every idea seemed ultimately destined to protect something or someone other than them and, to some extent, to exacerbate their environmental dispossession and perpetuate injustice.

DOI: 10.4324/9781003259466-19

The ephemeral nature of justice illuminates the limits of environmental justice in a liberal humanist frame—that is, the limits of the assumption and belief that all people have been bestowed with humanity, rights, and entitlements and are therefore autonomous, stable, equal, and free to exercise their rights when inclined to do so. The political systems surrounding Altgeld Gardens ask activists and residents to understand themselves as liberal subjects with equal rights who are therefore capable of making appeals for environmental justice. But such appeals for environmental justice and equality felt elusive to them; they were grasping at something that seemed concrete and matter-of-fact for white communities but abstract for them. "This would never happen in a white space," was a common refrain in that meeting and every meeting thereafter, a somber reminder that justice cherishes and protects white bodies and spaces, whereas justice for black bodies and spaces was tenuous at best.

In *Black Right/White Wrong: The Critique of Racial Liberalism*, Charles Mills describes precisely this challenge and refers to it as "racial liberalism" (2017). Mills argues that there can be no racial equality until US society adequately attends to and addresses the role of slavery and black subjugation in the development of the liberal state and its attendant discourse on justice and equality.

Echoing Mills, Saidiya Hartman notes that liberalism is a form of "abstract equality," based on the idea that to see everyone as persons and treat them equally, laws must be devoid of history or references to prior embodied and material realities. In other words, abstract equality is supposed to move beyond emancipation, which is "laden with the vestiges of slavery," and toward a narrative of blacks as subjects who should be treated "as if equal" to all others. Yet Hartman insists that abstract equality, as a requirement for formal equality, in reality produces white entitlement and black subjugation. She writes,

> It is not simply that rights are inseparable from the entitlements of whiteness or that blacks should be recognized as legitimate rights bearers; rather, the issue at hand is the way in which the stipulation of abstract equality produces white entitlement and black subjection in its promulgation of formal equality.
> (Hartman 1997: 116)

In other words, erasing the history of slavery and racial domination produces white entitlement rather than black subjectivity.

Mills and Hartman help to elucidate the disconnection activists at Altgeld Gardens felt from rhetoric that allowed them to assert their human rights and demand justice while they were being denied safe water, soil, and air. They saw that white spaces tended to be protected from pollution but theirs do not. This is the ruse of abstract equality and justice.

**BOX 15A**

Have you encountered abstract applications of justice, where rules or principles were applied "neutrally" in defiance of historical and systemic inequities? Have you encountered more concrete and fair applications of justice?

Much writing about environmental justice works within a liberalist framework and so produces white environmental entitlement. Under abstract justice, historical realities like the Middle Passage, slavery, the plantation system, Jim Crow segregation, and redlining are said to have nothing to do with how contemporary cities distribute their benefits and burdens. Under this (false) logic, it follows that black environmental degradation is the result of happenstance. This gives those in positions of power a license to continue to distribute environmental burdens unevenly in black communities. In other words, white spaces and white subjecthood are protected only through black ontological and environmental subjugation.

In working toward an ideal version of the human in Western societies, abstract forms of justice disregard the persistent pattern of black ontological and environmental subjugation. This chapter traces that pattern through decolonial theorist Sylvia Wynter's conceptualizations of "Man 1" and "Man 2," which describe ways the concept of "human" is a Western social construction that has shifted over time to subjugate people of color. Many scholars have already traced Wynter's understanding of the human to reveal black dehumanization; this chapter builds on that while also incorporating Wynter's discussion of the environment. I suggest that by placing Wynter's environmental analysis alongside her discursive tracing of the invention of the human, we get a better understanding of the roots, systems, and prevailing logics that tacitly organize environments to naturalize antiblackness in place.

To that end, instead of beginning with Man 1 or Man 2, I begin with Wynter's exposition of original sin, which created the pattern structuring the idea of Man 1 and Man 2. Abstract equality and justice, which stipulates black ontological and environmental subjugation, is not based completely on liberal humanism, or Man 1 or Man 2, but originates within the theological concept of original sin.

The second part of this essay invites you to consider whether justice is possible within a Christian settler-colonial state. I briefly introduce the concept of "justice otherwise"—that is, thinking about environmental justice outside or otherwise than the modes of the Christian colonial state. Interestingly, despite Wynter's sustained critique of religion, she finds within a religion the possibility to be otherwise. As Mayra Rivera has noted about Wynter's work, religion should be viewed "not only a tool of colonial ideology, but also a resource for its subversion" (2021: 58). In many ways, then, religion can offer us a way to think justice otherwise than within Christian and liberal humanist settler-colonial logics.

## The Pattern of Original Sin as Uneven Distribution of Being/Land

Sylvia Wynter draws from multiple fields to reveal a recurrent episteme that has shaped Western society. Specifically, her body of work maps the discursive invention of the human being in Western society, whom she identifies as types that she calls Man 1 and Man 2. According to Wynter, Man 1 emerged in the 15th century through European conquest, settler colonialism, and slavery and depicts white Christian rational subjects as the ideal normative being over and against Native Americans and Negros, whom white people by and large understood as irrational and depraved enemies of Christ (Wynter 2003: 265). Man 2 emerged in the 19th century with the advent of the biological sciences, depicting white subjects as the naturally selected normative subject in contrast to black subjects, whom these sciences deemed to be morally degenerate. Wynter's work reveals how both are products of a Christian humanism rooted in original sin, and that a persistent pattern of black ontological and environmental subjugation is prevalent in each.

Original sin refers to a Christian theological concept: because Adam disobeyed God, all human beings inherit a deficient or disproportionate nature that is enslaved to sin. In other words, all persons lack true being. The only way one can be redeemed from ontological depravity and achieve true being is through baptism into the Christian community. This idea presents "true" humanity as something that must be ascended to, which inherently dehumanizes those who have not ascended, those who are not Christian. For Wynter, what is important are the ways in which this Christian order of being is embodied and thus legitimated by medieval Christian society. For example, those who were baptized were understood as having true being, whereas those who were not baptized were understood as reflecting ontologically deficiency (Wynter 1989: 641). The basis of original sin, for Wynter, is a structural opposition between being/non-being that becomes embodied within medieval Christian society.

Structural ontological division between being and nonbeing was a totalizing episteme that the Church also used to divide the earth geographically. Because of Adam's sin, the Church understood the earth as "fallen." But parts of the earth had been "saved" and were inhabited by those who had "true being" (the redeemed Christians). Interestingly, such persons resided exclusively in mild or temperate climates and were thus said to be covered by God's grace. The remining half of the earth was occupied by those who were "ontologically depraved" (the fallen). They resided in inhabitable lands with a torrid or tropical climate, on the basis of that climate the Church deemed them to be outside and beyond God's grace. Wynter notes that "temperate regions centered on Jerusalem—regions that, because held up above the element of water by God's Providential Grace, were habitable—and, on the other, those realms that, because outside this Grace, had to be uninhabitable" (2003: 279). The center of the earth divided the two realms. Europe, with its mild temperature, was geographically fixed within God's grace; Africa, with its hotter climate, represented hell, a place devoid of God's grace. Wynter exemplifies this with

> the hitherto nonnavigable Cape Bojardor on the bulge of West Africa—a cape that had been projected, in the accounts of the earth's geography given by medieval Christian geographers, as being the *ne plus ultra* line and boundary between the habitable temperate zone of Europe and the [un]inhabitable torrid zones.
> (1995: 9)

This Christian humanist geographical praxis reveals a pattern of original sin—namely, a structural norm of uneven distribution of being/environments. It reveals a structural opposition in which Europeans/whites (and their environments) ascend to "true" being only through black ontological and environmental negation.

The Christian humanist geographical logic says that Europeans/whites are held in God's grace because they reside in Europe where the temperature is mild. Their geographic location and temperate climate allow their ascension to moral subjecthood, and their environmental spaces are protected by the fact that they are white and therefore fully human. In other words, they are environmentally privileged simply by being white. Since true being/land requires a structural opposition for it to be true, Wynter's exposition of original sin reveals that whites benefit environmentally from black environmental and ontological negation. This is evident in how Africa is imagined as an environmentally damned region that is uninhabitable by those other than the depraved fallen. The Church used the hot climate to further justify its understanding of African/black people and their environments as depraved and immoral.

In many ways, Lynn White Jr.'s infamous article "The Historical Roots of Our Ecological Crisis" is correct to highlight how Christian human-centeredness is to blame for our ecological crisis (1967). But he misses the point by not recognizing how human exceptionalism is achieved by positioning black peoples as nonbeing and their spaces as "wild," "irrational," and environmentally destitute.

### *Man 1*

Original sin also structures what Wynter calls Man 1. The idea of Man 1 emerged in parallel with the physical sciences during the 14th to 15th centuries when Copernicus and Galileo's theory that the earth was not fixed but moves overturned the legitimacy of Christian humanist geographical praxis. The shift dethroned "clergy man" and in its place instituted "rational man." In this new humanist order, baptism was no longer required for "true being." Instead, "man" was born from reason. To be human was to be reasonable. Importantly, Wynter notes that even though "rational man" displaced "clergy man," the birth of man as rational was "hybridly secular and religious." As Mayra Rivera notes, man as a rational creature "still depends on God to guarantee the rational nature of the human. Furthermore, humanism does not abandon the fundamental logic of original sin; it just displaces the realms of being and nonbeing from heaven and earth to the human" (2021: 62). In this way, the various reinventions of "man" in Western society continue to be informed by the theological concept of original sin.

> **BOX 15B**
>
> Can you think of examples in your own life or in broader culture where the most "rational" and "reasonable" people are considered the most human and/or given the most power?

For example, in this hybrid religio-secular humanism, Europeans reasoned not only that God created the vastness of nature to serve "man," but also that there was a rational divine design imbedded within nature that could be known. Wynter writes,

> It was the new premise that God had created the world/universe for mankind's sake, as a premise that ensured that [God] would have had to make it according to rational, nonarbitrary rules that could be knowable by the beings that [God] had made it for, that would lead to Copernicus's declaration . . . that since the universe had been made for our sake by the best and wisest of master craftsmen, it had to be knowable.
>
> (2003: 278)

This new understanding of "man" and the earth marked by a "rational divine design" legitimated Native American genocide, settler colonialism, and black slavery. The earth's center was no longer understood as a non-navigable region that Europeans avoided so as not to be near the "torrid"/"hell-like" spaces of the African "Adamic-fallen." Instead, Europeans now valorized countries in Africa as places to be explored, known, and—of course—exploited. The same was true for parts of the Western Hemisphere, which Christian humanist geographers had understood to be *terra nullius*. Wynter notes that the west of Europe had long been "known as being devoid of land . . . submerged in its 'natural place' under water" (ibid., 279). But the new rational understanding of the earth motivated Europeans to set out to "discover" new worlds, implementing their understanding of a rational divine design as a way to assert their humanity.

Although revised, "rational man" maintained the same pattern wherein whites ascend to the epitome of being and "discover"/conquer the environment through Native American genocide and black dehumanization and slavery. Wynter explains,

> Columbus would, on landing, at once take possession of the islands at which he had arrived, expropriating them in the name of the Spanish state, while offering in his first report home to ship back some of the indigenous peoples as slaves for sale on the "just" grounds that they were idolaters . . . [and] large numbers of peoples of African descent would be transshipped as the substitute slave labor force whose role would be indispensable to the founding of the new societies.
>
> (1995: 11)

In this new order, whites justified Native American genocide, conquering Indigenous land and enslaving Africans by again positioning themselves as rational and Native Americans and enslaved Africans as "irrational" enemies of Christ. This is most explicitly stated in the doctrine of discovery in which Pope Nicholas authorized King Alfonso to

> invade, search out, capture, vanquish, and subdue all Saracens and pagans whatsoever, and other enemies of Christ wheresoever placed, and the kingdoms, dukedoms, principalities, dominions, possessions, and all movable and immovable goods whatsoever held and possessed by them and to reduce their persons to perpetual slavery, and to apply and appropriate to himself and his successors the kingdoms, dukedoms, counties, principalities, dominions,

> possessions, and goods, and [the right] to convert them [those things] to his and their use and profit.
>
> (Davenport 1917: 17)

In the colonial context, enemies of Christ were those who did not exploit land and people for profit, appropriating and saving for their descendants. Because Native Americans had not exploited the land and people for profit, they and the land they inhabited were understood as wild, untamed, undeveloped. They and the land they inhabited were understood to be things that could be discovered and conquered. Indeed, part of the argument against Native Americans as rightful title bearers in the *Johnson v. McIntosh* case was that any reasonable human being (namely, a white one) would have worked the land and developed it into a source of wealth for "their use and profit." By Western European standards, Native Americans had not done so, and so they could not be considered rational humans. Andrea Smith notes,

> Native peoples were disqualified from being "discoverers" because they did not properly work . . . As they did not work, Native peoples had the ontological status of things to be discovered—the status of nature. By "work" [she means] the ability to transform nature into property.
>
> (Smith 2020: 118, 120)

Antiblackness and Native American genocide are woven together under settler colonialization and slavery. In *Black Shoals: Offshore Formations of Black and Native Studies*, Tiffany Lethabo King makes this clear when she identifies the 15th century as a form of conquistador humanism. She writes, "Conquistador humanism is the crafting and sustaining of European human life and self-actualization through Black and Indigenous death." This happened quite literally and also, King notes, cartographically when European settler colonialists wrote and drew themselves onto maps in a cartographic attempt to identify themselves as human subjects over and against the "chaotic" and "irrational" Indigenous and black people (King 2019: 84–6).

Transforming nature into property is rooted in antiblackness. Indeed, antiblackness had already been operating through Christian humanist geographical praxes that devalued African countries as "torrid" and "hellish" and African people as the "ontologically deficient Adamic-fallen," while valuing white spaces as temperate and insured under the grace of God. And so, with African land and bodies having already been positioned as enemies of Christ, the doctrine of discovery further justified their pillaging, "reducing [Africans] to perpetual slavery" (ibid.).

### *Man 2*

The early 19th century marked another shift, this time away from theology and reason and toward the human as a natural organism (natural man), what Wynter calls Man 2. Despite the shift, antiblackness persisted, this time based on logic derived from evolutionary science. Wynter notes that for the recently freed black population, “The negative inheritance was no longer from Adam in Genesis, but from the processes of natural dysselection within the new secular origin of the text of evolution” (1989: 642). Thus, the Christian humanist and geographic schema now operated through nature as that which “naturally selects” certain species for survival based on their alleged inherent superiority.

**BOX 15C**

Can you think of examples, in your own life or in broader culture, where those who have authority or control are assumed to be “naturally” more suited to it than others?

Race-based evolutionary science spouted many such racist theories. Most prevalent was the doctrine of environmental determinism popularized by French biologist Jean Baptiste-Lamarck. Environmental determinism is the idea that the environment or nature *caused* racial and cultural differences by providing conditions (climate, soil, etc.) under which cultures grew or declined. For Lamarck, a person’s mental and physical abilities were based on inherited characteristics one acquires from one’s environment, which he believed could be passed down from one generation to the next (Mitchell 2000: 18). Lamarck’s doctrine lost momentum in the 18th century, but neo-Lamarckians revived it a century later. Minister and social gospel leader Josiah Strong’s work had strong resonances to Lamarckian ideas. For example, in *Our Country*, Strong figures Anglo-Saxons as superior because the US climate acts as a stimulus that energizes and strengthens them. He writes,

> [N]othing more manifestly distinguishes the Anglo-Saxon than his intense and persistent energy; and he is developing in the United States an energy which, in eager activity and effectiveness, is peculiarly America. This is due . . . more largely to our climate, which acts as a constant stimulus.
>
> (Strong 1885: 173)

Strong understood the American climate as stimulating whites to conquer the “heathenistic” darker races. For him, the darker races reside in warmer climates and are therefore “enfeebled” by their hot temperaments. He furthermore notes that “even in warm climates, [the Anglo-Saxon] is likely to retain his aggressive vigor long enough to supplant races already enfeebled.” God’s solution to this problem, he contends, is to overthrow the darker races by populating the earth with “superior” Christian Anglo-Saxon people from cooler temperatures (ibid., 177, 165).

Strong here captures remnants of clergy man, rational man, and natural man all in one, revealing the persistence of black ontological and environmental negation en route to white self-actualization. The highly revered social gospel leaders Jane Addams and Graham Taylor later adopted similar logics. Addams and Taylor refused blacks residency in tenement housing because of a perceived lack of inherited moral resources from African countries (Addams 1911: 22–3). Ironically, social gospel leaders were known as progressive reformers in the same way liberal humanists are today. But in fact, Saidiya Hartman notes, "Progressive reformers and settlement workers were the architects and planners of racial segregation in northern cities" (Hartman 2019: 21).

Environmental sociologist Sylvia Hood Washington likewise shows that progressives provided the framework for environmental racism by "develop[ing] a paradigm of race and concomitant rights to American enfranchisement that became the operative and core episteme for determining the types of citizenry that would be entitled to salient 'green space' into the twenty-first century" (2004: 24). Further describing how this affects our everyday realities, cultural geographer Katherine McKittrick notes,

> Prevailing spatial organization gives a coherency and rationality to uneven geographic processes and arrangements: a city plan, for example, can (and often does) reiterate social class distinctions, race and gender segregation, and (in)accessibility to and from specific districts; the flows of money, spaces, infrastructure, and people are uneven, in that the built environment privileges, and therefore mirrors, white, heterosexual, capitalist, and patriarchal geopolitical needs.
>
> (McKittrick 2006: 6)

The prevailing spatial organization to which McKittrick points is one of unevenness of being/land within Christian humanist geographical praxis. Wynter notes this "continue[s] to provide the 'ultimate reference point' for Western societies" (1995: 13). The rationality of uneven environmental organization forms what political philosopher Michael Shapiro calls our moral geography—that is, a set of silent ethical assertions that organize our lives and our environment (1994: 482). In this way, the unquestioned and persistent pattern of black ontological and environmental subjugation is a silent assertion that organizes our lives, environments, and notions of justice and equality.

## What of Justice, Then?

Given this long history of the "crafting and sustaining of European human life and self-actualization through Black and Indigenous death" (King 2019: 84), one might be inclined to ask whether justice requires getting rid of the concept of the human altogether. In other words, should we aspire to live in a posthuman society?

Gestures toward posthumanism are similar to what is argued within liberal humanism. The liberal humanist idea that we are all human with equal rights is the same tune sung by posthumanists who argue that we should be *beyond* the human. Both seek to erase or ignore a history of colonization and racial domination that continues to structure our lives. In an effort to progress and go beyond, they leave structural oppositions and hegemonic systems like the Christian settler-colonial state fully intact. In that context, black and indigenous people are assumed to be less human, and so less capable of moving "beyond" the human. Attempts to transcend categories of the human only recreate a normative subject through black and Indigenous ontological and environmental negation. In other words, posthumanism creates more harm by "ask[ing] Indigenous and Black people who cannot seem to escape death to move beyond the human or the desire to be human" (King 2017: 167). Liberals who seek to disavow the category of human often turn a blind eye to or even negate actual racial and environmental harms, without taking accountability for doing so and without any form of redress. Tiffany King notes, "The erasure of the (white) body-as-subject-as-ontology has been more effective in covering the bloody trail of white/human-self-actualization than it has been at successfully offering a way around and beyond the entrapments of liberal humanism." King, reiterating Zakiyyah Iman Jackson's argument, further notes that "posthumanism is a ruse for white human ascendancy" (ibid., 178–9).

Part of the problem with trying to define environmental justice within a Christian settler-colonial nation is that our solutions will often rely on a colonizing impulse to erase difference (as in the case of posthumanists) or to reconfigure forms of antiblackness as a way to protect whiteness (as in slavery). Each work to maintain structural oppositions that privileges whites and dehumanizes blacks. As Frank Wilderson notes, "liberal discourses around community, accountability, innocence, and justice . . . sit upon anti-Black foundations and only go so far as to reconfigure, rather than abolish, the institutions that produce, control, and murder Black subjects" (2017: 11). If we trust King and Wilderson's insights, our task is to think and work toward environmental justice outside the modes of the Christian settler-colonial state. What would it mean to think outside the Christian settler-colonial state? And to cultivate moral commitments to each other and to the earth that did not simply reconfigure an antiblack and colonial relationship?

## Justice Otherwise

To think and work outside the modes of the Christian settler-colonial state is to be and do otherwise. The concept to be or do "otherwise" is rooted in many religions and philosophies. In Christianity, for example, the "otherwise" is reflected in the preferential option for the poor, or the biblical mandate that "the last will be first, and the first will be last" (Matthew 20:16). Throughout the biblical text, God and Jesus are revealed as overturning capitalist dehumanizing practices of the Roman Empire and offering new and more just possibilities based on those considered the "least" in society. Referring to these biblical precedents, Friedrich Nietzsche noted that Christianity is a religion that is based on the transvaluation of values, the reevaluation of predominant moral systems. In this way, to be otherwise is to operate outside of empires and colonial states, outside of what society has deemed normative and valuable. Only then can justice and liberation be achieved and new possibilities for caring for each other and the earth emerge. Indeed, as Mayra Rivera noted about Wynter's work, despite the violence and harm done under the banner of religion, it should be viewed "not only a tool of colonial ideology, but also a resource for its subversion" (2021: 58)

In practice, this entails churches and religious leaders taking accountability for their participation in Native American genocide, transatlantic slavery, and chattel slavery, reevaluating their racial and environmental commitments to reflect an abolitionist and anticolonial agenda. In practice, this also entails churches and religious leaders working with grassroots organizations to disentangle equity from land and property. Wealth building through home and land ownership is a product of the Christian settler-colonial state that implies that land is a thing that can be owned, land is a thing that must reap equity, and the purpose of land is to apply greater value and protection to predominantly white-occupied spaces (Smith 2020). These values were the justifications for Native American genocide, the theft of Indigenous land, chattel slavery, and the plantation economy. And they aided in maintaining the structural opposition between white space as valuable and held in God's grace and perceptions of black space as destitute and damned. As such, home and land ownership only work to reinforce black and Indigenous dehumanization and environmental degradation through gentrification, segregation, redlining, environmental racism, and other practices of settler colonialism.

The first step toward any kind of liberative justice is to become disenchanted with colonization, settler colonialism, and slavery, and the structures they have created, like land and homeownership, since they inevitably perpetuate black ontological and environmental subjugation.

Finally, to work toward justice otherwise from the modes of the Christian settler-colonial state is to privilege and prioritize how black and Indigenous people already work outside those modes and cultivate values for living on and with the earth. Practices of waywardness, revolt, and errancy are ways in which black communities operate outside normative colonial modes and refashion life in spaces meant for their social death. Any understanding of environmental justice must seriously take into account the knowledge and practices of those most affected by environmental harms.

**BOX 15D**

If you consider yourself a part of a black and/or Indigenous community, what lessons about environmental justice are central to your communal knowledge and practices? What, if anything, might your community offer to a wider audience on this topic? If you do not consider yourself part of such a community, how could you meaningfully and respectfully learn from black or Indigenous peoples?

### Case Study

Altgeld Gardens is a historically black public housing community on the southeast side of Chicago. Before it was a public housing community, the city had been using the land to dispose of its industrial waste. Instead of detoxifying the land, the city pressed the waste into the soil and discarded the remaining sewage into the nearby Calumet Lake before building Altgeld Gardens, a public housing community for black veterans, in 1945. Hazel Johnson, the mother of the environmental justice movement, galvanized her community to fight against environmental racism when she learned about this history and how 50 landfills and 382 industrial facilities, along with 250 leaking underground storage tanks, surround the housing community on all sides.

In response to what she learned, Hazel Johnson famously characterized Altgeld as the "the toxic doughnut" illustrating how polluting industries circle the housing community on all sides. This is one of many examples of environmental racism in the United States (Bullard 1993) but sadly among the very worst.

After many strategy meetings with the residents of Altgeld Gardens trying to understand how to get justice for communities plagued with antiblack environmental racism, activists organizing to improve their complex landed on a mission statement. It states that their purpose is to

> enhance the quality of life of residents living in communities affected by environmental pollution. We advocate, educate, and organize on community-identified priorities including environmental and climate justice, safe and affordable housing, economic equity and community health.

***Discussion Questions***

1. Based on this mission statement, what do you think are the primary concerns for the activists of Altgeld Gardens?
2. Why might the activist have listed both "environmental and climate justice"? How are these distinct concepts?
3. What does affordable housing and economic equity have to do with environmental justice for a community like Altgeld Gardens?
4. In what ways does this mission statement demonstrate the activists thinking and working toward justice *otherwise*, outside the modes of the Christian settler-colonial state?

## References

Addams, J. (1911) "Social Control," *Crisis* 1: 22–3.

Bullard, R. D. (ed) (1993) *Confronting Environmental Racism: Voices from the Grassroots*. Boston: South End Press.

Davenport, F. G. (1917) *European Treaties Bearing on the History of the United States and Its Dependencies to 1684*. Washington, DC: Carnegie Institution of Washington.

Hartman, S. (1997) *Scenes of Subjection: Terror, Slavery, and Self-Making in Nineteenth-Century America*. New York: Oxford University Press.

———. (2019) *Wayward Lives, Beautiful Experiments: Intimate Histories of Social Upheaval*. New York: Norton.

King, T. L. (2017) "Humans Involved: Lurking in the Lines of Posthumanist Flight," *Critical Ethnic Studies* 3(1): 162–85.

———. (2019) *Black Shoals: Offshore Formations of Black and Native Studies*. Durham, NC: Duke University Press.

McKittrick, K. (2006) *Demonic Grounds: Black Women, Geography, and the Cartographies of Struggle*. Minneapolis: University of Minnesota Press.

Mills, C. (2017) *Black Right/White Wrong: The Critique of Racial Liberalism*. New York: Oxford University Press.

Mitchell, D. (2000) *Cultural Geography: A Critical Introduction*. Malden, MA: Blackwell.

Pellow, D. N. (2018) *What Is Critical Environmental Justice*. Cambridge: Polity Press.

Rivera, M. (2021) "Embodied Counterpoetics: Sylvia Wynter on Religion and Race," in A. Younta and E. Craig (eds) *Beyond Man: Race, Coloniality, and Philosophy of Religion*. Durham: Duke University Press.

Shapiro, M. J. (1994) "Moral Geographies and the Ethics of Post-Sovereignty," *Public Culture* 6(3): 479–502.

Smith, A. (2020) "Sovereignty as Deferred Genocide," in T. L. King, J. Navarro, and A. Smith (eds) *Otherwise Worlds: Against Settler Colonialism and Anti-Blackness*. Durham, NC: Duke University Press.

Strong, J. (1885) *Our Country: Its Possible Future and Its Present Crisis*. New York: The American Home Mission Society.

Washington, S. H. (2004) *Packing Them In: An Archeology of Environmental Racism in Chicago, 1865–1954*. Lanham, MD: Lexington.

White, L. Jr. (1967) "The Historical Roots of Our Ecological Crisis," *Science* 155(3767): 1203–7.

Wilderson III, F. B. (2017) *Afro-Pessimism: An Introduction*. Minneapolis, MN: Racked & Dispatched.

Wynter, S. (1989) "Beyond the Word of Man: Glissant and the New Discourse of the Antilles," *World Literature Today* 63(4): 637–48.

———. (1995) "1492: A New World View," in R. Nettleford and V. L. Hyatt (eds) *Race, Discourse and the Origin of the Americas*. Washington, DC: Smithsonian Institution Press.

———. (2003) "Unsettling the Coloniality of Being/Power/Truth/Freedom: Toward the Human, After Man, Its Overrepresentation—An Argument," *The Centennial Review* 3(2): 257–337.

## Further Reading

Chavis, B. Jr., and Lee, C. (1987) *Toxic Waste and Race in the United States: A National Report on the Racial and Socio-economic Characteristics of Communities with Hazardous Waste Sites*. New York: Commission for Racial Justice United Church of Christ.

King, T. L. (2019) *Black Shoals: Offshore Formations of Black and Native Studies*. Durham: Duke University Press.

McKittrick, K. (2006) *Demonic Grounds: Black Women, Geography, and the Cartographies of Struggle*. Minneapolis: University of Minnesota Press.

Wynter, S. (2003) "Unsettling the Coloniality of Being/Power/Truth/Freedom: Toward the Human, After Man, Its Overrepresentation—An Argument," *The Centennial Review* 3: 257–337.

Yountae, A., and Craig, E. (2021) *Beyond Man: Race, Coloniality, and Philosophy of Religion*. Durham: Duke University Press.

# 16 Extinction

*Stefan Skrimshire*

## Studying Religion in an Age of Extinctions

Why now? Moral and religious concerns about extinctions have been with us for as long as any form of environmentalism. So why does a dedicated chapter on extinction appear only in the third edition of this book and still (at the time of writing) in no major handbooks on religion and ecology?

Let me qualify that observation. The subject of species extinctions *has* long been discussed under other headings: conservation, biodiversity, animals, or climate change, for instance. Extinction means the termination of a thing or group of things—usually an organism—and is discussed almost exclusively with reference to biological species. If there is a new kind of urgency surrounding the topic today, however, it is likely to be in response to the claim that human actions have precipitated what biologists are calling a *mass extinction event*. That is, a process of "biological annihilation" (Ceballos et al. 2017) comparable in scale to five previous catastrophes in the deep history of the Earth, each of which wiped out at least three-quarters of all living things. The last was triggered by the Chicxulub meteorite smashing into the Yucatan Peninsula of Mexico sixty-five million years ago. The destruction of life and life-forms in our present age, while not yet statistically equivalent, has an equally catastrophic trajectory. Sixty percent of vertebrates have gone extinct since 1970 (WWF 2018); insect populations are declining by 2.5% per year (*Guardian* 2019). Total species extinctions are occurring between a hundred and a thousand times their background historical rates (Sandler 2021). Such an alarming prognosis of global ecological collapse has amplified concerns about the potential extinction of human societies.

Clearly, then, extinction could not simply be considered one more ecological "area of concern" for religious studies. It requires a scalar shift to what we might call planetary thinking (Connolly 2016). Extinction has come to stand in as a signifier for the virtually unfathomable temporal and spatial scalar shifts in which climate crisis more broadly is narrated today. Consider this summary from a recent article on climate change ethics: "The scale of the challenge can be expressed in one sentence: *Humanity and life in general face a combination of converging catastrophes whose cumulative effects equal or dwarf anything since the volcanic mass extinction seventy-five thousand years ago*" (van Pelt 2018: 463, italics in the

DOI: 10.4324/9781003259466-20

original). Following this scalar shift, the focus of attention by scholars of extinction has widened accordingly. Not only biological species (in fact, often in resistance to that category—see Mitchell 2016) but also the loss of particular "life ways" (Van Dooren) of species in the particularities of their ecological interactions; peoples, cultures, and languages; and even natural formations, such as glaciers have become the objects of concern for an age of extinctions. When Ursula Heise writes that social and cultural narratives about extinctions "become part of the stories that human communities tell about themselves: stories about their origins, their development, their identity, and their future horizons" (Heise 2016: 5), we cannot, Willis Jenkins suggests, ignore the religiosity with which so many of those identities and horizons take place (Jenkins, forthcoming).

What, then, might we say about the *role* of religions in interpreting and responding to this now vastly expanded planetary phenomenon? One might begin by noting that religions are both impact*ful* and impac*ted* by mass extinction. Religious actors and institutions have certainly played their parts as drivers of extinction. Think, for instance, of the historical and ongoing religious justification for colonialism and associated acts of genocide against human and more-than-human populations. But religious actors have also been champions of a new kind of extinction resistance, such as the cases of faith-based activism, which I consider later in this chapter. Neither have religious institutions been silent on the challenges of mass extinction. The fourteenth Dalai Lama was outspoken against "the most massive wave of extinction in 65 million years" as early as 1992, at the Rio Earth Summit. That was over two decades before mass extinction became a focus of confessional declarations such as Pope Francis' *Laudato Si'* and *The Islamic Declaration on Climate Change*, both of which were published in 2015 and explicitly mention the global extinction crisis as a manifestation of a disordered and broken relationship between human beings and the earth. There are now well-established international religious and interfaith initiatives focused on combatting loss of biodiversity, such as the Alliance of Religions and Conservation and the Religion and Conservation Working Group of the Society of Conversation Biology, as well as faith-specific FBOs, such as the Christian organization A Rocha International.

Secular scientific and aid organizations are also increasingly recognizing the importance of engaging with religious networks and authorities to communicate and act upon extinctions locally, given that the parts of the world where its impacts are the most severe tend also to be the most religious. A few examples to demonstrate this point: across the Himalayan region of India, religious practices are seen as essential to the preservation of sacred groves. These are landscapes protected by local communities that encourage air, soil, and water conservation and are themselves essential habitats to endangered species, such as the pangolin and the hornbill (Singh et al. 2017). Worshippers believe that any damage to the groves would anger the local deity (such as the goddess Pallalama Devi, popularly known as the Nature Goddess); conversely, by revering the local species and ecosystems, worshippers also believe that the gods will protect and preserve their communities (Yarlagadda 2022). Ghanaian biologist and extinction activist Caleb Ofori Boateng, who champions the protection of Ghana's amphibians, relates how essential it is that he places such activism in religious contexts and speaking to church congregations, calling his work "conservation evangelism" (Future For Nature n.d.). And there are even increasing cases of Muslim religious authorities issuing fatwas to combat extinction, such as in Libya against illegal poaching (Almontaser et al. 2020: 198) and Indonesia against all acts that contribution to the extinction of wildlife (*The Guardian* 2014).

We should also consider that religious traditions and practices are themselves today counted among the potential *victims* of the extinction crisis. The Conceptual Framework of the Intergovernmental Panel on Biodiversity and Ecosystem Services (IPBES) included the following in its assessment of the costs of biodiversity loss to humanity: "spiritual and religious practices in which certain places, water bodies, forests, animals, trees are considered sacred, serve as totems, are protected by rituals and taboos, and/or are revered as gifts imbued with ancestral and divine presence and significance" (Diaz et al. 2015). Similarly, Todd LeVasseur (2021) wonders what will happen to religious practices and identities that are geographically specific—for instance, worship of the Ganges by Hindu traditions and pilgrimage to Mecca by Muslims across the world—when forces of climate and ecological crisis render those places extinct or inaccessible. Can we, and ought we, be talking about the extinction of religious lifeways in tandem with ecological lifeways as symptoms of our global crisis?

**BOX 16A**

How are religious traditions implicated, invoked, or affected by the claim that we are living in the sixth extinction event in the Earth's history?

## Reasons to Be Cautious About the Concept of Mass Extinction

There are good reasons to critically question references to mass extinction in contemporary environmental discourse. Some argue that focusing on this singular planetary "event" serves to mask the political and social drivers of extinction by likening it to a cosmic catastrophe. Most descriptions of the sixth extinction cite its perpetrators as humanity, humans, *Homo sapiens*, or simply *us*, thereby erasing the political critique of extinction as perpetrated by systems of injustice and as acts of violence by particular human groups against others. As McCullagh et al. put it, "there is nothing inherently human to blame for triggering and exacerbating extinctions and inequalities" (2021: 5). Generalized, too, are the victims of mass extinction. As Audra Mitchell and Noah Theriault argue, mass extinction discourses frame "all of humanity as the undifferentiated victim of ecological collapse" (2020: 179).

Mass extinction might also be a perfect example of what Kyle Powys Whyte calls the harmful effects of "crisis epistemology" operating in much Global North environmental discourse: "The presumption of unprecedentedness makes it possible to wilfully forget certain previous instances or lessons related to a crisis" (Whyte 2022: 55). The uses of crisis to erode other concerns, such as human rights, also have a long-standing relationship with religious identities, as millennial fears and anticipations of catastrophe become used to justify conflict or authoritarianism. As with the Anthropocene concept, mass extinction has enjoyed cultural and political success as symbolizing the exceptionality of the present moment. According to such a view, we are in unprecedented times in terms of threats against life on earth, but unprecedented too (according to some climate activists) is the opportunity for *us*, this present generation of humans or some subset thereof, to save it. Such rhetoric is undoubtedly supported as an essential tactic of galvanizing mass support for the environmental cause. But the danger is that a conception of imminent planetary catastrophe as "the extinction crisis" erases an already long memory of genocidal and ecocidal violence perpetrated against human and more-than-human communities. Several Indigenous scholars have explained this sense of erasure as a bias among white Western campaigners for framing extinction as an imagination of the future, as opposed to an experience of the past and present—the obliteration of animals, plants, lands, and languages essential to their way of life—which Indigenous peoples have *survived* and continue to survive (Mitchell and Theriault 2020; McCullagh et al. 2021).

It would be unfair to paint all discourses of mass extinction in this way, however. For many religious studies scholars, mass extinction awareness can generate a needed sense of "planetary solidarity" with creatures whose plight might otherwise not be felt by those sheltered from the impacts of ecological loss (Eaton 2017: 28). And Majority World scholars can and do also cite mass extinction as expressing a particularly acute kind of context-specific injustice, which jeopardizes first and foremost those vulnerable to loss of place, identity, and power (Natarjan). Religious studies has a crucial role to play here inasmuch as it contributes to understanding mass extinction as fundamentally a question of global injustice and inequality, and a breaking of bonds between creatures and creator.

**BOX 16B**

What reasons are there for critically questioning mass extinction as a focus of study in religion and ecology?

### Is Mass Extinction a Novel Problem for Religion and Religious Ethics?

Species extinctions have long generated a unique set of moral problems in the study of religion. This is due in part to the fact that it can result both from "natural" processes (biologists often refer to the "background rate" of species extinction) and also from acts of violence by one species against another. Is one form of extinction "good" (because part of the natural order) while the other is unequivocally bad? And what makes anthropogenic extinctions *especially* bad—worse, say, than harm done to individual creatures? Does stewardship of creation, a moral idea supported by several religious traditions, imply maintaining biodiversity at all costs (Deane-Drummond 2022)? Arguments for the special harm of species extinction have drawn upon a range of traditions to answer these questions: consequentialist arguments based on the harm that loss of species does to other individuals and to ecosystems as a whole, deep ecological arguments about the integral value of biodiversity for its own sake, and an appeal to the virtues from both secular (Bendik-Keymer 2009) and theological (Deane-Drummond 2021) perspectives—for instance, the virtues of mercy, prudence, and compassion. Religious ethics of various kinds have been called upon to support claims such as these. For instance, religious accounts of creation are invoked to imply that anthropogenic extinctions do violence to its integrity and completeness. Islamic traditions are strong on the concept of harmony in creation. For instance, the Qur'an teaches that Allah "created the balance (*mizan*), so that you would not tip the balance" (Khalid 2017). In Jewish and Christian traditions, some interpretations of the book of Genesis emphasize that humans are to be stewards not only of the sum of all creatures but of the very diversity of life upon which a flourishing earth depends. Jewish Kabbalists have found in their expression of the divine the importance of the diversity of life itself. Anthropogenic extinctions can thus be condemned as a form of idolatry, diminishing the image of God by separating it from this unique element of creation (Seidenberg 2017).

Does *mass* extinction represent an additional harm to that of an aggregate of species extinctions? In other words, is there something ethically significant about the "massness" of mass extinction? Ronald Sandler argues that there is, suggesting that the shift to a "radical state change" of the planet represents a special type of harm due to the loss of the specialness of *this* particular planetary system that a mass extinction event would irreversibly destroy—including the "associated biomes and biological communities with which peoples developed cultures, stories, histories, relationships, meanings and connections" (Sandler 2021). In a mass extinction event, not only biodiversity but "higher order taxonomic groups" upon which future evolutionary change depends are wiped out. What is uniquely bad about mass extinction is thus not only its scale of destruction, but its changing of the planet into one that may become, for any humanly imaginable future, inhospitable to much of life on Earth. One can certainly find parallels to this claim among religious ethical traditions. In global faith leaders' pronouncements on the subject, mass extinction is understood to be a special sort of harm in light of its breaking with some original goodness of creation that is a flourishing planetary system. Religious traditions can arguably state in far stronger terms than secular ones, in other words, that in triggering a planetary extinction event, the original "goodness" of creation is jeopardized. An Earth scarred by extinctions, writes Rabbi Zalman Schachter-Shalomi, "does not mediate the Creator to the extent it once did, nor is it able to reveal its own inner reality and what it has evolved to be . . . What God called 'very good' might more often be 'very harmful' in our age" (Schachter-Shalomi 2017).

**BOX 16C**

Is mass extinction a "new problem" for religious ethics? What new challenges does it pose, and what resources to religious traditions have to go about addressing them?

## Extinction: The Religious History of a Concept

To understand present cultural meanings of mass extinction, we need to understand its emergence as a scientific theory in a European context in which the twin influences of Christianity and imperialism dominated. Doing so can help us to understand the religious frameworks that might still underlie the narration of mass extinction today. But it is also essential for seeing the connection between extinction science and colonialism and the role that religious thought has played in both.

The "discovery" of species extinctions is often narrated as having been disastrous for religion for two main reasons. First, theories about extinction and evolution upset the biblical chronology on which geo-historical thought was based. Deep time, unfathomably long geological processes that took place prior to any kind of activity narrated in the Bible, posed a challenge to faith. Second, extinction threatened the belief in an order of creation that was perfect and complete and from which nothing could be removed.

It is also true that prior theological commitments fundamentally *shaped* the scientific discovery of extinction. In the 17th and 18th centuries, British and French naturalists debated whether changes in the earth could be explained by sudden ruptures and changes—what became known as catastrophism—or, on the other hand, by very long, gradual, and predictable changes in the earth's dynamics—the theory of uniformitarianism (sometimes referred to as gradualism). The contest revealed a split in religious commitments between its adherents. As David Sepkoski argues that "the balanced equilibrium of uniformitarianism sat more comfortably with those naturalists who reflected a deistic theology in which God acted on the universe through invariant natural laws" while "Catastrophism . . . found favor with scientists who sought to explain particular historical events described in scripture, such as the Noachian flood, that appeared to require special explanations" (Sepkoski 2020: 23).

While not mutually exclusive positions, Sepkoski argues that catastrophism's association with biblical literalism proved its downfall. It could be caricatured and ridiculed by opponents, as biblical literalism was falling quickly out of fashion. For a secularizing European audience, then, it was the uniformitarian theory of the earth that won the day. This was reinforced by the extinction science of the Victorian period and Darwin's gradualist picture of evolution for which extinctions were a necessary feature of natural history.

The main point of Sepkoski's thesis is to show how the success of scientific discoveries about the earth is dependent upon wider cultural commitments, including religious belief. However, it is equally important to see how theories about species decline informed racist theories about *human* evolution and how religion was used to support this. As Patrick Brantlinger observes, by the time of Darwin's voyage of the *Beagle*, theories about a hierarchy of purity in the human races were already dominant in Europe. They found justification in biblical interpretation of the antediluvian descendants of Noah by the very same theorists of geo-history, such as Georges Cuvier, who are among the first to propose a theory of extinction (Brantlinger 2003). Darwin reflected around the time of that voyage that inferior human races appeared to suffer the same evolutionary fate as any other creature:

"the stronger always extirpating the weaker" (cited in Brantlinger 2003: 23). Eventually such a view would come to express the explicit belief that primitive, savage races were naturally bound for extinction upon contact with colonizers, according to processes of evolutionary competition. Darwin had noted in secular terms that the "rapid decline" of populations of aboriginal peoples in Australia since the arrival of Europeans displayed the working of some secret "destructive force" in nature in its process of self-improvement. For others, such as the geologist Charles Lyell and the economist Thomas Malthus before him, such observations demonstrated divine providence and the overall harmony of God's creation (Brantlinger 2003: 34).

This background history of the science of extinction should be considered alongside some of the critical comments mentioned earlier about the focus on mass extinction in contemporary environmentalism. As scholars and students of religion and ecology, we should ask ourselves: are secular scientific accounts of extinction, and even discourses of mourning and loss that accompany it (which I discuss further here), serving a narrative of global extinction as tragic inevitability—the capitulation of weaker species/races to forces beyond anyone's control rather than the result of systemic violence perpetrated by some human populations against others?

And what of catastrophism, which (as suggested) had more purchase among literalist interpreters of the Bible? Sepkoski argues that catastrophism is enjoying a revival with the popularization of mass extinction theories, and so it follows that we ought to be interested in the role that religious frameworks might be continuing to play. The emergence of the idea of mass extinction is linked to the Alvares hypothesis. In 1980, the physicist Luis Alvares and his son Walter, the geologist, discovered "an anomalous layer of iridium at the stratigraphic break between the Cretaceous and Tertiary periods." That period coincided with the disappearance of most terrestrial and marine life from the fossil record. They argued that the only plausible explanation was an asteroid or comet striking Earth, causing a mass extinction event. But the hypothesis was all the more compelling, argues Sepkoski, because its evocation of a planetary cataclysmic event resonated with a threat that was very much live in Western imaginations of the 1980s and particularly in the USA: the possibility of all-out nuclear warfare between the world's two global superpowers. The connection between those two "discoveries" is made all the more poignant by the fact that Luis Alvares himself had worked with Robert Oppenheimer on the Manhattan Project during World War II and had personally observed the Trinity nuclear test and the bombing of Hiroshima. Thus, the imagination of world cataclysm in the deep history of the earth was brought into contact with the new human capacity to bring about a world cataclysm of our own making. It is significant that the Alvareses were not the first to propose a planetary cataclysm as the explanation for the mass extinction event that wiped out the dinosaurs. But their timing was perfect, coinciding with Cold War anxieties about nuclear annihilation, thus galvanizing support for the hypothesis among scientists (Sepkoski 2016: 172) where others had failed to do so.

Millennial anxieties are demonstrable in much of American popular culture of course—a wave post-apocalyptic films, novels, and artworks inspired by nuclear scenarios, as well as fears of social and ecological collapse linked to the new environmental movement. But in American culture, these are inextricable from the influence of millennialism in a more literal sense. The 1980s were a particularly prolific period for the generation and popularity of millennialist predictions in America among predominantly Protestant Christian denominations. Premillennialism, the model of eschatological (end-time) belief that expects earthly catastrophes to announce Christ's return as a prelude to the final judgement day, was particularly prevalent among Evangelical Christians that became associated with the Christian "New Right" who lobbied for American political influence throughout the 1980s.

Thus, if Sepkoski is right that a scientific theory of earthly mass extinctions only found professional and public support on the back of an ascendant apocalyptic imagination, we must take note of the religious contours of that imagination. Especially given the American context (where millennial beliefs are arguably most influential), we can say without hyperbole that religious belief played a key role in facilitating a modern mass extinction imaginary. Just as fears of nuclear annihilation in the mid-20th century had "resonated deeply with the linear, progressive narrative of Judaeo-Christian history" (Sepkoski 2020: 265), in our own age, the threat of a new mass extinction event might also resonate with religious beliefs of different kinds and find more purchase in the cultures for which those beliefs still have power.

What ought we to make of this association with a mass extinction imaginary and religious belief? We should be critical for the reasons that are suggested earlier: framing extinction in eschatological terms as a futural, millennial catastrophe can erase the experience of extinction as present and ongoing injustice. Nevertheless, we ought also to be interested in the coinciding of public concern for mass extinction and a flourishing of religious forms of activism, which I now consider.

**BOX 16D**

What do the intwined histories of extinction science and Christianity teach us about contemporary ideas about extinction?

### Extinction Activism as the New Visibility of Religious Protest

Political activist responses to mass extinction are embracing, reviving, and innovating religious modes of public engagement. The most obvious example of this can be seen in public expressions of ecological lament, or eco-grief. Alongside the phenomenon that has become known as eco-anxiety, there has been a proliferation of public actions and rituals that allow ordinary people to come to terms with, resist, or lament species extinction. Many of these engage either overtly or implicitly with religious practices. Some of these practices are connected explicitly to faith traditions, especially those for whom practices of remembrance, lament, and reflection upon mortality are (albeit in different ways) integral. (For more on this, please see the final chapter of this volume.)

For instance the Work That Reconnects Network in the USA, inspired by Joanna Macy, for several decades developed an "engaged Buddhist" training model for environmental activists coming to terms with ecological loss, and these are being reconsidered in the context of mass extinction (Strain 2016). Christian groups have turned a number of its liturgies to specific use in addressing the subject of extinction. For instance, Operation Noah used its Ash Wednesday Declaration to help churches integrate awareness of the extinction crisis into their services. Most recently, Christian Climate Action (CCA) organized extinction-themed services at Extinction Rebellion (XR) protests in London and elsewhere, including Stations of the Cross (in which each station identified victims of mass extinction with the suffering of Christ), Eucharistic liturgies, and Maundy Thursday and Good Friday services. And Jewish Extinction XR groups hosted an extinction-themed Seder to commemorate Passover (Skrimshire 2019).

As with previous generations of environmental protest, extinction activism in the Global North has also produced hybrid and new religious identities that consciously adopt, resist, or synchronize traditions and practices according to the specific demands of the extinction crisis. For instance, Maria Nita (forthcoming) has observed the prevalence of contemporary paganism in XR protests, particularly those focusing on ritual and performative engagements with death in the context of the extinction crisis. She argues that XR death rituals—die-ins, funeral coffin processions, and ghostly death-figure performances of the Red Rebel Brigade—visibly combine both "pagan" elements of belief in death as a natural cycle and rite of passage on the one hand and "post-Christian" symbols of death such as the crucifix and hourglass, as well as aesthetic references to the symbols of Christian apocalypse (e.g., the Four Horsemen). Such hybridities are of course not new in the history of religious environmental activism. Nevertheless, Nita suggests that they take on new meaning in the specific context of contemporary extinction activism. Extinction activists today grapple with the difficult perspectives on death that extinction can generate, from the desire to rage against the violence of extinction to an attempt to confront its reality with honesty: "a complex symbolism intersecting a wide array of themes, such as illness, healing, vulnerability, as well as murder or the culpability for murder, suicide, sacrifice, and the absence of memorialisation" (Nita forthcoming).

Nominally secular groups exploring ritual performative responses to extinction also reference religious practices obliquely. For instance, the UK-based Feral Theatre were one of the first to respond to the call from Persephone Pearl (of ONCA gallery in Brighton, UK) to commemorate extinct species on November 30 each year, by establishing a "funeral for lost species" in public places. The building of "life cairns" in remembrance of lost species has also become popular in the UK, especially in places of ancestral and ancient significance such as those established in Sussex, UK, and Totnes in Devon (Brewster 2020). In Boston, USA, XR groups collaborated with Latin American performing artists to stage a ceremony inspired by Mexican and Central American Day of the Dead celebrations, including an altar that "offers a sacred space to feel grief, connect with the spirits around us—of humans, animals and nature—and celebrate the cycle of life" (Honkfest! 2019).

And Jeremy Kidwell considers the religious contours of public ceremonies of witness to extinction, such as the unveiling of the memorial to the disappearing Icelandic glacier, Okjokull (Kidwell, forthcoming).

It is also important to recognize religious, spiritual, and ceremonial practices that implicitly or explicitly contest the use of mourning in the context of extinction activism. As with the critique considered earlier, we might suspect that an emphasis on mourning tends to portray extinction as a tragic inevitability as opposed to a site of active resistance by those peoples who have, and are, surviving extinction. It might also be that mourning reflects the same Western bias for temporal framings of extinction that we critiqued earlier.

What other ceremonial and activist framings might be sought? Oneida scholar Roberta Hill suggests there is interest in the uses of the Haudenosaunee Thanksgiving Address in today's extinction context for its ability to "focus the community's attention to the interconnected relationships between the Earth, sky and all that is in-between, to generate a communal vision of these relationships, and to have people let go of their resentments and hostility in order to generate gratitude for the Earth's power" (Hill 2020: 160).

Some scholars also express concern at the ease by which Minority World environmental cultures feel able to express personal outpourings of grief without their daily lives being personally impacted in the same way that those in Majority World societies are more likely be impacted. Deborah Bird Rose, for instance, draws attention to the difference between the experiences of Aboriginal peoples who have grown up "already looking into the possibility of their own extinction" and the experience of many of us in the Global North who may "get occasional glimpses of terrible, faraway processes of extinction" (Rose 25: 28). It is important, then, that scholars of religion seek to understand the phenomenon of extinction through the voices and traditions of those closest to its consequences. For instance, Hannah Malcom's stirring collection of essays, *Words for a Dying World*, provide a platform for (largely Christian) activists of the Global South to witness to ecological grief in ways that are at times thoroughly specific to cultural context.

Neither are ecological rituals of lament confined to Jewish and Christian traditions. Writing from the premise that practices of mourning are essential for activists confronting cultures of denial and fostering deeper levels of connectedness, Nancy Menning has compared different religious approaches to mourning as resources for eco-grief. For instance, mourning ceremonies of the Dagara Indigenous people of West Africa are marked by outpourings of great emotion, which is needed to "carry the dead home." Emotion is also required to build a strong connection between mourners and the dead, revealing "relationships disrupted by death" and reviving "bonds of friendship" with the living (Menning 2017: 49). By contrast, Tibetan sky burials, in which corpses are left as food for the vultures, seem to emphasize almost opposite, encouraging the living to let go of their emotional attachment to the physical body of the deceased and ultimately of human existence altogether (Menning 2017: 53). Menning asks: what lessons can be learned from the ritual enactment of the impermanence of existence in the light of a mass extinction event, and what would constitute the "unproductive attachments to what once was" in the context of extinction activism?

By their very diversity, then, religious traditions can be seen as resources for expressing the complex and multivalent nature of grief and its application to the context of extinction: from the imperative to hold past sufferings in memory, to the chastening of one's attachment to bodily existence, to the need to work through personal and corporate guilt and atonement. Are these the building blocks of forms of extinction activism, too?

## Case Study

Helen Burnett is a parish priest in the Church of England in Chaldon, South East England. I first met her during one of the first "rebellions" of Extinction Rebellion (XR)—gatherings of civil disobedience at which thousands of activists from around the UK occupied roads and bridges across the capital for over a week, forcing climate change onto the media and political agenda. As suggested in the previous section, faith-based activists have comprised a visibly significant number among these activists, and Helen had quickly become involved in both Christian Climate Action (CCA), the main hub for Christian activists of XR, and an interfaith XR network marching under the banner of the Faith Bridge. In November 2019, Helen organized a Requiem for Lost Species at her parish church. The idea was inspired by the rituals and performances that have taken place every November 30 as Remembrance for Lost Species Day, launched in 2016 by Persephone Pearl of ONCA gallery in Brighton in response to the lack of public engagement—and perhaps a lack of ideas about *how* to engage—with the mass extinction crisis.

Events running under this banner have ranged quite widely in content and rationale: from overtly secular forms of expression (processions of puppets representing extinct birds) to the nominally spiritual (such as the funeral processions and "life cairn" monuments established in Totnes and Sussex). At XR events, too, the use of ritual acts of grieving or lament to engage activists and passersby with mass extinction had become increasingly prevalent.

Helen's service was held in the 11th-century church where she serves, but the extinction-themed liturgy and the use of "verse, meditation, music, procession, bells and candles" (Burnett 2020: 5) were expressly designed to speak to "all faiths and none." There were readings from Greta Thunberg, David Attenborough, and Simon Armitage. After readings, attendees were invited to place local stones to construct a cairn in memory of extinct species. Headstones for extinct species were placed around the churchyard.

Helen's conscious attempt to channel both the resources of Christian liturgical space and the possible concerns of non-religious activist participants make this an interesting case study in thinking about religious practice in the context of mass extinctions. She writes of her own motivations for the event: "human activity had provided a sacred space whilst at the same time desecrating that space. How could this discrepancy between the beauty of human creativity, and the human capacity to destroy, be marked and mourned?" (Burnett 2020: 4). In an interview I conducted before this event, Helen had spoken with some amazement about how she had encountered a genuine thirst by non-religious XR activists for rituals and practices that drew upon the Christian tradition. For instance, at one XR protest, she celebrated Eucharistic communion at the base of a "lock-on tower," a built structure obstructing traffic to which activists had chained themselves (having first checked with those who were locked on that they were happy for her to do so). Those who joined in were mainly but not exclusively members of CCA. In the desire for a memorial service, she interpreted a need from a broad section of activists to create a space to "feel difficult feelings" that, while not monopolized by religious traditions, finds a particular home in Christian services, such as Good Friday and November All Souls celebrations. These, in her words, were liturgical and sacramental forms that seemed powerfully relevant to the sort of reflection required of extinction activists: a process of inhabiting deeply an awareness of death and loss followed by a re-emergence to life, inhabiting a "new space" to think, reflect and act following that initial requiem process.

Interestingly, however, Helen reports of a hesitancy among Christians of her own parish for the "gloomy stuff," whereas the non-religious XR activists who attended expressed gratitude for the "regenerative nature of the time and space offered" via the service.

Helen's requiem service at Chaldon represents a flourishing of memorial practices within activist cultures focused on the global extinction crisis: as mentioned, the ritual and performative elements of Lost Species Day, XR actions, and a legacy of environmental activist movements that precede it. Christian theologians emphasize the importance of the publicness of liturgy (*litous ergos* means "public works"), its role in bearing witness to that which is lost. Eco-theologians are keen to channel this tradition for extinction activism, noting that to bear witness to environmental loss is to acknowledge the divine which is revealed in creation itself (Hessel-Robinson 2011).

But some of the questions raised above should also provide grounds for critical reflection. Is an emphasis on mourning the most appropriate emotional, moral, or religious register for responding to mass extinction? Who has a right to grieve, and do we really know what is being grieved? What attention to ongoing struggles for survival, justice, and reparation are masked by such a focus on loss? What becomes of the religious emphases on hope, reparation, or forgiveness in such a context? How does grief lead to action, and in the context of the planetary extinction crisis, what does that action look like?

### *Discussion Questions*

1. To what extent do the examples discussed earlier demonstrate that there is a desire for specifically religious modes of engagement among environmental activists? Is this something that is generated by the crisis of mass extinction in particular, or is it a long-standing element of the environmental movement more broadly?

2. What do you make of the appeal to ritual forms (whether overtly religious or not) of lament or mourning, in the context of extinction activism? Are there ethical or political reasons for encouraging or discouraging such forms?
3. The case study indicates the public role of a specific religious tradition (Christianity) in a specific geographical context (UK). Can you think of comparable, or contrasting, uses of religion to respond to extinction from different traditions and contexts? What different questions do they raise?

## References

Almontaser, T., Atkins, J., Elfadi, A., Eskandrany, A., Hassan, A., Mowafi, O., Norton S., and Saeudy, M. (2020) "Middle Eastern Extinctions: Building a Religious Motivation for Species Protection," in J. Atkins and M. Macpherson (eds) *Extinction Governance, Finance and Accounting: Implementing a Species Protection Action Plan for the Financial Markets*. London: Routledge.

Bendik-Keymer, J. (2009) "Species Extinction and the Vice of Thoughtlessness: The Importance of Spiritual Exercises for Learning Virtue," *Journal of Agricultural and Environmental Ethics* 23: 61.

Brantlinger, P. (2003) *Dark Vanishings: Discourse on the Extinction of Primitive Races, 1800–1930*. Ithaca, NY: Cornell University Press.

Brewster, S. (2020) "Remembrance Day for Lost Species," *Performance Research* 25(2): 95–101.

Burnett, H. (2020) "Requiem for Lost Species," *Green Christian* 89.

Ceballos, G., Ehrlich, P., and Dirzo, L. (2017) "Biological Annihilation via the Ongoing Sixth Mass Extinction Signaled by Vertebrate Population Losses and Declines," *PNAS* 113:(30): E6089–E6096.

Deane-Drummond, C. (2021) "Paying Attention to Biological Diversity and Its Theological Significance," *New Blackfriars* 103(1104): 171–88.

Diaz, S. et al. (2015) "The IPBES Conceptual Framework—Connecting Nature and People," *Current Opinion in Environmental Sustainability* 14: 1–16.

Eaton, H. (2017) "An Earth-Centric Theological Framing for Planetary Solidarity," in K. Grace Ji-Sun (ed) *Planetary Solidarity*. Minneapolis, MN: Fortress Press.

Future for Nature. (n.d.) https://futurefornature.org/ffn_winner/caleb-ofori-boateng/

The Guardian. (2014) "Indonesian Clerics Issue Fatwa to Protect Wildlife," *The Guardian*, March 5, www.theguardian.com/environment/2014/mar/05/indonesia-clerics-fatwa-illegal-wildlife-trade

———. (2019) "Plumetting Insect Numbers Threatent Collapse of Nature," *The Guardian*, www.theguardian.com/environment/2019/feb/10/plummeting-insect-numbers-threaten-collapse-of-nature (accessed July 29, 2022).

Heise, U. (2016) *Imagining Extinction: The Cultural Meanings of Endangered Species*. Chicago: Chicago University Press.

Hessel-Robinson, T. (2011) "Requiem for the Baiji: Liturgical Lamentation and Species Extinctions," in T. Hessel-Robinson and R. M. McNamara (eds) *Spirit and Nature: The Study of Christian Spirituality in a Time of Ecological Urgency*. Eugene, OR: Pickwick Publications.

Hill, R. (2020) "The Haudenosaunee Thanksgiving Address and Its Relevance for Futures and Learnings," in L. L. Lopez and G. Coello (eds) *Indigenous Futures and Learnings Taking Place*. London: Routledge.

Honkfest! (2019) https://honkfest.org/archive/2019-festival/saturday-in-davis-square-2019/2019-elm-street-interactive-area/

Jenkins, W. (Forthcoming) "Loving Swarms: Religious Ethics amidst Mass Extinction," in J. H. Kidwell and S. Skrimshire (eds) *Extinction and Religion*. Bloomington: Indiana University Press.

Khalid, F. (2017) "Exploring Environmental Ethics in Islam," in J. Hart (ed) *Wiley Blackwell Companion to Religion and Ecology*. Oxford: Blackwell.

Kidwell, J. (Forthcoming) "Absence and (Unexpected) Presence: Reflecting on Cosmopolitical Entanglements Across Time," in J. Kidwell and S. Skrimshire (eds) *Extinction and Religion*. Bloomington: Indiana University Press.

LeVasseur, T. (2021) *Climate Change, Religion and Our Bodily Future*. Lanham, MA: Lexington Books.

McCullagh, S., Pradanos, L., Marcyan, I. T., and Wagner, C. (2021) *Contesting Extinctions: Decolonial and Regenerative Futures*. Lanham, MA: Lexington Books.

Menning, N. (2017) "Environmental Mourning and the Religious Imagination," in C. A. Willox and K. Landman (eds) *Mourning Nature*. Kingston: McGill-Queen's University Press.

Mitchell, A. (2016) "Beyond Biodiversity and Species: Problematizing Extinction," *Theory, Culture & Society* 33(5): 23–42.

Mitchell, A., and Theriault, N. (2020) "Extinction," in C. Howe and A. Pandian (eds) *Anthropocene Unseen*. Santa Barbara, CA: Punctum.

Nita, M. (Forthcoming) "Sacred Waters, Sacred Earth. Contemporary Paganism Inside Extinction Rebellion: A Relational Analysis of Protest Death Rituals," in J. Kidwell and S. Skrimshire (eds) *Extinction and Religion*. Bloomington: Indiana University Press.

Sandler, R. (2021) "On the Massness of Mass Extinction," *Philosophia* 50: 2205–0.

Schachter-Shalomi, Z. (2017) "A New Partzuf for a New Paradigm Living Earth—an Icon for Our Age," in J. Hart (ed) *Wiley Blackwell Companion to Religion and Ecology* (In Conversation with J. Hart). Oxford: Blackwell.

Seidenberg, D. M. (2017) "Eco-Kabbalah: Holism and Mysticism in Earth-Centered Judaism," in J. Hart (ed) *Wiley Blackwell Companion to Religion and Ecology*. Oxford: Blackwell.

Sepkoski, D. (2016) "Extinction and Biodiversity: A Historical Perspective," in J. Garson, A. Plutynski and S. Sarkar (eds) *The Routledge Handbook of Philosophy of Biodiversity*. London: Routledge.

Sepkoski, D. (2020) *Catastrophic Thinking: Extinction and the Value of Diversity from Darwin to the Anthropocene*. Chicago: Chicago University Press.

Singh, S., Youssouf, M., Malik, Z. A., and Bussmann, R. W. (2017) "Sacred Groves: Myths, Beliefs, and Biodiversity Conservation—A Case Study from Western Himalaya, India," *International Journal of Ecology* 2017: 12.

Skrimshire, S. (2019) "Extinction Rebellion and the New Visibility of Religious Protest," *Open Democracy*, May 12.

Strain, C. (2016) "Reinventing Buddhist Practices to Meet the Challenge of Climate Change," *Contemporary Buddhism* 17(1): 138–56.

van Pelt, J. (2018) "Climate Change in Context: Stress, Shock, and the Crucible of Livingkind," *Zygon* 53(2).

Whyte, K. (2022) "Against Crisis Epistemology," in B. Hokowhitu et al. (eds) *Routledge Handbook of Critical Indigenous Studies*. London: Routledge.

WWF (2018) *Living Planet Report—2018: Aiming Higher*. M. Grooten and R. E. A. Almond (eds) Gland: WWF.

Yarlagadda, K. (2022) "How Religious Worship Is Boosting Conservation in India," *BBC*, July 27, www.bbc.com/future/article/20220726-how-religious-worship-is-boosting-conservation-in-india

## Further reading

Kidwell, J., and Skrimshire, S. (eds) (Forthcoming) *Extinction and Religion*. Bloomington, IN: Indiana University Press.

Rose, D. B. (2011) *Wild Dog Dreaming: Love and Extinction*. Charlottesville: Virginia University Press.

Willox, A. C., and Landman, K. (eds) (2017) *Mourning Nature*. Montreal: McGill-Queen's University Press.

# 17 Biodiversity and Cultural Diversity

*Maria Nita*

This chapter considers links between biodiversity on one hand and religious and cultural diversity on the other. To study biodiversity we will examine human culture using the tools of anthropology.

At the foundations of anthropology, the science of humanity, is the idea that religion is an essential part of human culture. The so-called father of anthropology, the first chair of anthropology at the University of Oxford in the UK, Edward Bernard Tylor (1832–1917), defined culture as

> that complex whole which includes knowledge, belief, art, morals, law, custom, and any other capabilities and habits acquired by man as a member of society.
>
> (2010 [1871]: 1)

This definition clearly includes religion and assumes that religion is a key element in shaping cultures. But the definition appears in a text that Tylor titled *Primitive Culture*, and he assumed, as did most late 19th- and early 20th-century anthropologists, that Indigenous and aboriginal cultures were "less advanced" than the cultures of Europe and European descendants. Their work assumed a trajectory of development in religion and all other aspects of culture, treating North American and European religion and culture as the most developed and higher than others on an evolutionary scale.

Later anthropologists have rejected the linear and ethnocentric notion that cultures "develop" along a pre-ordained track. Instead, thinkers like Frantz Boas understand cultures as changing and adapting on many scales of development rather than just one and avoid simplistic claims that rank cultures against one another (2008 [1911]).

But anthropology has continued to insist that religion is an important part of culture. According to the influential 20th-century anthropologist Clifford Geertz, cultures are made up of *structures of meanings* that allow participants in the same culture to correctly interpret the words, gestures, activities, or symbols that were part of their own cultural context (2000 [1973]: 7). Cultures allow people to make meaning together.

DOI: 10.4324/9781003259466-21

This chapter argues that if we want to understand biodiversity, biodiversity loss, and cultural diversity, we need to understand cultural structures of meaning, many of which are religious. I argue here that, just as biological diversity makes ecosystems more resilient, cultural and religious diversity make human systems more resilient and better able to work with ecological systems. Given that we now live in the Anthropocene, a geological era in which human culture is shaping the future of the planet, understanding human structures of meaning has never been more important.

## Biodiversity

> **BOX 17A**
>
> When you hear or read the word "biodiversity," what do you think of? Does biodiversity include the wildlife near you or mostly distant places? Does it include pets and farm animals? Does it include human beings?

The concept of biodiversity refers to the millions of diverse and interconnected life-forms—it is estimated around fourteen million species—that make up the biosphere of the Earth. Biodiversity refers to the variability among living organisms, including the diversity within and between species and organisms (Dahiya 2006: 1). Some ecosystems—like coral reefs and the Mediterranean heathland—are more diverse than others, with tropical forests being the most species rich environments on the planet. All these living organisms are connected by key planetary cycles and processes, such as the water cycle, regulation of the climate system, soil conservation, and regulation of the gaseous composition of the atmosphere (Wilson 1999).

An increasing number of species of all kinds are now in decline, both in terms of the number of species going extinct and the population numbers within each species. This is biodiversity loss. The biodiversity crisis is connected to the climate crisis, but it is not solely caused by climate change. For example, the number of insect species has been in decline for some decades now due to habitat loss, urbanization, and industrial agriculture, as well as the use of pesticides in industrial agriculture (Milman 2022). Some six decades ago, in her influential *Silent Spring* (1999 [1962]), American scientist and conservationist Rachel Carson powerfully made a case that the indiscriminate use of pesticides was affecting not only insect populations but also those who relied on them for food, such as birds. These populations continue to decline today, creating a biodiversity crisis.

So how is the biodiversity crisis affecting human and non-human life on our planet?

The previous chapter of this book discussed the ecological and cultural consequences of extinction. But even when species continue to exist in smaller numbers, the loss of diversity in the natural world poses threats to both humans and non-humans. Localities with a high degree of biodiversity are better able to adapt to the challenges posed by a changing climate. This is because the resilience of an ecosystem, its ability to resist or recover quickly from change like the erratic weather patterns caused by global warming, depends on the diversity of species in that ecosystem. Therefore, biodiversity is hugely important in the fight against the climate crisis.

Since the Industrial Revolution, increased urbanization and technical advancements have led to the growth of cities into huge, interconnected metropolises, giving rise to "human-dominated ecosystems" (Ernstson 2021: 1639). These huge urban jungles are changing both the planetary ecology and human cultures. Even before such growth, human habitats posed a threat to biodiversity. Humans have long cultivated certain crops and farmed certain animals, to the detriment or exclusion of others. Over the past eleven thousand years, humans have domesticated more and more species of animals, keeping them for food, labor, and/or companionship (Zeder 2012). As populations of domestic animals grow, populations of wild animals shrunk. Factory farming of animals and overconsumption pose severe threats to biodiversity. Areas of wilderness where biodiverse ecosystems can thrive without human interference are becoming increasingly rare (Watson et al. 2016).

It is perhaps very telling that the land around the Chernobyl nuclear disaster, which took place in 1986 in what used to be the Union of Soviet Socialist Republics, is now a thriving and biologically diverse area precisely because it has since been restricted from human interference. The industries and technologies of human beings have been a growing threat for the planet's biodiversity.

## Globalization and Cultures of Residence

One term that can help us think about the effects of growing urbanization and ever-more sophisticated digital technologies is "globalization." Globalization is an intersection of political, economic, and cultural processes that weaken national and local boundaries through the growth of global processes and networks. These processes include global information technology, global media, transnational migrant networks, world corporations, and banks—institutions and trends that heavily influence almost every human culture. Today one can find surprising vestiges of urban, consumeristic, modern cultures—such as a disposable Starbucks coffee cup—almost anywhere in the world.

These globalizing processes should always be understood from the perspective of unequal power dynamics, whereby richer and more influential nations—such as group of seven nations that make up the G7 intergovernmental political forum: Canada, France, Germany, Italy, Japan, the United Kingdom, and the United States—drive political and economic forces, often against other cultures of resistance (de Sousa Santos 2006).

### BOX 17B

When you think about the decline in biodiversity in contemporary times, where do you place primary responsibility? Is it better to think of biodiversity loss as occurring because of actions by all of humanity? The industrialized world? A few elites? Why?

But what cultures are resisting globalization and what role can they play in preserving and restoring biodiversity?

Here our discussion becomes more complex. We frequently see the globalized world caricatured as if there are only two groups: First are contemporary Indigenous peoples in the Global South who attempt to preserve their local cultures, ways of life, environments, and ecosystems' biodiversity. Second, in competition with the first, are the globalizing, urbanizing, and exploitative forces of modernity in the Global North. Blockbusters like *Avatar* (2009) present this duality quite plainly.

However, significant cultures of resistance against both globalizing processes and biodiversity loss have emerged precisely from the cultural diversity brought about by globalization. The cultural diversity of the new urban jungles of modernity gave birth to new cross-cultural movements, creating new cultures of resistance. For example, 20th-century new religious movements like contemporary paganism became instrumental in taking the green movement to the streets, providing activists with material culture, an iconography for the planet Earth as the Goddess, and key cultural practices for reconnecting to nature. Before looking at some examples and a case study exploring the links between biodiversity and cultural diversity in more depth, let us first examine the concepts of cultural and religious diversity.

## Cultural and Religious Diversity

Cultural and religious diversity are not new. Throughout the ancient, medieval, and pre-modern periods, major cities like Rome, Mecca, Baghdad, or Cordoba, were, at various times, thriving multicultural centers. While most were dominated by a particular religious tradition, other minority religious groups always coexisted within and alongside them. For example, in the early Roman Empire public or official religion revolved around the emperor, yet many other religious traditions and movements were recognized and tolerated at different times and by different emperors. Some of these made spectacular turnarounds: Christianity started as a persecuted movement within Judaism yet later became a cultural heir of the Roman Empire. Today, Christianity is one of the most influential and diverse religious traditions in the world, and it continues to influence and be influenced by many other religions.

This diversity among religions leads to change: countercultural ideas develop and bring about resistance and sometimes adaptations to dominant culture. For example, in Europe Christianity dominates the cultural and material urban landscape, perhaps most notably through its imposing cathedrals. However, European Christianity coexists with every other global religion and increasing trends of secularism, leading to vast cultural changes and hybridization.

In my own research, climate activists who come from secular and various faith perspectives (Buddhism, paganism, Islam) have been welcomed by many Christian communities who provide protesters with respite and spaces to gather during actions. Some climate activists in my research meet weekly inside church buildings to share food, read poetry, and organize protests. This is not too different from the ways Christian communities use the same spaces. This is hybridization, a natural and essential process in all human cultures.

Perhaps the most famous period of Western and Eastern cultural hybridization came in the countercultural movements of the 1950s and 1960s. New religious movements emerging at this time, like the Hare Krishna movement or eco-paganism, were cultures of resistance against the hegemonic or dominant global cultural forms that had taken shape with the advent of modernity. Eco-pagans are part of a broader indigenizing movement that seeks to either counter or resist industrial culture's assault on nature. Similarly, Hare Krishnas aspired to a pre-modern communal model of living, which was and is disappearing as increasingly alienated nuclear families live in urban environments.

But while these movements resisted dominant cultures, they also very much grew out of globalization and urbanization, which are essential for such countercultural networks to take root. Eco-paganism would have been impossible without mass media that spread its ideas; Hare Krishnas required the cultural combination of East and West that came from increased trade and communication. Therefore, the broad religious and cultural diversity of the contemporary world is a direct result of globalization, and dominant religions helped to produce the cultures that continuously fragment their traditions into the pulverized, "pick and mix" spirituality that is so common today.

This hybridized world means that the fight to preserve biodiversity is not exclusively from Indigenous peoples in the Global South. Significant mobilization has also emerged in the Global North as globalization increased the cultural diversity of industrialized Northern countries. These movements have based themselves in part on the material and technological resources of their cultures, including the internet and other tools for mass communication. They also had rich and diverse cultural resources.

My argument is that this geographic and cultural diversity is important. Just as biodiversity can improve an ecosystem's resilience, cultural diversity can intensify new movements' ability to resist dominant cultures and adapt to political, economic, social, or environmental change. Before we go deeper into this discussion, though, a disclaimer: I do not mean to suggest that cultures of resistance in the Global South—Indigenous groups opposing deforestation in South America, climate activists in India fighting for their very lives, and many others—are insignificant! Of course not! And I suspect they will be more significant in the future, as the geopolitical status quo changes and countries in the Global South, certainly including India, become more and more influential world powers.

However, looking back at the past century when the biodiversity crisis peaked, at the 1960s counterculture with its catalog of new religious movements, we see an important culture of ecological resistance that developed partly in the Global North. The cultures whose growing economies drove the biodiversity and climate crises also produced resistance.

## Biodiversity, Religion, and Culture

The intersection between biodiversity and cultural diversity is one example of the key question asked throughout this book: what is the relationship between religion and nature? One answer comes from an influential book by American scholar Catherine Albanese, *Nature Religion in America: From the Algonkian Indians to the New Age* (1990). Albanese suggests that scholars should look for specific characteristics of so-called nature religions, rooted in relationships to the environment rather than in history. Based on this approach, Abrahamic traditions—Judaism, Christianity, and Islam—are often set in opposition to nature religions, and nature religionists are reported to be critical of Abrahamic religions for their anthropocentrism, patriarchal attitudes, and arrogance (Taylor 2010a: 5, 8, 36, 163).

While Albanese makes a compelling case for understanding "nature religions" as a continuing tradition that goes back to early Indigenous cultures, her interpretation can be critiqued for representing Indigenous cultures as a golden age of human and nature harmony. Such arguments can be Orientalist or embrace a simplistic idea of a "noble savage."

As mentioned earlier, Indigenous cultures were understood by Taylor and other early anthropologists as primitive and inferior. In the 20th and 21st centuries many postcolonial critiques, like Edward Said's book *Orientalism* (2003 [1978]), illuminated and critiqued the colonial Western lens through which other cultures were observed and measured, classified, stereotyped, and dominated.

Today, Indigenous religions and cultures are no longer seen by serious scholars as primitive or archaic. However, even favorable understandings of Indigenous religions and cultures, like that of "nature religion," can be guilty of misrepresentation. For example, scholars and activists still sometimes speak of Indigenous cultures as if they remain unchanged, "frozen in time," and unimpacted by globalizing cultures. This rather idealized view of Indigenous cultures is another form of Orientalism (Belich 1996: 19–22). Any fixed archetype that reduces Indigenous peoples to a simplistic explanation maintains a colonial, othering view.

## BOX 17C

Indigenous cultures and communities can be erased and dismissed by those who see them as "less developed" than others. These cultures and communities can also be erased and dismissed by those who see them as "ecological" and somehow purer than others. Have you seen either kind of dismissal in your own reading and cultural analysis? Is one more present or dangerous than the other?

Simplistic cultural divisions also lead to broad generalizations that Western culture, and specifically Western religion, is at the root of our ecological crisis. This well-known critique of the Judeo-Christian roots of the ecological crisis was most famously articulated by American historian Lynn White Jr. in the late 1960s. He argued that the ecological crisis was a result of inculcated Judeo-Christian beliefs and values, mainly the belief in a transcendent God whose most valued creation (and the only one created in God's own image), "man," was given dominion over the rest, and was thus separated from it (White 1967).

White was not the first to have made such a claim. The prominent conservationist and ethicist Aldo Leopold had already suggested that "conservation is getting nowhere because it is incompatible with our Abrahamic concept of land" (Leopold 1989 [1949]: viii). Yet White's articulation has become iconic, and he made an extremely important claim that heavily influenced subsequent work:

> Human ecology is deeply conditioned by beliefs about our nature and destiny—that is, by religion [and since] the roots of our troubles are so largely religious, the remedy must also be essentially religious, whether we call it that or not.
>
> (White 1967: 1207)

This argument produced a massive response from historians, environmentalists, philosophers, and theologians, who debate what role Christianity played in causing environmental problems and what role it should or should not play in responding to them. White inspired many Christian theologians, who often disagreed with his critique of their tradition but, like him, sought to make Christianity part of environmental solutions.

Other scholars writing in White's wake extended the search for culprits. For example, Carolyn Merchant's *The Death of Nature: Women, Ecology and the Scientific Revolution* (1980) aimed to demonstrate that the patriarchal advances of mechanistic science and scientific inquiry were important in the domination of women and nature. This helped to shape the growing field of ecofeminism, which has since become a leading environmental perspective. Ecofeminist Anne Primavesi developed an argument against the patriarchal aspects of Christianity, showing that images of heaven in Christian cosmography and cosmology opposed it to the earth. She argued that such imagery teaches Christians to see this world as a place of exile, a lesser place on a qualitative axis. Primavesi argued that if God is understood to be present in heaven and absent on earth, the earth can easily be dismissed as a body without mind, without rationality, without self, and ultimately without self-worth. In other words, the earth could be dismissed in all the same ways that patriarchy has long sought to dismiss women (2003: 79–90).

In my own work, I have responded to these claims and argued that Christianity has in fact been the very model of countercultural reformulation in the ecological cultures of resistance in the Global North (Nita 2016, 2018). This is not to say that Christianity has never offered problematic ideas. But Christianity is not and has never been a single and monolithic tradition. This is why the perspective introduced earlier, that religion is an inseparable and evolving part of human culture, is so important. No aspect of culture is immutable, including religion. Dismissals of Christianity tend to treat it as singular and always resisting change. That not only misrepresents rich and diverse global Christian cultures but also fails to take into account the ways that Christian cultures have evolved and changed as they interact with a multitude of other ideas and material cultures.

If we understand religion as integral to and generative of wider cultural repertoires, we can discharge the simplistic argument that Abrahamic religions are maladaptive and cannot produce an adequate response to the urgent ecological crisis. This view, first articulated by the environmental anthropologist Roy Rappaport (1999), was also explored by Bron Taylor in his article "Earth Religion and Radical Religious Reformation" (Taylor 2010b). Taylor articulated the possibility that existing major religious traditions may be obsolete and incapable of change on the scale required by the ecological crisis:

> [L]ongstanding religions have more historical and conceptual obstacles to overcome than do post-Darwinian forms of nature spirituality, and this is why very little of the energy expended by participants in the world's religions is currently going toward the protection and restoration of the world's ecosystems. Conversely, participants in nature spiritualities steeped in an evolutionary-ecological worldview appear to be more likely to work ardently in environmental causes than those in religious traditions with longer pedigrees.
> (Taylor 2010b: 6)

My own work suggests that in fact eco-paganism and intersecting nature spiritualities are fundamentally rooted in a plural Christian tradition. The "nature spirituality" that Taylor studies often draws on Christian resources for its countercultural reformulation. The most influential Christian model of resistance was developed by the early Christian movement that attempted to oppose dominant Jewish and Greco-Roman cultures. It emphasizes not direct opposition to one's enemies but instead the reframing of a culture's emotional landscape. Cultural theorist Raymond Williams refers to such landscapes as "structures of feelings" within cultures (Williams 1961).

We find this model and other deeply rooted Christian discourses in the movements and currents that have shaped the green movement, like the 19th-century Romantic movement and the 20th-century hippie counterculture. For example, the British historian Sharif Gemie and I have argued that the sweeping late 20th-century free festival movement, which gestated in today's burgeoning festival cultures, represented a reinvention of Christian pilgrimage praxis (Nita and Gemie 2020). These festivals drew on a Christian vernacular and anti-materialism of a simple Eden imagery to reframe festivals as a return to a sacred nature.

Empirical research (Wilkinson 2012; Nita 2018), shows that contemporary Christianity incorporates a great diversity of cultural and political reformulations—from Christian anarchists in Europe to Christian Evangelicals in the US. Many, although certainly not all, of these Christians advocate for environmental reforms. Such green Christians represent a great example of cultural and religious diversity as a deeply cross-fertilized and syncretic movement. They bring together environmental movements with Christian denominations through a variety of internal outreach campaigns and eco-missionary activities.

## Return to Nature: The Forest Church and the Greenbelt Festival

The environmentalist argument about biodiversity is that more diverse systems are more resilient. This chapter has suggested that the same is true of cultures and that cultural perspectives combining diverse origins and perspectives have the best chance of responding constructively to environmental degradation. This includes Western cultures shaped by Christianity, and the internal diversity of Christian traditions means that they, too, can be resilient and adaptive in a world of climate change, extinction, and biodiversity loss.

The culture of environmental protest changes and adapts, as well. Phil Macnaughton and John Urry (1998) discuss the implications of living with unprecedented global risk in a "detraditionalized society." They argue that environmentalism before the 1990s could be characterized by discrete issues: "road rage," "animal rage," and "oil rage," for example (Macnaughton and Urry 1998: 70). But in the 1990s, a different kind of environmentalism took shape, positioning itself more broadly "against the system" and demanding global change across all sectors. The emphasis in this type of environmentalism is grassroots organizations and direct action. We can see such activism in the contemporary climate movement, which at the time of this writing is spearheaded in the United Kingdom by Extinction Rebellion (XR). This is a very urban movement—protesting on the British High Street and on London bridges and engaging mass media—but it also preserves the "back to nature" elements of earlier environmental protests.

**BOX 17D**

What "cultures" of environmental protest are you aware of in your own community? How do they interact with other aspects of the cultures there? How, if at all, do they interact with the biological diversity around them?

One Christian expression of the countercultural movement that aligns with contemporary protests is the Greenbelt Festival in the UK, a decidedly Christian expression of countercultural environmentalism (Nita 2016, 2018). Participants in the Greenbelt Festival, which began in the 1970s, borrowed features from the broader hippie movement, but they also remained explicitly connected to Christian churches. Organizing in those churches, they also began to gather and conduct rituals outdoors in an effort to return to sacred nature through festivals and retreats.

Some five decades on, the Greenbelt Festival is still offering a pastoral reimagination of the early Church, sometimes by constructing a Christian landscape during its annual enactment. For example, we can see in Figure 17.1, a landscape garden of the stately home in England where the festival has been hosted since 2014, which has been turned into The Mount in preparation for the festival. The Mount is of course a reference to Jesus' sermon of the Mount in the text of the Gospels very much part of the biblical nature landscape alongside other sacred sites, such as the Gethsemane Garden.

In Figure 17.2 we see a workshop at the 2018 Greenbelt Festival with members of the Forest Church. The Forest Church, also known as the Communities of the Mystic Christ, started in Wales in 2010 and has since rapidly established many groups around the UK and is beginning to extend across Europe. The Church seeks to recover monastic spiritual practices from the Christian tradition, like contemplation, while also adapting new practices from other green networks, like walking barefoot to connect to the earth. Members of the Forest Church worship

*Figure 17.1* The Mount, Greenbelt Festival, 2015. (Photo by the author.)

*Figure 17.2* Forest Church workshop, the Greenbelt Festival, 2018. (Photo by the author.)

outdoors and often include the natural environment in their practices, including, for example, praying and communing with trees.

The Forest Church is a countercultural reformulation in response to the ecological and biodiversity crisis, as well as broader phenomena of urbanization and globalization. It is part of the broader green and climate movements. While eco-pagans seek to directly challenge dominant religious understandings of the earth from outside of mainstream Christian traditions, the Forest Church offers the same challenge while remaining anchored in and seeking to shift the culture of the Christian tradition.

### Case Study: Rewilding Nature Spirituality

Could religious/cultural diversity help to preserve and promote biodiversity in the Anthropocene?

The following text comes from a 2018 advertisement inviting people to a weekend retreat in Wales, UK, to learn about "rewilding spirituality." The retreat was supported by a Christian church in London, St. Ethelburga, which has a long tradition of involvement with and support of the green and peace movements.

The concept of rewilding refers to combating biodiversity loss by "assisting natural regeneration of forests and other natural habitats." The idea of rewilding parts of Europe and North America has developed since the 1960s, and while it has support from many environmental writers, it has encountered some resistance from both the public and scientific community, given that it proposes reducing human habitat and involves the loss of the traditional agricultural landscape (Carey 2016: 806; Pereira and Navarro 2015: 5).

The following text does not mention a particular religious tradition, showing that green spirituality is a common currency that can bring together people from different faiths and those who do not identify with a particular tradition.

As you read three excerpts from the advertisement, remember the parallel suggested earlier between biodiversity and cultural diversity. I propose that, just as biodiversity improves and ecosystem's resilience, so could cultural diversity and syncretic encounters between cultures make human beings more resilient. Is this "rewilding spirituality" an example of a spirituality that brings and weaves together different traditions, such as Christianity and Indigenous cultures? Do you believe it could contribute to a more resilient culture?

**BOX 17E**

***Rewilding Spirituality: A Spiritual Exploration of Our Connection to the Natural World***

Imagine if everything in the world around you was conscious—every tree sacred, every rock, every falling leaf. Imagine if you felt they were closely related to you, like cousins, always available to offer wise guidance, gentle healing, fierce protection and a deep sense of belonging. How differently might we treat each other, the non-human world, and ourselves? . . . The recent surge in interest in "rewilding" reveals a yearning for a different way. Rewilding aims to regenerate, reconnect and restore, to create healthy, functional ecosystems.

. . .

But, as key parts of the ecosystems we dominate, humans must be part of the rewilding. A rewilding of the self is a re-enchantment with the natural world, a re-awakening of our senses and intuition, a dissolving of the false boundaries between our atomised selves and our Earthly home. It is a restoration of meaningful connections with nature, ourselves and each other. Ultimately, it is a regeneration of our sacred relationship with the natural world; our spiritual selves must too be rewilded. . . . As individuals, communities and society, we must build resilience to withstand the challenges of transitioning to a life within ecological limits. To build a life-affirming society from the ashes of a dying system will require great skill, creativity and courage. We can tap into vast resources by connecting with nature. Nature's ways are powerful and wise, and we can take part in that web of power and wisdom. The wise guidance, gentle healing and fierce protection are all there if we develop the humility to hear it.

. . .

Through meditation and reflection, discussion, ritual, experiential activities and play, together we will live simply as a community and explore what a spiritual connection with the earth means for each of us and how we can bring this into our daily lives. We'll work on the land to participate in the creation of wildness, exploring the inseparability of rewilding land and ourselves. Held in a stunning wild valley in West Wales, this retreat is for people of any or no particular spiritual tradition who want to bring the Earth more explicitly into their practice, as well as those without any formal practice who wish to explore nature-based spirituality.

*Source:* https://rewildeverything.wordpress.com/rewilding-spirituality

***Discussion Questions***

1. Can the extracts from this invitation to take part in the "rewilding retreat" be understood as religious? Why or why not?
2. Do you think the desire for rewilding is a yearning for a pre-modern world? What signs of this do you see in the invitation? What signs of globalization do you see?
3. Do you see specifically Christian influences in this invitation? Is the fact that the event is sponsored by a Christian church important to your understanding? After reading this chapter, how much do you think that eco-paganism and green Christianity are distinct, and how much do you think they can combine?
4. How does "rewilding spirituality" relate to the biodiversity crisis? Do you think that a belief in the sacredness of every tree would help to fight the climate and biodiversity crises?

## References


Albanese, C. L. (1990) *Nature Religion in America: From the Algonkian Indians to the New Age*. Chicago: University of Chicago Press.

Belich, J. (1996) *Making Peoples: A History of the New Zealanders*. Honolulu: University of Hawaii Press.

Boas, F. (2008 [1911]) *The Mind of Primitive Man*. New York: Macritchie Press.

Carey, J. (2016) "Rewilding," *Proceedings of the National Academy of Sciences—PNAS* 113(4): 806–8.

Carson, R. (1999 [1962]) *Silent Spring*. London: Penguin.

Dahiya, M. P. (2006) *Biodiversity Conservation*. New Delhi: Pragun Publications.

de Sousa Santos, B. (2006) "Globalizations," *Theory, Culture & Society* 23(2–3): 393–9.

Ernstson, H. (2021) "Ecosystems and Urbanization: A Colossal Meeting of Giant Complexities," *Ambio* 50(9): 1639–43.

Geertz, C. (2000 [1973]) *The Interpretation of Cultures*. New York: Basic Books.

Leopold, A. (1989 [1949]) *A Sand County Almanac and Sketches Here and There*. New York: Oxford University Press.

Macnaughton, P., and Urry, J. (1998) *Contested Natures*. London and Thousand Oaks, CA: Sage.

Merchant, C. (1980) *The Death of Nature: Women, Ecology and the Scientific Revolution*. San Francisco: Harper & Row.

Milman, O. (2022) *The Insect Crisis: The Fall of the Tiny Empires that Run the World*. London: Atlantic Books.

Nita, M. (2016) *Praying and Campaigning with Environmental Christians: Green Religion and the Climate Movement*. New York: Palgrave Macmillan.

———. (2018) "Christian Discourses and Cultural Change: The Greenbelt Art and Performance Festival as an Alternative Community for Green and Liberal Christians," *Implicit Religion* 21(1): 44–69.

Nita, M., and Gemie, S. (2020) "Counterculture, Local Authorities and British Christianity at the Windsor and Watchfield Free Festivals (1972–5)," *Twentieth Century British History* 31(1): 51–78.

Pereira, H. M., and Navarro, L. M. (2015) "Introduction," in H. M. Pereira and L. M. Navarro (eds) *Rewilding European Landscapes*. Cham: Springer International Publishing.

Primavesi, A. (2003) *Gaia's Gift*. London and New York: Routledge.

Rappaport, R. A. (1999) *Ritual and Religion in the Making of Humanity*. Cambridge: Cambridge University Press.

Said, E. W. (2003 [1978]). *Orientalism*. London: Penguin Classics.

Taylor, B. (2010a) *Dark Green Religion: Nature, Spirituality, and the Planetary Future*. Berkeley: University of California Press.

Taylor, B. (2010b) "Earth Religion and Radical Religious Reformation," in K. D. Moore & M. P. Nelson (eds) *Moral Ground: Ethical Action for a Planet in Peril*. San Antonio, TX: Trinity University Press, 306–79.

Tylor, E. B. (2010 [1871]) *Primitive Culture: Researches into the Development of Mythology, Philosophy, Religion, Art, and Custom*. Cambridge: Cambridge University Press.

Watson, J. et al. (2016) "Catastrophic Declines in Wilderness Areas Undermine Global Environment Targets," *Current Biology* 26(21): 2929–34.

White, T. L. (1967) "The Historical Roots of Our Ecological Crisis," *Science* 155(3767): 1203–7.

Wilkinson, K. (2012) *Between God & Green: How Evangelicals Are Cultivating a Middle Ground on Climate Change*. Oxford: Oxford University Press.
Williams, R. (1961) *Culture and Society: 1780–1950*. London: Penguin.
Wilson, E. O. (1999) *Biodiversity*. Washington, DC: National Academies Press.
Zeder, M. A. (2012) "The Domestication of Animals," *Journal of Anthropological Research* 68(2): 161–90.

# 18 Politics

*Emma Tomalin*

## Introduction

This chapter examines the intersection between politics and discourses about religions and ecology. I ask, in what ways are religions and ecology discourses, which have emerged alongside the birth of modern environmental movements, political? Since the late 1960s, religious traditions have responded to the increasing awareness that human interaction with the natural world has consequences that are damaging to other species and to human well-being and security (White 1967). As a reflection of the emergent awareness that humans needed to change their values and behaviors with respect to nature, religious traditions enthusiastically entered moral debates and calls for practical action, and a field of "religions and ecology" arose (Jenkins et al. 2017). This involved religious practitioners, activists, and scholars seeking to examine the ways in which religious teachings and traditions could be directed toward establishing a moral framing for environmental action and imperatives for individuals and communities to change their behavior. Religions and ecology discourse today inspires a wide range of expressions of religious environmentalism across the globe as forms of civil society political action. These seek to address environmental destruction and climate change at the individual and community level and at the level of formal politics and multilateral cooperation between states (Kidwell 2020).

Given the interest in this volume in approaching the religions and ecology nexus in an *antiracist and anticolonial way*, my aim in this chapter is to think about politics in terms of examining the power relations underpinning religions and ecology discourse, particularly the notion that religions are inherently environmentally friendly. I ask, who is involved in constructing religions and ecology discourse and to what ends? What are the implications of this for the communities that it seeks to represent? While religious traditions can be interpreted to support care for nature, the more radical claim that they are inherently environmentally friendly has been critiqued for promoting the "neotraditionalist" view that the small-scale, sustainable livelihoods that communities apparently followed in the past were a direct result of people following the injunction of their religious traditions to treat nature with respect but that processes of colonialism and industrialization have severed their sacred link with the natural world (Tomalin 2011; Baviskar 1999;

DOI: 10.4324/9781003259466-22

Guha 1989). Colonialism and industrialization have of course played a significant role in the shift to a capitalistic economic system that has undermined more sustainable livelihoods. However, the over-determination of the role that religion played in maintaining sustainable livelihoods in the way that is imagined by some contemporary environmentalists reveals more about their political agenda than that of the people being represented by these claims (Guha 1989).

Against the backdrop of rising forms of nationalist and populist politics globally, I argue that the power relations involved in neotraditionalist religions and ecology discourse take on a new significance. To examine this, I focus on the case study of the engagement of Hindu nationalism in India with religions and ecology discourse. Both religious environmentalists and Hindu nationalists resort to romantic images about India's ecologically harmonious past, made possible by virtue of Hindu teachings about care for the natural world.

The chapter begins with an examination of this neotraditionalist construction of religious traditions as inherently environmentally friendly as political, arguing that this move reflects powerful, often neo colonial, interests. Neotraditionalism refers to "the deliberate revival and revamping of old cultures, practices, and institutions for use in new political contexts and strategies" (Galvan 2007: 399). To unpack and understand the politics surrounding this use of religions and ecology discourse, I adopt a political ecology lens. The interdisciplinary field of political ecology emerged in the 1980s and is concerned with "societies' relationships with the nonhuman environment" (Bridge et al. 2015: 3) in ways that draw attention to power relations "rooted in political economy, marginalization, colonial capitalism, and the abuses of predatory states" (2015: 5). Wilkins has drawn attention to the overall neglect of religion in the field of political ecology, which, he argues, has led "political ecologists to neglect important factors in their analyses and has resulted in incomplete conceptualizations of interpersonal power relations" (2021: 276). However, where Wilkins argues that "political ecology would benefit from stronger engagements with religion" (2021: 277), my argument is that the study of religions and ecology would benefit from a stronger engagement with political ecology for its leverage of critical social theory, its strong emphasis on learning from empirical research (rather than assumptions and myths), and its commitment to social change (Bridge et al. 2015: 7).

To highlight the importance of being attuned to the "politics" behind the construction of religions as inherently environmentally friendly, the case study presented at the end of the chapter explores overlaps between religions and ecology discourse and right-wing movements as an important example of how particular manifestations of political rhetoric and action are engaging with religions and ecology discourse. Populist parties and governments are typically known for rejecting environmentalist causes and for being suspicious of the science underpinning climate change, where they construct environmentalists and scientists as meddling "others" who are against the interests of the "people." However, today they are increasingly engaging with ecological themes to boost their populist agendas. While this is part of a broad trend, the case study will focus upon the example of the Hindu nationalist movement in India, which, since the 1980s, has taken up ecological themes that are underpinned by the portrayal of Hinduism as inherently environmentally friendly.

I ask, is the Hindu nationalist engagement with religions and ecology discourse an example of the "greening" or the "greenwashing" of religion? Does religions and ecology discourse have a role to play in efforts to achieve sustainable development in India or does the political context render it counterproductive?

## Outlining the Political Ecology Approach

Political ecology emerged in the 1980s to provide a counterpoint to "apolitical views about ecological relations," which often blame local communities for the problems they face rather than the wider socio-political structures that lead to their disadvantage (Robins 2004: 12). Even though many communities in the Global South, who are experiencing the worst impacts of environmental degradation and climate change, are deeply religious, and even though religion plays a key role in shaping the social and political structures that impact their lives, Wilkins points out that political ecology has tended to ignore religion as a relevant factor (2021). Within such communities, religion influences people's relationships to the natural resources that they rely upon, where features of the natural world are considered as sacred and are the focus of ritual and worship. Religion also shapes the social structures that influence the different forms of inequality, including gender inequality, that cause people to experience the impact of environmental degradation and climate change in different ways. This neglect of religion within political ecology is due to a reliance on Marxian-influenced political economy, resulting in secularist framings that render the religious or the spiritual invisible.

### BOX 18A

How do you think about the relationship between religion and politics? Between the environment and politics? How might these relationships change based on what you have read in this book about the ways religion and environmental thought shape one another?

While the field of political ecology has not engaged seriously with religion, its approach to the topic of what has been called local environmental knowledge (LEK)[1] offers some tools for thinking about and responding to religions and ecology discourse as political, in terms of considering the operation of power relations that potentially benefit some groups but can marginalize and disempower others. LEK is defined as "a cumulative body of knowledge, practice, and belief, evolving by adaptive processes and handed down through generations by cultural transmission, about the relationship of living beings (including humans) with one another and with their environment" (Berkes 2012: 7). However, as Horowitz explains, by the early 1990s, "political ecologists began cautioning . . . against an overly-romanticized and ultimately constraining view of local, particularly indigenous, knowledge" (2015: 236) and drew attention to what Blaikie referred to as "neo-populist developmentalism" that "reifies and idealizes indigenous knowledge" (1996: 84).

This idealization is not only a misrepresentation but also has a concrete impact on people's lives because portrayals of "traditional ecological wisdom" are sometimes employed by conservationists in ways that do not represent the interests or inputs of local communities. For instance, as Horowitz writes, the "view of ecosystems and their components as possessing intrinsic, aesthetic, and/or recreational values that must be protected from any exploitation, as conservationists may insist," does not always match the perspective of local communities who view ecosystems as possessing "resources 'to be respected and used responsibly' in accordance with locally developed management practices and/or ancestral taboos" (2015: 241). Nonetheless, while a political ecology approach makes visible the power relations involved in constructions of traditional ecological wisdom, it also draws attention to the ways in which such discourses can be strategically useful where they enable alliances to be forged that can give communities a voice in international political fora within which such discourses "have gained traction" (2015: 242; Brosius 1999). As Milton (1996) indicates, some indigenous peoples actively portray themselves as ecologically wise, appropriating the "myth of primitive ecological wisdom" for strategic ends.

## Applying a Political Ecology Lens to Religions and Ecology Discourse

This political ecology critique of LEK is also useful in unpacking the power relations involved in religions and ecology discourse. Some commentators have argued that the depiction of religions as inherently environmentally friendly, within which Asian or Eastern religions are portrayed as particularly so, amounts to "anachronistic projections of modern phenomena onto the screen of tradition" (Pederson 1995: 264; Tomalin 2004). This is viewed as part of a neotraditionalist discourse and a form of Orientalism that silences the voices of the poor, where "Eastern man exhibits a spiritual dependence with respect to nature . . . denying agency and reason to the East and making it the privileged orbit of Western thinkers" (Guha 1989: 7; Baviskar 1997; Sinha et al. 1997). For instance, Freeman is critical of the way in which the protection of sacred groves in India is frequently taken as evidence of the existence of an environmental ethic both in the past and where they continue to exist to this day, albeit in dwindling numbers (1994). He argues that

> cultural values are being imputed to populations not on the evidence of their actually espousing and expressing those values, but on the basis of inferring that they must hold some such values and beliefs from the requirements of the analyst's own ecological model.
>
> (1994: 7–8)

He suggests instead that, although there is a strong tradition of sacred grove preservation in India, people have traditionally worshiped these forests because they are the abode of the deity rather than to conserve their biodiversity *per se* (1994). This matters because there is a danger that when assumptions are made by powerful outsiders about the significance of local environments to people in ways that do not include them in decision-making processes or involve evidence-based policy-making, this can lead to outcomes that do not meet people's needs. For instance, conservationists are increasingly recognizing the ecological value of sacred groves, but it cannot be assumed that the goals of scientific conservation will necessarily match the cultural and economic needs of local communities, particularly where these deny any human interference whatsoever. By contrast, Freeman notes that different degrees of human interference in sacred groves in India may well be accommodated with the "cultural framework of the grove as the deities' preserve" (1994: 11).

One of the earliest invocations of neotraditionalist religions and ecology discourse is found in Lynn White Jr.'s famous article, "The Historical Roots of Our Ecological Crisis," in the journal *Science* in 1967. He argues that Christianity had played a role in establishing the conditions for the human exploitation of nature that led to the Industrial Revolution of the 18th century. According to this view, Christianity has created dualisms between nature and humanity and between humanity and the divine, establishing damaging hierarchies that led humans to exploit nature for its own ends. By contrast, Asian or Eastern traditions are depicted as promoting the view that humans are interconnected with nature and the divine, and that the Earth is afforded intrinsic value, which encourages people to treat the natural world with respect and limit their interference.

However, neotraditionalist religions and ecology discourse is not just the preserve of Western thinkers. Baviskar and others argue that it has also become absorbed by "bourgeois" or "middle-class" Indian environmentalists, who engage with global environmentalist discourse, more than the lower classes, who are focused on day-to-day survival (2003; Mawdsley 2004, 2006; Sinha et al. 1997; Guha and Martinez-Alier 1997). At the same time, these "bourgeois environmentalists" are motivated to seek alternatives to the destructive forces of Western colonialism and capitalism, using the notion of "Hindu civilization" to constitute "a critique of ecologically destructive development and an alternative model of ecologically-sound development" (Baviskar 1999: 24). Baviskar argues that this amounts to " 'inverted Orientalism,' which homogenizes and glorifies India as the mirror opposite of the West" (1999: 21) and underpins what she calls the "Hindu civilizational" response to ecological problems promoted by both middle-class environmentalists and Hindu nationalists. This is seen, for instance, in the Hindu contribution to the Assisi Declarations. These declarations, presented at a gathering in Assisi, Italy, in 1986, come from one of the first attempts to bring together representatives from different world religions seeking to establish the environmentalist credentials of their religious traditions, employing strongly neotraditionalist themes. Consider part of the contribution by Dr. Karan Singh, president of the Hindu Virat Samaj:

> In the ancient spiritual traditions, man [*sic*] was looked upon as a part of nature, linked by indissoluble spiritual and psychological bonds with the elements around him. This is very much marked in the Hindu tradition, probably the oldest living religious tradition in the world . . . [T]he natural

> environment also received the close attention of the ancient Hindu scriptures. Forests and groves were considered as sacred, and flowering trees received special reverence . . . The Hindu tradition of reverence for nature and all forms of life, vegetable or animal, represents a powerful tradition which needs to be re-nurtured and re-applied in our contemporary context.
>
> (WWF 1986: 17–19)

This quotation is a powerful expression of neotraditionalist discourse that romanticizes the past and essentializes Hinduism as inherently environmental, selectively filtering out elements of the tradition that would not meet environmentalist credentials. For instance, Nelson is concerned that the frequent disregard for the material world in Hinduism clashes with claims that the tradition is environmentally friendly. Nelson notes that Hinduism also includes perspectives that suggest nature is irrelevant to spiritual life:

> Pure non-attachment is disregard for all objects—from the god Brahma down to plants and minerals—like the indifference one has toward the excrement of a crow.
>
> (From the Aparokshanubhuti, a text associated with the 8th-century Indian philosopher Shankara; cited in Nelson 1998: 81)

**BOX 18B**

Have you encountered any examples of neotraditionalist thinking—which simplifies and valorizes past ideas—in your life? In your community? In this book? Who tends to appeal to such thinking, and why?

### Hindu Nationalism and Religions and Ecology Discourse

Since the 1990s, scholars and activists have drawn attention to the overlaps between the ways in which religious environmentalists and Hindu nationalists construct Hinduism as inherently environmentally friendly. While not all environmentalists who invoke neotraditionalist discourse are necessarily supporters of Hindu nationalism, some scholars tend to portray them as such (Baviskar 1999; Nanda 2002, 2005), whereas others question whether there is an inevitable "guilt by association" (Mawdsley 2006: 388). As we will see in the case study at the end of the chapter, concern for nature and Hindu nationalist politics are multidimensional, and it can sometimes be hard to see the line between the greening and the greenwashing of religion, as well as to untangle the interplay of different agendas. However, given the need for practical responses to the pressing climate crisis, I return to the question posed earlier: is the Hindu nationalist engagement with religions and ecology discourse an example of the greening or the greenwashing of religion? Does religions and ecology discourse have a role to play in efforts to achieve sustainable development in India or does the political context render it counterproductive?

To address this question, I argue that the engagement between populist politics and religion and ecology discourse in India should be understood with a political ecology approach. This involves the application of critical social theory to understand the underlying power relations involved in the dynamic and the promotion of empirical research rather than a reliance upon assumptions and myths to understand how religion and culture intersect with people's livelihoods and relationships to their environment. Whether or not religious beliefs promote social and environmental change that will reduce social inequality and increase the health of the planet is an empirical question.

The political ecology approach lays bare the interplay of the colonial, class, and nationalist dynamics involved when certain groups are considered environmentally friendly due to their religious beliefs. Such assumptions have implications for the communities so represented. These communities do sometimes strategically develop and employ neotraditionalist discourses, but when powerful outsiders romanticize their livelihoods as ecologically harmonious, it can lead to policies that do not meet people's needs and silence the voices of those whose interactions with the environment do not meet standards set by a "myth of primitive ecological wisdom" (Milton 1996).

Although Hindu nationalism and environmentalism are not necessarily mutually exclusive, any short-term ecological gain that comes from their combination is outweighed by the "political damage" (Sharma 2011: 50) caused by divisive ideology that seeks to establish boundaries between "us" and "them," apportioning blame for the climate crisis by constructing an "other" who threatens the Hindu nation. The view that the Hindu nationalist engagement with environmentalism amounts to greenwashing seems to be supported by the mismatch between the rhetoric and actions of Prime Minister Narendra Modi, who frequently invokes neotraditionalist Hinduism and ecology imagery while enacting policies that are widely considered to be counterproductive to achieving sustainable development.

**BOX 18C**

Are you aware of other examples of nationalism outside of India that resonate with what you have read here? Do those examples also engage in environmental rhetoric as part of political discourse?

This does not mean that we should abandon research on religions and ecology. It is important to understand where religion plays a role in supporting more sustainable livelihoods. It is important to do robust research that involves local communities and can feed into policies that have the potential to reduce social inequality alongside sustainable development. Such a critically informed, grounded and socially responsible approach to religious and ecology research is essential to resist and counter populist appropriations. But political ecology suggests that when the discourse of religions and ecology adopts the same neotraditionalist rhetoric as the Hindu nationalist movement, it is compounding a political ideology that is primarily driven by nationalism rather than the interests of the poor or the environment.

## Case Study—the Greening or Greenwashing of Religion? The Engagement of Populist Politics with Religions and Ecology Discourse in India

Populist politics have typically rejected environmentalism and environmental science. As Machin and Wagerner write, "environmentalists often feature as part of the unresponsive international elites, accused of asserting policies that work against the interests of 'ordinary people'" and their "common sense," and scientists are also "seen as suspicious and politicised actors who use their expertise in the interest of a biased agenda" (2019). However, right-wing groups are increasingly adopting environmental concerns as part of their political agendas. In particular, according to Machin and Wagerner, "landscapes, forests, and animals resonate with 'the people' and become important unifying symbols" (2019).

For example, De Nadal explores the shift made by the Spanish right-wing party VOX, which used to apparently deny climate change, but now leader Santiago Abascal places "the preservation of the 'natural heritage' at the core of the group's 'patriotic' solution to climate change" (2021). Defending the previous stance of VOX, Abascal argued that they had not disagreed with the "evidence" of climate change but rather the " 'totalitarian' tendency to submit climate policy to the dictates of the scientific community. 'Our concern,' he insisted, 'is with the rise of a climate religion with which one is not allowed to disagree'" (2021).

It is compelling to label such examples of rightwing populist environmentalism as greenwashing, broadly defined as the "practice of promoting environmentally friendly programs to deflect attention from an organization's environmentally unfriendly or less savoury activities" (*Webster's New Millennium Dictionary of English* cited in de Freitas Netto et al. 2020: 6). In practice, however, it is difficult to differentiate between the co-option of environmentalist discourse as part of populist rhetoric and a genuine concern to address ecological concerns; the two are not necessarily mutually exclusive.

Nonetheless, the use of neotraditionalist environmentalist discourse by right-wing groups to help their broader populist and nationalist project to establish "us" and "them," through recourse to romantic images of the past bolstered by selective appropriations of history and culture, is arguably counterproductive to longer term goals that address social inequality and environmental degradation. Given that climate change already exacerbates group tensions over access to increasingly scarce natural resources and that this is likely to worsen, political responses that feed on divisiveness ought to be resisted, despite any short-term commitments to environmentalist goals.

This embrace of environmental issues by populist politics is seen not only in Europe but also in Global South countries, such as India, where at the time of this writing the government is led by the Hindu nationalist Bharatiya Janata Party (BJP) under Prime Minister Narendra Modi, which had electoral success in 2014 and 2019. Hindu nationalism emerged as a response to the British presence in India and was a movement calling for India to be established as a Hindu state following independence, achieved in 1947. While Sikhs, Buddhists, and Jains are viewed as within the Hindu fold by virtue of their shared Indic origins, Muslims and Christians were viewed as colonialists who "suppressed Hindu nationhood" (Khan et al. 2017: 494; Jaffrelot 2007).

In contrast to the classic populist attitude toward environmentalism outlined earlier, Narendra Modi is not publicly a skeptic about climate change, despite some instances where this has been in doubt. For example, in a widely criticized speech to school children in November 2014 in Delhi, he claimed, "Climate has not changed. We have changed . . . our tolerance and habits have changed. If we change then God has built the system in such a way that it can balance on its own" (Mehra 2014). But Modi has marketed himself as a champion of climate change action—for instance, by changing the name of the Ministry of Environment and Forests to the Ministry of Environment, Forests, and Climate Change in May 2014. Writing in the *Financial Times* just before the 2015 United Nations Climate Change Conference held in Paris, Modi asserted that "we will play our part" in a "common but differentiated approach" (Modi 2015). While controversial, this approach recognizes that, in the interests of equity, developing countries should not be expected to assume the same burden for change mitigation as those that are already developed (Modi 2015; Gupta et al. 2015: 592). However, in this article Modi exemplifies what Baviskar (1999) has called the "Hindu civilizational response" to climate change action where he states:

> The instinct of our culture is to take a sustainable path to development. When a child is born, we plant a tree. Since ancient times, we have seen humanity as part of nature, not superior to it. This idea, rooted in our ancient texts, endures in sacred groves and in community forests across the land.
>
> (Modi 2015)

Sharma, writing before the recent and rapid ascendency of the BJP, refers to this Hindu nationalist engagement with religions and ecology discourse as the "greening of saffron" (2011). Saffron is the color of the clothing traditionally worn by renunciates within Hinduism, but here is used to denote the "political practice of Hindutva, or 'Hinduness,' which deploys the religious associations of the colour saffron for mobilizations" (2011: 32). Against the backdrop of the rise of Hindu nationalist politics, it has become increasingly difficult to differentiate between those who invoke religions and ecology discourse from a conservationist concern and those who do it to future their exclusionary nation building political ideology (Baviskar 2004; Nanda 2002; Mawdsley 2006: 382).

One of the most striking examples of the Hindu nationalist entry into environmental politics was the campaign to prevent the construction of the Tehri Dam on the Bhagirathi River in Garhwal, in the state of Uttarakhand. Construction began in 1978 and was completed in 2006. In the interim period, a strong protest movement against the dam emerged, led by the veteran campaigner Sunderlal Bahuguna, also known for his involvement in the Chipko forest protection movement in the Himalayan region of Uttarakhand in the 1970s (Guha 1989; Rangan 2000). From the earliest days of the protest, Bahuguna was well known for invoking Hindu teachings and myths, opposing the dam in part based on the sacredness of the Ganges River, the holiest river for Hindus, into which the Bhagirathi River flows. However, by the 1980s, Sharma observes that the BJP and other nationalist groups began to show interest in the anti-dam movement and joined forces with Bahuguna and others, who in "invoking certain metaphors, myths, emotions and faith . . . came close in their worldview to Hindu nationalist forces and their communal agenda" (2011: 150–1). Thus, Sharma also notes that there has been a "saffronizing of green" where environmental movements and groups refer to the same discourses employed by Hindu nationalists, which "fabricates glorifications of 'Hindu' land, rivers, forests, community, tradition, self-reliant villages, and ancient nature philosophy" (2011: 38). Sharma argues that this engagement of Hindu nationalists with ecological causes where they invoke the Hindu civilizational response is not only a means of securing votes, although there is evidence that this does play a role (Alley 2000). As Sharma suggests, the saffronizing of the green movement has become a "Trojan Horse to carry an authoritarian ideology into the citadels of ordinary discourse and political debate" (2011: 43).

Given the increasing political success of Hindu nationalists since the 1980s, there has been a strong backlash in India against neotraditionalist religions and ecology discourse, with Sharma arguing that "it is not only unnecessary to valorize the past in order to critique modern development paradigms, but that such valorization needs to be exposed for the political damage that it does" (2011: 50; Nanda 2002, 2005). Although, as I have suggested, genuine commitment to environmentalism and populism are not necessarily mutually exclusive, Sharma notes that a "socially just and ecologically sustainable society cannot be created via the atavistic recrudescence implied in postulating the value of traditional socio-ecological relations, nor by religious, economic, and cultural nationalism" (2011: 50).

A number of commentators have argued that the BJP's politics in fact stand in the way of progress tackling environmental degradation and climate change. For instance, Agrawal has pointed out that the BJP's dislike of NGOs has meant that important organizations such as Greenpeace and Amnesty International can no longer function effectively in India where "any opposition, whether it be institutional, civil, or political, represents a difficulty for populists, as it undermines their claim to be the sole representatives of the people" (2020: 119). Moreover, the fact that populists prefer solutions with short-term benefits is in tension with "pro-environment decisions" that "yield slow results, while causing immediate pain . . . in complete contradiction to the populist impatience" (2020: 142).

Chandra proposes four concrete reasons why Modi's Hindu nationalism impairs the global fight against climate change. First, the "spurious science" advanced by Hindutva proponents has the effect of "structurally impairing prospects for combating climate change" (2021). For instance, Modi and others associated with the BJP "have frequently argued, without evidence, that ancient India mastered modern scientific achievements" and more recently one of Modi's former health ministers "helped launch a suspect COVID-19 cure" (2021). He concludes that in "such a scientifically spurious context, the pursuit of a hard-nosed, consistent approach to fighting climate change becomes challenging" (2021). Second, Chandra (2021) proposes that the culture war that rages in modern India, fueled by Hindu nationalism, "distracts attention from pressing issues, including climate change." Third, its authoritarian nature means that there is "limited questioning, discussion, and accountability over important issues such as climate change" (2021). Finally, "the tensions that Hindutva nurtures, regionally and internationally, weakens the capacity for concerted action against climate change" (2021).

However, just as there are those who are critical of the problems that Hindu nationalism poses for social and environmentalist goals, others praise Modi and the BJP for their approach to addressing climate change. This suggests that politics shapes views on both sides. For example, in contrast to the negative accounts outlined earlier, Saryal writes about the "deep interest in climate change of Prime Minister Narendra Modi," recent evidence of "ecologically inspired action that now seems to spearhead a new 'green revolution'" under the Modi government, and the image of Modi as "a doer rather than a vain talker" (2018: 2, 11, 15). Taking the example of the run up to the 2015 United Nations Climate Change Conference held in Paris, where Modi engaged in various activities to draw attention to the synergies between Indian culture and environmentalism, Saryal is critical of "outsiders" for their "short-sighted" dismissal, arguing instead that "ecological awareness is an ancient Asiatic and not just Indic topic on which there is much literature" (2018: 12). He concludes,

> Along with this historical responsibility argument and equity frame, however, India now also projects itself as a guardian of Nature, remembering and invoking Indic cultural elements that symbolise Nature as a power beyond humans, considered sacrosanct and to be respected, not destroyed.
> (2018: 12–13)

Saryal's very positive account is at odds with the view of other commentators who draw attention to India's worsening environmental conditions. While we need to be cautious not to over-determine the impact of populism on India's poor environmental record—previous governments also failed to make necessary improvements and were equally prone to short-termism and vote bank politics—a number of commentators suggest that the situation is declining under the BJP leadership and that populist policies play a role (Elliot 2020). For instance, Rathee (2019) offers statistical evidence from the Environmental Performance Index, on which India dropped from the 25th worst country (out of 180) in 2013 to the 4th worst in 2018. He notes that since 2014, legislation to limit factories in particularly polluted areas has been removed, thermal power units have been allowed to exceed legal levels of pollutants, inner-city forests in Delhi and Mumbai have been destroyed, and the government has allowed coal mining in one of India's most pristine, dense forests, in the state of Chhattisgarh (2019). This is starkly at odds with the valorization of India's forests by Modi and other Hindu nationalists. So too is the way that

Hindu nationalist religions and ecology discourse romanticizes past Hindu communities that are portrayed as living in harmony with nature while at the same time enacting policies that undermine the more sustainable livelihoods of tribal and pastoralist communities.

There are an estimated thirteen million pastoralists in India who, under the policies of the BJP, are finding it ever more difficult to pursue their traditional livelihoods by herding goats, camels, and sheep (Kishore and Kóhler-Rollefson 2020). They are increasingly forced to sedentarize as they lose access to their traditional grazing lands. Pastoralism is frequently dismissed by policymakers as "unproductive," "fragile," "marginal," and "remote" (Krätli 2014: 10; Sharma et al. 2003), and pastoralists are depicted as "backward" and "hard to reach" (Dyer 2014). Against the backdrop of the BJP's embrace of sustainable development and rhetoric about traditional Indian cultures of nature conservation, one might expect promotion and support for a livelihood suited to dryland environments that draws on traditional knowledge systems rooted in religious and cultural heritage. On the contrary, pastoralists' contributions to India's regional rural economies go largely unrecognized (Sharma et al. 2003: iii; Dyer 2014; Jitendra 2019).

While the Modi government portrays itself to both domestic and international audiences as a leading champion for sustainable development, its drive for a modern market economy alongside the pursuit of Hindu nationalist politics is having an impact on communities with livelihoods and religious identities that do meet the ambitions of the BJP (Jaffrelot 2021; Chacko 2019). Its embrace of the "myth of primitive ecological wisdom" becomes a proxy that deflects attention away from policies and actions that are at odds with the values supposedly being promoted.

For instance, while research with pastoralist communities[2] highlights the role that religion plays in their relationships with the land and their animals and how this supports their livelihood, it does not suggest that they are inherent environmentalists in the modern sense and as implied by the "myth of primitive ecological wisdom." Their religious beliefs and practices do play a practical role in conserving and protecting some features of the natural world, where patches of forest, for example, are protected from human interference because of the presence of shrines to the deities and saints and are used as places where sick animals can go to recuperate or where they can be grazed if other land was not available (e.g., during a drought) (Tambs-Lyche 2019: 5). However, as communities sedentarize, they are shifting their religious identities toward the Hindu nationalist mainstream and away from a style of religious practice that is nature focused.

### *Discussion Questions*

1. In what ways is it appropriate for scholars and citizens outside of the nation of India to critically examine Indian politics and its environmental implications?
2. Based on what you have read, do you consider the Hindu nationalist engagement with religions and ecology discourse an example of the greening or the greenwashing of religion?

3. In what ways can the academic study of religions and ecology contribute to better environmental politics? What are the limits of such study?
4. Have you experienced other examples where green politics is employed by conservative or right-leaning politics?

## Notes

1 Local environmental knowledge (LEK) is among a number of terms used interchangeably in the literature to refer to similar phenomena, including traditional ecological knowledge (TEK), Indigenous knowledge (IK), or Indigenous technical knowledge (ITK) (Horowitz 2015: 235; Onyancha 2022).

2 This was part of a larger ethnographic study of dignity, heritage, and sustainable development among pastoralist women in India in Gujarat, Maharashtra, and Himachal Pradesh, funded by the British Academy. It was led by Professors Caroline Dyer and Emma Tomalin at the University of Leeds and involved other collaborators, including Dr. Archana Choksi, Sushma Iyenga, and a number of local researchers.

## References


Agrawal, B. (2020) "Regaining Control Over the Climate Change Narrative: How to Stop Right-Wing Populism from Eroding Rule of Law in the Climate Struggle in India," *Fordham Environmental Law Review* 32(1): 134–48.

Alley, K. D. (2000) "Separate Domains: Hinduism, Politics and Environmental Pollution," in C. Chapple and M. E. Tucker (eds) *Hinduism and Ecology*. Camrbidge, MA: Harvard U Press, 355–88.

Baviskar, A. (1997) "Tribal Politics and Discourses of Environmentalism," *Contributions to Indian Sociology* 31(2): 195–224.

———. (1999) "Vanishing Forests, Sacred Trees: A Hindu Perspective on Eco-Consciousness," *Asian Geographer* 18(1–2): 21–31.

———. (2003) "Between Violence and Desire: Space, Power, and Identity in the Making of Metropolitan Delhi," *International Social Science Journal* 55(1): 89–98.

———. (2004) *In the Belly of the River Tribal Conflicts Over Development in the Narmada Valley*. Delhi: Oxford University Press.

Berkes, F. (2012) *Sacred Ecology*. London and New York: Routledge.

Blaikie, P. (1996) "Post-Modernism and Global Environmental Change," *Global Environmental Change* 6(2): 81–5.

Bridge, G., McCarthy, J., and Perreault, T. (2015) "Editors' Introduction," in G. Bridge, J. McCarthy, and T. Perreault (eds) *The Routledge Handbook on Political Ecology*. London and New York: Routledge, 3–18.

Brosius, P. (1999) "Analyses and Interventions: Anthropological Engagements with Environmentalism," *Current Anthropology* 40(3): 277–309.

Chacko, P. (2019) "Marketising Hindutva: The State, Society and Markets in Hindu Nationalism," *Modern Asian Studies* 53(2): 377–410.

Chandra, A. (2021) "How Modi's Hindu Nationalism Impairs Global Fight Against Climate Change," *Chicago Sun-Times*, https://chicago.suntimes.com/2021/7/29/22600092/narendra-modi-hindu-nationalism-climate-change-india (accessed June 16, 2022).

de Freitas Netto, S. V., Falcão Sobral, M. F., Bezerra Ribeiro, A. R., and de Luz Soares, G. R. (2020) "Concepts and Forms of Greenwashing: A Systematic Review," *Environmental Sciences Europe* 32(1): 1–19.

de Nadal, L. (2021) "Spain's VOX Party and the Threat of 'International Environmental Populism'," *Open Democracy*, www.opendemocracy.net/en/can-europe-make-it/spains-vox-party-and-the-threat-of-international-environmental-populism/ (accessed August 24, 2022).

Dyer, C. (2014) *Livelihoods and Learning: Education for All and the Marginalisation of Mobile Pastoralists*. London and New York: Routledge.

Elliot, J. (2020) "Modi: Six Years and the Environment," *The Round Table: The Commonwealth Journal of International Affairs*. www.commonwealthroundtable.co.uk/commonwealth/eurasia/india/modi-six-years-and-the-environment/# (accessed August 23, 2022).

Freeman, J. R. (1994) "Forests and the Folk: Perceptions of Nature in the Swidden Regimes of Highland Malabar," *Pondicherry: Pondy Papers in Social Sciences* 15.

Galvan, D. (2007) "Neotraditionalism," in M. Bevir (ed) *The Encyclopedia of Governance*. Thousand Oaks, CA: Sage, 599–601.

Gupta, H., Kohli, R. K., and Ahluwalia, A. S. (2015) "Mapping 'Consistency' in India's Climate Change Position: Dynamics and Dilemmas of Science Diplomacy," *Ambio* 44(6): 592–9.

Guha, R. (1989) "Radical American Environmentalism and Wilderness Preservation: A Third World Critique," *Environmental Ethics* 11: 71–83.

Guha, R., and Martinez-Alier, J. (1997) *Varieties of Environmentalism: Essays North and South*. London: Earthscan.

Horowitz, L. S. (2015) "Local Environmental Knowledge," in G. Bridge, J. McCarthy, and T. Perreault (eds) *The Routledge Handbook on Political Ecology*. London: Routledge, 235–48.

Jaffrelot, C. (2007) *Hindu Nationalism: A Reader*. Princeton, NJ: Princeton University Press.

———. (2021) *Modi's India: Hindu Nationalism and the Rise of Ethnic Democracy*. Princeton, NJ: Princeton University Press.

Jenkins, W., Tucker, M. E., and Grim, J. (2017) *Routledge Handbook of Religion and Ecology*. London and New York: Routledge.

Jitendra. (2019) "Recognize Environmental Contribution of Pastoralists: Experts," *Down to Earth*, www.downtoearth.org.in/news/wildlife-biodiversity/recognize-environmental-contribution-of-pastoralists-experts-67077#:~:text=Their%20traditional%20profession%20helps%20in,regeneration%20of%20grasses%20and%20trees (accessed April 3, 2022).

Khan, S., Svensson, T., Jogdand, Y., and Liu, J. (2017) "Lessons from the Past for the Future: The Definition and Mobilisation of Hindu Nationhood by the Hindu Nationalist Movement of India," *Journal of Social and Political Psychology* 5(2): 477–511.

Kidwell, J. (2020) "Mapping the Field of Religious Environmental Politics," *International Affairs* 96(2): 343–63.

Kishore, K., and Köhler-Rollefson, I. (2020). "Accounting for Pastoralists in India," www.pastoralpeoples.org/wp-content/uploads/2020/09/Accounting4pastoralists-IN.pdf (accessed August 24, 2022)

Krätli, S. (2014) *If Not Counted Does Not Count? A Programmatic Reflection on Methodology Options and Gaps in Total Economic Valuation Studies of Pastoral Systems*. IIED Issue Paper. London: IIED, https://pubs.iied.org/sites/default/files/pdfs/migrate/10082IIED.pdf?

Machin, A., and Wagerner, O. (2019) "The Nature of Green Populism," *Green European Journal*. www.greeneuropeanjournal.eu/the-nature-of-green-populism/ (accessed August 23, 2022)

Mawdsley, E. (2004) "India's Middle Classes and the Environment," *Development and Change* 35(1): 79–103.

Mawdsley, E. (2006) "Hindu Nationalism, Postcolonialism and Environmental Discourses in India," *Geoforum* 37(3): 380–90.

Mehra, M. (2014) "The Miseducation of Narendra Modi on Climate Change," *Climate Home News*, www.climatechangenews.com/2014/09/08/the-miseducation-of-narendra-modi-on-climate-change/ (accessed August 23, 2022).

Milton, K. (1996) *Environmentalism and Cultural Theory: The Role of Anthropology in Environmental Discourse*. London and New York: Routledge.

Modi, N. (2015) "The Rich World Must Take Greater Responsibility for Climate Change," *Financial Times*, www.ft.com/content/03a251c6-95f7-11e5-9228-87e603d47bdc (accessed August 24, 2022).

Nanda, M. (2002) *Breaking the Spell of Dharma and Other Essays*. New Delhi: Three Essays Press.

———. (2005) "Hindu Ecology in the Age of Hindutva: The Dangers of Religious Environmentalism," in M. Nanda (ed) *The Wrongs of the Religious Right: Reflections on Science, Secularism and Hindutva*. New Delhi: Three Essays Collective, 63–88.

Nelson, L. (1998) "The Dualism of Nondualism: Advaita Vedanta and the Irrelevance of Nature," in L. Nelson (ed) *Purifying the Earthly Body of God: Religion and Ecology in India*. Albany: State University of New York Press, 61–88.

Onyancha, O. (2022) "Indigenous Knowledge, Traditional Knowledge and Local Knowledge: What Is the Difference? An Informetrics Perspective," *Global Knowledge, Memory and Communication*. https://doi.org/10.1108/GKMC-01-2022-0011

Pederson, P. (1995) "Nature, Religion and Cultural Identity: The Religious Environmentalist Paradigm," in O. Bruun and A. Kalland (eds) *Asian Perceptions of Nature: A Critical Approach*. Richmond, Surrey: Curzon Press, 258–76.

Rangan, H. (2000) *Of Myths and Movements: Rewriting Chipko into Himalayan History*. London: Verso.

Rathee, D. (2019) "Environment Is the Most Under-Reported Disaster of Narendra Modi Government," *The Print*, https://theprint.in/opinion/environment-is-the-most-under-reported-failure-of-narendra-modi-government/223670/ (accessed August 24, 2022).

Robins, P. (2004) *Political Ecology: A Critical Introduction*. Malden, MA: Wiley and Sons.

Saryal, R. (2018) "Climate Change Policy of India: Modifying the Environment," *South Asia Research* 38(1): 1–19.

Sharma, M. (2011) *Green and Saffron: Hindu Nationalism and Indian Environmental Politics*. Ranikhet: Permanent Black.

Sharma, V. P., Köhler-Rollefson, I., and Morton, J. (2003) *Pastoralism in India: A Scoping Study*. Indian Institute of Management (IMM and League for Pastoral Peoples. https://assets.publishing.service.gov.uk/media/57a08ce2e5274a31e00014fa/ZC0181b.pdf (accessed April 3, 2022)

Sinha, S., Gururani, S., and Greenberg, B. (1997) "The 'New Traditionalist' Discourse of Indian Environmentalism," *The Journal of Peasant Studies* 24(3): 65–99.

Tambs-Lyche, H. (2019) "Hindu Pastoralists of Western India," in M. Carrin (ed) *Encyclopedia of the Religions of the Indigenous Peoples of South Asia*. Leiden: Brill. www.academia.edu/39787644/Hindu_Pastoralists_of_Western_India_Encyclopedia_of_the_Religions_of_the_Indiginous_Peoples_of_South_Asia_Leiden_Brill_Available_online_to_be_published_on_paper_shortly (accessed January 2, 2023).

Tomalin, E. (2004) "Bio-Divinity and Biodiversity: Perspectives on Religion and Environmental Conservation in India," *Numen* 51(3): 265–95.

——— (2011) *Bio-Divinity and Biodiversity: The Limits of Religious Environmentalism for India*. Aldershot: Ashgate.

White, L. (1967) "The Historical Roots of Our Environmental Crisis," *Science* 155(3767): 1203–7.

Wilkins, D. (2021) "Where Is Religion in Political Ecology?" *Progress in Human Geography* 45(2): 276–97.

World Wildlife Fund. (1986) *The Assisi Declarations: Messages on Man and Nature from Buddhism, Christianity, Hinduism, Islam and Judaism*. London: WWF.

# 19 Place

*Brian G. Campbell*

## Place Matters

Like some of the other key concepts in this book, place is important in part because it is so commonplace. We take it for granted without thinking about what it means or why it matters. Place can refer to *spatial* relationships, describing a physical, geographical location: "Let's meet at my place" or "I want to buy a hotel on Park Place." Place also refers to *social* relationships, especially one's position or rank in a social hierarchy: "That ought to keep her in her place" or "I finished in first place." Thinking critically about place demands sorting out the ways social and spatial relationships are often intertwined.

Both senses of place are key to the study of religion and ecology. We have geographic locations that matter to us personally—sites that hold memories and meanings and that shape our ethical commitments. This is true collectively as well. American environmentalism, for example, traces its history through particular sites such as Walden Pond, Yosemite Park, Warren County in North Carolina, and the Oceti Sakowin Camp at Standing Rock. Religious traditions ground their concern for the natural world in particular places, whether these exist in sacred texts and myths (Eden, New Jerusalem) or as sacred sites (Mecca, the Ganges.) Religions also teach us how we should understand our place in the social sense, mapping norms within human communities, and situating humans within broader more-than-human worlds, both natural and supernatural.

This chapter introduces critical perspectives and theories for thinking about place in the study of religion and ecology, with an emphasis on three: phenomenology, bioregionalism, and cultural geography. Each of these stresses the social and spatial aspects of place in different ways. As you consider these differences, think about how each approach defines this common and complex category. What does place mean for each and why does place matter? What aspects of religion does each approach emphasize? Rather than think about these approaches in the abstract, try to keep in mind particular places you care about. What are the strengths and weaknesses of each approach for thinking about those places, about particular religious beliefs and practices, and about particular environmental issues you can examine in place?

DOI: 10.4324/9781003259466-23

## Phenomenology: Perceiving and Experiencing Place

Phenomenology is a philosophical tradition that examines the human experience and perception of the world. Rooted in the thought of Edmund Husserl, Martin Heidegger, and Maurice Merleau-Ponty, this approach seeks to describe the pre-theoretical, embodied experience of a place. Here, the human person is not a subject separate from the objectively real world. Instead, the human being is always already a "being-in-the-world" (from Heidegger's term "Dasein"), in-the-world not just in the sense of being spatially situated in a physical world of objects but indivisibly involved in the world, which we actively encounter with and through our ideas and values and our perceptual and sensory capacities.

Philosophers and geographers have applied the methods and ideas of phenomenology to issues of place and the environment. Humanistic geographer Yi Fu Tuan makes a key distinction between space and place (Tuan 1977). While *space* is undifferentiated, abstract, and empty (think outer space), *place* is particular, familiar, and endowed with meaning and significance (think home place). In much of Western history, space has been treated as philosophically superior—an objective, universal container for all reality. In contrast, phenomenologists argue that place is always primary. In David Casey's words, "To live is to live locally, and to know is first of all to know the place one is in" (Casey 1996: 18). Tuan develops a concept he calls "topophilia" to describe this "affective bond between people and place." This critical form of attachment shapes one's identity and one's capacity to care for the broader world (Tuan 1974).

Phenomenology aims to understand the essence of what makes a place a place, the particular qualities that give it a distinctive identity and facilitate such topophilia. We recognize places by their distinctive physical features: a well-worn, fading sofa or a smooth, sloping granite dome. The essence of a place is not only a matter of features we passively perceive. We actively encounter place, with intentionality and with particular behaviors and practices: the sofa as the place where dad naps; the mountain as the place we climb to watch the Easter sunrise. Self-consciously or not, *people* make places significant.

Phenomenologist Edward Relph stresses that people also create "placeless" places, which lack the rich, authentic identity that gives rise to topophilia (1976). He argues that placelessness is a key ailment in the modern industrialized world. The landscape is sprawling with places built to look alike—strip malls, chain stores, and suburban developments. We build structures like airports, skyscrapers, and highways whose scale overwhelms us. We also invest in "other-directed" places, which appeal to outside tourists, spectators, and consumers rather than local communities. Relph laments such "disneyfication" and "museumification" of places, which makes them feel shallow and superficial. Relph's critique of the placelessness of mass, consumer culture is an invitation and a challenge to local communities, including religious communities. How can they preserve and produce more authentic places, drawing on their deeper traditions of place-making? What models do religions provide for navigating the intersection of culture and commerce, sanctification, and commodification?

**BOX 19A**

Edward Relph and other phenomenologists of place are critical of mass-produced aesthetics, including pedestrian-friendly new urbanist developments and energy-efficient prefab buildings. What are the positive and negative consequences of mass-produced buildings and places like these? Can they promote an authentic sense of place and a sustainable lifestyle?

While Relph's work focuses primarily on architecture and the built environment, another group of thinkers has developed an explicitly ecological phenomenology, focused on nature. These thinkers argue that the human experience of the more-than-human environment, the encounter with place, is the strongest foundation for environmental ethics and politics. This "eco-phenomenology" asserts that perception is *inter*-subjective and *inter*-corporeal. Philosopher David Abram writes,

> To touch the coarse skin of a tree is thus, at the same time, to experience one's own tactility, to feel oneself touched *by* a tree. And to see the world is also, at the same time, to experience oneself as visible to feel oneself *seen* . . . We can perceive things at all only because we ourselves are entirely a part of the sensible world that we perceive! We might as well say that we are organs of this world, flesh of its flesh, and that the world is perceiving itself *through* us.
>
> (Abram 1996: 68)

Asserting the human body is thoroughly intertwined with the "flesh of the world," eco-phenomenology rejects dualistic worldviews that imagine the human mind (soul, spirit, etc.) as something separate from the embodied, en-fleshed places we inhabit. People are part and parcel of nature, situated in particular places that shape the totality of our experience. This perceptual interconnectedness provides a basis for an environmental ethic; concern for nature emerges from the encounter with place. Abram asserts that

> the "new environmental ethic" toward which so many environmental philosophers aspire . . . will not come through the logical elucidation of new philosophical principles and legislative structures, but through a renewed attentiveness to this perceptual dimension that underlies all our logics, through a rejuvenation of our carnal, sensorial empathy with the living land that sustains us.
>
> (Abram 1996: 69)[1]

Belden Lane's *Landscapes of the Sacred* is one example of a phenomenological approach to the study of religion and the environment. Throughout the text, he uses his own personal experiences to highlight the "sensory exchanges" between people and place. Places are not passive material for cultural construction but participate in a "dynamic reciprocity." He describes his experience in Utah's Canyonlands National Park:

> Your first impression is one of being trapped at the end of the earth in a dry canyon carved by the distant memory of water. Slickrock winds its way along meanders traced by the forgotten music of swirling streams. The silence of the place is unnerving. That distracting echo you occasionally hear is but the sound of blood pumping through your own temples. But if you are patient, you become gradually attentive to the way aging juniper trees speak to the rock, how wind whispers along canyon walls and morning sunlight dances on yucca plants and Mormon tea. You flinch, startled as Raven, the Trickster, comes out of nowhere, soaring overhead with the audible, rhythmic beating of feathers on air. You begin slowly to move through the place as part of its own distinctive pattern.
>
> (Lane 2002: 57)

The experience of place cannot be reduced to purely cultural or material factors. Every place, in the words of Edward Casey, "retains a factor of wildness, that is, of the radically amorphous and unaccounted for" (Casey 1996). In Lane's terms, we must leave room for the sacred, for the messy and inexplicable. We need a phenomenological and poetic sensitivity, attentive to the voice of the place itself, speaking through our embodied experience.

## Bioregionalism: Reinhabiting Place

Like phenomenology, bioregionalism is concerned with the authenticity and integrity of places in a rapidly modernizing, urbanizing, globalizing world. Both perspectives highlight the potentially powerful bonds between people and place as a resource for environmentalism. We act ethically because we care about the place we call home. While phenomenology began as an intellectual tradition, bioregionalism developed out of a grassroots movement beginning in the 1970s among artists, activists, writers, natural scientists, and back-to-the-landers. Concerned about social and environmental challenges, they saw themselves as part of a long tradition of living rooted in place.

Bioregionalism asserts that the most important response to the ecological crisis is to "reinhabit" place. To do this, we must rethink our sense of scale, sinking deep roots in the local environment we call home. Peter Berg, one of the key leaders of the movement, explains the term:

> A bioregion is defined in terms of the unique overall pattern of natural characteristics that are found in a specific place. The main features are generally found throughout a continuous geographic terrain and include a particular climate, local aspects of seasons, landforms, watersheds, soils, and native plants and animals.

Rather than political names and borders, places are mapped and named according to their ecological identities and natural boundaries. The Cascadia Bioregion, for example, stretches across Canada and the US Pacific Northwest. Like phenomenology, bioregionalism emphasizes that humans are part of nature, "an integral aspect of a place's life," and Berg calls for "present day reinhabitants" to learn from "ecologically adaptive cultures of early inhabitants" as they "attempt to harmonize in a sustainable way with the place where they live" (Berg 2002).

Gary Snyder is another prominent writer who has articulated the ideas of bioregionalism, including the link between spirituality, place, and indigenous culture. After decades exploring the wilds of his native Cascadia, the Beat counterculture scene of the San Francisco Renaissance, and Zen meditation in Japan, Snyder was ready to establish deeper roots in a place. He and his family settled down with a community of like-minded back-to-the-landers in the Shasta bioregion at the foothills of the Sierra Nevada Mountains. Snyder describes this region as one part of "Turtle Island," an "old/new name for the continent based on many creation myths of the people who have been living here for millennia" (1974). In a 1992 talk, Snyder stated,

> I don't know if I'm an Indian or not. I do know that I'm a Native American. Here again is a Turtle Island bioregional point. Anyone is, metaphorically speaking a Native American who is "born again of Turtle Island." Anyone is a Native American who chooses, consciously and deliberately, to live on this continent.
>
> (Snyder 1999: 336)

Leslie Marmon Silko and a number of Native American writers have criticized Snyder, and bioregionalism more broadly, for this appropriation of the term "native," calling it a "new version of cultural imperialism."[2] Bioregionalism movements, remapping place through indigenous and ecological identities, have the potential to align with movements against colonization, but it is difficult to sustain partnerships among scholars, activists, first nations, and indigenous leaders, especially when wrestling with the fact that "decolonization is not a metaphor" (Tuck and Yang 2012).

Snyder and Berg developed bioregionalism in California and the movement quickly spread through grassroots groups around the country and the world. Bioregionalism also developed a growing body of writing, including cultural historian Kirkpatrick Sale's *Dwellers in the Land.* Sale situates bioregionalism within a centuries-old tradition of decentralized resistance against industrialization civilization and globalization. He calls readers to be "dwellers in the land . . . once again comprehending the earth as a living creature" and "contriving the modern equivalent of the worship of Gaea." For him, this means not an occasional act of devotion but a wholesale transformation our lifestyle to fit the "immediate and specific place where we live" (Sale 1985: 41–2). Sale summarizes the bioregional alternative, one that touches every aspect of the social order (Table 19.1)

"Geologian" Thomas Berry was another key voice spreading bioregionalism, and his ideas have been especially influential for the study of religion and ecology.

*Table 19.1* The Bioregional Alternative

| | *Bioregional Paradigm* | *Industrio-Scientific Paradigm* |
|---|---|---|
| *Scale* | Region<br>Community | State<br>Nation/World |
| *Economy* | Conservation<br>Stability<br>Self-sufficiency<br>Cooperation | Exploitation, change/progress<br>World Economy<br>Competition |
| *Polity* | Decentralization<br>Complementarity<br>Diversity | Centralization<br>Hierarchy<br>Uniformity |
| *Society* | Symbiosis<br>Evolution<br>Division | Polarization, growth/violence<br>Monoculture |

*Source*: Sale 1985: 50

His book *The Dream of the Earth* at once focuses on the vast scale of the cosmic "universe story" and the particular context of the bioregion. Within this framework, Berry reimagines the whole of civilization, including religion, economics, and technology. He also proposes a total transformation of American college education to include not just education about the earth, but education from and through the earth itself. Higher education should be holistic, fostering ecological and spiritual wisdom, not through detached abstraction and analysis but through direct experience with one's immediate environment (Berry 1988).

Berry's attention to both bioregional and cosmic scales points to an important challenge for thinking about place. How can we think and act locally but also take seriously our place in broader global, even cosmic processes? Both phenomenology and bioregionalism prioritize the local. We know a place through direct, embodied experience with its distinctive features. We care about a place because it is familiar, and because it is home. This commitment to the local is perhaps the greatest strength and greatest weakness of these perspectives, which distinguishes them from cultural geography.[3]

**BOX 19B**

Look online for a copy of "Where You At? A Bioregional Quiz." How well do you know your bioregion? What additional bioregional wisdom would you add to tailor this quiz to your context? What questions would you include on a quiz testing your phenomenological awareness or your attention to the cultural geography of a place?[4]

### Cultural Geography: Power, Difference, and Global Connections

Cultural geography focuses attention on global dynamics, especially the ways global capitalism is transforming place. This approach examines not experience or ecology but material practices and spatial structures that shape our relationship to one another and the environment. Cultural geography asserts that places should not be taken for granted as "natural," with obvious boundaries and essential qualities, but instead places are constituted and constructed through complex social, economic, and political processes. The goal in studying place is to understand and respond to these processes.

Cultural geographer David Harvey describes places as "permanences within the flux and flow of capital circulation" (1996: 295). He insists it is precisely because of globalization's flux and flow that place has become such an important locus of popular and scholarly concern. We construct these "permanences" as sites of relative stability, meaningful and secure refuges in a rapidly changing world. Harvey describes the power of "militant particularism," especially among radical environmentalist and environmental justice groups, who resist the negative forces of globalization by appealing to their deep, distinctive, and often sacred bond with place.

Harvey warns, though, that such embrace of place is fundamentally conservative and reactionary. Such efforts to protect and preserve a place can also serve to make permanent its particular social hierarchies of power and difference. He describes, for example, a neighborhood in the Baltimore suburbs that elected to become a gated community. Residents appealed to their sense of the *place* as safe, familiar, and culturally coherent (and racially homogenous), over and against the specter of chaotic, uncontrollable, and racially mixed *space* (Harvey 1996: 291–3). Similar processes are often at play in the creation of wilderness areas, national parks, and conservation preserves. These places may serve to protect the environment, but also to control social and economic access to a space. Though environmental groups may have the best of intentions, their place-based politics often reinforce problematic structural inequalities of race and class.

Geographer Doreen Massey has a more optimistic view of what place can mean in a complex, pluralistic context. She calls for a "global" and "progressive" sense of place as an alternative to the conservative notions of place that include "reactionary nationalisms to competitive localisms, to sanitized, introverted obsessions with 'heritage.'" Massey develops this approach using her London neighborhood as an example. She argues that places are defined not by some essential, bounded identity but by their distinctive combination of differences and their dynamic connections with the broader world. On her walk down a single street, Massey encounters people and products from all corners of the planet. Places, in fact, have quite permeable boundaries, with webs of social and material relations extending across vast expanses of time and space. She notes, "People's routes through the place, their favorite haunts within it, the connections they make (physically, or by plane or post, or in memory or imagination) between here and the rest of the world vary enormously." Places, in fact, have multiple identities that coexist, and diverse groups often contest these meanings. Massey also stresses the importance of seeing historical forces at play in the ways place is structured in the present. "It is (or ought to be) impossible even to begin thinking about Kilburn High Road without bringing into play half the world and a considerable amount of British imperialist history." As powerful as this past is, it does not determine the future. People actively construct and reconstruct the history and identity of a place in response to contemporary challenges (Massey 1993: 64–5).

Globalization creates new configurations of time and space, with constantly changing networks and flows of highly mobile information, capital, and people. Cultural geography calls for global thinking, but it is not enough to simply recognize that interconnectedness. Individuals and groups exercise very different kinds of power over global issues and changing patterns. Massey experiences globalization quite differently from the Arab immigrant she encounters at the newsstand. The global economy recognizes and rewards a certain cosmopolitan class, whose privilege enables them to cross borders legally, whether for leisure, work, or religious pilgrimage. Meanwhile, millions of refugees, migrants, and global poor lack this legal freedom of movement. Massey argues that we must be attentive to the power dynamics among these diverse groups not only at the local level but also in the ways people engage global structures and processes. Each place has an embedded "power-geometry" that reflects and reinforces social differences like race, class, gender, and citizenship (Massey 1993: 61).

## BOX 19C

Draw a map of the place you call home. Note how differences like race, class, religion, and ethnicity are reflected in the spatial structure of the place. What sorts of boundaries mark the areas where different groups live, work, or socialize? What do you know about the history of how these communities came to be located in this way? What do you know about where environmental burdens and benefits are located in this place? Do you see connections between these social and environmental patterns?

Cultural geographers echo environmental justice advocates, urging environmental groups to analyze the "power-geometry" of a place rather than ground their politics solely in romantic feelings toward nature and personal connections with a place. Harvey acknowledges the "depth and intensity of feeling" people have in "intimate and immediate relations to nature," and he warns that precisely because this phenomenological experience of one's immediate environment feels so "authentic," it tempts us to ignore larger material processes and structures (Harvey 1996: 313–14). Just as Marx warns against the "fetishism of commodities," Harvey warns of similar fetishism of both "nature" and "the local." Historically, American environmentalism has fetishized a particular kind of nature, protecting remote, pristine wilderness areas, meanwhile ignoring the health of urban ecosystems and places where people live, work, play, and worship.

Sociologist Robert Bullard has been one key voice drawing attention to urban environments and rural communities of color as key sites too often overlooked by mainstream environmentalism. His research has consistently demonstrated the spatial patterns of environmental injustice. Which places get access to environmental benefits like parks, public transit, fresh foods, and clean air and water? Which places get stuck with environmental burdens like toxic waste facilities, dirty industries, and mega-highways? Bullard urges us to pay attention how places are physically constructed and how this reinforces cultural constructs, with particular ideas of "nature" built into the infrastructure of a place to make particular social ideologies and inequalities seem "natural." Paying attention to nature, especially in a diverse, urban context, requires more than simply sensing what is immediately observable but also investigating the history and politics that is intentionally hidden from view (Bullard 2007; Bullard and Wright 2009).

Urban planning scholar Julian Agyeman warns against a similar "scalar fetishism" in environmentalism, which increasingly celebrates "the local" without interrogating the power geography of a place. This is particularly visible in the local food movement, which touts the value of eating with a sense of place, buying foods grown close to home, preserving heirloom plants adapted to local conditions, and celebrating local culinary traditions. Local food campaigns often represent the interests of elite middle- and upper-income consumers who prioritize environmental sustainability more than social justice. The local food movement, Agyeman argues, makes localization an end rather than a means to the more important goal of a more sustainable and socially just food system. The key issue, he contends, should be "who is empowered and disempowered by food system localization," which requires interrogating the social relationships, inequalities, and politics embedded in a place (Agyeman 2013: 65).

Adrian Ivakhiv's *Claiming Sacred Ground: Pilgrims and Politics at Glastonbury and Sedona* provides one model of religion and ecology scholarship that incorporates the perspectives of cultural geography. This ethnographic study examines the "spatial practices" or "practices of place" of New Age pilgrims: hiking, meditation, visualization, chanting, "chakra activation," invocation or channeling of guides or spirits, and the arrangement of stone or rocks in medicine wheels and the conducting of ceremonies within them. Grounding his research in two prominent pilgrimage sites, Ivakhiv stresses that New Age practices must be interpreted within the context of "interpretive disputes with other groups, and broader sets of socioeconomic relations." At Glastonbury and Sedona, Forest Service bureaucrats, tourism promoters, real estate developers, Native Americans, and Evangelical Christians produce their own senses of place, often contesting the practices and politics of one another. Ivakhiv argues that in addition to these local ways place is contested, New Age pilgrims also challenge the perspectives and practices of transnational capitalism and science. They create competing ways of knowing nature and alternative economies. Like Belden Lane, Ivakhiv is attentive to the textures of place and his own embodiment as an ethnographer, but he also stresses the necessity for analyzing experiences of place as dynamically situated within complex global flows of culture and capital (Ivakhiv 2002: 191–3).

## Place in the Study of Religion

Religion scholars have long stressed the importance of place. Mircea Eliade argues that sacred space orients all of reality. The sacred *irrupts* into a particular place, making it the *axis mundi*, the center and origin of the world, the zone of absolute reality, radically set apart from everything profane (Eliade 1954). Subsequent scholars stress the social processes and politics underlying this mapping of the sacred. Jonathan Z. Smith argues that constructing a place as sacred simultaneously constructs other places as profane, as religiously and politically marginal. The mapping of the sacred is always a mapping of social power (1987: 104). David Chidester and Edward Linenthal focus on the "symbolic labor" by which sacred space is constructed—the "choosing, setting aside, consecrating, venerating, protecting, defending and refining" of sacred spaces. They argue that because sacred space asserts a particular symbolic and social order, it is inherently contested. Sacred spaces mark "hierarchical power relations of domination and subordination, inclusion and exclusion, appropriation and dispossession" (Chidester and Linenthal 1995: 17).

These contrasting approaches within religious studies mirror the approaches outlined earlier and raise some of the same questions about how we should think about place. What defines a place as sacred? In what ways is this sacredness a cultural phenomenon (constructed through particular stories, practices, and politics), a natural phenomenon (produced by experiencing the distinctive features of the place itself), or a supernatural phenomenon (a religious reality that cannot be reduced)? Where should we focus our attention when studying place: locally or globally, on the perceiving person on the broader cultural context? What tools and sensitivities are most helpful for understanding the nature of place: the perspectives of social or natural sciences or the aesthetic capacities of the poet?

Increasingly, scholars are interested in how digital technologies mediate the connections between individuals and communities and their place. Mobile devices, from smartphones and fitness trackers to virtual reality goggles, shape how we experience the environment around us. We now often visit national parks, neighborhood restaurants, and religious communities online before we visit them in the flesh. During and after our visits, we share images and video on social media, documenting and authenticating the experience. Meanwhile, the internet enables entirely new kinds of online worlds and identities, including new kinds of sacred cyberspaces and virtual religious communities. Social networking sites, blogs, online role-playing games are all part of a "digital reformation" of religion that is reshaping our cultural, ecological, and spiritual connections with place (Drescher 2011; Campbell 2013).

## BOX 19D

What insights do each of these approaches to place offer as you think about your college campus? What is the essence of the place? How is it embedded in a particular bioregional context? How are power and difference structured spatially? What is the relationship between your campus and global flows of information, capital, human, and natural resources? How is your everyday experience on campus mediated by digital technologies and online interactions? How has your education been shaped by the particulars of the place?

The approaches outlined in this chapter provide multiple ways to analyze the importance of place. As we confront increasingly complex environmental issues, with local and global causes and effects, we need such contrasting approaches to place. We must learn to think both spatially and socially about the environmental challenges we face. This means thinking carefully about scale, power, and difference. It means paying attention to what we sense directly, in our bodies, and to the forces and flows that are hidden from view.

## Case Study—Stone Mountain: A Sacred Site, Commodified and Contested

The world's largest piece of exposed granite, Stone Mountain is a dramatic landmark among the gently rolling hills of the Georgia piedmont that are now sprawling suburbs of Atlanta. Stone Mountain also has a long history as a sacred place where surrounding communities negotiated their relationships with one another and with nature. Atop the mountain, early indigenous groups erected large stone formations whose purpose is now a mystery. Creek and Cherokee leaders used the peak for political gatherings and religious rituals.

Stone Mountain was later transformed into a different kind of sacred site, a memorial to the Confederacy and its "Lost Cause." In the 1920s, renowned sculptor Gutzon Borglum removed what remained of Native American stone formations atop the mountain and began carving enormous statues of Robert E. Lee, Jefferson Davis, and Stonewall Jackson right into the granite dome. Promoter E. Lee Trinkle described Stone Mountain as "consecrated ground that God himself has raised up," a "mecca of glory," a "sanctuary of truth," and a "sermon in stone," where the South's "golden age . . . defied the future" (Trinkle 1923). In 1915, William J. Simmons chose Stone Mountain as the place to reawaken another potent symbol of Southern identity, the Ku Klux Klan, marking this new beginning with a complex weaving of racial and religious symbolism, including the Klan's first cross-burning. The KKK spread and splintered, but for decades the group continued to return to Stone Mountain for its annual pilgrimage, the Klonvocation.

This sacred site also developed into a highly commercialized tourist destination, where visitors flock to enjoy both nature and Southern nostalgia. In 1958, the State of Georgia purchased Stone Mountain to preserve its natural wonder and cultural meaning but also with the stated purpose of generating revenue. Over the next decade, at the height of the civil rights movement, the state completed the Confederate carving and, inspired by the popularity of *Gone With the Wind*, erected an antebellum style plantation in the meadow below. To increase its "authenticity," officials hired actress Butterfly McQueen, who had played house slave Prissy in the movie, to greet visitors. The state also enhanced Stone Mountain's "natural" qualities, constructing a large lake and adding a driving loop, scenic railroad, campground, picnic shelters, hiking trails, petting zoo, horseback riding academy, and game ranch.

In 1998, the state privatized management of the park, partnering with Herschend Family Entertainment, a Christian company that operates Dollywood and a number of theme parks in Branson, Missouri. Herschend soon began construction of a $100 million theme park celebrating the "fun side of the Southern story." Not everyone embraced these changes, and among the loudest opponents was a

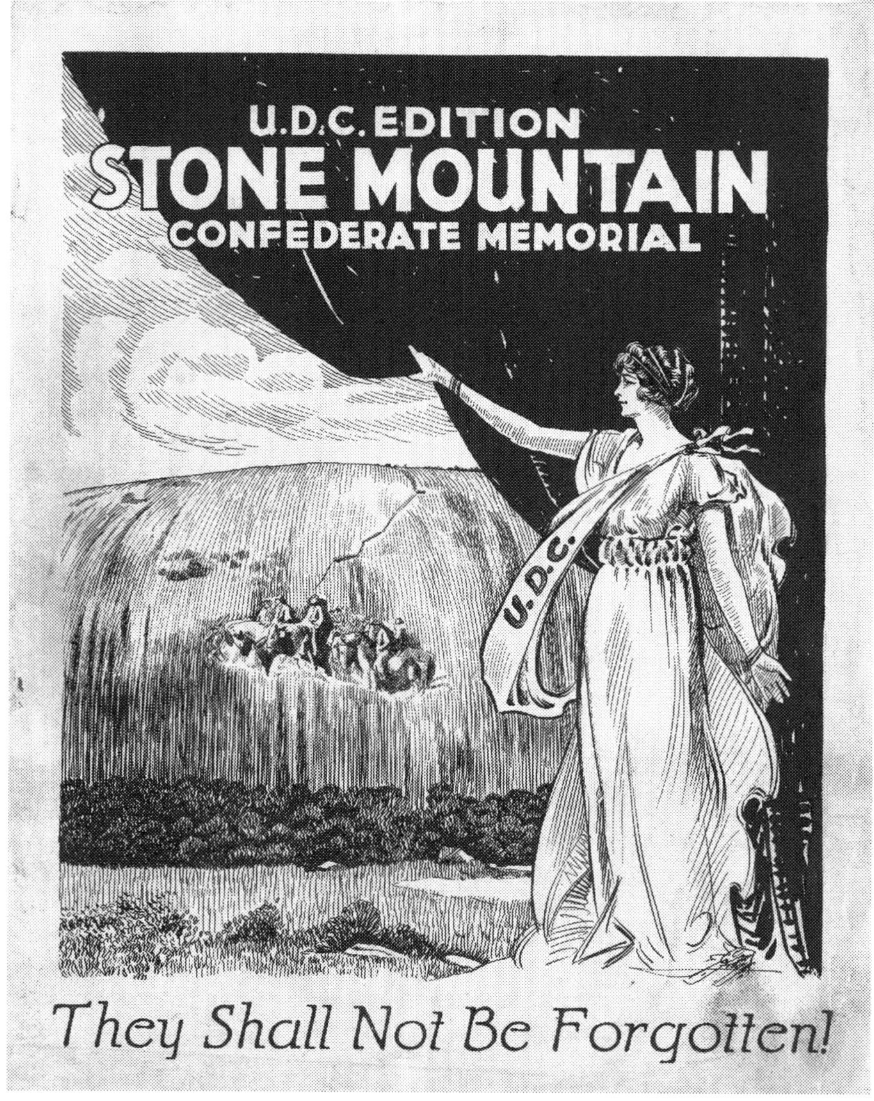


*Figure 19.1* Stone Mountain's quarries provided granite for confederate memorials throughout the South. By 1915, the United Daughters of the Confederacy envisioned the mountain itself into an icon of the Lost Cause, and they led efforts to promote and pay for the massive memorial. (Poster courtesy of the Stone Mountain Collection; Manuscript, Archives, and Rare Book Library, Emory University.)

group of hikers who for years met each morning at 6:00 a.m. to climb Stone Mountain. The mountain had special memories for these long-time white residents of the town, and they were the heart and soul of a watchdog group, the Friends of Stone

Mountain. Originally formed in 1992 to resist development of Olympic venues in the park, the group vigorously defended the mountain's natural beauty, leading protests alongside environmentalist allies including EarthFirst! One member of the Friends group explained, "I am not a tree hugger, but . . . I will always fight for the park." Another added, "We connect with places with a tendency that some people don't understand. It's a Southern thing. You fight even though you know you can't win. You're fighting after it's lost, and you'll fight after you know it's hopeless" (Smith 2003). Here, Lost Cause values memorialized at Stone Mountain provided the model for protecting the sacred site from the profane forces of commercialization and development.

Diverse other groups also seek to protect nature at Stone Mountain. A small Evangelical Christian ministry called "Creation Science Defense" uses geologic evidence embedded in the granite of Stone Mountain to demonstrate that the earth is quite young and not the result of a distant big bang. They publish a field guide and lead field trips for homeschoolers, promoting a biblical environmental ethic of human dominion and care for creation. Another group, the psychics and energy workers of the First Georgia Dowsers, also offers an alternative to mainstream scientific ideas of nature. Through careful attention to patterns of earth energy, they identify places of disharmony, often caused by past pollution and violence, and they concentrate their psychic energy to heal the earth. For this group, too, Stone Mountain is a spiritual focal point, with powerful energy patterns and immense potential for healing.

Stone Mountain, like other sacred sites, attracts and amplifies divergent religious understandings of nature and also divergent visions of culture. The monument has long been a place where public and private values, memories, and meanings come in contact and at times into conflict. After the state took ownership, authorities began restricting the Klan's access to the park, prompting a 1962 struggle between state troopers—with clubs and teargas—and a crowd of hooded Klansmen, who eventually forced their way to the mountain for what they called a "religious ceremony." For decades, the Klan was blocked from entering but continued to gather on private land at the base of the mountain. Meanwhile, the area surrounding Stone Mountain changed dramatically, growing from a small, largely white town to a booming, largely African American Atlanta suburb. This community has asserted their power to inscribe new meanings at Stone Mountain. In 1994, a black civic group sponsored an integrated, community-wide picnic at Leila Mason Park, adjacent to the private land where the Klan continued to gather for its annual Klonvocation and cross-burning. What was long a place of exclusion and hate, they now claimed as a place of harmony and integration.

In 1997, when Chuck Burris was elected the first African American mayor of the town, he struck a deal with the daughter of former mayor and KKK Imperial Wizard James Venable, agreeing to keep her father's name on a city street if the family would stop hosting Klan rallies on its property. A year later, Burris purchased Venable's house. The first thing he did when moving in was to hang on the bedroom wall a picture of Martin Luther King, who himself had subverted the racist history of this place. In 1963, from the steps of the Lincoln Memorial, King ascended to the climax of his most famous speech saying, "Let freedom ring from Stone Mountain of Georgia." Fully aware of the Klan history and Confederate commemoration, he declared the sacred significance of this as a place not fixed in a racially segregated past but one ushering in a future of justice and equality. In 2000, Burris dedicated a "Freedom Bell" in the heart of Main Street as a kind of counter-monument representing King's vision.

This conflict over the Confederate legacy at Stone Mountain intensified yet again in 2015, following the massacre of black churchgoers at Emanuel African Methodist Episcopal Church in Charleston, South Carolina. When images emerged linking perpetrator Dylan Roof to white supremacist symbols, including the Confederate flag, calls erupted across the country to take down Confederate flags and memorials, and Stone Mountain became a key place in this struggle. Protests against Confederate memorials intensified even more following the 2020 murder of George Floyd.

Georgia activists called for boycotts of the park and its corporate sponsor Coca-Cola until Confederate flags were removed. Others demanded sandblasting the carving from the mountain. Meanwhile, groups calling themselves "pro-flag" and "pro-white" repeatedly rallied at Stone Mountain, defending their right to celebrate Southern heritage and white identity as the history of the place. Each rally attracted counter-protesters from the Black Lives Matter movement and other antiracism groups, with antagonistic protesters separated by barricades and well-armed law enforcement. Rival groups utilized social media sites to organize, confronting each other in dueling videos and posts and in the comments sections of local media sites.

The Stone Mountain Memorial Association (SMMA), the state authority charged with managing the park, has rejected calls to remove the monument and instead offered various forms of compromise. In 2015, they proposed erecting a "freedom bell" atop the mountain, with SMMA CEO Bill Stephens saying, "We're into additions and not subtractions" (Faucett 2015). The Sons of Confederate Veterans issued a statement opposed to the idea, insisting, "The park was never intended to be a memorial to multiple causes but solely to the Confederacy" (GASCV 2015). Richard Rose, president of the Atlanta NAACP, also rejected the proposal, saying, "It's an insult to the legacy of Dr. King to put a tribute to him up there alongside those warmongers . . . You can't make hate more inclusive" (Jarvie 2015).

In 2021, after years of sustained pressure, SMMA announced it would relocate Confederate flags away from the current location at the start of the park's most popular hiking trail to a designated area for monuments. Rev. Abraham Mosley, SMMA's first African American chair, announced they would also create a new exhibit telling "the whole story" of Stone Mountain, "the good, the bad, and the ugly." These changes are not enough to satisfy groups like the Stone Mountain Action Coalition, which is calling for removal of all Confederate symbols, including flags, names, and merchandise and eventually the carving itself. Meanwhile, the pressure on corporate groups has created change too. Coca-Cola is no longer listed as an official sponsor, and both Marriott and Herschend have announced they will end their operations in the park, the latter explaining that the place "feels increasingly less family-friendly, welcoming, and enjoyable, as the park is frequently the site of protests and division." The case of Stone Mountain, Georgia, shows the struggle among multiple meanings of a place, and it shows how ideas of nature and culture take on sacred significance in these competing claims.

***Discussion Questions***

1. In what sense would you say Stone Mountain is a place that is "natural"? Based on this short case study, which groups involved with the mountain do you think of as "religious"?
2. Who should have the power to make decisions about how the park is managed? Why?
3. For the past few decades, most visitors to Stone Mountain Park saw no mention of the Ku Klux Klan's history at the site. There was one small photograph of a Klan gathering in an out-of-the-way corner of the museum, but otherwise, the park seemed to hope this bad memory would simply be forgotten. As they enlist the help of "credible and well-established historians" to design a new exhibit, what do you think is the best way to deal with this aspect of the place's history and identity?

## Notes

1 Christian Diehm elaborates this eco-phenomenological ethics of encounter. Drawing on the work of Emanual Levinas, he argues we should aim to see the natural world as we see the human other: intimately, face-to-face, beautiful and vulnerable, like a mirror of our own self. See Diehm, C., ibid., "Natural Disasters."

2 For a more detailed discussion of this debate, see Gray (2006) and Wiebe (2021).

3 A number of scholars have proposed models of bioregionalism that account for this global scale. Mitchell Thomashow develops a "cosmopolitan bioregionalism" (2002). Adrian Ivakhiv calls for a "nonessentialist bioregionalism" that includes "an ethical and critical appreciation of difference of plurality, and a non-essentialist understanding of place which recognizes the ambiguity and mutability of borders and cross-border movements, territorialities and deterritorializations" (2002).

4 "Where You At?" was developed by Leonard Charles, Jim Dodge, Lynn Milliman, and Victoria Stockley, originally published in *Coevolution Quarterly* 32 (Winter 1981): 1.

## References


Abram, D. (1996) *The Spell of the Sensuous: Perception and Language in a More-Than-Human World*. New York: Pantheon Books.

Agyeman, J. (2013) *Introducing Just Sustainabilities: Policy, Planning, and Practice*. London: Zed Books.

Berg, P. (2002) *Bioregionalism (a Definition)*. San Francisco Diggers Archives. www.diggers.org/freecitynews/_disc1/00000017.htm (accessed July 1, 2016).

Berry, T. (1988) *The Dream of the Earth*. San Francisco, CA: Sierra Club Books.

Bullard, R. D. (2007) *The Black Metropolis in the Twenty-First Century: Race, Power, and Politics of Place*. Lanham: Rowman & Littlefield Publishers.

Bullard, R. D., and Wright, B. (2009) *Race, Place, and Environmental Justice After Hurricane Katrina: Struggles to Reclaim, Rebuild, and Revitalize New Orleans and the Gulf Coast*. Boulder, CO: Westview Press.

Campbell, H. (2013) *Digital Religion: Understanding Religious Practice in New Media Worlds*. London and New York: Routledge.

Casey, E. (1996) "How to Get from Space to Place in a Fairly Short Stretch of Time: Phenomenological Prolegomena," in S. Feld & K. H. Basso (eds) *Senses of Place*. Santa Fe, NM: School of American Research Press.

Chidester, D., and Linenthal, E. T. (1995) "Introduction," in *American Sacred Space*. Bloomington: Indiana University Press.

Diehm, C. (2003) "Natural Disasters," In C. S. Brown and T. Toadvine (eds) *Eco-Phenomenology: Back to the Earth Itself*. Albany: State University of New York Press.

Drescher, E. (2011) *Tweet if You [Love] Jesus: Practicing Church in the Digital Reformation*. Harrisburg, PA: Morehouse Pub.

Eliade, M. (1954) *The Myth of the Eternal Return*. New York: Pantheon Books.

Faucett, R. (2015) "A Plan to Honor Martin Luther King at a Southern Civil War Symbol," *New York Times*, October 21, www.nytimes.com/2015/10/22/us/a-plan-to-honor-martin-luther-king-at-a-southern-civil-war-symbol.html? (accessed July 1, 2016).

GASCV (Georgia Sons of Confederate Veterans) (2015) "SCV Responds to Attempt to Place MLK Statue on Stone Mountain," http://gascv.org/scv-responds-to-attempt-to-place-mlk-statue-on-stone-mountain/ (accessed July 1, 2016).

Gray, T. (2006) *Gary Snyder and the Pacific Rim: Creating Countercultural Community*. Iowa City: University of Iowa Press.

Harvey, D. (1996) *Justice, Nature, and the Geography of Difference*. Cambridge, MA: Blackwell Publishers.

Ivakhiv, A. J. (2002) *Claiming Sacred Ground: Pilgrims and Politics at Glastonbury and Sedona*. Bloomington, IN: Indiana University Press.

Jarvie, J. (2015) "Time to Honor Martin Luther King at Confederate Memorial in Georgia?" *Los Angeles Times*, October 14, www.latimes.com/nation/la-na-stone-mountain-martin-luther-king-20151013-story.html (accessed July 1, 2016).

Lane, B. C. (2002) *Landscapes of the Sacred: Geography and Narrative in American Spirituality*. Baltimore, MD: Johns Hopkins University Press.

Massey, D. (1993) "Power-Geometry and a Progressive Sense of Place," in B. C. Jon Bird, T. Putnam, G. Robertson, and L. Tickner (eds) *Mapping the Futures: Local Cultures, Global Change*. London and New York: Routledge.

Relph, E. C. (1976) *Place and Placelessness*. London: Pion.

Sale, K. (1985) *Dwellers in the Land: The Bioregional Vision*. San Francisco: Sierra Club Books.

Smith, B. (2003) "The Battle for Stone Mountain; Watchdog Group That Opposed Rent Cut Undeterred by Setback," *The Atlanta Journal-Constitution*, July 31.

———. (1987) *To Take Place: Toward Theory in Ritual*. Chicago: University of Chicago Press.

Snyder, G. (1974) *Turtle Island*. New York: New Directions Pub. Corp.

———. (1999) *The Gary Snyder Reader: Prose, Poetry, and Translations, 1952–1998*. Washington, DC: Counterpoint.

———. (2002) *Bringing the Biosphere Home: Learning to Perceive Global Environmental Change*. Cambridge, MA: MIT Press.

Trinkle, E. L. (1923) *Stone Mountain Collection*. Address by Governor E. Lee Trinkle of the Commonwealth of Virginia on the occasion of the first carving on the Stone Mountain Confederate Memorial at Stone Mountain, GA. Atlanta: Manuscript, Archives and Rare Book Library, Emory University, June 18.

Tuan, Y. (1974) *Topophilia: A Study of Environmental Perception, Attitudes, and Values*. Englewood Cliffs, NJ: Prentice-Hall.

———. (1977) *Space and Place: The Perspective of Experience*. Minneapolis: University of Minnesota Press.

Tuck, E., and Yang, K. W. (2012) "Decolonization Is Not a Metaphor," *Decolonization: Indigeneity, Education & Society* 1(1): 1–40.

Wiebe, J. (2021) "Cultural Appropriation in Bioregionalism and the Need for a Decolonial Ethics of Place," *Journal of Religious Ethics* 49: 138–58.

## Further Reading

- To learn more about Stone Mountain, visit the website of the privately managed park (www.stonemountainpark.com) or the state agency, the Stone Mountain Memorial Association (www.stonemountainpark.org). The Stone Mountain Action Coalition (https://stonemountainaction.org) maintains links to media coverage of the latest protests and proposals for transforming the park.
- The best scholarly treatment of Stone Mountain's history is Hale, G. E. (2003), "Granite Stopped Time: Stone Mountain Memorial and the Representation of White Southern Identity," in C. Mills and P. H. Simpson (eds.), *Monuments to the Lost Cause: Women, Art, and the Landscapes of Southern Memory*, Knoxville: University of Tennessee Press. For a more general, book-length history, see Freeman, D. B. (1997), *Carved in Stone: The History of Stone Mountain*, Macon, GA: Mercer University Press. Another useful resource is "Shades of Gray: The Changing Focus of Stone Mountain Park," a website produced as a student project, which includes a timeline, primary documents, and historic images (http://xroads.virginia.edu/~ug97/stone/home.html).
- For a survey of place from the perspective of academic geography, see Cresswell, T. (2015), *Place: A Short Introduction*, 2nd ed., Malden, MA: Wiley Blackwell.
- For more on bioregionalism, see Thayer, R. L. (2003), *LifePlace: Bioregional Thought and Practice*, Berkeley: University of California Press, and Mcginnis, M. V. (ed.) (1999), *Bioregionalism*, New York: Routledge.
- For more essays on place, religion, ecology, and the South, see Johnston, L., and Aftandilian, D. (2019), *Grounding Education in Environmental Humanities: Exploring Place-Based Pedagogies in the South*, New York: Routledge.

# 20 Canceling the Apocalypse

## Defiant Hope as a Call to Action in the Climate Era

*Sarah McFarland Taylor*

### Introduction

"We are *all* Amabella."

This was our topic of conversation in my Media, Earth, and Making a Difference class after we viewed a clip from the HBO series *Big Little Lies* (2017–2019). The series centers on a group of families in the prosperous and progressive coastal community of Carmel, California. Amabella is an 8-year-old girl who ends up hospitalized with a sudden panic attack when she collapses unconscious on the floor of a classroom closet. What in her young life could be making her so anxious? Her second-grade teacher has been tying together the story of *Charlotte's Web* with the class's ongoing lessons on climate crisis. When discharged from the hospital, the doctor recommends counseling, which the parents administer in the form of a child-appropriate play therapist dressed as Little Bo Peep. After exploring Amabella's feelings, Dr. Peep reports her findings to Amabella's parents: "Nobody is bullying her. She's worried about the end of the planet. Her class is evidently talking about climate change and she's gotten the message that we are doomed . . . She's worried about the end of the world."

Amabella is not alone. She has become an avatar for our age (Ballhaus 2019). In fact, this scene from the episode, "End of the World" (season 2, episode 3), resonated so much with viewers that an outpouring of social media posts and blogs followed its airing. *Esquire*'s Justin Kirkland proclaimed, "Amabella's *Big Little Lies* anxiety attack over climate change made me feel seen. Her boots sticking out of the closet are little, metallic metaphors for living in 2019" (Kirkland 2019). Twitter lit up with #Same sentiments, such as "Amabella fainting because she thinks the end of the world is near. Me too, baby, me too"; "Amabella having a panic attack after discussing climate change is the most relatable thing I've ever witnessed on TV"; and "Nice to see myself represented on TV in Amabella collapsing in the closet after having a panic attack about the environment" (Ballhaus 2019).

Amabella may be a fictionalized character and her faint during the apocalyptic climate reading of *Charlotte's Web* may seem a tad hyperbolic, but her distress and despair are all too real. Researchers in Human and Planetary Health at Stanford's Center for Innovation and Global Health conducted the largest study investigating

DOI: 10.4324/9781003259466-24

levels of climate anxiety among young people, surveying more than ten thousand 15-to-25-year-olds from more than ten countries (Marks et al. 2021; Veidis 2021). Three-quarters of the young people surveyed reported feeling that "the future is frightening," half said "humanity is doomed" and reported that climate anxiety impacts their day-to-day lives, and 39% fear bringing children into a world beset by climate crisis.

In 2020, climate writer Elin Kelsey was asked by a journalist to respond to a real-life Amabella-like incident in connection with a school in Toronto. Kelsey was contacted because, in her many educational workshops and residences (Rachel Carson Center in Munich, Stanford University School of Education, University of Victoria's School of Environmental Studies, the Rockefeller Foundation, the Monterey Bay Aquarium, and more), she focuses on the emotional implications of the narrative of environmental doom and gloom, especially its impacts on children. In this case, a Toronto second-grader had come home from school visibly shaken and announced to her mother, "We're all going to die in eight years." Kelsey recounts,

> The girl had attended a climate change presentation at school that featured Greta Thunberg's emotional speech to the UN Climate Action Summit . . . "You have stolen my dreams and my childhood," Greta said. "People are suffering. People are dying. Entire ecosystems are collapsing. We are in the beginning of a mass extinction, and all you can talk about is money and fairy tales of eternal economic growth." After watching the video of the speech, the children were shown the climate change doomsday clock as it rapidly counts down the years, days, and seconds we have left. Imagine being a kid seeing this and believing we are literally moments from the end of the world. When teachers and other trusted adults take on the role of telling kids just how wrecked the world is, in the name of *telling them the facts so they will be inspired to act*, they fuel the cycle of fear, anxiety, and hopelessness.
>
> (Kelsey 2020: 64–5)

It is not surprising, then, that there has been pushback from even progressive-leaning writers and pundits, not to mention climate scientists themselves, against feeding children a steady diet of climate apocalypse and doom. *New York Times* columnist Ezra Klein penned an opinion piece, "Your Kids Are Not Doomed," which quotes climate scientist Kate Marvel: "I unequivocally reject, scientifically and personally, the notion that [due to climate change] children are somehow doomed to an unhappy life" (Klein 2022). Klein goes on to detail evidence for optimism that people can rise to the challenge of climate change. He is clearly walking a fine line here, as it is very difficult to achieve a "Goldilocks" approach to climate messaging. Yes, climate advocates want to rouse complacent publics by conveying an urgent, imminent, dire, global, existential threat. But too much impending apocalypse talk paralyzes people with fear. They shut down, tune out completely, or simply cannot function (Boykoff 2019: 63; Kelsey 2020: 33–7; Hayhoe 2021: 63–71; Ray 2020). In other words, inspiring terror and hopelessness can be counterproductive, while impressing upon young generations of humans that they have no future to look forward to can backfire, if not be lethal.

Hannah Ritchie is a senior researcher at Oxford University and head of research at *Our World in Data*, a scientific online publication that provides data and analysis in addressing global problems, such as poverty, hunger, war, and climate change. In "Stop Telling Kids They'll Die From Climate Change," Ritchie, like Klein, tries to make a nuanced intervention in the prevailing messaging:

> Let's be clear: Climate change is one of the biggest problems we face. It comes with many risks—some certain, some uncertain—and we are not moving anywhere near fast enough to reduce emissions. But there seems to have been a breakdown in communication of what our future entails. None of the climate scientists I know and trust—who surely know the risks better than almost anyone—are resigned to a future of oblivion. Most of them have children. In fact, they often have several . . . it signals that those who spend day after day studying climate change are optimistic that their children will have a life worth living.
> (Ritchie 2021)

Ritchie goes on to cite evidence-based data to support climate hope, but she also calls out a 2021 video "Advice to Young People as They Face Annihilation," produced by the climate action group Extinction Rebellion and featuring its founder Roger Hallam, for promulgating the now commonplace narrative that doom inexorably looms and we are already "too late." Ritchie writes,

> [Hallam] claims that we must get emissions to zero within months, otherwise humanity will be wiped out. He claims that this annihilation is now locked in. The worst thing about this message is that, rather than inspiring actions, it resigns us to the falsehood that we are already too late.

More importantly, says Ritchie, while it might be easy to dismiss this messaging as extreme or an outlier, Hallam is "the founder of one of the world's largest environmental movements . . . a movement whose name is hinged on this premise that we're heading for a total wipeout" (Ritchie 2021).

Ritchie, like a growing number of climate thinkers (Hasso and Mann 2022; Mitchell and Chaudhury 2020; Heglar 2019a; Piper 2022; Hayhoe 2021; Klein 2017; Hawken 2007; 2021) is skeptical that this apocalyptic approach is even effective in driving change: "It often makes us feel like any effort is futile. That we're already out of time . . . And once anger transitions into hopelessness, we struggle to achieve much at all." Hopelessness, contends Ritchie, "is no better than denial."

Back in my classroom at Northwestern University, after our own watching of the Amabella scene from *Big Little Lies*, a debate ensued among students over how much young children like Amabella should be steeped in an apocalyptic climate change curriculum that may well evoke despondency, hopelessness about the future, or even suicidal thoughts. During this discussion, some of the young women in the class shared that they already decided not to bear any children because it is unethical and cruel to bring new lives into a world of climate chaos and because additional humans on the planet would only make things worse. I looked around at the faces in the classroom and realized that the question of how much doomerist climate change messaging Amabella should be subjected to and imbibe is not heuristic. "Amabella" is here, sitting in the desks right in front of me.

In *Hope Matters: Why Changing the Way We Think Is Critical to Solving the Climate Crisis* (2020), Elin Kelsey makes the case for "*evidence*-based hope" in motivating substantive climate action. Kelsey emphasizes that, far from being misguided, Pollyannaish, or mere wishful thinking, evidence-based hope *fuels* the kind of work on systemic change that can successfully tackle the climate crisis. Building on this, I argue that interventionary, engaging mediamaking is fundamental to the project of reframing climate change in the public imagination as a formidable but "solvable problem" that we *can* do something about (Gibson 2021; Mann 2021; Gates 2021; Hawken 2021, 2017; Jacobson 2023). Both widely circulated and more niche-targeted media works, if strategically crafted and made easily accessible, can inspire and advance a compelling call to climate action. Doing so transforms the apathy and despondency that fosters climate paralysis. Indeed, intervening, countering, and reframing "doomerism" and "climate fatalism" is just as important as addressing sources of climate denial. These are two sides of the same coin that result in inaction.

As prominent climatologist/geophysicist Michael Mann, director of University of Pennsylvania's Center for Science, Sustainability, and Media, cautions,

> Doom-mongering has overtaken denial as a threat and as a tactic. Inactivists know that if people believe there is nothing you can do, they are led down a path of disengagement. They unwittingly do the bidding of fossil fuel interests by giving up.
>
> (Watts 2021)

Mann points to this as a perniciously effective tactic because it succeeds in neutralizing and taking out of the game environmental progressives, "who would otherwise be on the frontline demanding change." Pervasive circulating narratives that communicate it is "too late" or proclaim a finite closing window of no turning back the apocalypse, a resolved fatalism now promoted by fossil fuels interests themselves, inevitably base such claims on "false science," says Mann. "If the science objectively demonstrated it was too late to limit warming below catastrophic levels," he points out, "that would be one thing and we scientists would be faithful to that. But science doesn't say that" (Watts 2021).

I argue in this chapter that, by telling and transmediating stories of evidence-based hope and by highlighting examples of those who are boldly going about the work of "canceling the apocalypse," mediamakers and educators alike can "flip the script" and cultivate agency, empowering citizens to work toward meaningful climate action. While most of the chapters in this book have focused on the ways religious communities and religious ideas relate to environmental problems, my focus is on media, which play an enormous role in the lives of contemporary people and will be essential to understanding and building the courage required in these times. As Susan Sontag famously argued, "the courage of an example" inspires communities, and courage engenders a powerful viral quality; "for courage is as contagious as fear" (Sontag 2007: 182).

## Alternative Energies: Defiant Badass Hope and a Dose of Unapologetic Joy

I specifically design the syllabus for my Media, Earth, and Making a Difference course with the acute conviction that having "Amabella" collapse unconscious from a panic attack in the classroom closet does not do anyone any good, most of all the planet. Instead, I focus the class on action as an antidote to despair. This action takes the form of learning and then applying skills, tools, and strategies for effective climate messaging and mediamaking. Students take on the challenge of designing and producing the kind of climate media that morally engages publics and moves them from mere "concern" (72% of the US population, according to 2021 Pew polling data [Bell et al. 2021]) into substantive action. This often includes a series of what we call "ridiculously easy," accessible, concrete, actionable steps to systemic change. What this might look like: working to get climate defenders into every level of public office to pass rigorous climate decarbonization/drawdown policies and adaptation measures; educating publics about the hows and whys of supporting effective carbon pricing; and lobbying strategies for systemic transformation of our energy, food, and agricultural systems/infrastructure, not to mention the conservation, care, and regeneration of healthy, biodiverse, functioning ecosystems, critical to avoiding climate disaster. What this does not look like: touting the virtues of paper straws, canvas grocery bags, purchasing all-natural products, popping plastic water bottles into recycling bins, and other personal lifestyle microchanges, which are inadequate to the speed, scope, and scale needed to address the climate crisis. Debunking the personal, consumerist microchanges narrative is the major intervention and throughline of my book *Ecopiety: Green Media and the Dilemma of Environmental Virtue* (2019). Here is that same argument succinctly expressed by world-renowned climatologist Michael Mann:

> Of course lifestyle changes are necessary, but they alone won't get us where we need to be. They make us more healthy, save money and set a good example for others. But we can't allow the forces of inaction to convince us these actions alone are the solution and that we don't need systemic changes. If they can get us arguing with one another, and finger pointing and carbon shaming about lifestyle choices, that is extremely divisive and the community will no longer be effective in challenging vested interest and polluters.
>
> (Watts 2021)

Keeping the need for systemic changes at the forefront, students can learn and practice effective mediamaking approaches that soften their target audience's climate paralysis. In the process, they learn strategies to unpack their own climate paralysis. As they craft climate media, they also get a sense of the radical political nature of defiant hope and the ways it can fuel hard-core climate action. We thus explore and analyze both the mobilizing rhetorical and action strategies of what I call "anti-doomers." These are climate scientists, eco-designers, environmental engineers, environmental economists, climate writers, city planners, artists, activists, and mediamakers, who are all defiantly rejecting the climate fatalism of the "it's already too late" crowd. Instead, these proponents of "defiant hope" are getting on with the business of repairing the world, as they build the foundations and infrastructure for a better future. For students' midterm projects, they analyze a variety of anti-doomerist media, including solutions-based documentaries, such as *2040* (Gameau 2019), *Tomorrow* (Dion and Laurent 2015), *Kiss the Ground* (Tickell and Tickell 2020), *The Biggest Little Farm* (Chester 2018), and *This Changes Everything* (Lewis 2015).

We also study storied media, like feature film *Black Panther* (Coogler 2018), looking at the ways the visual rhetoric of sustainability in the Afrofuturistic portrayal of Wakanda has inspired real-life city planners, transportation designers, and environmental design engineers. Streaming videos, podcasts, memes, tattoos, TikToks, hip-hop music, mobile apps, art installations, flashmobs, and public space guerilla projections all become rich primary source materials for exploring and evaluating climate messaging. Which media works present fatalistic "doomer porn" with few or no pathways to action? Which media works convey a message of agency, defiant hope, and issue a call to action, empowering and mobilizing publics to work on a formidable but solvable problem?

Are hope-based climate media works all rainbows, unicorns, and rose-colored glasses? Hardly. But too many of us are pickled in catastrophe on a daily basis in a pervasive apocalyptic newsfeed we carry around 24/7. Elin Kelsey points out that there is space, between cynicism and naivete, for the kind of engaged hope that is required for vision, for creatively and actively imagining something beyond what is (Kelsey 2020: 55–6). Hope is not passive but goal-directed for Kelsey, who invokes environmental writer David Orr's definition: "Hope is a verb with its sleeves rolled up" (54).

Evidence-based, goal-directed, active-verb-form hope, an amalgamated form of hope that I am calling here, "defiant hope," is also not mutually exclusive from grief, anger, and outrage (43). As Sarah Jacquette Ray, in *Climate Anxiety: A Field Guide* (2020), argues, to combat climate change, we can harness the resources of hope, humor, play, wonder, and optimism, together with resources like sadness, anger, and mourning. Marshaling myriad resources, defiant hope is a commitment to persevering no matter what the obstacles. Defiant hope is *badass*. Defiant hope is real-life middle-aged mother Angela Cavallo lifting a 1964 Chevy Impala off her pinned teenage son (Beck 2011; Cottrell 2021). Defiant hope is revolutionary. Defiant hope is the harder path than the resignation and inaction of climate fatalism.

And yet, within the dominant culture of the environmental movement, climate hope more generally has been denigrated as "soft," foolish, or a childish delusion. Climate writer Mary Annïse Heglar, who is African American, observes that she often finds herself in the company of (predominantly white and male) "doomer dude" environmentalists and climate writers. Heglar came to work on climate justice through her work combating eco-racism. In her essay "Home Is Always Worth

It" (2019b), she calls out what she encounters as a kind of weird self-satisfaction—"wistfulness," "joyful nihilism," and even "glee"—expressed by her white male environmental colleagues about how "There's really no point anymore. Humans are done for." "Don't worry," they go on to smugly console, "the earth will be just fine. She just needs to get rid of *us*!"

In my own work in the eco-scholarship space, I too have encountered variations of this narrative—that our planet is doomed and *we* humans, well, "get what we deserve." That is, *we* have had our chance as humans, *we* have screwed things up, and now the earth will be better off without *us*. As a mother, more than determined to lift a climate-sized Chevy Impala off my son and his generation, I confess that this "*We*'ve had our chance" routine *really* ticks me off. How have children had their chance on this planet? How have people who have not had political, economic, and social power because of unjust structures "had their chance"?

Heglar raises the question in her work of just *who* is this "us" that has ostensibly had their chance? She bristles at the casual fatalism of climate "doomer dudes" who "smack of the privilege wrought from the deluded belief that this world has ever been perfect and that, therefore, an imperfect version of it is not worth saving, or fighting for." Heglar recounts,

> Since becoming a part of the climate justice movement in earnest, I've come across a good share of climate de-nihilists. They have books. They host panels. They are prolific Tweeters. They are legion. In my opinion, they are a problem. And they're almost always white men because only white men can afford to be lazy enough to quit . . . *on themselves*. . . . We, quite literally, have no time for nihilism. . . . I've never seen a perfect world. I never will. But, I know that a world warmed by 2 degrees Celsius is far preferable to one warmed by 3 degrees, or 6. And that I'm willing to fight for it, with everything I have, because it *is* everything I have . . . We don't know how this movie is going to end, because we're in the writers room *right now*. We're making the decisions *right now*. Walking out is not an option. We don't get to give up. This planet is the only home we'll ever have. There's no place like it. And home is always, always, always worth it.

Many of us in academic circles can likely relate to Heglar's frustration, especially when we raise reasons for hope and/or point to examples of constructive headway being made on drawdown. Such interjections can be branded as unsophisticated, denialist, counterproductive, or even self-delusional. Articulations of even evidence-based hope, whether in the classroom or at an academic conference, can be shamed and devalued, asking people to feel guilty for daring to express hope in what is legitimately a formidable crisis but not one without pathways forward to mitigation, adaptation, and regeneration (Hawken 2017, 2021; Jacobson 2023).

Like Heglar, Karen Waldron came to be a writer and advocate for interlocking issues of justice, peace, and liberation, through her work as a civil rights and Black Lives Matter activist. In *The Lightmaker's Manifesto: How to Work for Change Without Losing Your Joy* (2021), Waldron offers sage advice on how to maintain hope in the midst of despair. She acknowledges just how guilty activists can feel about espousing both hope and joy during enormously challenging times of violence, injustice, and suffering (2021: 176). Defiantly, Waldron declares, "I will never apologize for embracing joy and beauty—even when the world is falling apart—because joy and beauty are my fuel for activism."[1] Her sentiment, as it relates to hope, is shared by the likes of famed conservationist Jane Goodall in *The Book of Hope* (Goodall and Abrams 2021). Goodall and her coauthor, Abrams, point to the science of hope in the emergent field of "hope studies" and how, qualitatively different from "wishing" or "fantasizing," hope "sparks us to take action directed toward the hoped-for goal" (26). As with Waldron's observations on joy, Goodall acknowledges a deep human pleasure in espousing hope, but hope research also suggests that "more hopeful people actually anticipate setbacks along the way and work to remove them" (27). That is, rather than a "Pollyanna avoidance of the problems," consciously embracing hope is a way of *engaging* problems while persevering through the inevitability of concomitant challenges (27). So hope might feel good to us, but it is also a powerful and practical functional tool for perseverance and resilience.

Climate advocates can find a powerful example of defiant, persevering hope in the face of devastation, annihilation, and collapse in *Radical Hope: Ethics in the Face of Cultural Devastation* (2008), Jonathan Lear's anthro-philosophical study of Crow indigenous resilience to cultural catastrophe. Lear analyzes Crow Chief Plenty Coups' (1848–1932) life story, as told to Western writer and friend Frank B. Linderman (1930). Lear is taken with Plenty Coups' radical form of hopefulness that "even with the death of the traditional forms of Crow subjectivity, the Crow can nevertheless survive and flourish again" (Lear 2008: 99). In his chapter on the "legitimacy of radical hope," Lear points to what a powerful, agential force for survival radical hope has been historically for the Crow people. But in studying Plenty Coups' story, Lear is also interested in our time of planetary challenges and existential threats and how radical hope can offer a path forward when life as we have always known it turns upside down or passes away. That is, how do people go on after collapse, when the world that has defined us is gone? In Plenty Coups' case, Lear argues that the chief responded to the total collapse of Crow civilization with radical hope, which Lear defines as hope "directed toward a future goodness that transcends the current ability to understand what [that] is" (2008: 103). Lear's analysis here is somehow sanguine and yet grief-filled, with faith in "radical hope" as the "secret sauce" in humanity's capacity for resilience.

A more contemporary indigenous meditation on the power of hope in the climate age can be found in the work of Choctaw elder and Episcopal bishop Steven Charleston. In *Ladder to the Light: An Indigenous Elder's Meditations of Hope and Courage*, Charleston draws wisdom for dealing with the daunting planetary challenges of our time from the ceremonial experience of descending into the earthy subterranean darkness of the prayer kiva. "We are all in the kiva together," he writes. "Whatever our politics, whatever our religion, whatever our culture, we are all in the place of darkness together" (2021: 15). The bishop acknowledges that the darkness is frightening but reminds us that it can also be a place of profound spiritual transformation. Amid our immersion in the darkness, one thing we can discover is hope. Charleston does not invoke this dimension of hope flippantly but from the context of a people who are no stranger to apocalypse and for whom "apocalypse" is not an abstract. "In 1831," recounts Charleston,

> The world came to an end for my family—and for all the families that were part of the Choctaw nation. That year, we were forced off our ancestral homeland and made to walk a death march we called the Trail of Tears. Thousands of our people died. We lost our homes, our way of life, even our graveyards, we lost everything. Everything, that is, except the one thing they could not take from us: hope. Hope kept us going, kept us climbing toward the light, even though the world seemed to be filled with nothing but darkness.
>
> (57–8)

Charleston qualifies that when he speaks of "hope," he is not talking about "wishful thinking" or "miracles" but of tangible signs, actions, and transformations we can see all around us:

> People who had fallen asleep are waking up. People who had been content to watch are wanting to join. People who never said a word are speaking out . . . Look and see the thousands of new faces gathering from every direction. There is the sign of hope for which you have been waiting.
>
> (60–1)

We can, Charleston suggests, allow ourselves to become immersed in the darkness, to sit in and with its womb-like/tomb-like oblivion, to be transformed by it (147–56) and then to climb the ladder purposefully back into light and into the "next cycle of emergence" (170). The kiva reminds us, Charleston keenly observes, "that we have been in the darkness before. It is nothing new" (170). Speaking about the state of our world in the climate age, he counsels, "Do not be afraid. Do not be tricked into thinking what has been broken can never be fixed . . . Honor the earth. Respect the wisdom of elders. Speak the truth." Charleston urges us each to *be* the ladder to the light in dark times, to be that conduit of hope. "A new faith is emerging," proclaims the Choctaw elder, "not for the few, but for all, the great tribes of life assembled, beneath the single blessing . . . uniting our family once again and forever, light flowing like a river, hope beating like a drum" (171).

If this vision of a better future amid the dark realities of climate crisis sounds beautiful and poetic but wildly unachievable, consider climate scientist Katharine Hayhoe's bold vision of hope for the future. With a doctorate in atmospheric science, as the director of the Climate Center at Texas Tech University, and as the 2019 winner of the United Nations' Champions of the Earth's highest honor in the category of science and innovation, Hayhoe has "the receipts," as it were, to lend credibility to her assessments of what is and is not achievable. She envisions systemic transitioning and adaptation so we do not get to a point of the kind of total catastrophe and devastation that Lear anticipates. In *Saving Us: A Climate*

*Scientist's Case for Hope and Healing in a Divided World*, Hayhoe contends, "Real hope provides a vision of the future that we want to live in, where energy is abundant and available to all, where the economy is stable, where we have resources we need, where our lives are not worse but better than they are today" (2021: 243).

Hayhoe's friend and colleague Peter Kalmus matches step, proclaiming, "We're not just fighting for a 'livable planet.' We're fighting for a riotous, wild, gorgeous, generous, miraculous, life-cradling planet that's home to a society that works for everyone" (ibid.). Kalmus is a data scientist for NASA and a project scientist at UCLA in Earth System Science and Engineering, but he is probably most famous for chaining himself to the JP Morgan Chase building in Los Angeles to protest the bank's bankrolling of new fossil fuel projects in April 2022. Both Hayhoe's and Kalmus' visions of the future are goal-directed, sleeves-rolled-up, hope-as-a-verb kind of big visions—those that unapologetically embrace and inspire contagious courage. Both have written very readable books articulating their case for the future and the kinds of actions they advocate for bringing about a better world. Both also demonstrate that, in the digital age, a different kind of storytelling can be more powerful (Jenkins et al. 2013, 2020). In the next section, we will explore storytelling further and its implications for transmediating defiant hope messaging as a call to climate action.

## Case Study: Canceling the Apocalypse and Rejecting the Strategic Weaponization of Hopelessness

In the spring of 2022, the audacious galvanizing vision of "canceling the apocalypse" first popped up in my classroom as a clarion call. One of my students presented a media analysis project on a viral climate video produced by the German animation group, Kurzgesagt (German for "Shortly Said"). Kurzgesagt makes captivating, highly accessible, science-based, educational video shorts that are fact-checked by experts in the relevant subject field.[2] The group then posts these videos to their YouTube channel, which has a substantial following of more than twenty million subscribers. The group's call to climate action video, "We WILL Fix Climate Change!" has nearly ten million views and educates viewers about the threat of human-caused climate change, while also highlighting positive news and data emerging regarding our successes in reducing carbon emissions.

In a rousing section of this video titled "Canceling the Apocalypse," the creators make the case that "earth is not doomed and humanity is not doomed." We are indeed drawing down greenhouse-producing gasses, they point out, especially as renewables become considerably cheaper than coal. The video pointedly qualifies that there is still massive and daunting work to be done, but we are moving in the right direction to mitigate climate warming, and goals such as those outlined in the Paris Accords are indeed *achievable*. Kurzgesagt also cites a series of climate projection studies calculating that the strides we are making in our current trajectory, which vastly reduce the likelihood of truly apocalyptic scenarios (about 4–8°F of warming) (Plumer and Popovich 2021; Hausfather and Peters 2020; Harvey 2020; Gearino 2022). To be clear, the animated video recognizes that there is still a world of pain in the 1.5- and 2-degree warming scenarios, much less that of 3 degrees. However, the presentation also cautions viewers that falling into the "trap of hopelessness" that precipitates apathy and inaction *plays right into the interests of a fossil fuel industry* that strategically "weaponizes hopelessness" in order to maximize profits by suppressing meaningful climate action. Kurzgesagt's aim is to intervene in that weaponization, to umask it, and to reframe it. Working together, the video urges, we can (and will!) radically defy the trap of hopelessness and *cancel the apocalypse.*

If "canceling the apocalypse" as a *cri de coeur* sounds audacious or even comical, that is precisely the point. Communications scholar Maxwell Boykoff (2019) argues that, precisely because the nature of climate change is so dire and scary, we need to infuse elements of humor and levity into our climate communications as a social and psychological lubricant to soften the public's hardening carapace of eco-anxiety paralysis (Kelsey 2020; Ray 2020; Polle 2016). And so it is with humorous audacity and a good dose of cheekiness, combined with serious intent and commitment, that my students and I subsequently affirmed Kurzgesagt's proclamation with an overwhelming cheer in class, "YES! Let's *cancel the apocalypse* and *not* schedule a rain date!" In fact, since that time, I have now explicitly added to the "Course Objectives" section of my syllabus, as the very first stated course objective: "Canceling the environmental apocalypse."

Embedded in the declaration of "canceling the apocalypse" are powerful emotional resonances for a culture steeped in action movies, whose plots turn on the well-worn trope of a band of ragtag underdogs pulling off a seemingly impossible mission against much more powerful, well-funded, and better-armed forces that appear to be the sure-bet winners. In fact, the phrase "canceling the apocalypse!" does not originate with Kurzgesagt's climate video; it is borrowed from the (now cult favorite) science fiction/monster/disaster film, *Pacific Rim* (2013). Director Guillermo del Toro brings us the world of 2025 (now right around the corner), in which earth-killing monsters have invaded the planet through an interdimensional portal in the earth's ocean floor called the Breach.

Screenwriter Travis Beacham wrote his first treatment for *Pacific Rim* in 2010, during British Petroleum's Deepwater Horizon Macondo prospect's massive oil breach, the largest environmental disaster in US history (Essman 2013). The oil rig explosion killed eleven workers and blasted the prospect's wellbore, hemorrhaging 210-million gallons of sticky, black, toxic oil into the Gulf of Mexico ecosystem (Chow 2020). To get a sense of scale, the breach gushed more than twelve times the amount of oil spilled in the Exxon Valdez 1989 disaster (Borunda 2020). Though Beacham's film is set in the Pacific, the screenwriter's imagined gaping hole in the ocean floor, spewing forth earth-killing monsters, not only closely resembles the BP Macondo oil disaster but simultaneously (and ominously) nods to the popular *Godzilla* films made in the shadow of the Atomic Era, another time of seemingly imminent apocalypse. In the original 1954 *Gojira*, directed by Ishirō Hondo, the awakening *kaiju*, or monster, served as a 1950s dark allegory for nuclear weapons and their existential threat to humans and to all life on the planet.

Scholars of monster studies remind us that monsters come in multiple forms and contexts, depending on their era and their usefulness to its prevailing crises (Laycock and Minkle 2021: 3–16; Gloyn 2019; Mittman and Dendle 2012: 1–16; Auerbach 1995). Today, just one hundred companies around the world are responsible for generating 71% of global carbon emissions (Shen 2017; Meredith 2017). Collectively, these companies have relentlessly shelled out billions of dollars to sow climate denial via high-paid public relations firms and front groups (Supran and Oreskes 2021; Oreskes and Conway 2011; Mitchell 2021). Like the fossil fuel industry and the gushing offshore ocean drilling platforms that feed it, *Pacific Rim*'s *kaiju* pose an existential threat to humanity and to life on earth as we know it. But how might mere citizens prevail in a seemingly hopeless battle against such formidable monsters?

To fight the *kaiju*, the humans in the film must put their differences aside, work together, and even create collaborative interpersonal "mind melds" to wield monster-vanquishing mechanisms. This raises the question of what our own monster-vanquishing mechanisms might be in an age of climate crisis. The tools of media, I contend, are core to developing those mechanisms, even as (or perhaps especially because) the monsters who threaten our climate also expertly wield the same tools.

Kurzgesagt's climate change video call to action, its urging of viewers defiantly to resist the "trap of hopelessness" engineered by our own climate "monsters," echoes *Pacific Rim*'s movie trailer. The narrator recounts that the monsters "counted on humans to hide, to give up, to fail. They never considered our ability to stand, to endure—that we would rise to the challenge." In other words, the monsters count on humans losing hope and succumbing to fatalism. It is the film's hero, aptly named Stacker Pentecost, who ultimately issues the *cri de coeur*: "We are canceling the apocalypse!" Since the film's release, this phrase has become iconic and seemingly infinitely malleable, as it is referenced and remediated via memes and hashtags across the digital mediaverse, persisting as a popular meme even a decade after the film's release. As Stacker Pentecost rallies his team of earth defenders for an against-all-odds mission to close the breach in the earth that is leaking monsters, he cries out, "Today, at the edge of our hope. At the end of our time. We've chosen to believe in ourselves and each other. Today, we face the monsters at our door. And we bring the fight to them. Today, *we are canceling the apocalypse*!" (Loud cheers ensue.)

The cultural meme of "Cancel the Apocalypse" has also now become one of the marketing taglines for the organization Films for Action, an online library of hope-inspiring films. Directed toward cultivating positive social change, the library collection promotes documentaries on individuals and communities hard at work canceling the apocalypse as they build in the present the foundations for earth repair for a more positive future.

The library offers a curated list titled "Thirty Documentaries to Unlock a Good Ending," pointing out to viewers, "Our present moment is saturated in dystopian, apocalyptic fantasies of the future." Films for Action concertedly counters doomerist media images with ones steeped in defiant hope, arguing that, if humanity is going to alter catastrophic trajectories for the future, then we need to be able to imagine that better ending first: "We've got to imagine ten thousand localized versions of it. That's how things change" (Film for Action 2021). This is the power of media storytelling, and the film library's mission tracks with Elin Kelsey's contention that "[h]ope lies in the capacity of stories to transform" and that "[w]e need to nurture the capacity to imagine something beyond what is" (2020: 56, 102).

Embracing the adage that you cannot be what you cannot see, Films for Action concertedly curates and promotes films that feature human actors choosing defiant hope, imagination, and resourcefulness over fear, fatalism, and paralysis:

> They're imagining the future they want, not the future they're afraid of, and they're bringing that future into being. Whether we're ultimately successful is not the point, and beyond anyone's ability to truly know. The point is that our true nature calls us to choose determination over defeat, and resilience over despair. We hope these films inspire the former—that place in your heart that knows a better world *is* possible and is ready to make it happen.
>
> (Films for Action 2021)

Ultimately, it is this heart-stirring ideal of a brighter and more beautiful future that is still possible that my students and I actively work toward in Media, Earth, and Making a Difference. Drawing upon their diverse concentrations of academic specialization, these environmentally committed students are working on mending the planet's many "breaches"—wielding the tools of media to communicate and galvanize support for their proposed solutions to urgent environmental engineering, ecosystem, eco-policy, eco-ethical, and economic climate challenges. In the process, they are engaging hope and telling the apocalypse to go take a hike. If we learn nothing else from *Pacific Rim* and its apparent endless legacy of viral memes, it is that monster slayers need good mediamaking strategies and skills to spur concerned citizens into substantive action and to *keep* them engaged over the long haul.

For those of us who are academics highly invested in our students' futures, for those of us who are parents who would lay down our lives to ensure that our children get their chance to grow up and thrive on this planet, and for those of us who are simply unabashed, unapologetic lovers of this good green earth in all its terrible, beautiful, messy miraculousness, giving up hope is *not* an option.

So with a nod to *Pacific Rim*'s Stacker Pentecost: Today, at the edge of our hope, at the end of one era and perhaps the start of another, we can choose to believe in ourselves and each other. Today, we can face the climate monsters at our door. And we can boldly proclaim, "Today, *we are canceling the apocalypse*!" Audacious? Presumptuous? Grandiose? Precisely. It is all these things, and this is the kind of radical, badass hope—hope as an indefatigable call to action—that the climate era calls for. Even in the midst of the daily diet of "doomer porn" that pervades our newsfeeds and populates our devices, let us courageously go about the business of healing the breach. What second-grader Amabella and all of earth's denizens most need from us right now is *defiant verb-form hope*—hope with its sleeves rolled up.

***Discussion Questions***

1. What are three things that give you hope for the world and the future of our planet?
2. What tools, skills, or abilities that you see demonstrated by people you know are most useful for healing and repairing the world?
3. When you encounter story after story in your daily news feed of dire environmental problems, how do you respond? Are there ways to stay informed about our world without getting sucked into a vortex of hopelessness?
4. Climate change is serious business, but climate communications scholars like Max Boykoff argue that messages infused with humor and playfulness can be more effective in moving people into action than those that spark terror. Why do you think that might be? What is your experience with climate media?

## Notes

1 See Brene Brown's March 9, 2022, interview with Waldron on her podcast *Unlocking Us* here: https://brenebrown.com/podcast/accessing-joy-and-finding-connection-in-the-midst-of-struggle.

2 See the group's main website (https://kurzgesagt.org) and the group's YouTube channel (www.youtube.com/channel/UCsXVk37bltHxD1rDPwtNM8Q).

## References

Auerbach, N. (1995) *Our Vampires, Ourselves*. Chicago: University of Chicago Press.

Ballhaus, L. (2019) "Twitter Can't Stop Talking About Amabella's Climate Change Panic on 'Big Little Lies'," *She Knows*, June 24, www.sheknows.com

Beck, J. (2011) "FYI: Can a Woman Really Life a Car Off Her Pinned Child?" *Popular Science*, August 11, www.popsci.com/science/article/2011-07/fyi-can-woman-really-lift-car-her-pinned-child/

Bell, J. et al. (2021) *In Response to Climate Change, Citizens in Advanced Economies Are Willing to Alter How They Live and Work*. Pew Research Center, September 14, www.pewresearch.org

Borunda, A. (2020) "We Still Don't Know the Full Impacts of the BP Oil Disaster, Ten Years Later," *National Geographic*, April 20, www.nationalgeographic.com/science/article/bp-oil-spill-still-dont-know-effects-decade-later?loggedin=true

Boykoff, M. (2019) *Creative (Climate) Communications: Productive Pathways for Science, Policy, and Society*. New York: Cambridge University Press.

Charleston, S. (2021) *Ladder to the Light: An Indigenous Elder's Meditations on Hope and Courage*. Minneapolis: Broadleaf Books.

Chester, J. (dir) (2018) *The Biggest Little Farm* (Film). Moorpark, CA: FarmLore Films.

Chow, D. (2020) "Ten Years After the Deepwater Disaster, Scientists and Activists Worry No Lessons Have Been Learned," *NBC News*, April 20, www.nbcnews.com/science/science-news/ten-years-after-deepwater-disaster-scientists-activists-worry-no-lessons-n1187741

Coogler, R. (dir) (2018) *Black Panther* (Film). Burbank, CA: Marvel Studios.

Cottrell, S. (2021) "This Mom Lifted a Car Off Her Trapped Son, and so Can You," *Medium*, January 23, www.medium.com

Dion, C. and Laurent, M. (dirs) (2015) *Tomorrow* (Film). Paris, France: Move Movie, Mars Films.

Essman, S. (2013) "Travis Beacham on *Pacific Rim*," *CreativeScreenwriting.com*, August 3, www.creativescreenwriting.com/travis-beacham-on-pacific-rim/

Films for Action. (2021) "Cancel the Apocalypse: Here Are 30 Documentaries to Help Unlock the Good Ending," October 22, www.filmsforaction.org/articles/cancel-the-apocalypse-documentaries-to-help-unlock-the-good-ending/

Gameau, D. (dir) (2019) *2040* [Film]. Victoria: Good Things Productions.

Gates, B. (2021) *How to Avoid a Climate Disaster: The Solutions We Have and the Breakthroughs We Need*. New York: Knopf.

Gearino, D. (2022) "Finally, Some Good Climate News: The Biggest Wins in Clean Energy 2022," *Inside Climate News*, December 8, https://insideclimatenews.org/news/08122022/inside-clean-energy-2022-good-news/

Gibson, K. (2021) "Bill Gates: Climate Change Is a Formidable but Solvable Problem," *Stanford University Energy Reports*, February 28, https://energy.stanford.edu/news/bill-gates-climate-challenge-formidable-solvable

Gloyn, L. (2019) *Tracking Classical Monsters in Popular Culture*. London: Bloomsbury.

Goodall, J., and Abrams, D. (2021) *The Book of Hope: A Survival Guide for Trying Times*. New York: Celadon Books.

Harvey, C. (2020) "The Worst Climate Scenarios May No Longer Be the Most Likey," *Scientific American*, January 30, www.scientificamerican.com/article/the-worst-climate-scenarios-may-no-longer-be-the-most-likely/

Hassol, S. J., and Mann, M. E. (2022) "Now Is Not the Time To Give in to Climate Fatalism," *Time*, April 12, www.time.com

Hausfather, Z., and Peters, G. (2020) "The 'Business as Usual' Story Is Misleading," *The Journal Nature*, January 29. www.nature.com/articles/d41586-020-00177-3

Hawken, P. (ed) (2007) *Blessed Unrest: How the Largest Social Movement in History Is Restoring Grace, Justice, and Beauty to the World*. New York: Penguin Books.

———. (2017) *Drawdown: The Most Comprehensive Plan Ever Proposed to Reverse Global Warming*. New York: Penguin Random House.

———. (2021) *Regeneration: Ending the Climate Crisis in One Generation*. New York: Penguin Books.

Hayhoe, K. (2021) *Saving Us: A Climate Scientist's Case for Hope and Healing in a Divided World*. New York: One Signal Publishers.

Heglar, M. A. (2019a) "Climate Change Isn't Racist—People Are," *Medium*, August 13, https://medium.com/zora/climate-change-isnt-racist-people-are-c586b9380965

———. (2019b) "Home Is Always Worth It," *Medium.com*, September 12, https://medium.com/@maryheglar/home-is-always-worth-it-d2821634dcd9

Jacobson, M. (2023) *No Miracles Needed: How Today's Technology Can Save Our Climate and Clean Our Air*. New York: Cambridge University Press.

Jenkins, H., Ford, S., and Green, J. (2013) *Spreadable Media: Creating Value and Meaning in a Networked Culture*. New York: New York University Press.

Jenkins, H., Peters-Lazaro, G., and Shresthova, S. (eds) (2020) *Popular Culture and the Civic Imagination: Case Studies of Creative Social Change*. New York: New York University Press.

Kelsey, E. (2020) *Hope Matters: Why Changing the Way We Think Is Critical to Solving the Environmental Crisis*. Berkeley: Greystone Books.

Kirkland, J. (2019) "Amabella's Big Little Lies Anxiety Attack Over Climate Change Made Me Feel Seen," *Esquire*, June 23, ww.esquire.com

Klein, E. (2022) "Your Kids Are Not Doomed," *New York Times*, June 5, www.nytimes.com
Klein, N. (2014) *This Changes Everything: Capitalism vs. The Climate*. New York: Simon & Schuster.
———. (2017) *No Is Not Enough: Resisting Trump's Shock Politics and Winning the World We Need*. Chicago: Haymarket Books.
Laycock, J., and Minkle, N. (eds) (2021) *Religion, Culture, and the Monstruous: Of Gods and Monsters*. London: Rowman & Littlefield.
Lear, J. (2008) *Radical Hope: Ethics in the Face of Cultural Devastation*. Cambridge: Harvard University Press.
Leiserowitz, A. et al. (2022) "Global Warming's Six Americas, 2021," Climate Change Communication Program (Yale University), January 12, https://climatecommunication.yale.edu/publications/global-warmings-six-americas-september-2021/
Lewis, A. (dir) (2015) *This Changes Everything* (Film). Toronto: Klein Lewis Productions.
Linderman, F. B. (1930) *American: The Life Story of a Great Indian, Plenty Coups, Chief of the Crows*. New York: John Day Company.
Mann, M. (2021) *The New Climate War: The Fight to Take Back Our Planet*. New York: Public Affairs.
Marks, E. et al. (2021) "Young People's Voices on Climate Anxiety, Government Betrayal, and Moral Injury: A Global Phenomenon," *The Lancet*, September 7, https://papers.ssrn.com/sol3/papers.cfm?abstract_id=3918955
Meredith, S. (2017) "Just 100 Firms Attributable for 71% of Global Emissions, Report Says," *CNBC News*, July 10, www.cnbc.com/2017/07/10/just-100-firms-attributable-for-71-percent-of-global-emissions-report-says.html
Mitchell, A., and Chaudhury, A. (2020) "Worlding Beyond 'the' 'End' of 'the World': White Apocalyptic Visions and BIPOC Futurisms," *International Relations* 34(3): 309–32.
Mitchell, S. (2021) "Tracing Big Oil's PR War to Delay Action on Climate Change," *The Harvard Gazette*, September 28, https://news.harvard.edu/gazette/story/2021/09/oil-companies-discourage-climate-action-study-says/
Mittman, A., and Dendle, P. (2012) *The Ashgate Research Companion to Monsters and the Monstrous*. New York: Routledge.
Oreskes, N., and Conway, E. (2011) *Merchants of Doubt: How a Handful of Scientists Obscured the Truth on Issues from Tobacco Smoke to Climate Change*. New York: Bloomsbury.
Piper, K. (2022) "Stop Telling Kids That Climate Change Will Destroy Their World," *Vox*, June 8, www.vox.com
Plumer, B., and Popovich, N. (2021) "Yes, There Has Been Progress on Climate: No, It's Not Nearly Enough," *The New York Times*, October 25, www.nytimes.com/interactive/2021/10/25/climate/world-climate-pledges-cop26.html
Polle, C. P. (2016) "Unfreeze Yourself: Five Ways to Take On Climate Change Now for the Sake of Your Family, Your Health, and the Planet," www.tappingcourage.com
Ray, S. J. (2020) *A Field Guide to Climate Anxiety: How to Keep Your Cool on a Warming Planet*. Oakland: University of California Press.
Ritchie, H. (2021) "Stop Telling Kis They Die from Climate Change," *WIRED*, November 1, www.wired.com
Shen, L. (2017) "These 100 Companies are Responsible for Most of the World's Carbon Emissions," *Forbes Magazine*, April 20, www.nationalgeographic.com/science/article/bp-oil-spill-still-dont-know-effects-decade-later?loggedin=true

Sontag, S. (2007) *At the Same Time: Essays and Speeches*, eds. P. Dilonardo, A. Jump, and D. Rieff. New York: Farrar, Straus & Giroux.

Supran, G., and Oreskes, N. (2021) "Rhetoric and Frame Analysis of ExxonMobile's Climate Change Communication," *One Earth* 4(5), www.sciencedirect.com/science/article/pii/S2590332221002335

Taylor, S. M. (2019) *Ecopiety: Green Media and the Dilemma of Environmental Virtue*. New York: New York University Press.

Tickell, J., and Tickell, R. (dirs) (2020) *Kiss the Ground* [Film]. San Francisco: The Redford Center and Big Picture Ranch.

Veidis, E. (2021) "New Study Finds High Levels of Climate Anxiety in Youth," *Stanford Center for Innovation and Global Health*, September 30, https://globalhealth.stanford.edu/

Waldron, K. (2021) *The Lightmaker's Manifesto: How to Work for Change Without Losing Your Joy*. Minneapolis: Broadleaf Books.

Watts, J. (2021) "Climatologist Michael E. Mann: 'Good People Fall Victim to doomism. I Do too, Sometimes' [Interview]," *The Guardian*, February 27, www.theguardian.com

Yang, M. (2022) "Six in Ten Americans 'Alarmed' or 'Concerned' About Climate Change," *The Guardian*, January 13, www.theguardian.com/environment/2022/jan/13/record-number-americans-alarmed-about-climate-crisis

# Index

Note: Page numbers in *italic* indicate a figure and page numbers in **bold** indicate a table on the corresponding page.

Printed in the United States
by Baker & Taylor Publisher Services